Gleipnir 9 is a work of fiction. Name
places, and incidents are the products of the
or are used fictitiously. Any resemblance to a
persons, living or dead, is entirely c

A Kodansha Comics Trade Paperback Original
Gleipnir 9 copyright © 2020 Sun Takeda
English translation copyright © 2021 Sun Takeda

Published in the United States by Kodansha Comics, an imprint of
Kodansha USA Publishing, LLC, New York.

Publication rights for this English edition arranged through
Kodansha Ltd., Tokyo.

First published in Japan in 2020 by Kodansha Ltd., Tokyo.
as Gureipuniiru, volume 9.

ISBN 978-1-64651-199-0

Printed in the United States of America.

www.kodanshacomics.us

9 8 7 6 5 4 3 2 1
Translation: Iyasu Nagata
Lettering: Daniel Lee
Editing: Jordan Blanco
Kodansha Comics edition cover design by Phil Balsman

Publisher: Kiichiro Sugawara

Director of publishing services: Ben Applegate
Associate director of operations: Stephen Pakula
Publishing services associate managing editor: Madison Salters
Production managers: Emi Lotto, Angela Zurlo

<PREVIEW OF NEXT VOLUME>

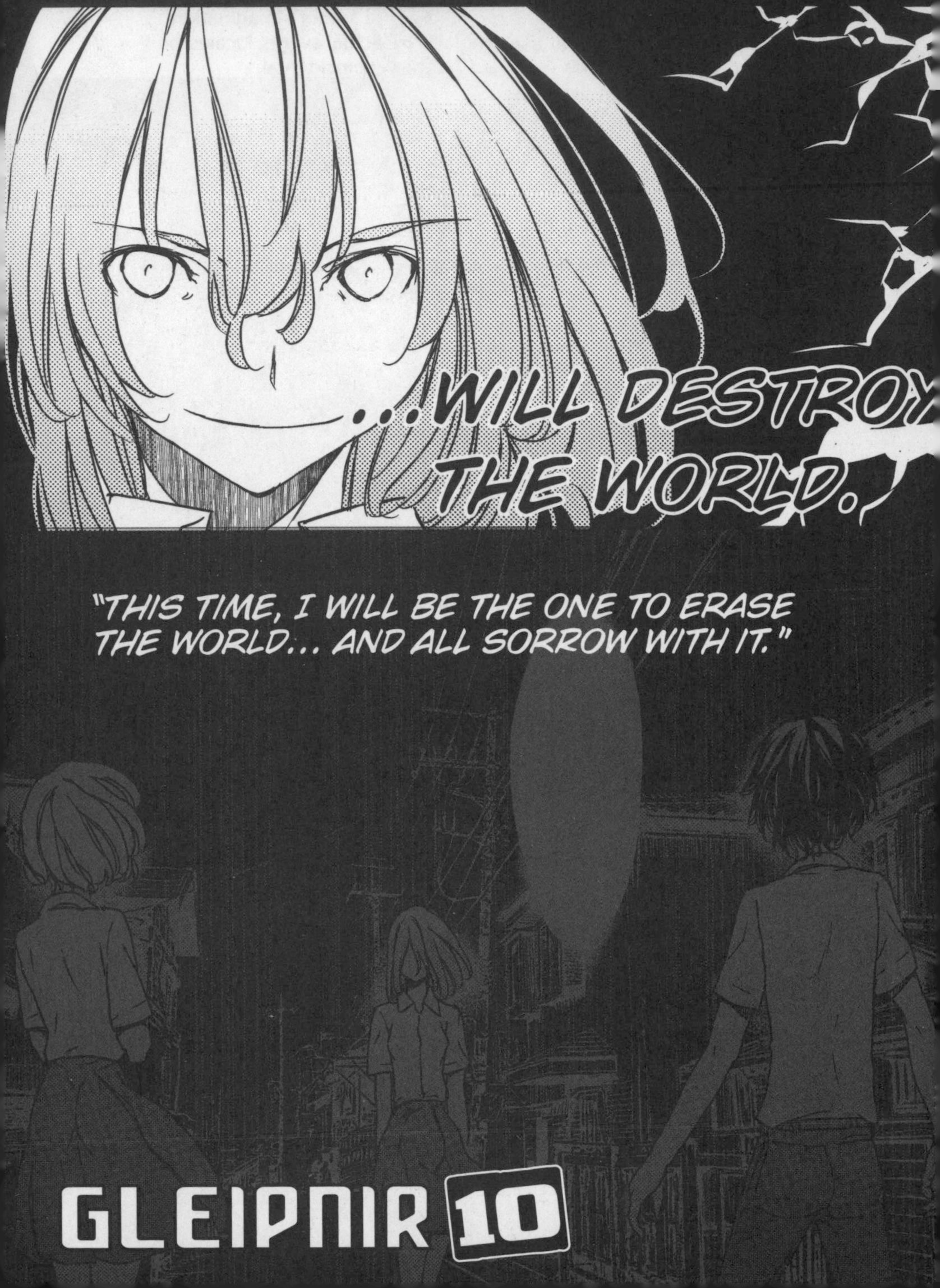
...WILL DESTROY THE WORLD.
"THIS TIME, I WILL BE THE ONE TO ERASE THE WORLD... AND ALL SORROW WITH IT."
GLEIPNIR 10

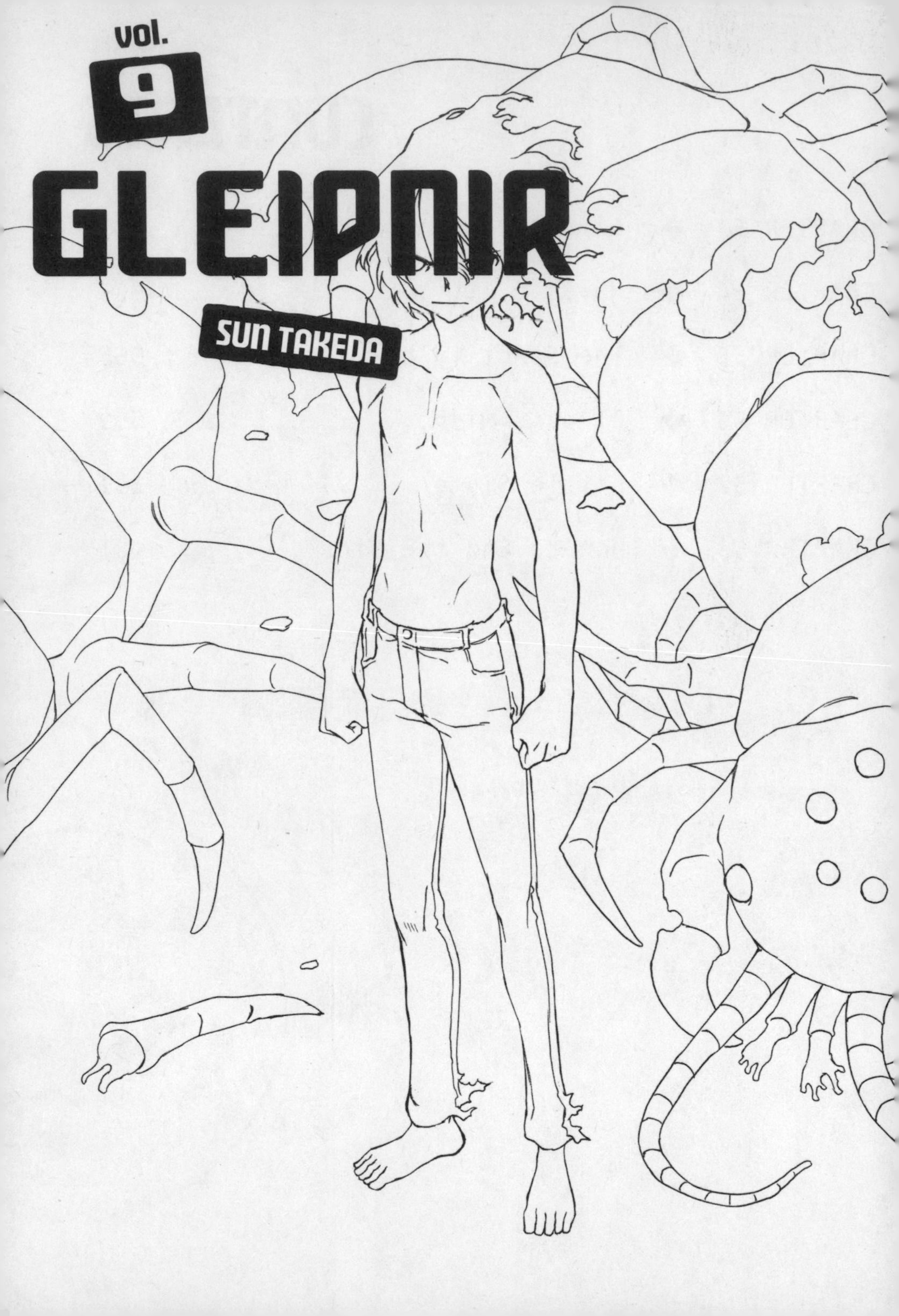
vol.
9
GLEIPNIR
SUN TAKEDA

CONTENTS

G L E I P N I R

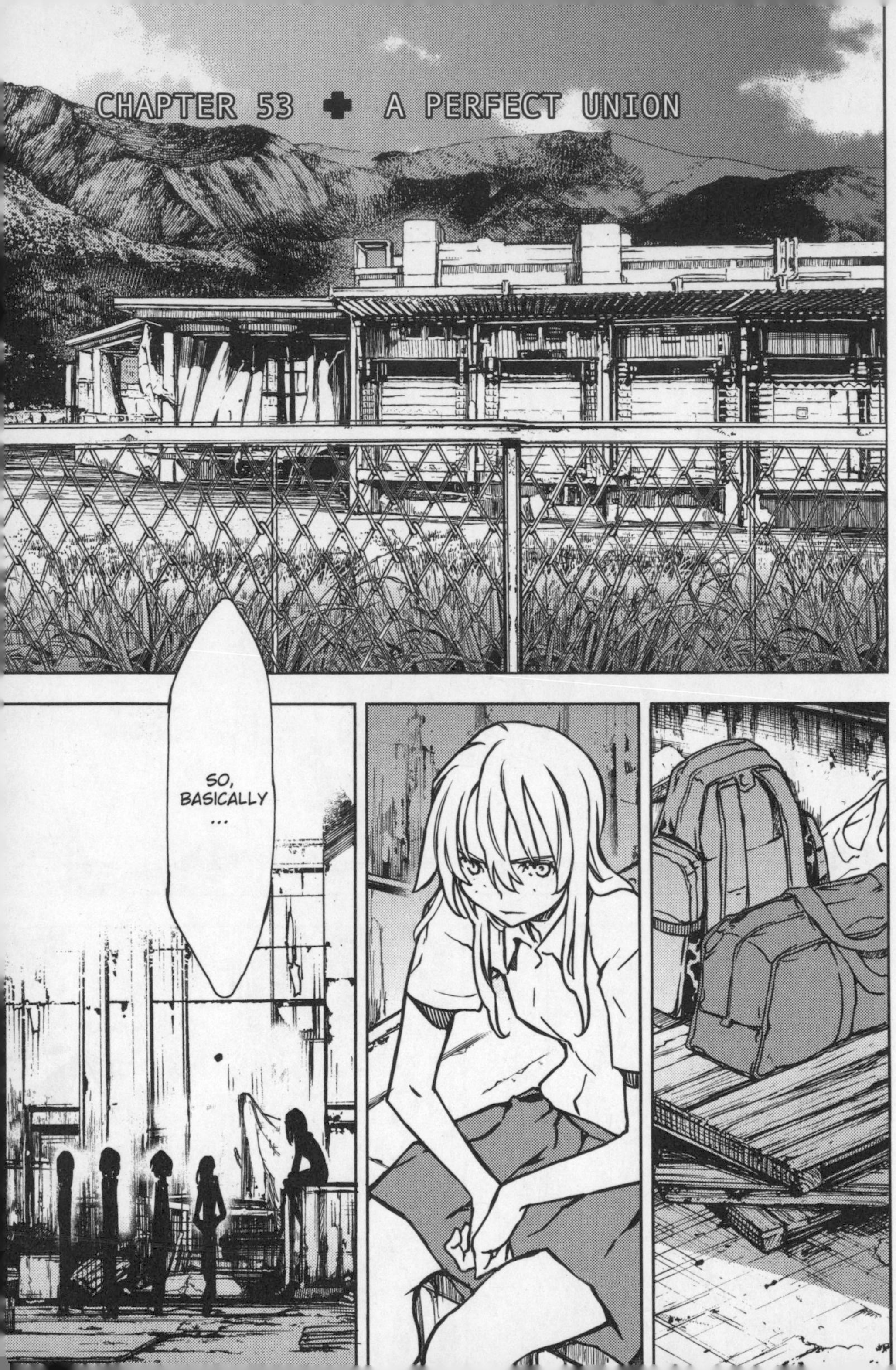
CHAPTER 53 ✚ A PERFECT UNION
SO, BASICALLY ...

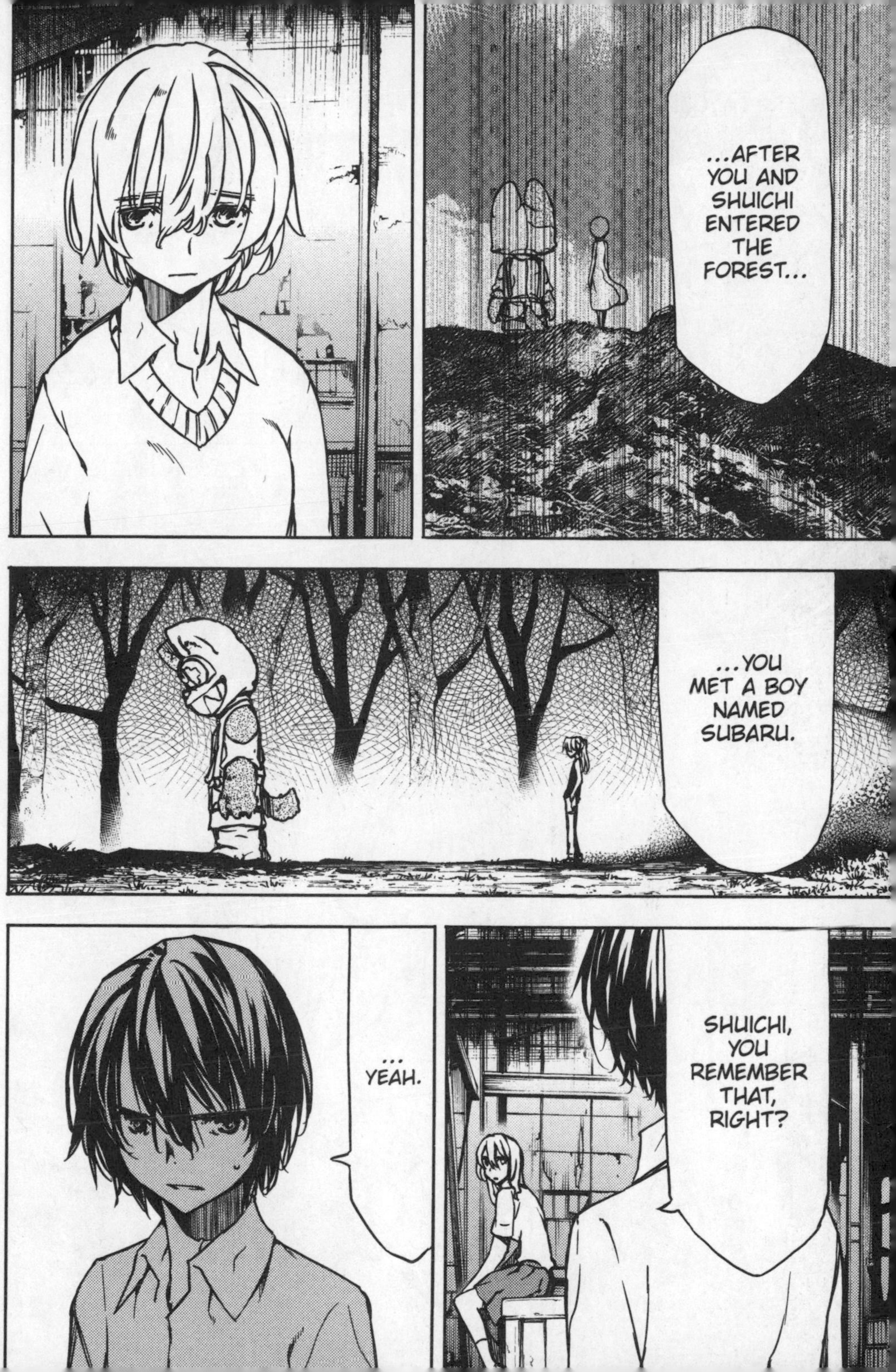
...AFTER YOU AND SHUICHI ENTERED THE FOREST...
...YOU MET A BOY NAMED SUBARU.
SHUICHI, YOU REMEMBER THAT, RIGHT?
... YEAH.

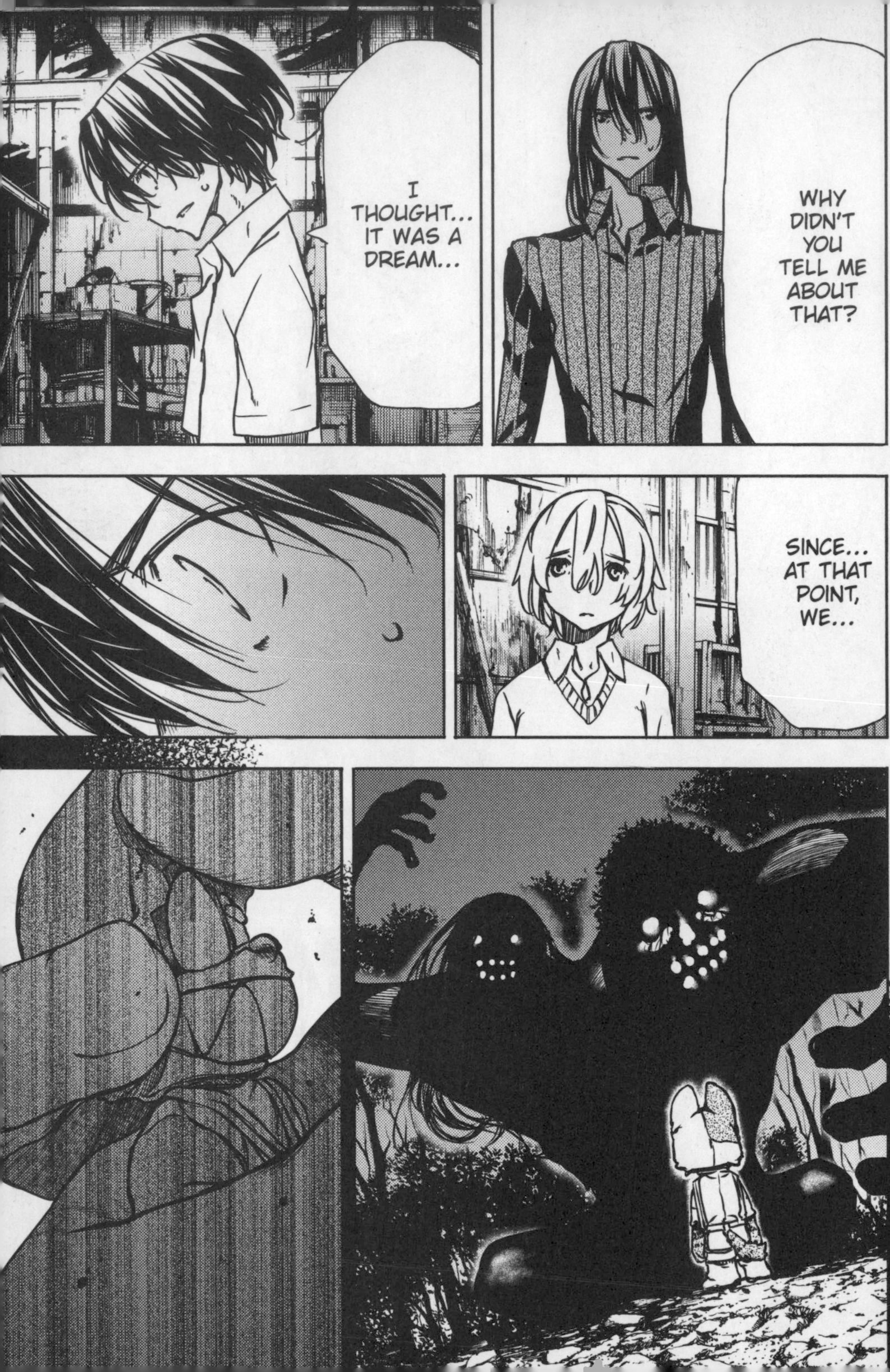
WHY DIDN'T YOU TELL ME ABOUT THAT?
I THOUGHT... IT WAS A DREAM...
SINCE... AT THAT POINT, WE...

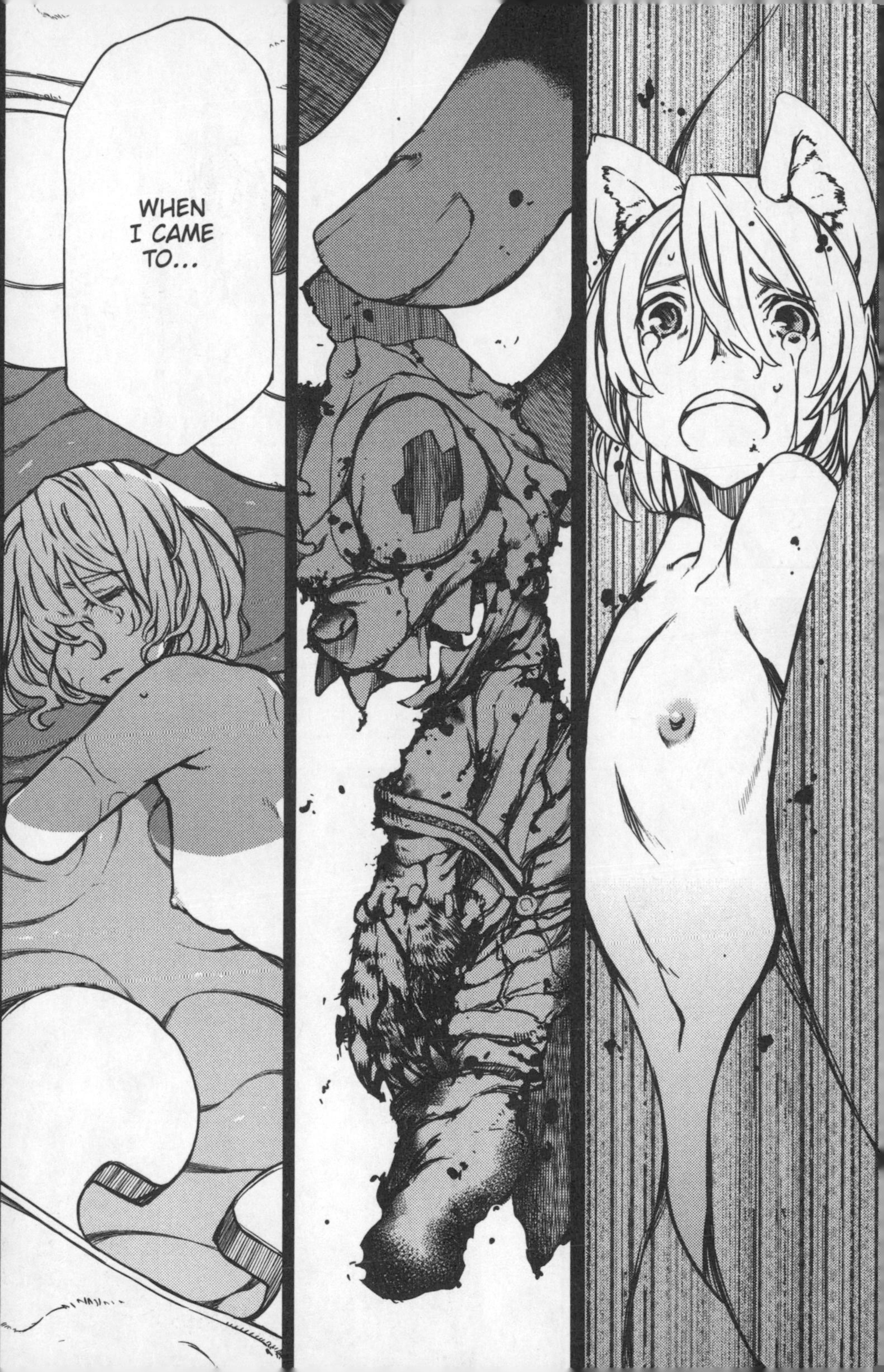
WHEN I CAME TO...

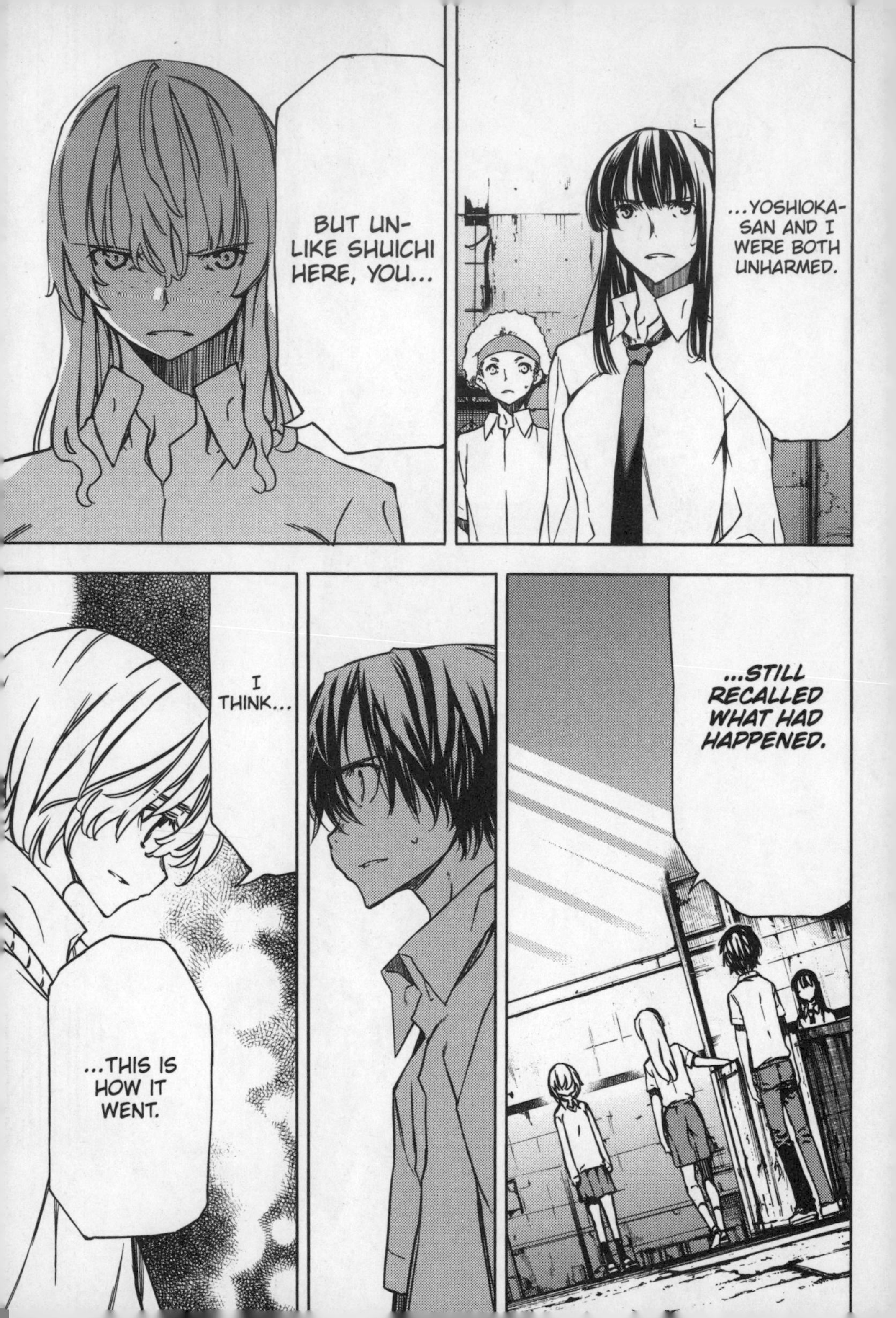
...YOSHIOKA-SAN AND I WERE BOTH UNHARMED.
BUT UN-LIKE SHUICHI HERE, YOU...
...STILL RECALLED WHAT HAD HAPPENED.
I THINK...
...THIS IS HOW IT WENT.

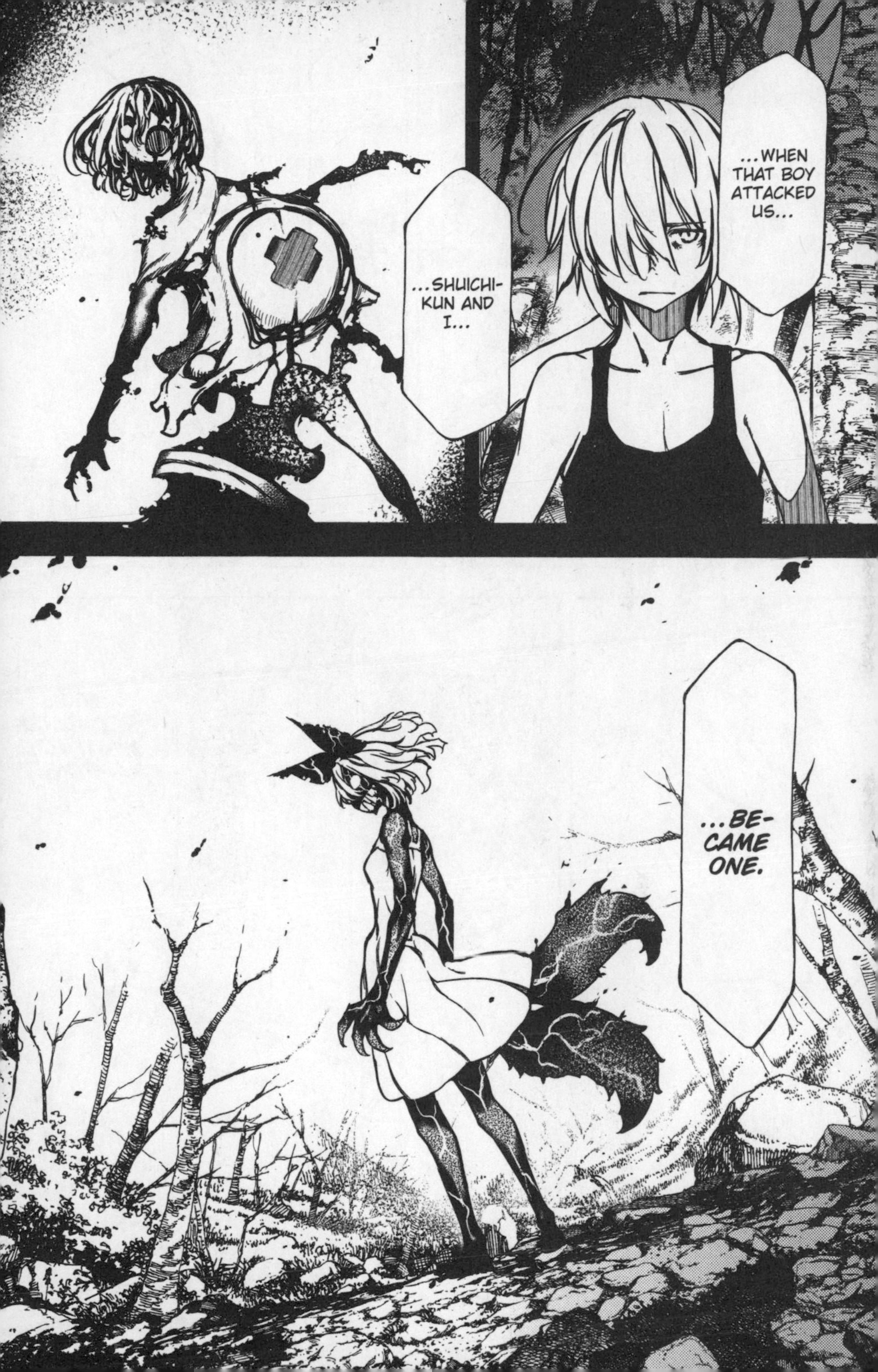
...WHEN THAT BOY ATTACKED US...
...SHUICHI-KUN AND I...
...BE-CAME ONE.

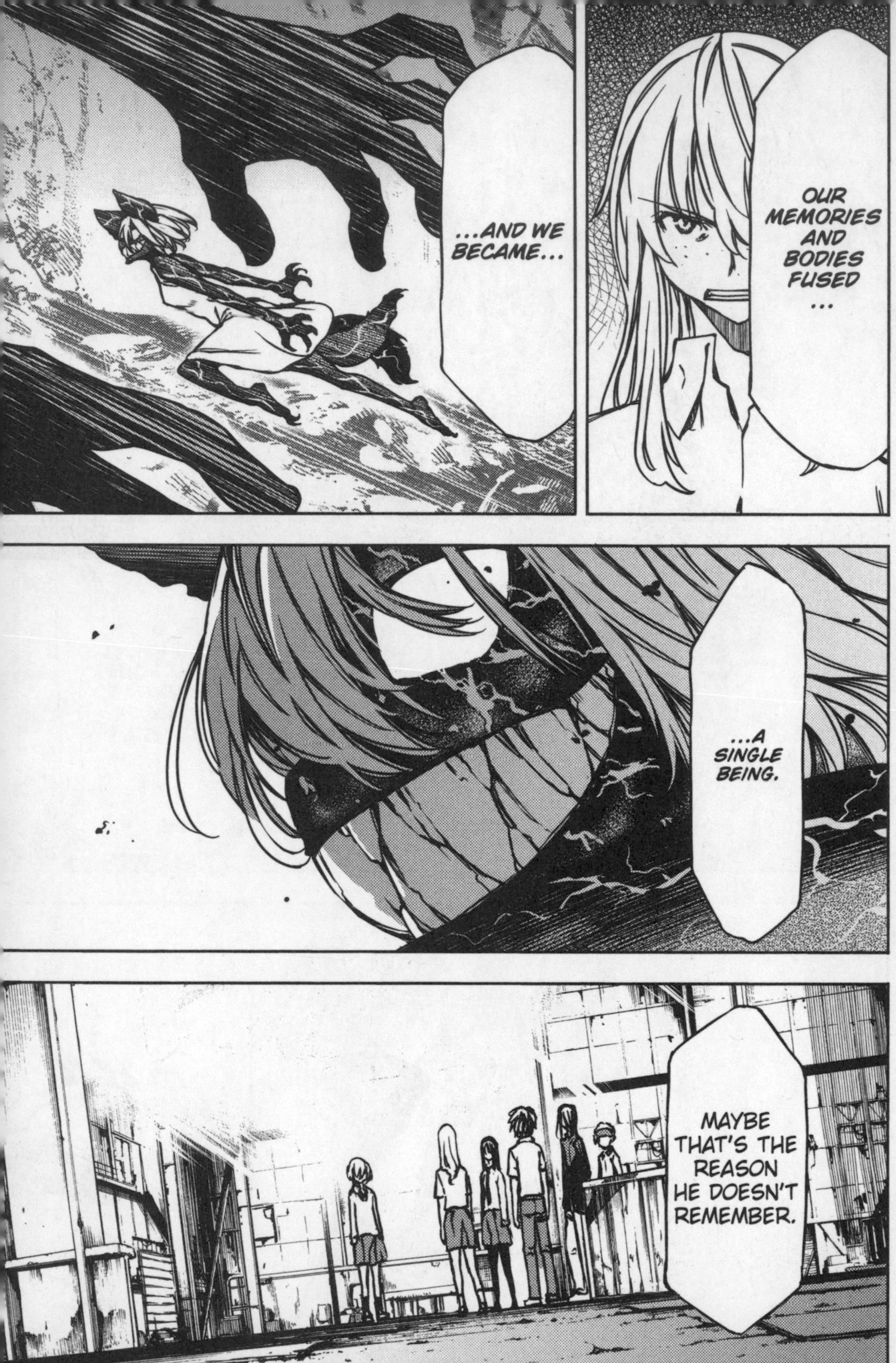
OUR MEMORIES AND BODIES FUSED ...
...AND WE BECAME...
...A SINGLE BEING.
MAYBE THAT'S THE REASON HE DOESN'T REMEMBER.

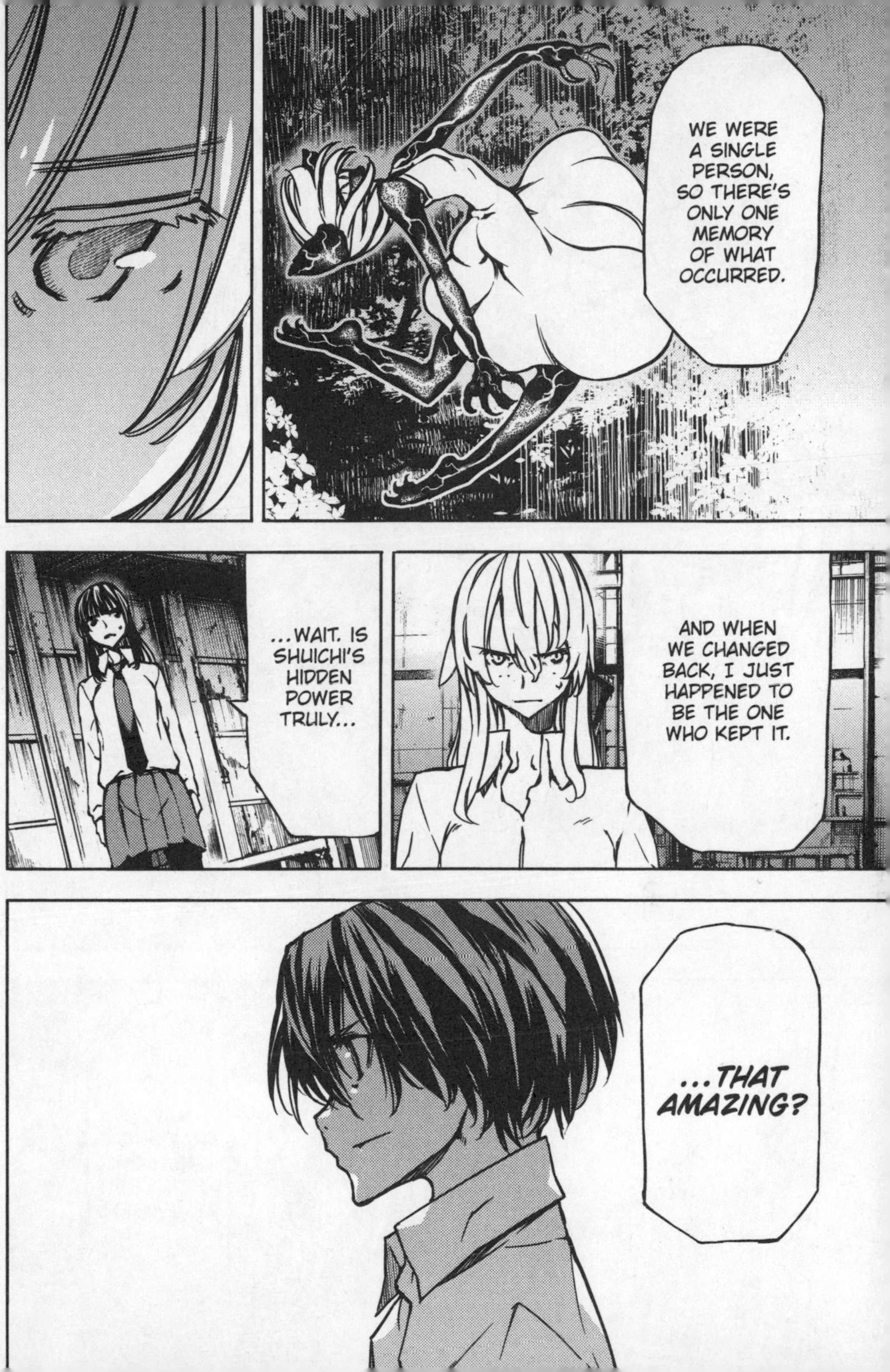
WE WERE A SINGLE PERSON, SO THERE'S ONLY ONE MEMORY OF WHAT OCCURRED.
AND WHEN WE CHANGED BACK, I JUST HAPPENED TO BE THE ONE WHO KEPT IT.
...WAIT. IS SHUICHI'S HIDDEN POWER TRULY...
...THAT AMAZING?

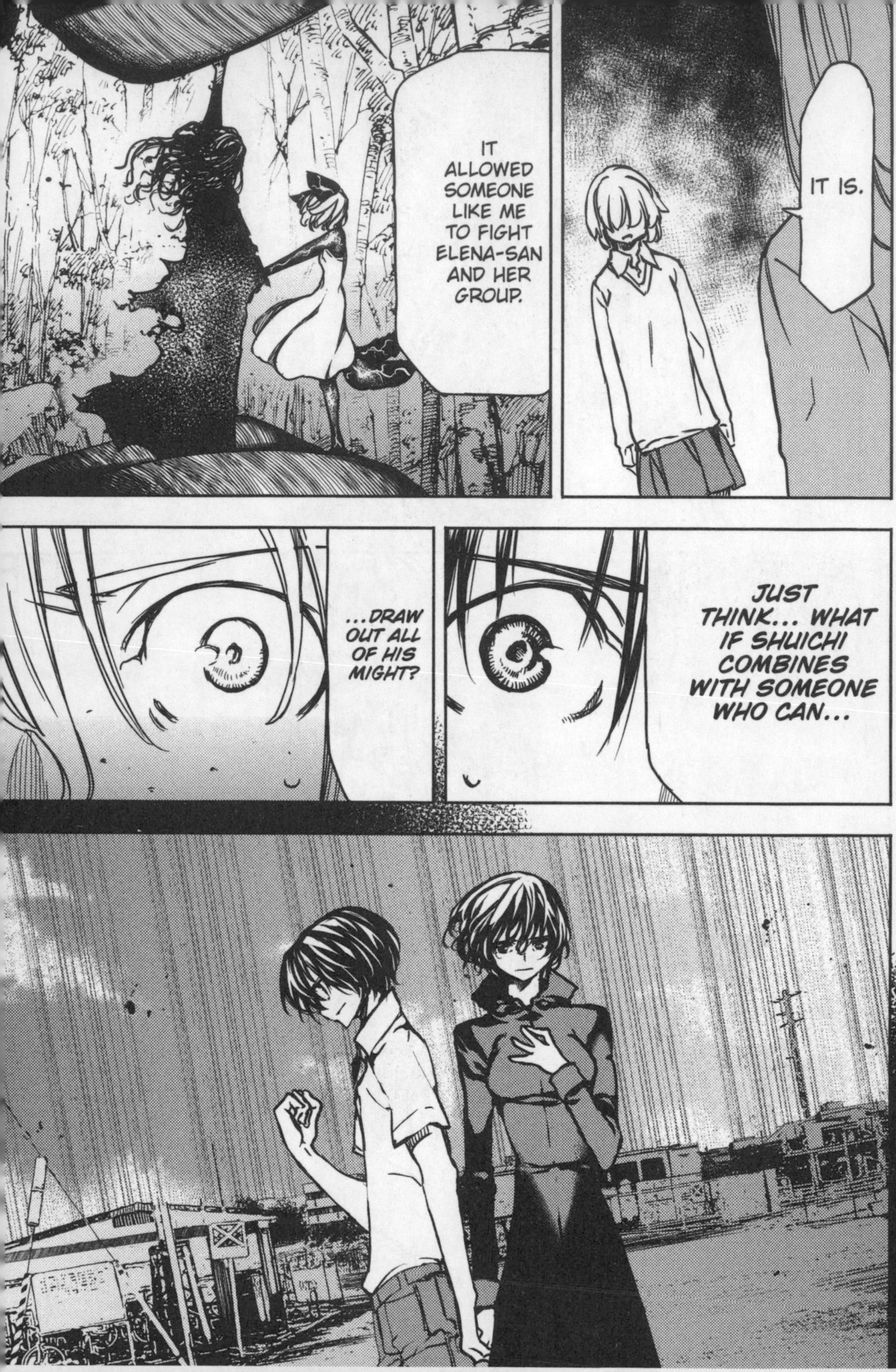
IT IS.
IT ALLOWED SOMEONE LIKE ME TO FIGHT ELENA-SAN AND HER GROUP.
JUST THINK... WHAT IF SHUICHI COMBINES WITH SOMEONE WHO CAN...
...DRAW OUT ALL OF HIS MIGHT?

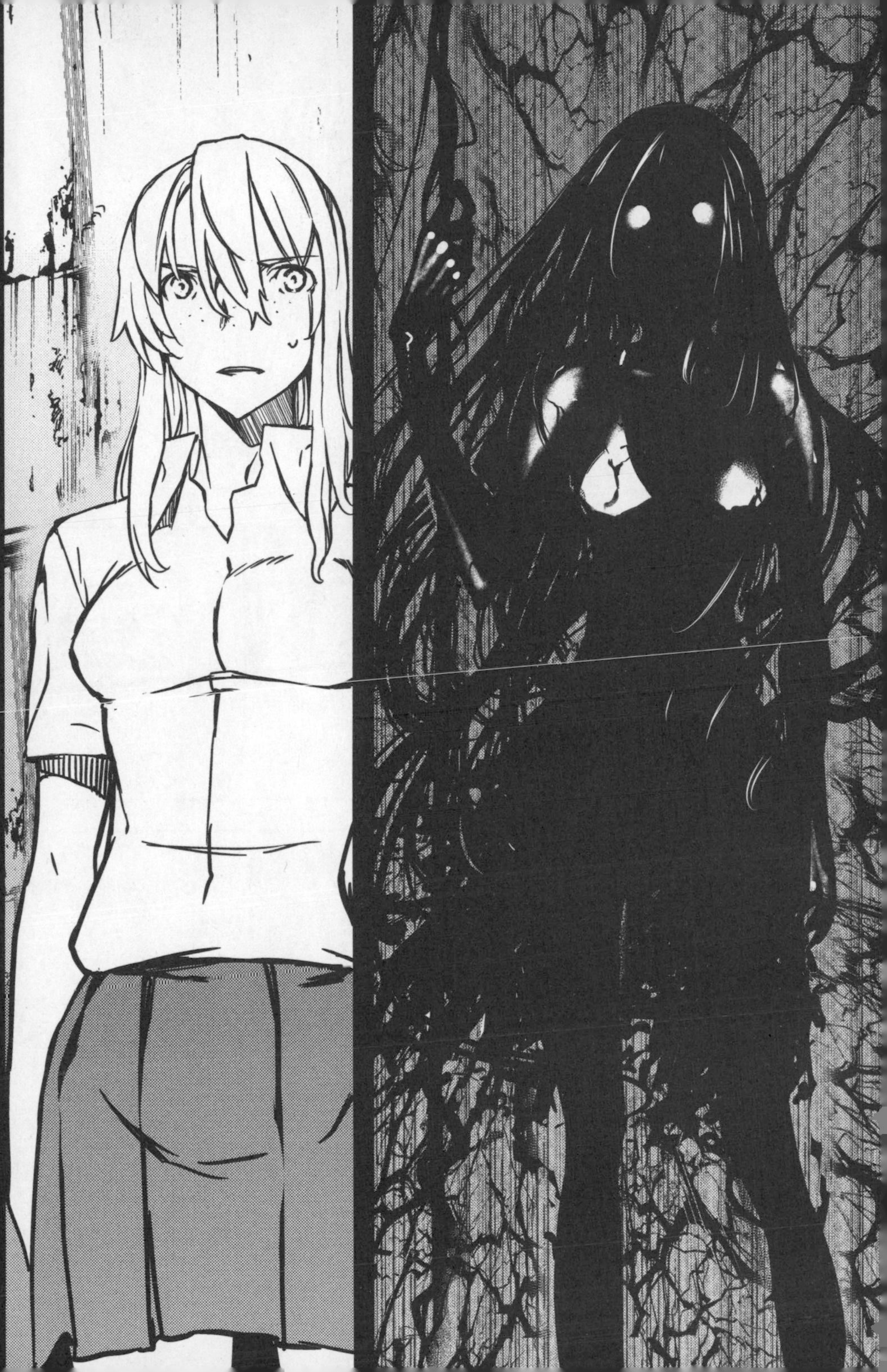

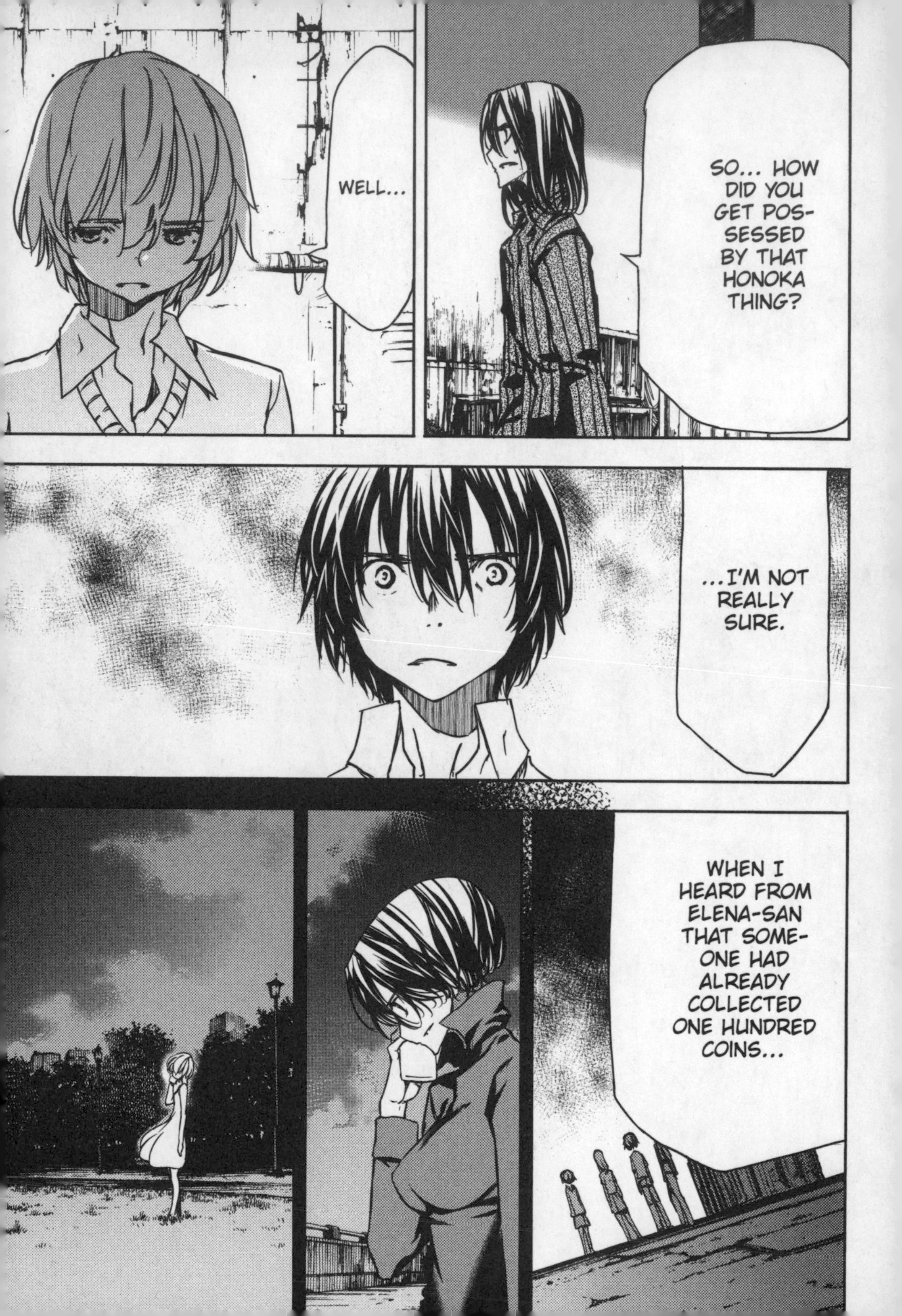
SO... HOW DID YOU GET POSSESSED BY THAT HONOKA THING?
WELL...
...I'M NOT REALLY SURE.
WHEN I HEARD FROM ELENA-SAN THAT SOMEONE HAD ALREADY COLLECTED ONE HUNDRED COINS...

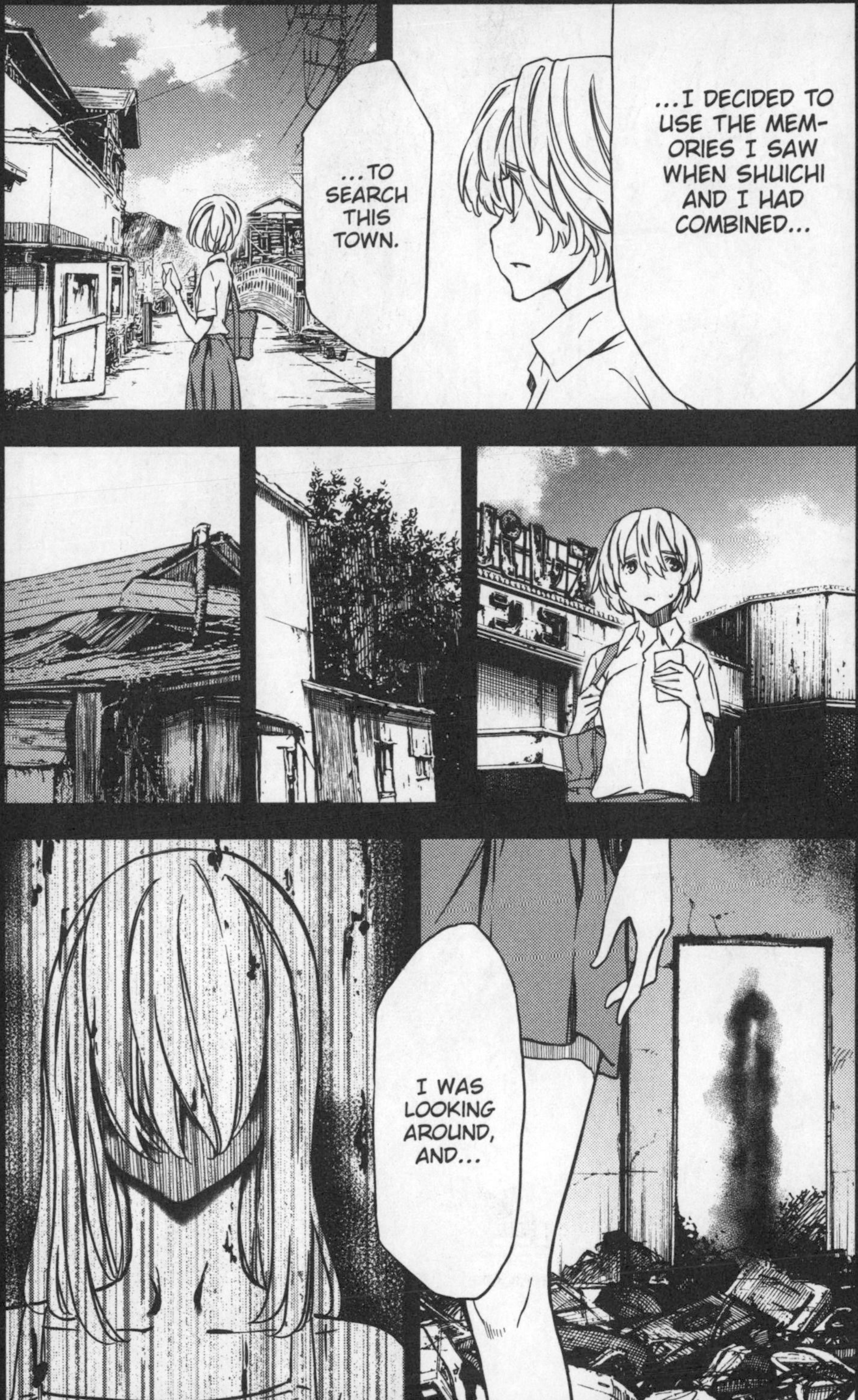
...I DECIDED TO USE THE MEM-ORIES I SAW WHEN SHUICHI AND I HAD COMBINED...
...TO SEARCH THIS TOWN.
I WAS LOOKING AROUND, AND...

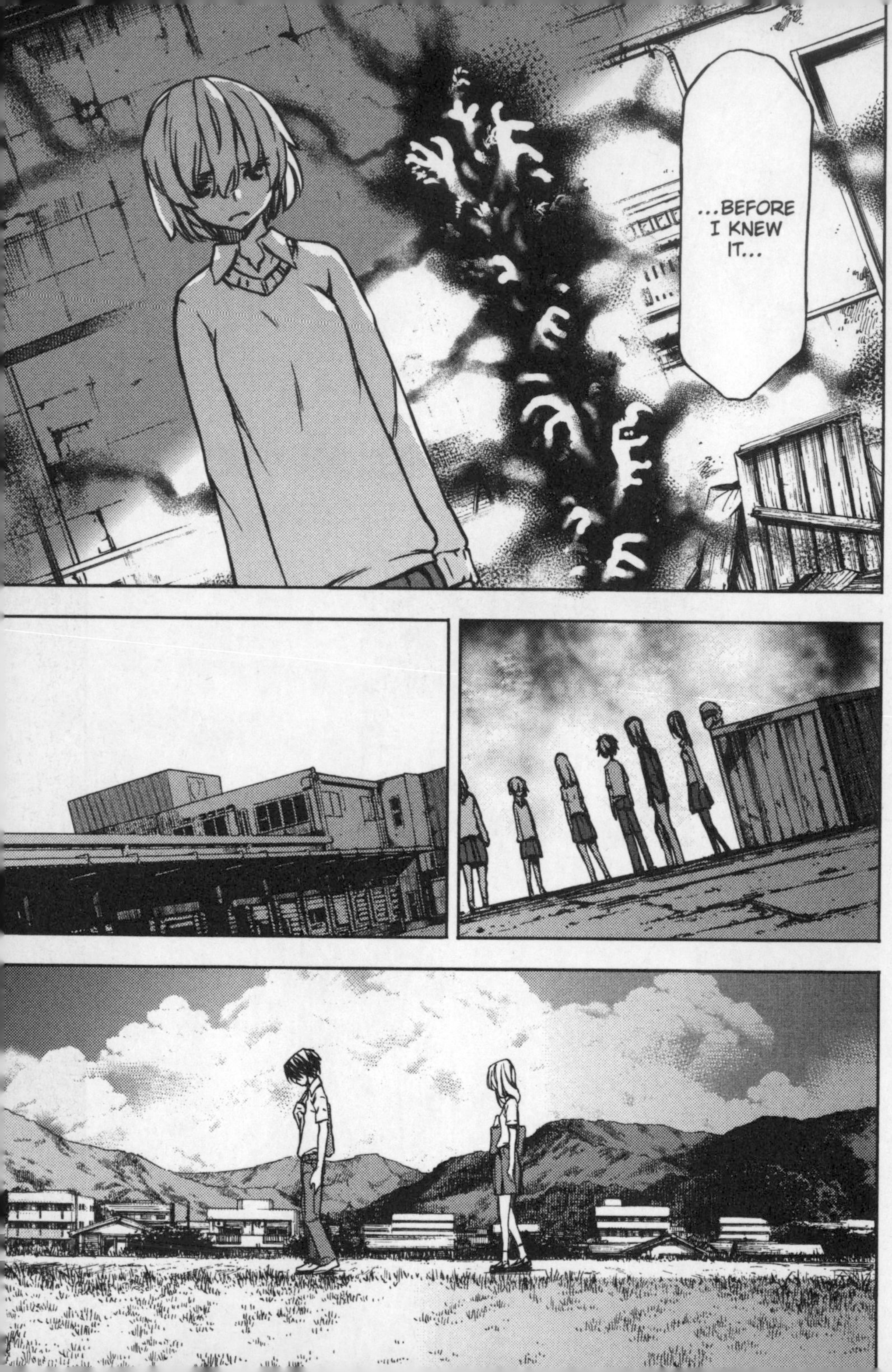
...BEFORE I KNEW IT...

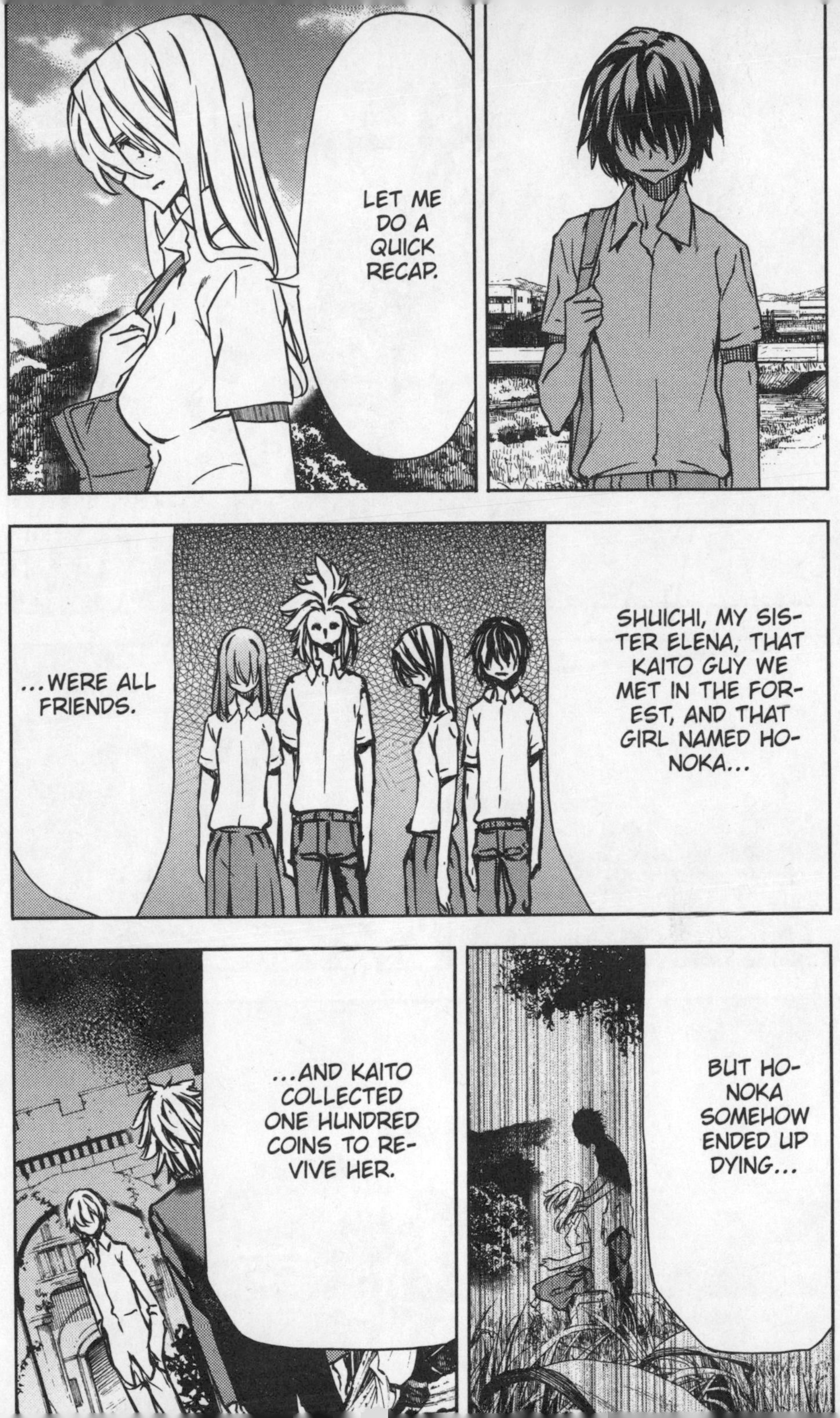
LET ME DO A QUICK RECAP.
SHUICHI, MY SISTER ELENA, THAT KAITO GUY WE MET IN THE FOREST, AND THAT GIRL NAMED HONOKA...
...WERE ALL FRIENDS.
BUT HONOKA SOMEHOW ENDED UP DYING...
...AND KAITO COLLECTED ONE HUNDRED COINS TO REVIVE HER.

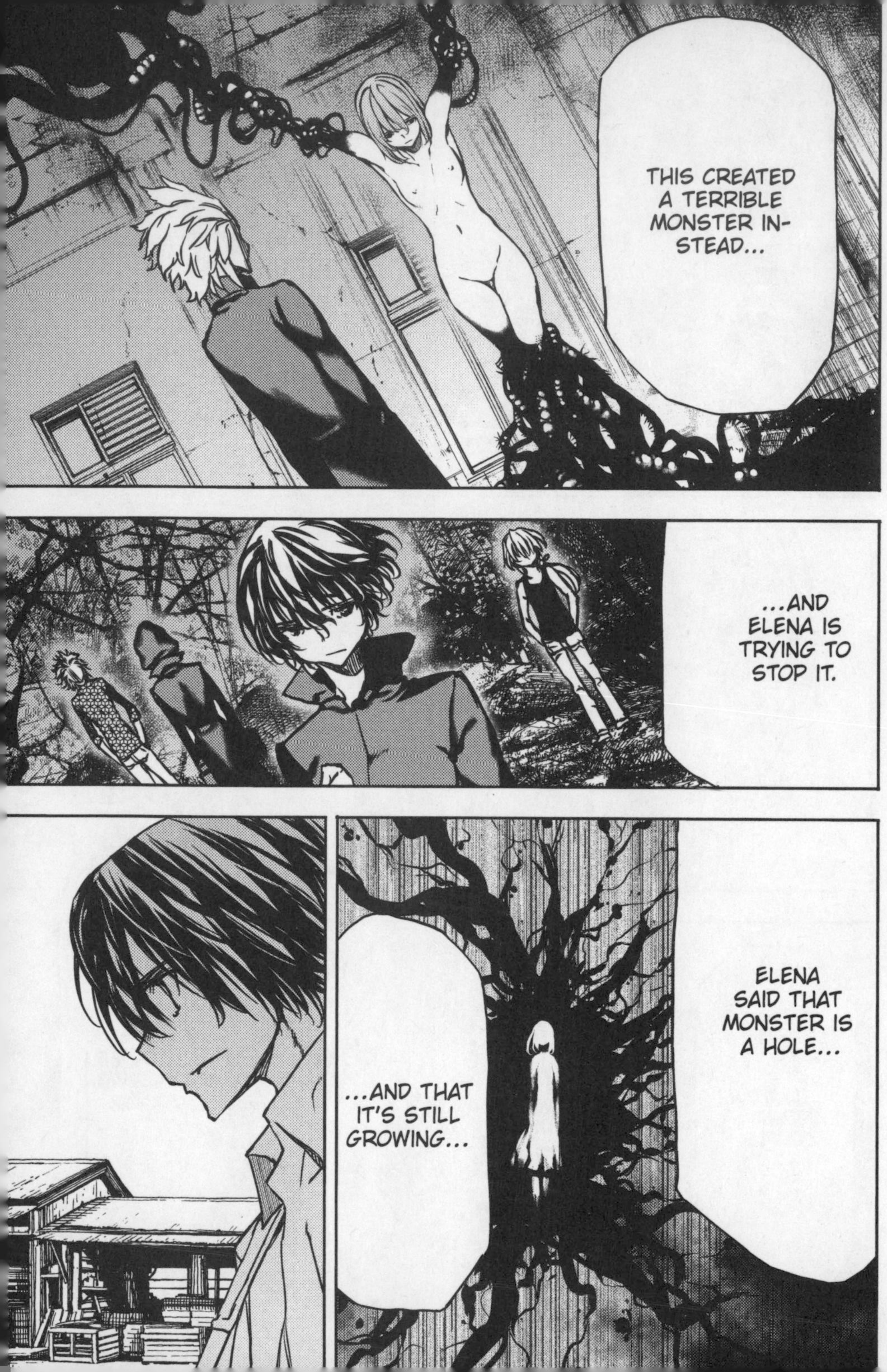
THIS CREATED A TERRIBLE MONSTER IN-STEAD...
...AND ELENA IS TRYING TO STOP IT.
ELENA SAID THAT MONSTER IS A HOLE...
...AND THAT IT'S STILL GROWING...

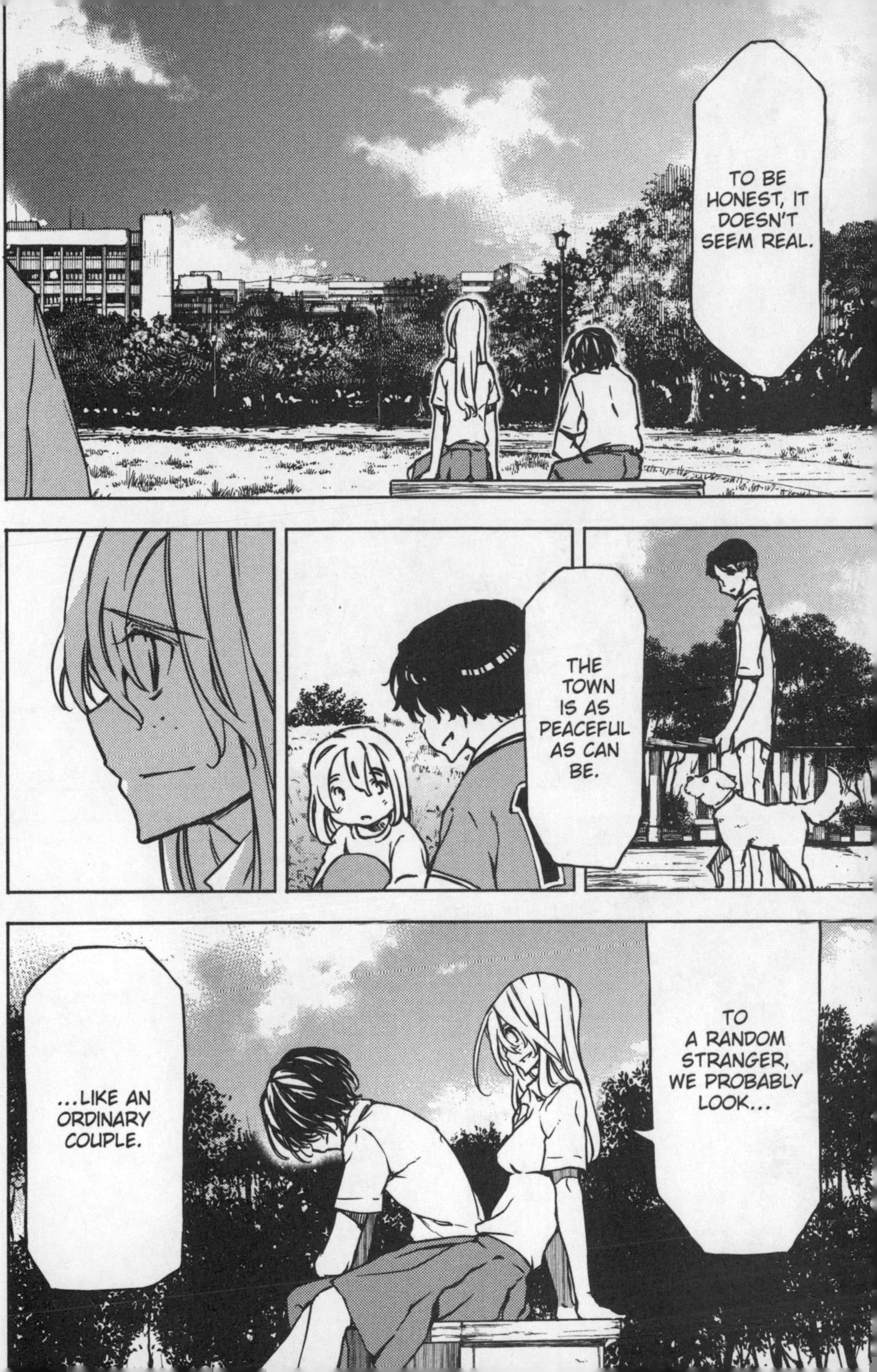
TO BE HONEST, IT DOESN'T SEEM REAL.
THE TOWN IS AS PEACEFUL AS CAN BE.
TO A RANDOM STRANGER, WE PROBABLY LOOK...
...LIKE AN ORDINARY COUPLE.

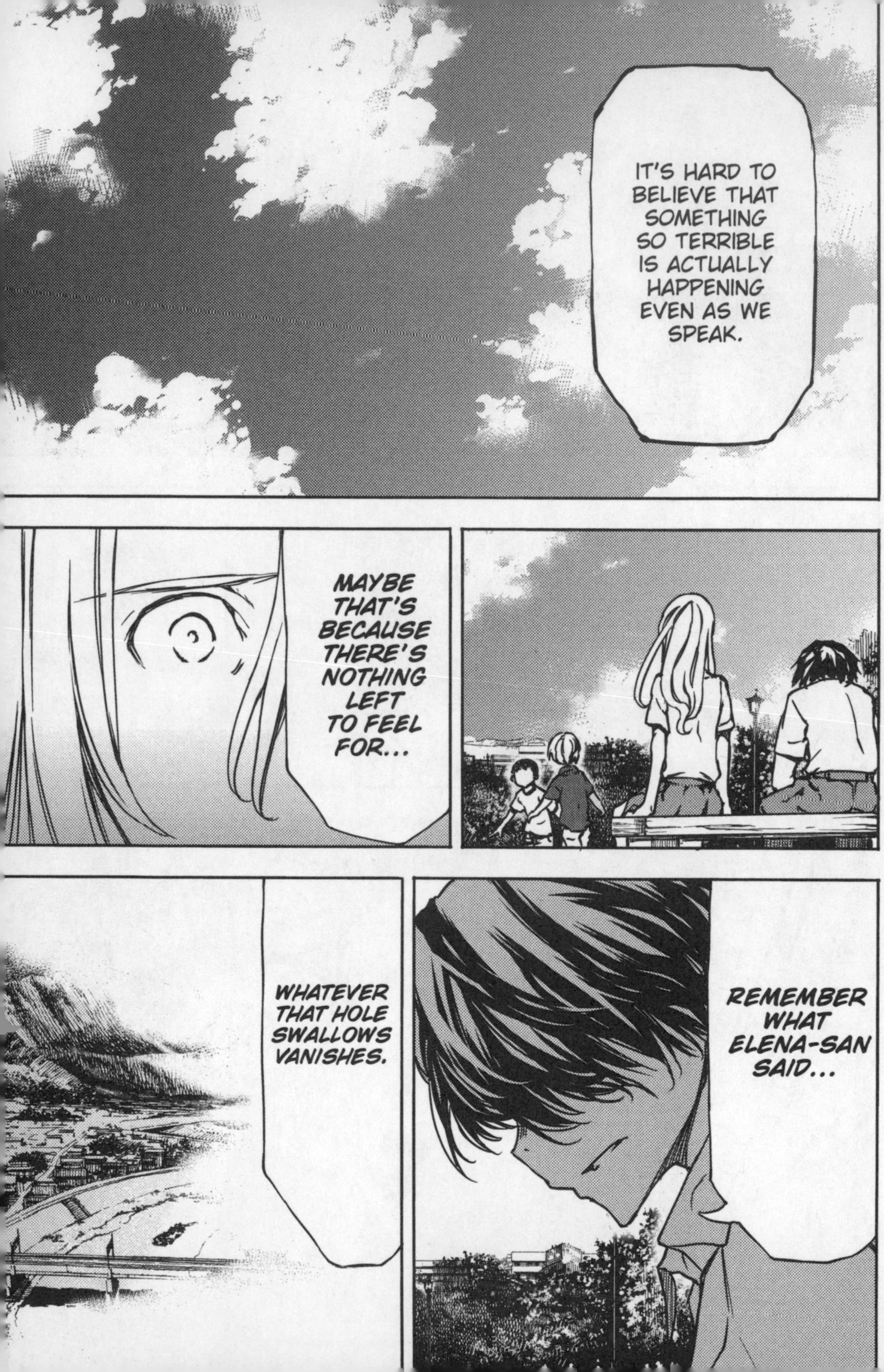
IT'S HARD TO BELIEVE THAT SOMETHING SO TERRIBLE IS ACTUALLY HAPPENING EVEN AS WE SPEAK.
MAYBE THAT'S BECAUSE THERE'S NOTHING LEFT TO FEEL FOR...
REMEMBER WHAT ELENA-SAN SAID...
WHATEVER THAT HOLE SWALLOWS VANISHES.

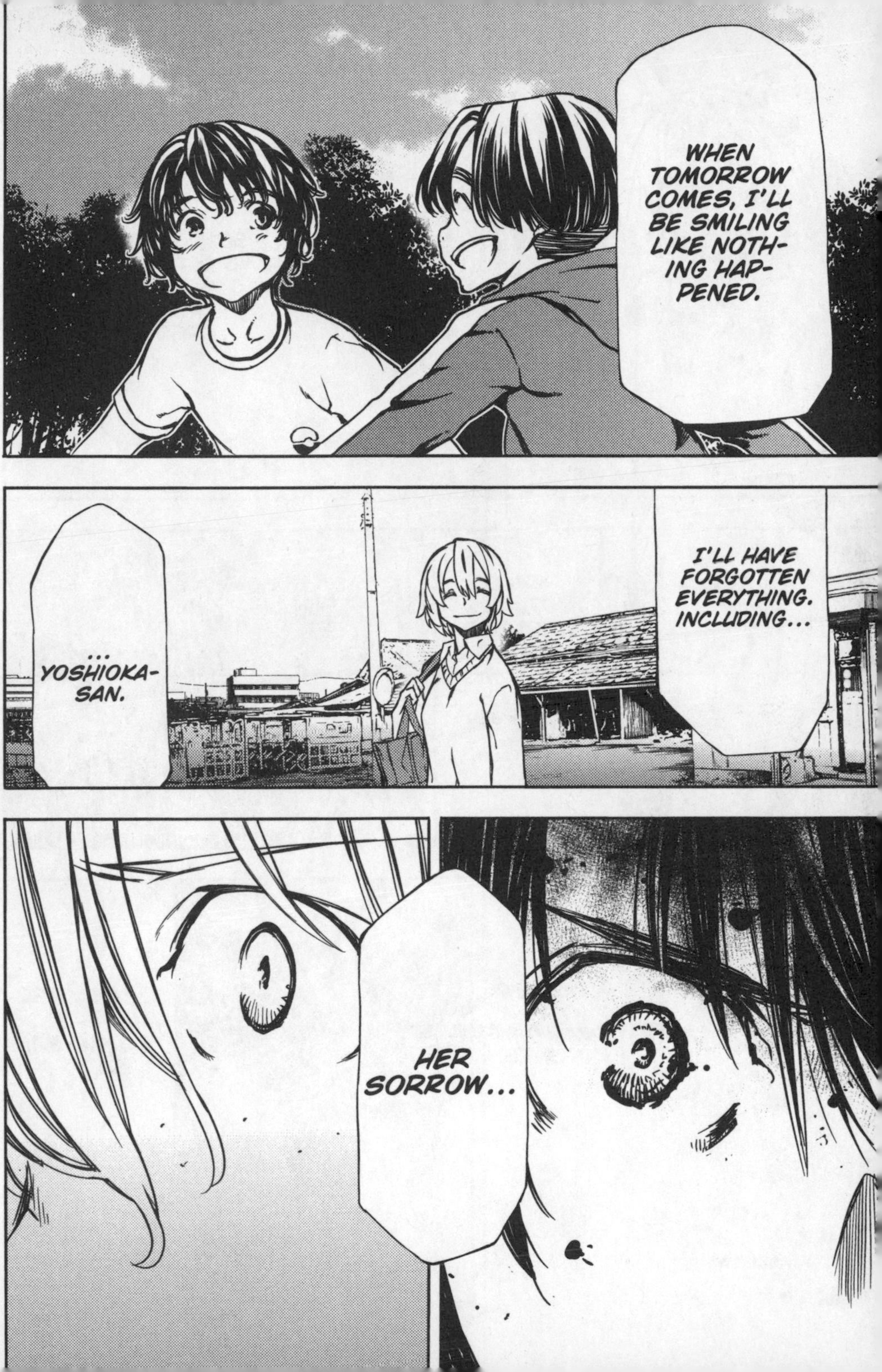
WHEN TOMORROW COMES, I'LL BE SMILING LIKE NOTHING HAPPENED.
I'LL HAVE FORGOTTEN EVERYTHING. INCLUDING...
... YOSHIOKA-SAN.
HER SORROW...

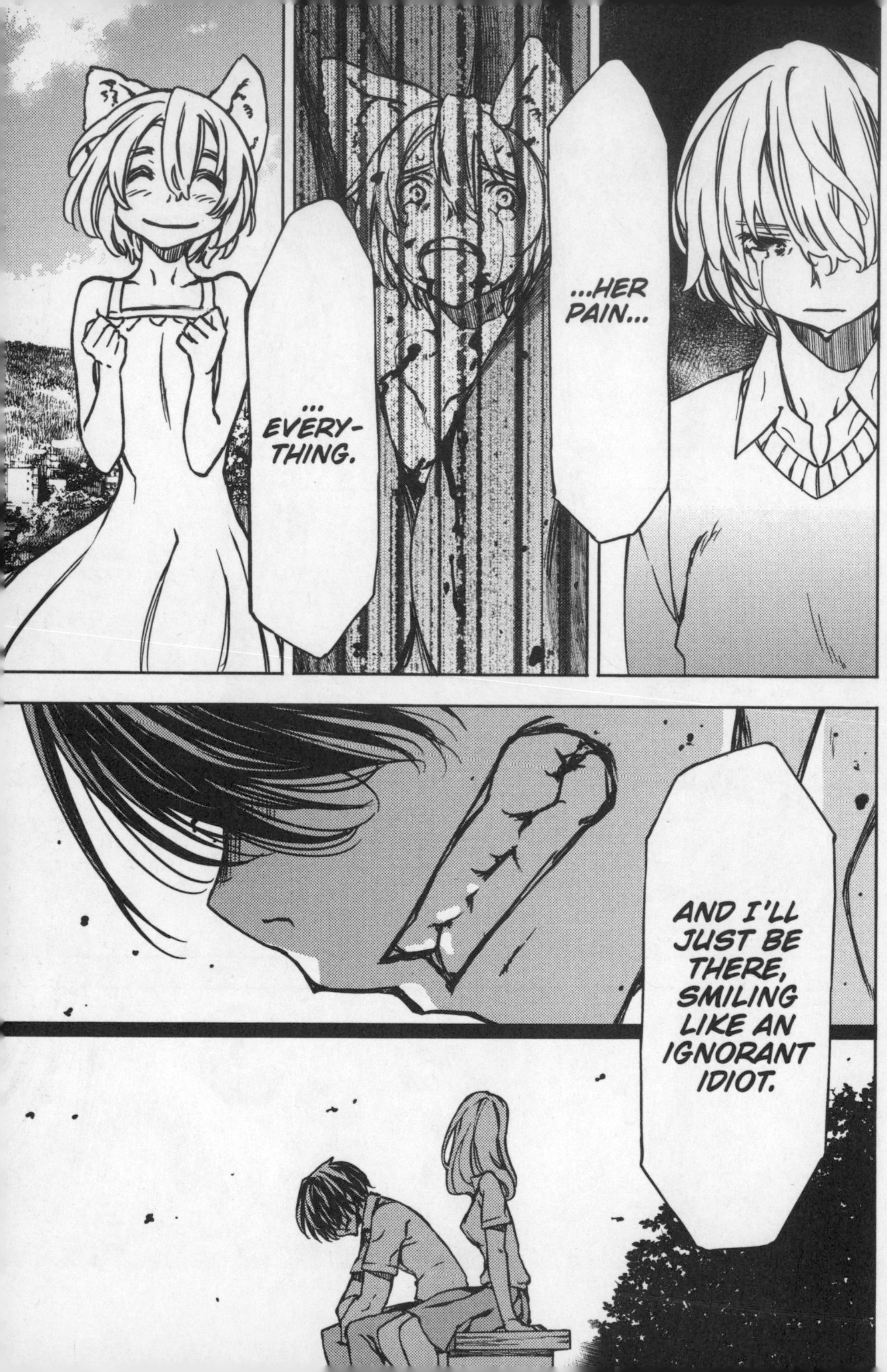
...HER PAIN...
... EVERY-THING.
AND I'LL JUST BE THERE, SMILING LIKE AN IGNORANT IDIOT.

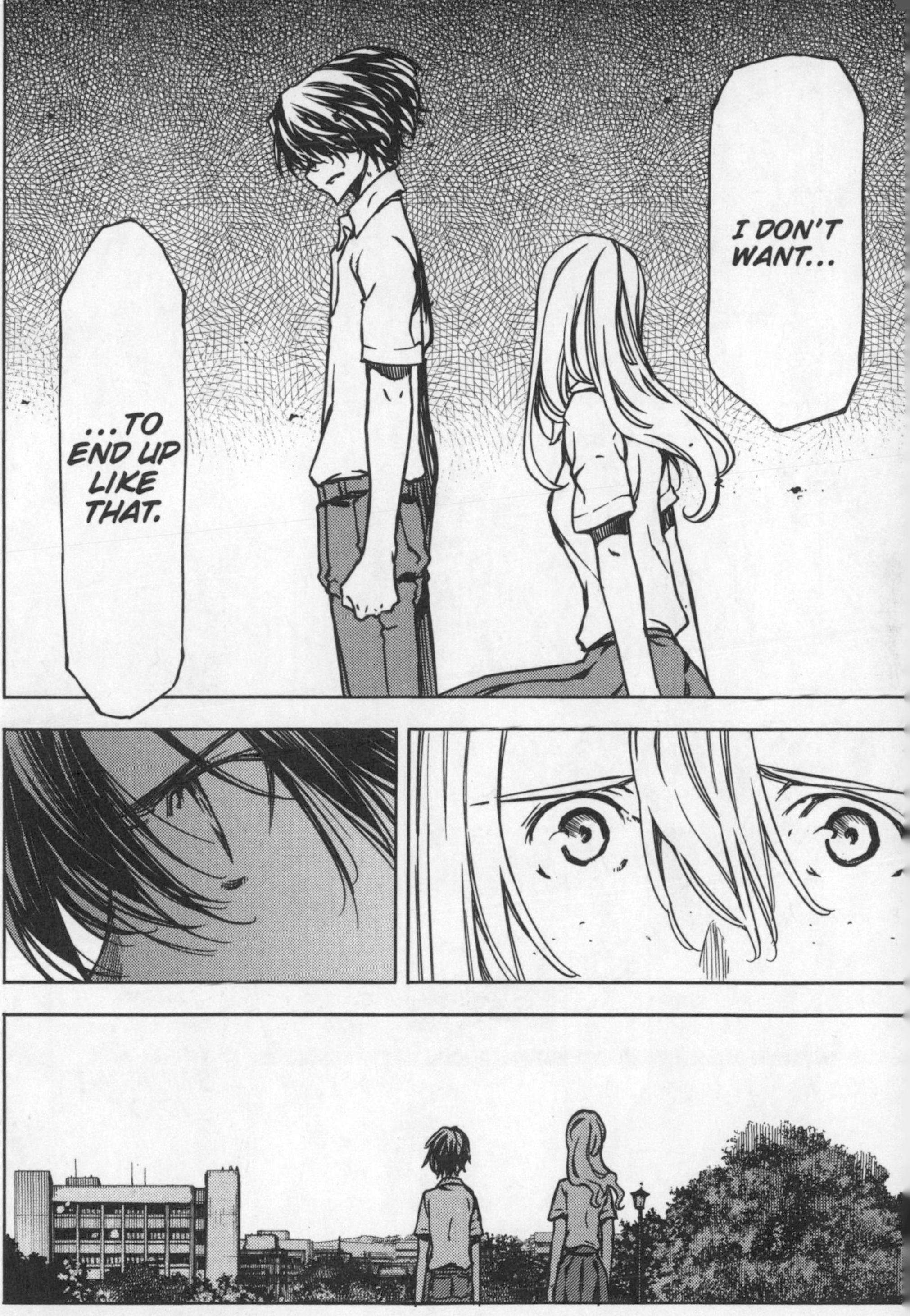
I DON'T WANT...
...TO END UP LIKE THAT.

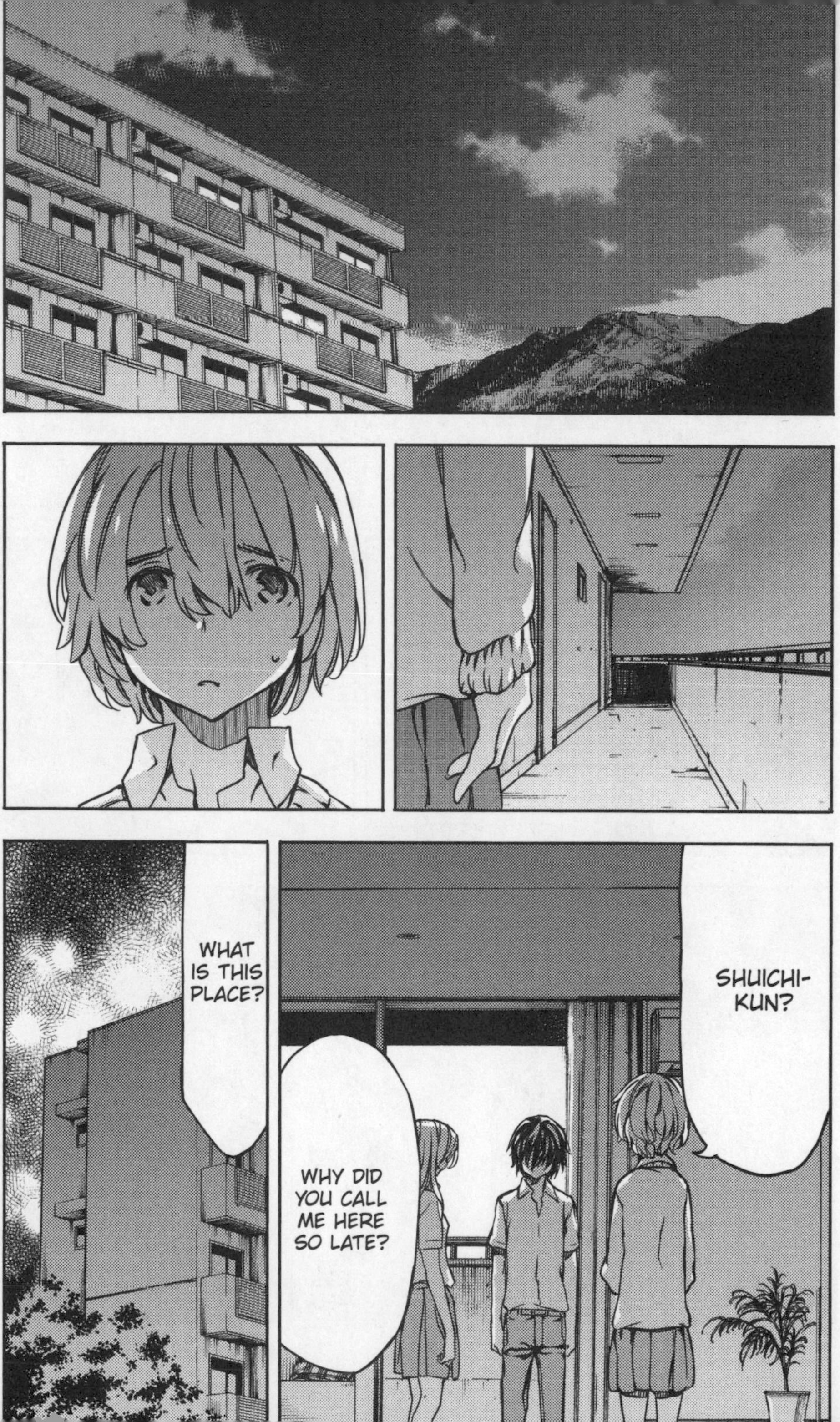
SHUICHI-KUN?
WHY DID YOU CALL ME HERE SO LATE?
WHAT IS THIS PLACE?

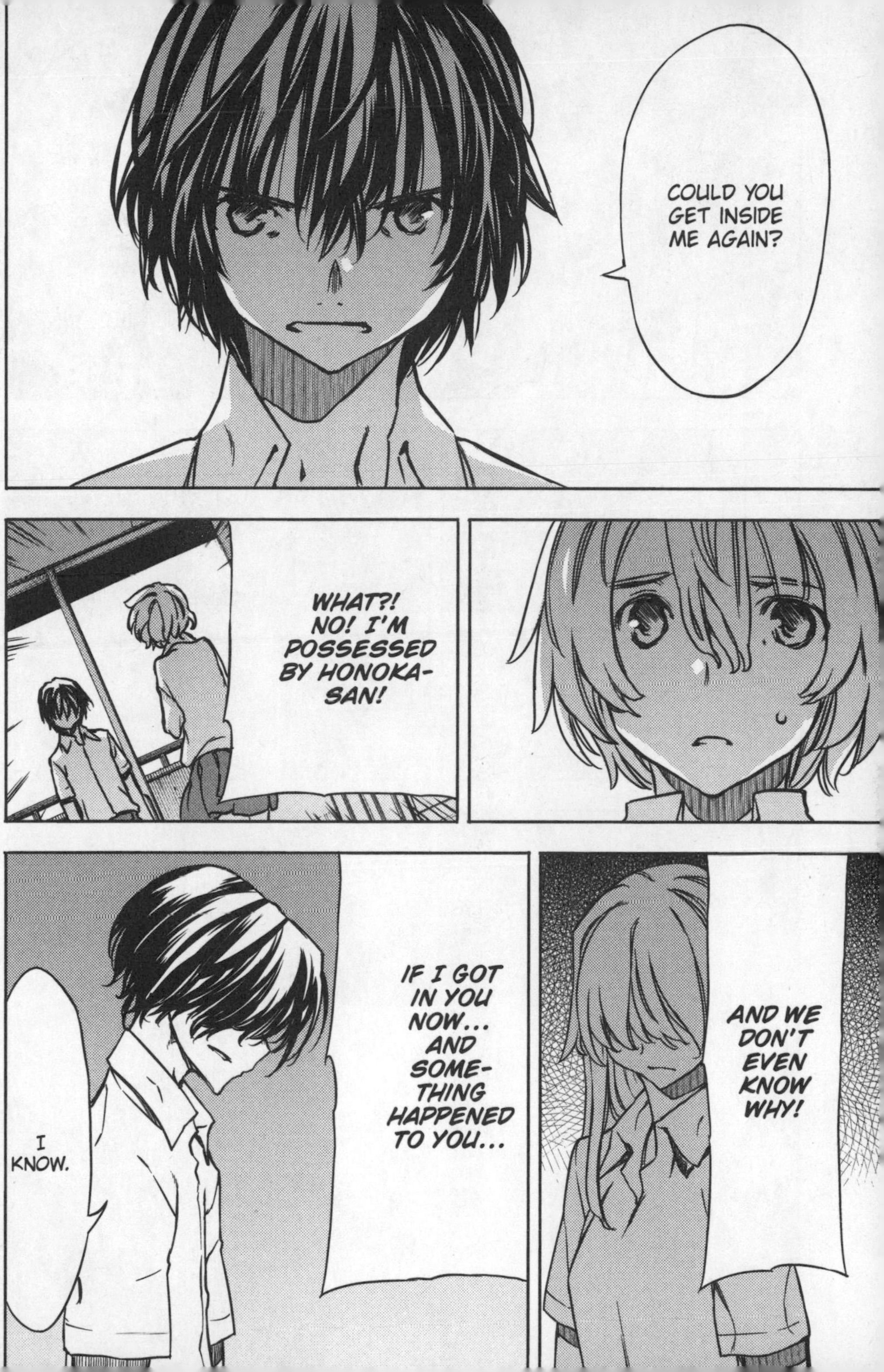
COULD YOU GET INSIDE ME AGAIN?
WHAT?! NO! I'M POSSESSED BY HONOKA-SAN!
IF I GOT IN YOU NOW... AND SOMETHING HAPPENED TO YOU...
AND WE DON'T EVEN KNOW WHY!
I KNOW.

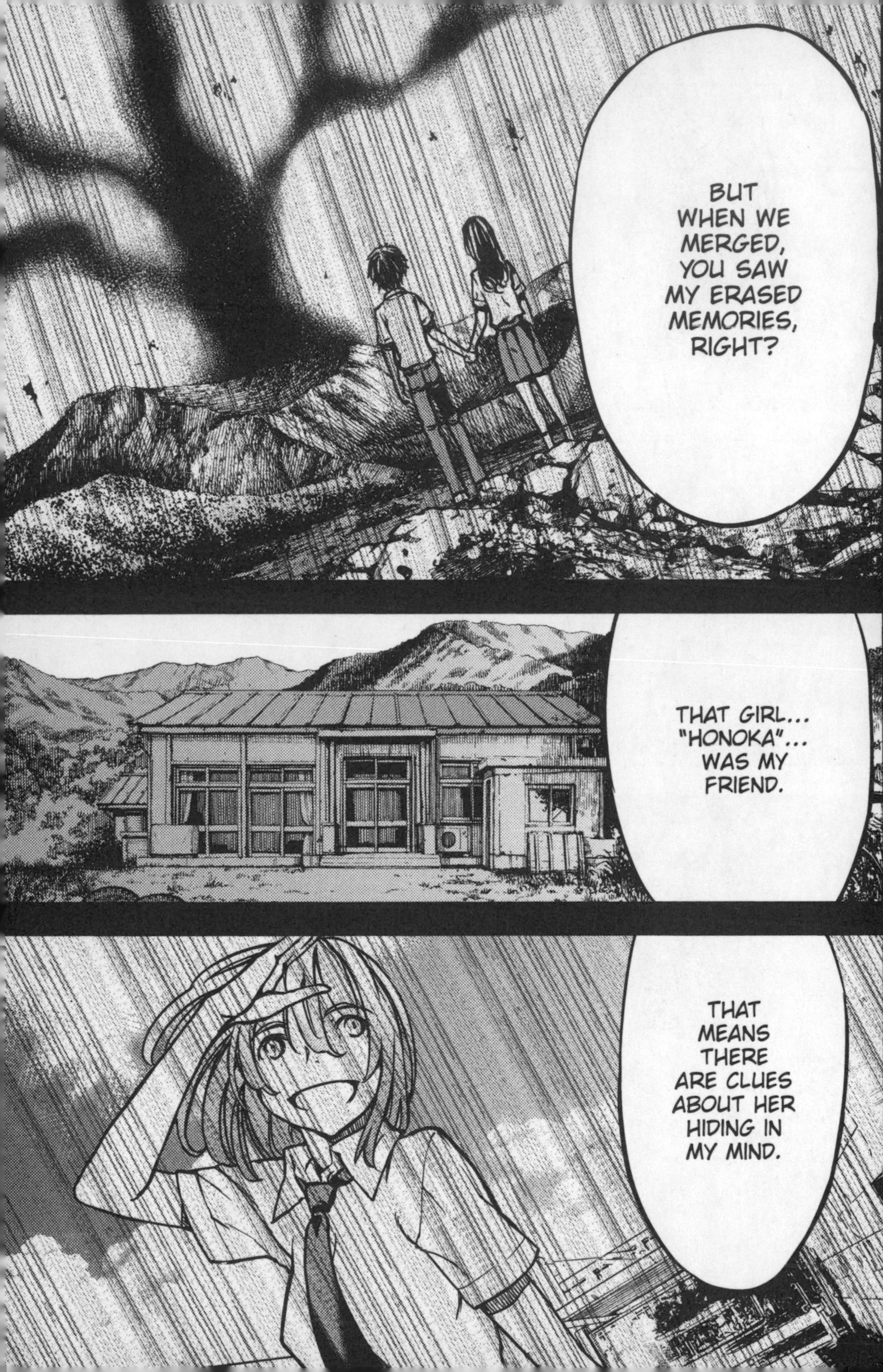
BUT WHEN WE MERGED, YOU SAW MY ERASED MEMORIES, RIGHT?
THAT GIRL... "HONOKA"... WAS MY FRIEND.
THAT MEANS THERE ARE CLUES ABOUT HER HIDING IN MY MIND.

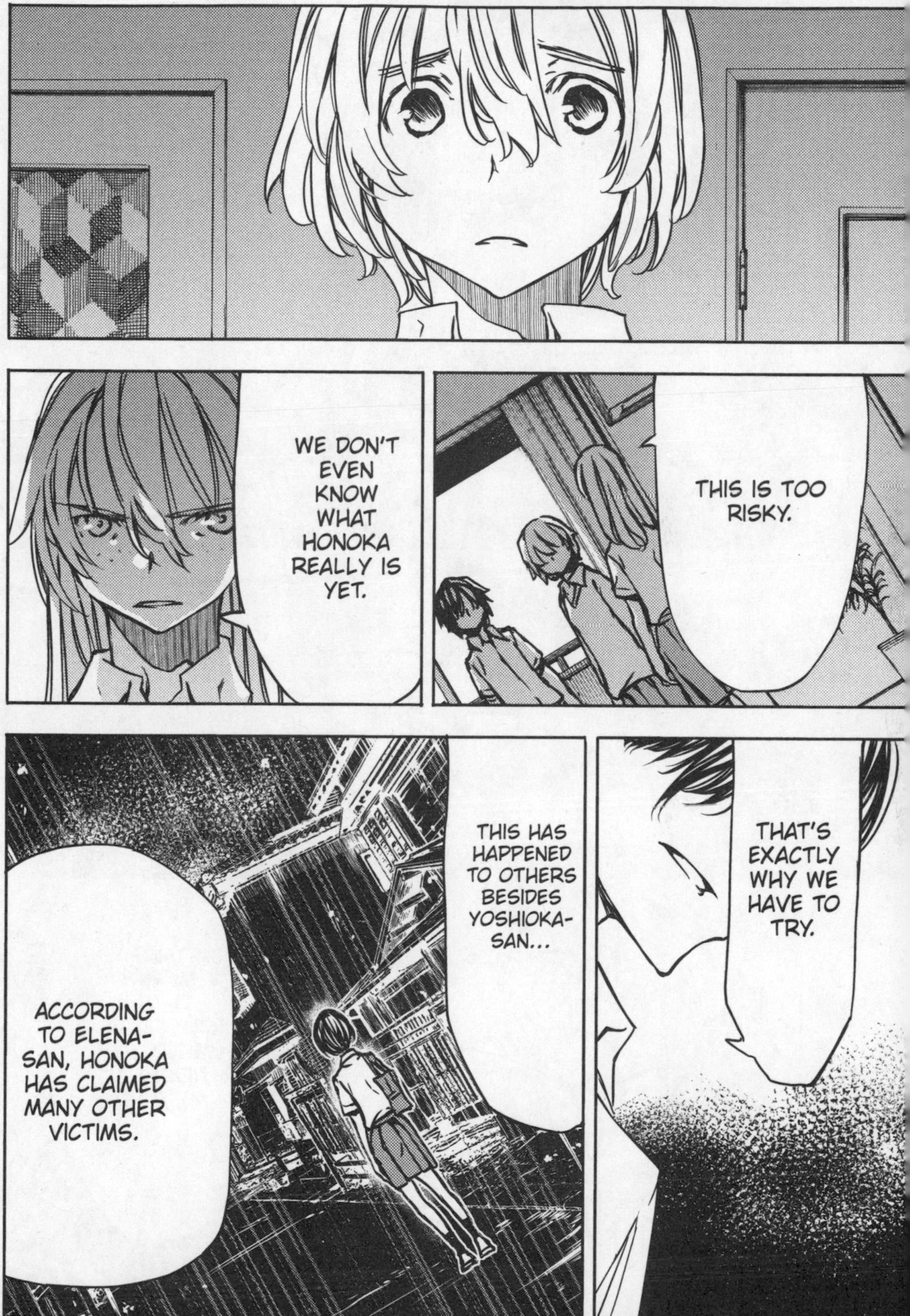
THIS IS TOO RISKY.
WE DON'T EVEN KNOW WHAT HONOKA REALLY IS YET.
THAT'S EXACTLY WHY WE HAVE TO TRY.
THIS HAS HAPPENED TO OTHERS BESIDES YOSHIOKA-SAN...
ACCORDING TO ELENA-SAN, HONOKA HAS CLAIMED MANY OTHER VICTIMS.

PLEASE, YOSHIOKA-SAN...

I NEED YOUR HELP.

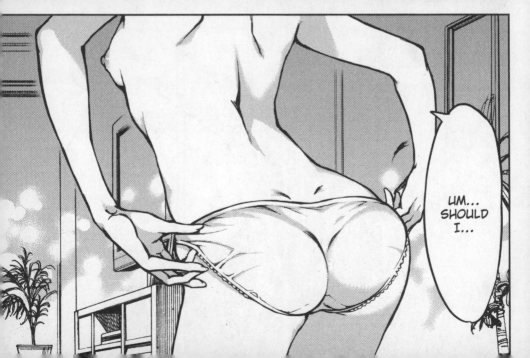

UM... SHOULD I...

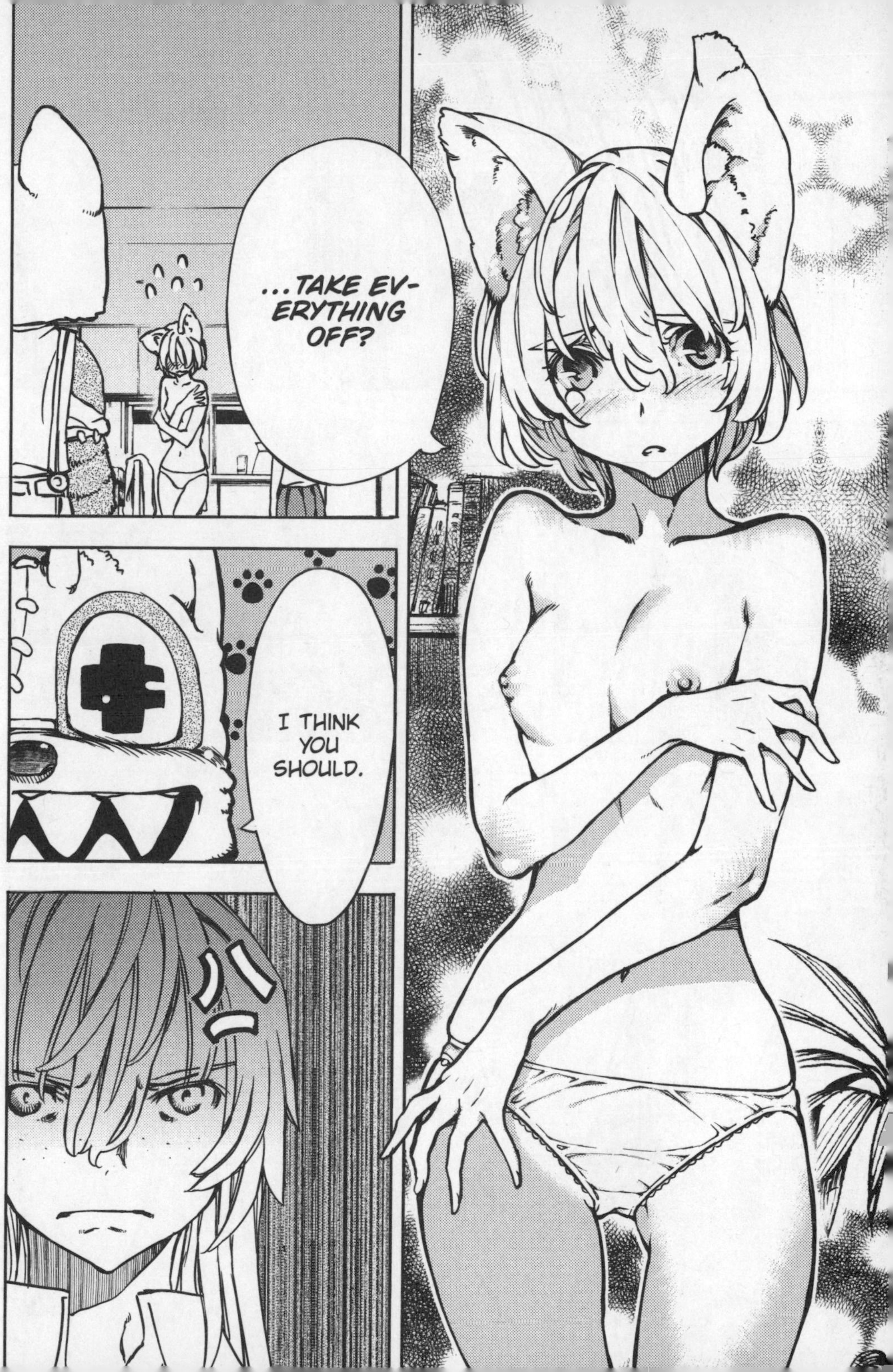
...TAKE EV-ERYTHING OFF?
I THINK YOU SHOULD.

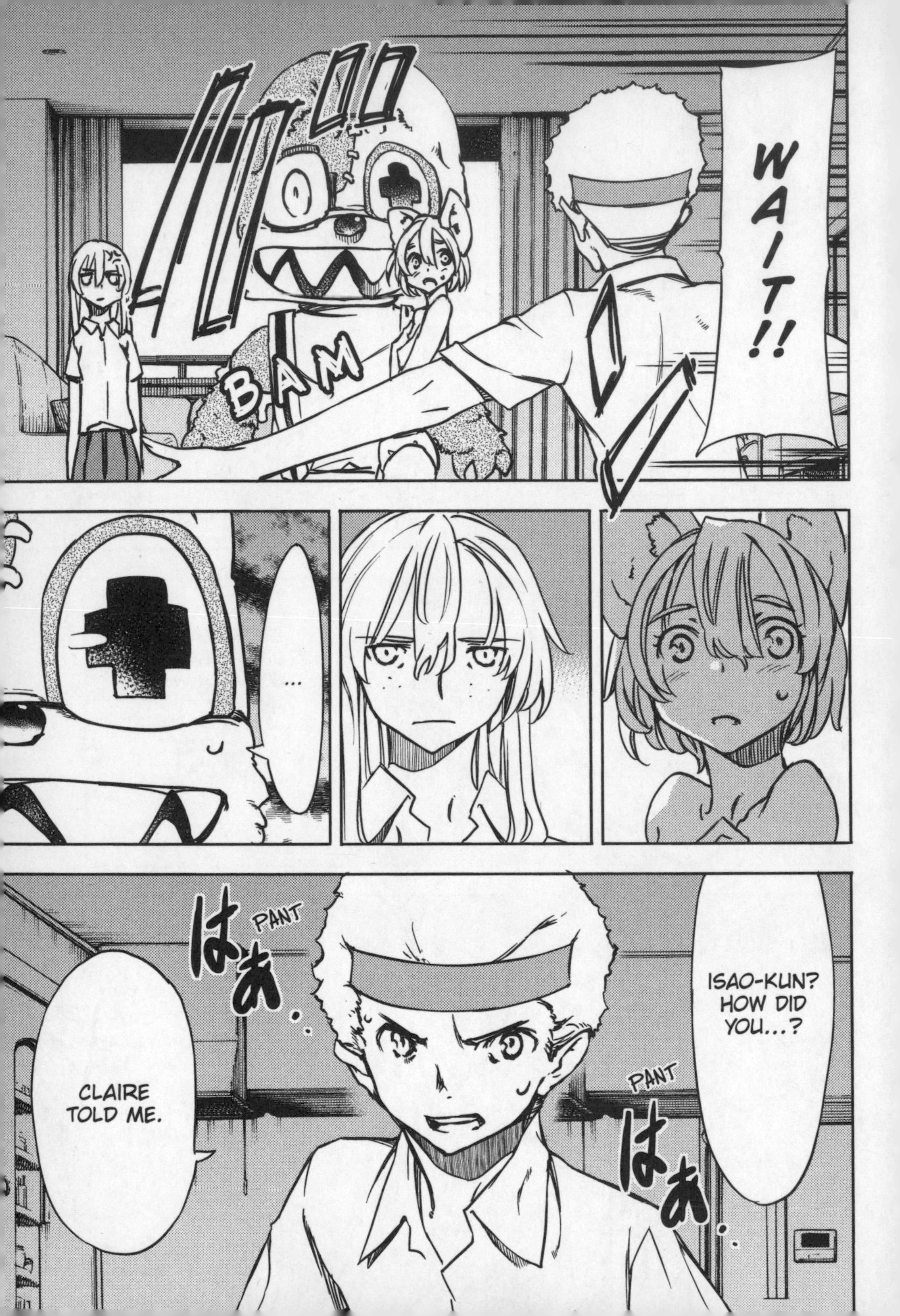
WAIT!!
BAM
...
ISAO-KUN? HOW DID YOU...?
PANT
はぁ..
PANT
はぁ..
CLAIRE TOLD ME.

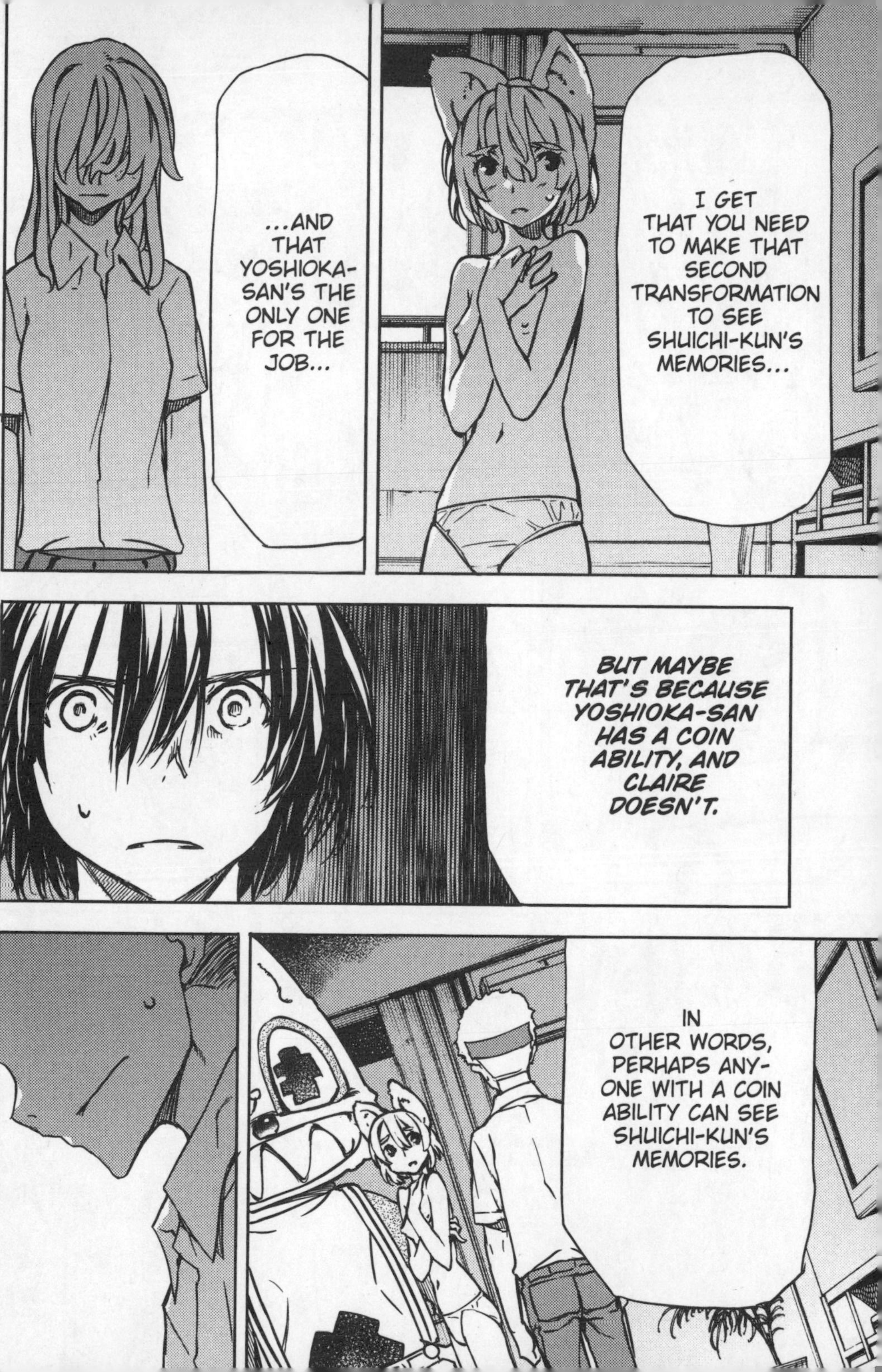
I GET THAT YOU NEED TO MAKE THAT SECOND TRANSFORMATION TO SEE SHUICHI-KUN'S MEMORIES...
...AND THAT YOSHIOKA-SAN'S THE ONLY ONE FOR THE JOB...
BUT MAYBE THAT'S BECAUSE YOSHIOKA-SAN HAS A COIN ABILITY, AND CLAIRE DOESN'T.
IN OTHER WORDS, PERHAPS ANY-ONE WITH A COIN ABILITY CAN SEE SHUICHI-KUN'S MEMORIES.

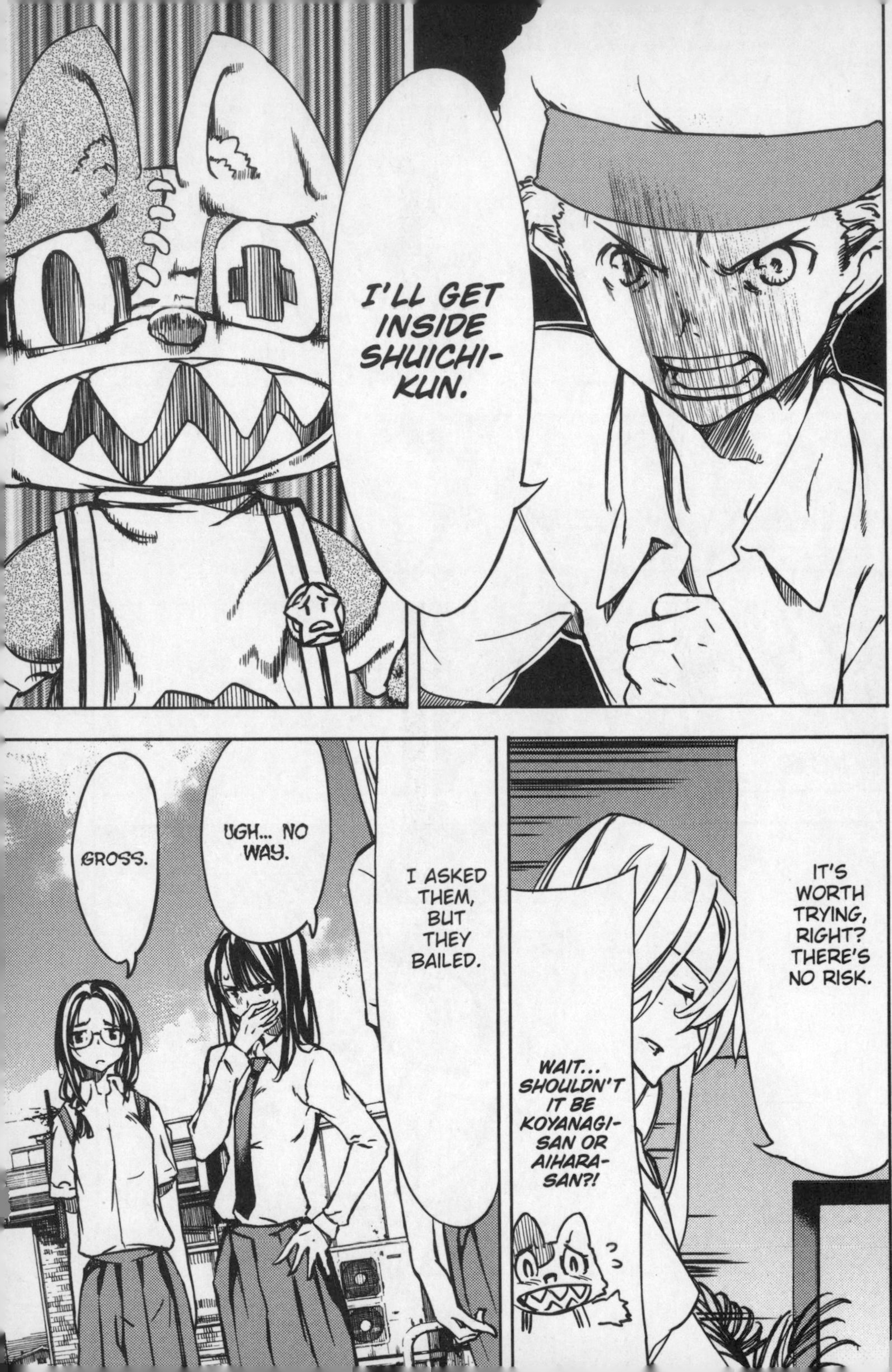
I'LL GET INSIDE SHUICHI-KUN.
IT'S WORTH TRYING, RIGHT? THERE'S NO RISK.
WAIT... SHOULDN'T IT BE KOYANAGI-SAN OR AIHARA-SAN?!
I ASKED THEM, BUT THEY BAILED.
UGH... NO WAY.
GROSS.

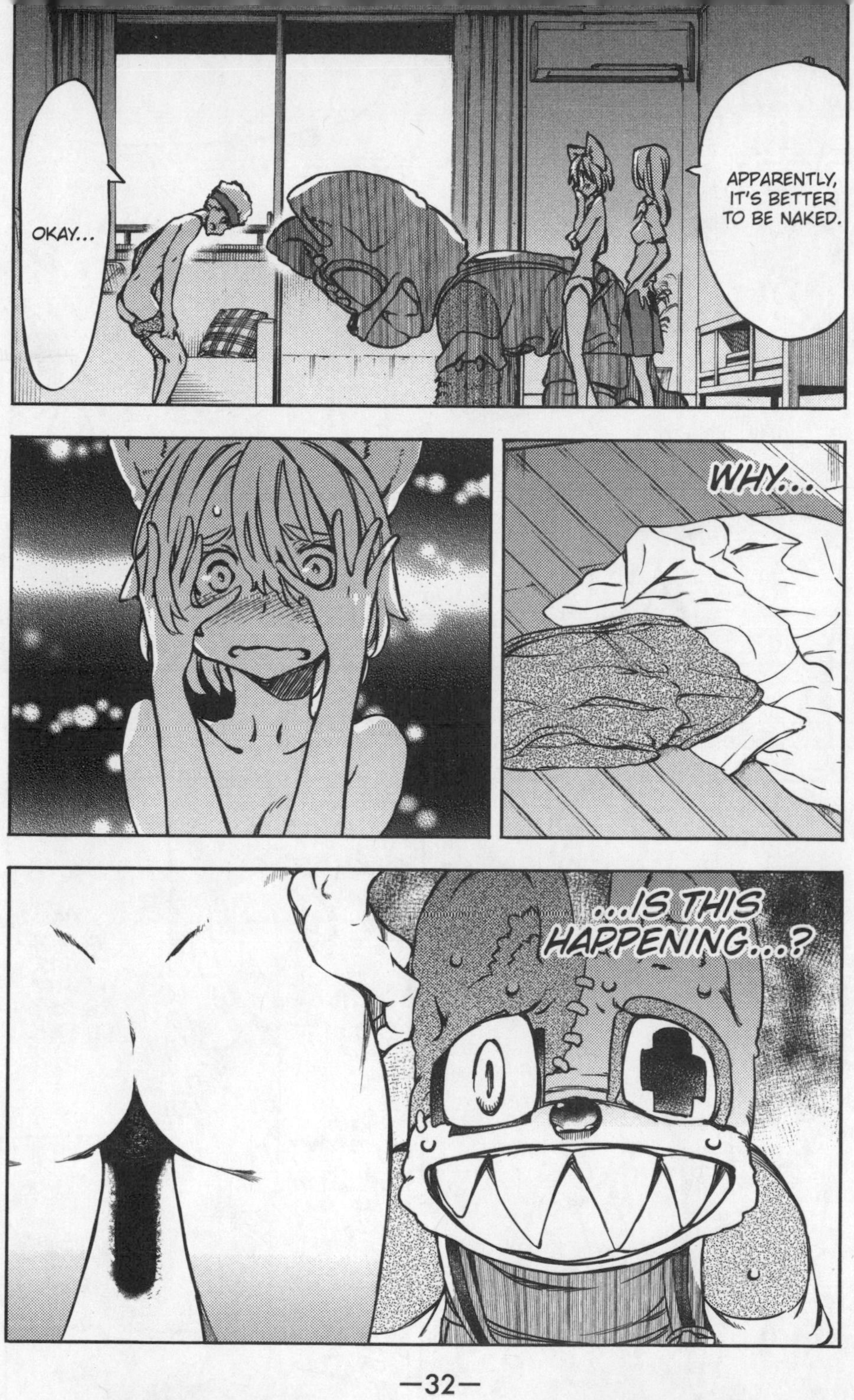
APPARENTLY, IT'S BETTER TO BE NAKED.
OKAY...
WHY...
...IS THIS HAPPENING...?

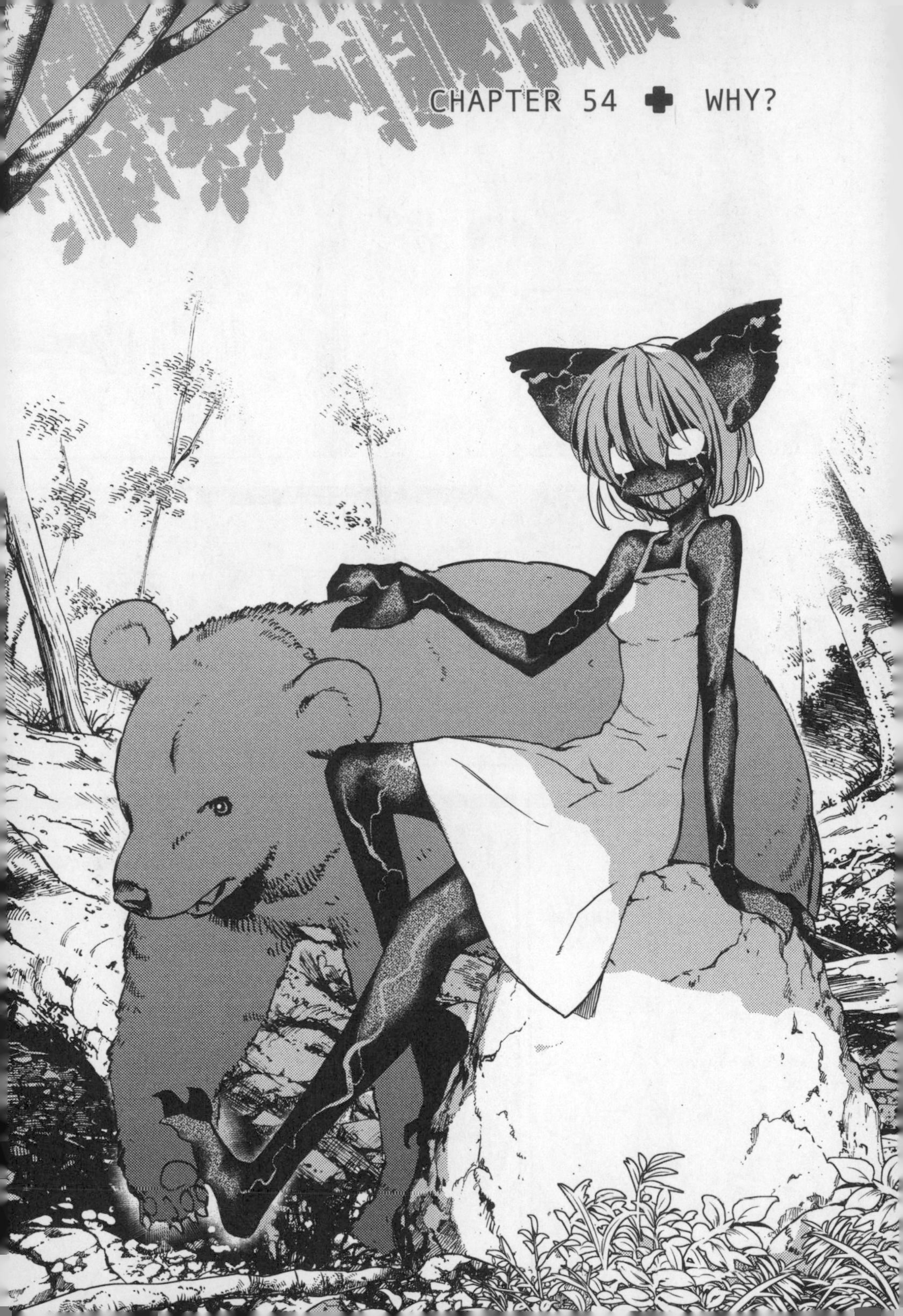
CHAPTER 54 ✚ WHY?

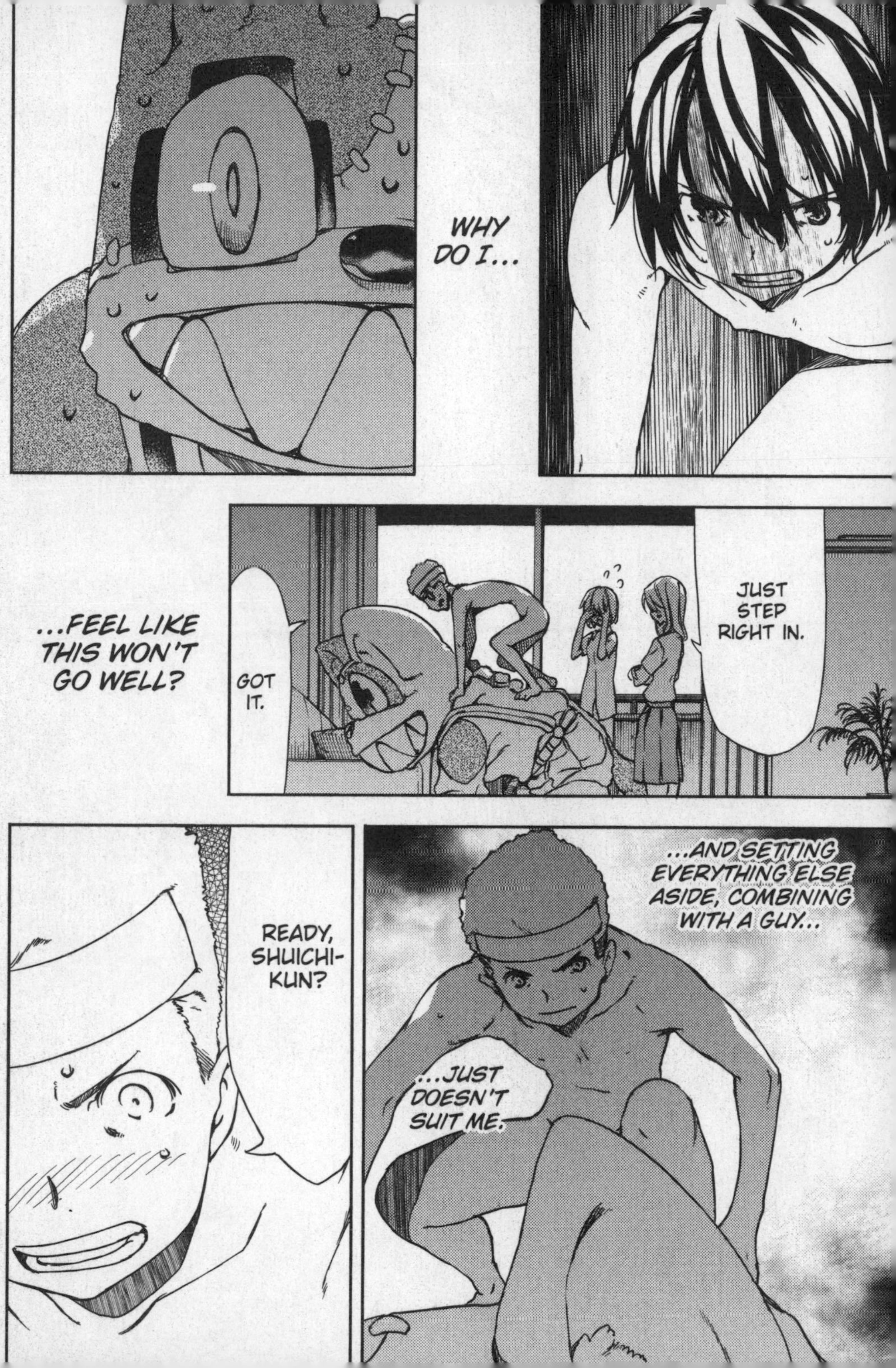
WHY DO I...
JUST STEP RIGHT IN.
GOT IT.
...FEEL LIKE THIS WON'T GO WELL?
...AND SETTING EVERYTHING ELSE ASIDE, COMBINING WITH A GUY...
...JUST DOESN'T SUIT ME.
READY, SHUICHI-KUN?

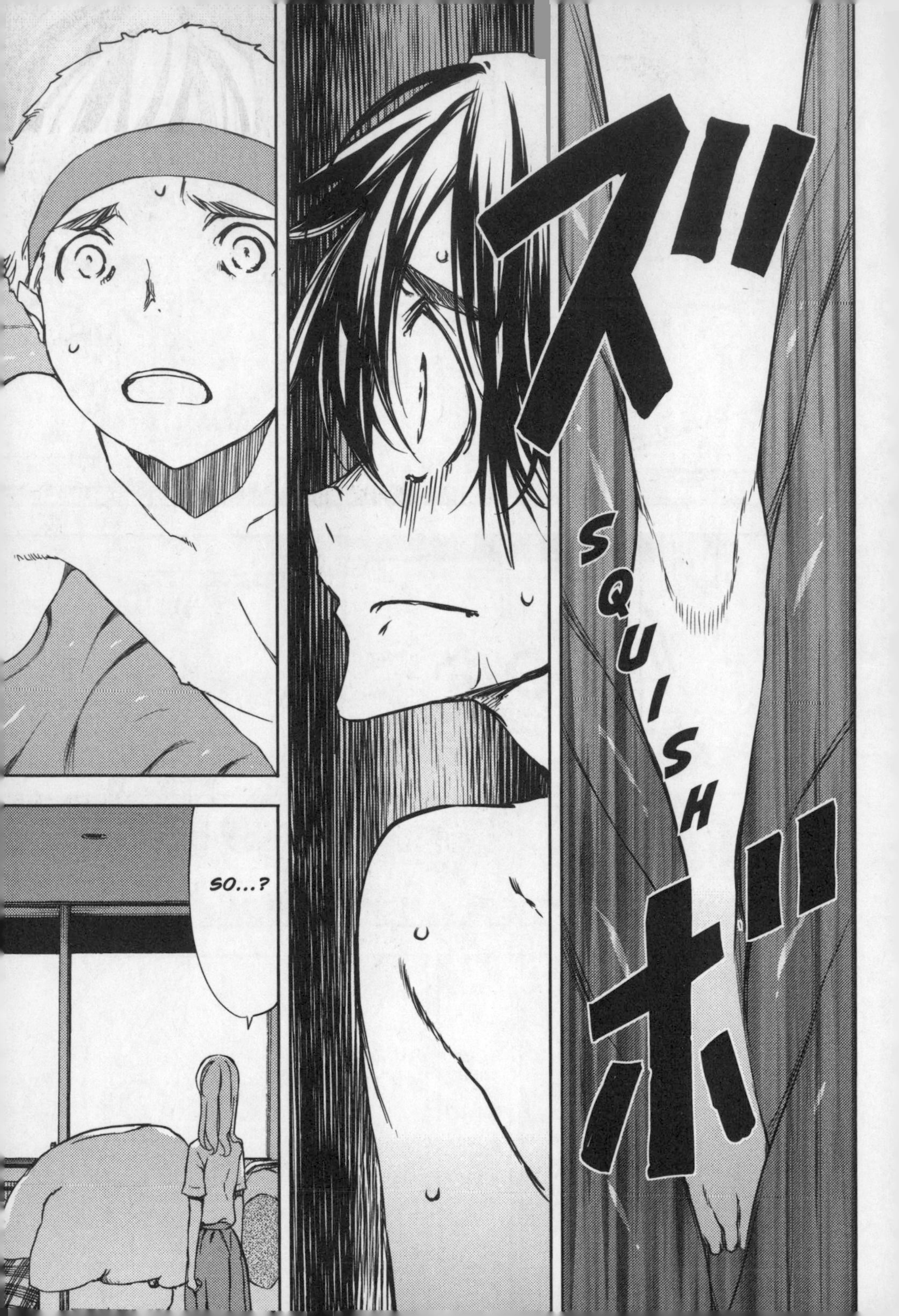
ズボ
SQUISH
SO...?

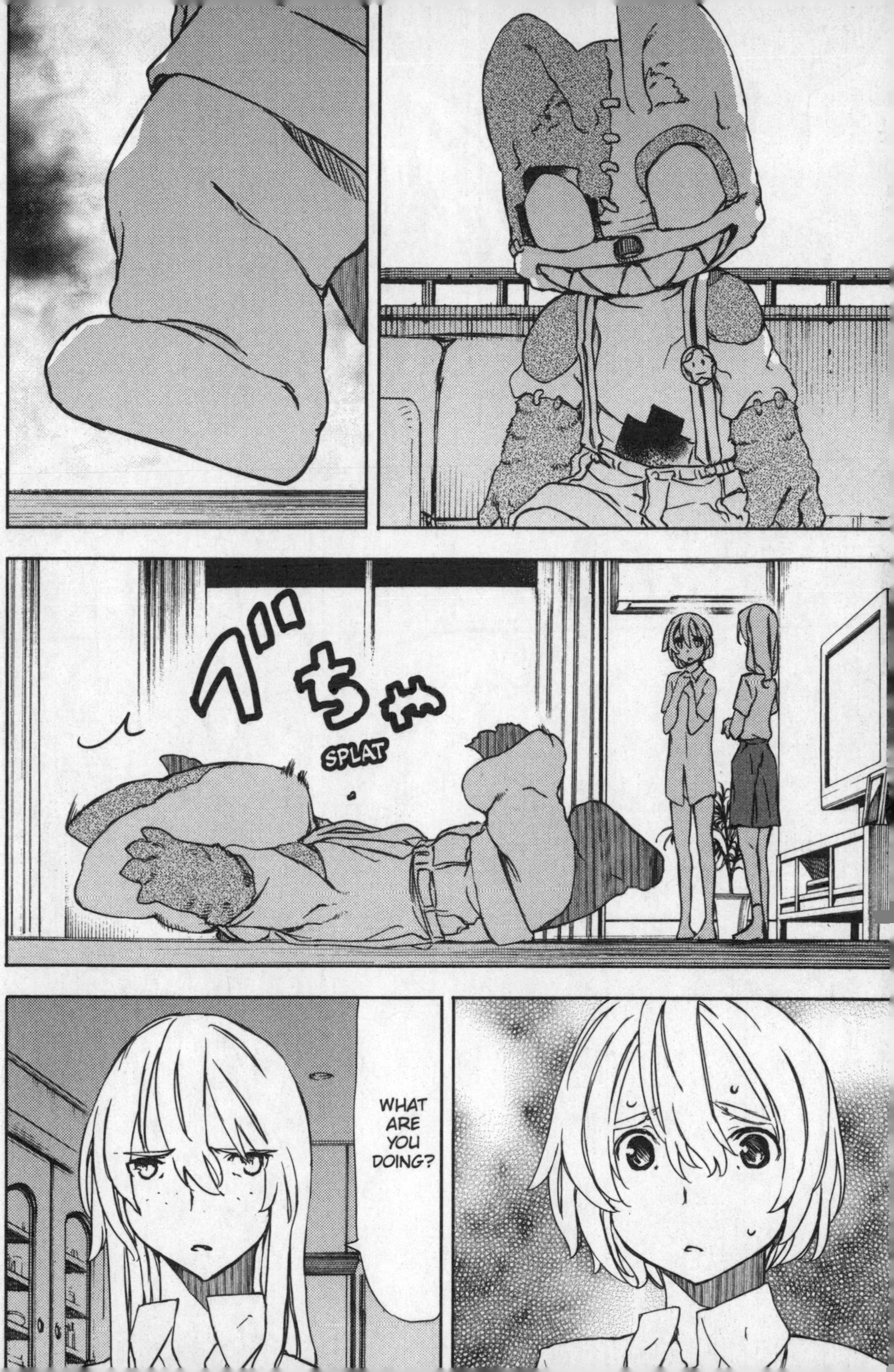
グちゃ
SPLAT
WHAT ARE YOU DOING?

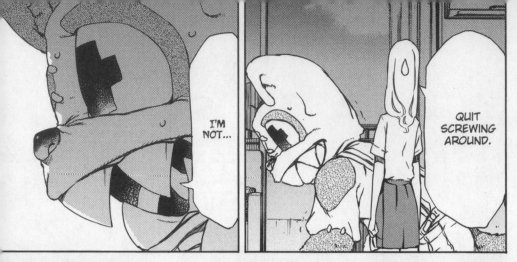

I'M NOT...

QUIT SCREWING AROUND.

...MOVE VERY WELL...

I CAN'T...

ELENA-SAN DID MENTION...

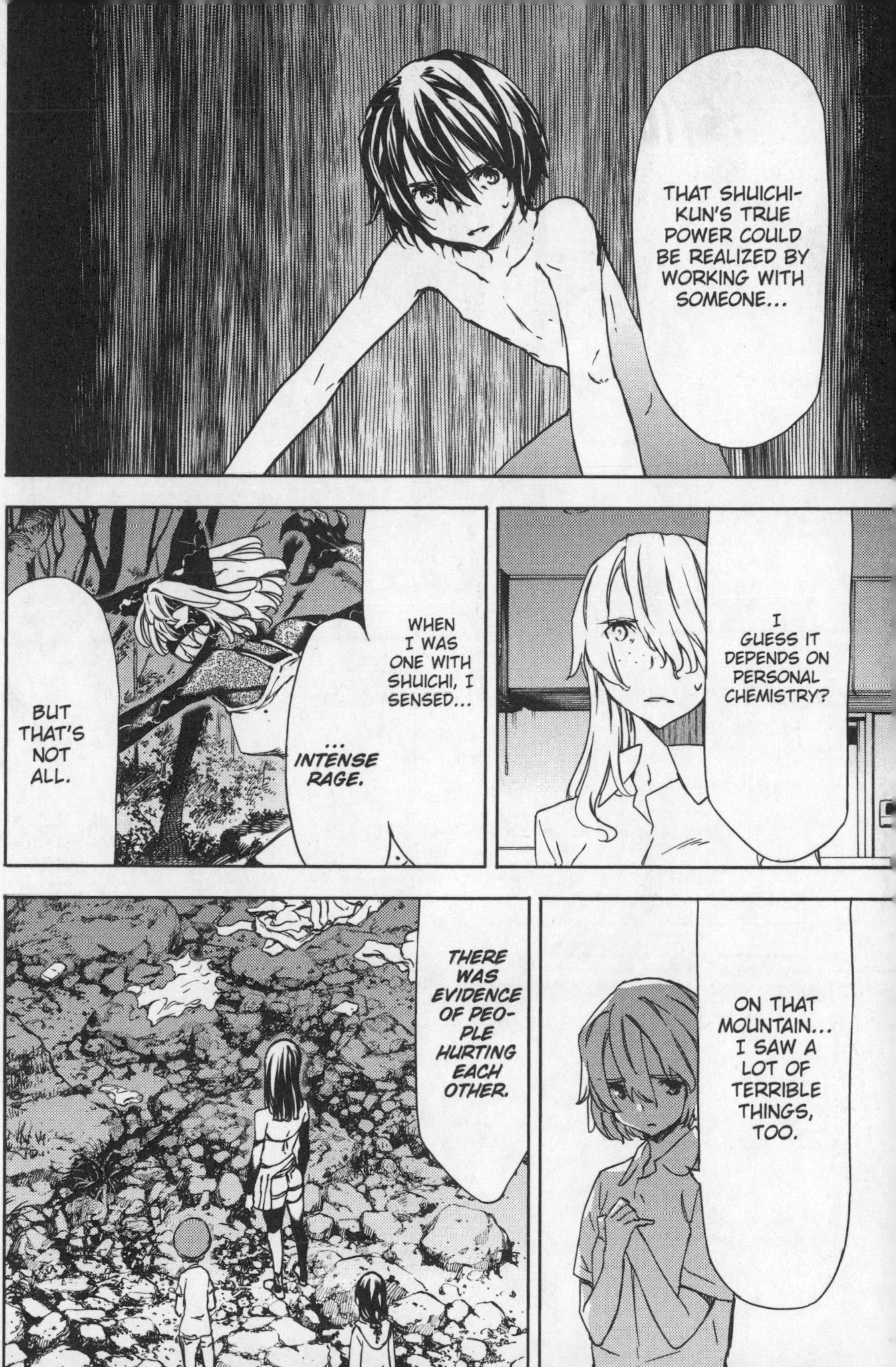
THAT SHUICHI-KUN'S TRUE POWER COULD BE REALIZED BY WORKING WITH SOMEONE...
I GUESS IT DEPENDS ON PERSONAL CHEMISTRY?
WHEN I WAS ONE WITH SHUICHI, I SENSED...
...INTENSE RAGE.
BUT THAT'S NOT ALL.
ON THAT MOUNTAIN... I SAW A LOT OF TERRIBLE THINGS, TOO.
THERE WAS EVIDENCE OF PEO-PLE HURTING EACH OTHER.

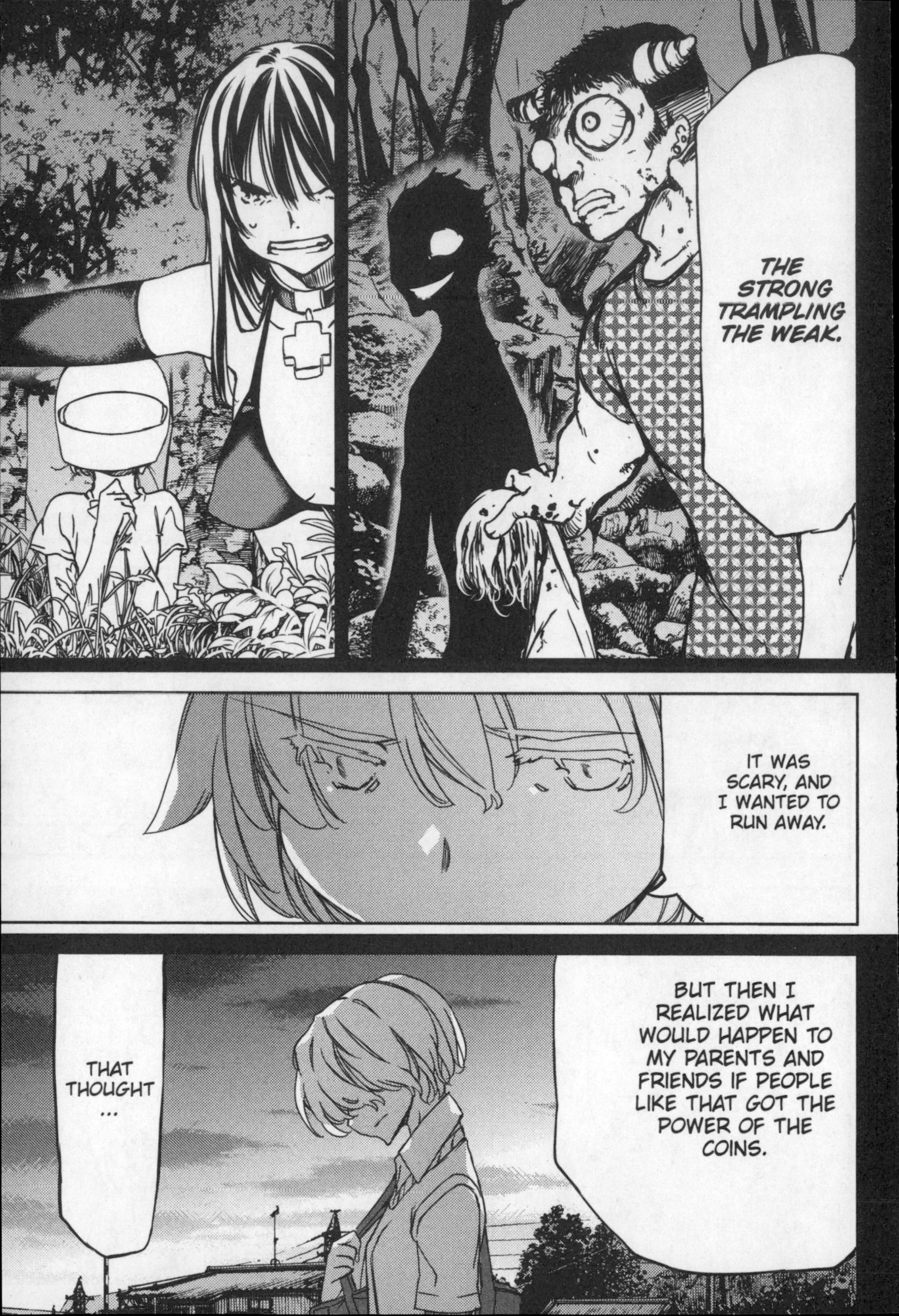
THE STRONG TRAMPLING THE WEAK.
IT WAS SCARY, AND I WANTED TO RUN AWAY.
BUT THEN I REALIZED WHAT WOULD HAPPEN TO MY PARENTS AND FRIENDS IF PEOPLE LIKE THAT GOT THE POWER OF THE COINS.
THAT THOUGHT ...

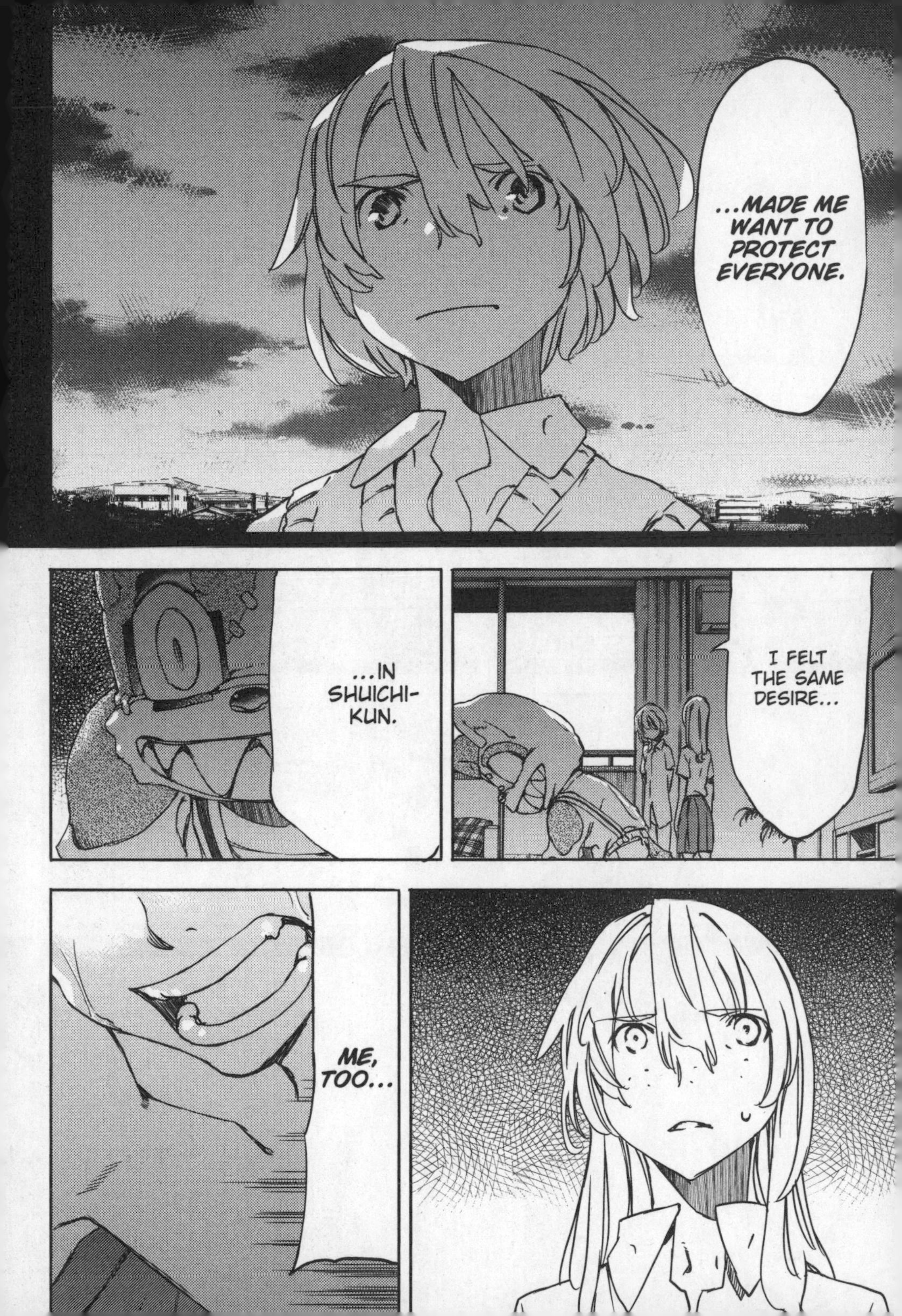
...MADE ME WANT TO PROTECT EVERYONE.
I FELT THE SAME DESIRE...
...IN SHUICHI-KUN.
ME, TOO...

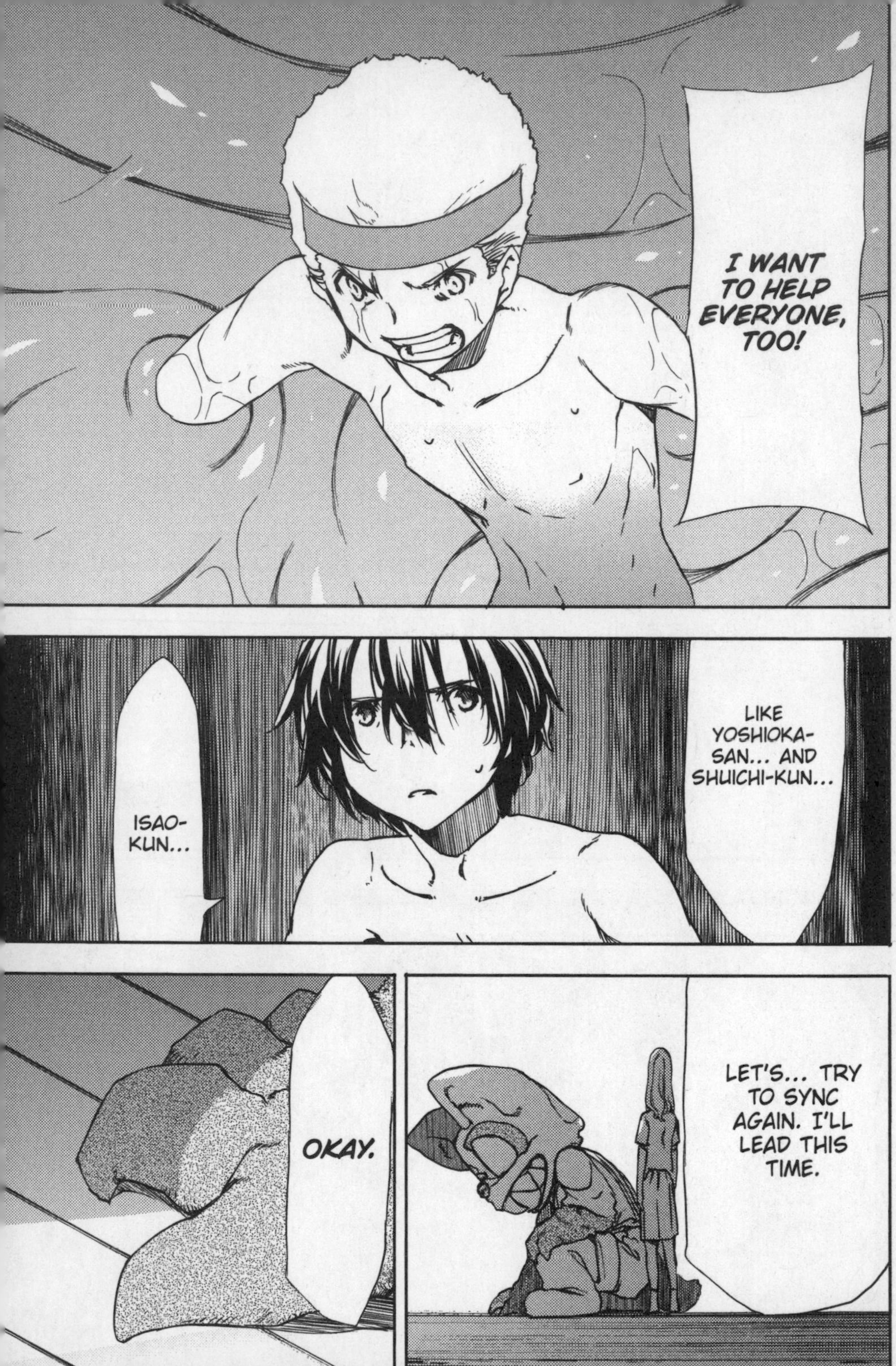
I WANT TO HELP EVERYONE, TOO!
LIKE YOSHIOKA-SAN... AND SHUICHI-KUN...
ISAO-KUN...
LET'S... TRY TO SYNC AGAIN. I'LL LEAD THIS TIME.
OKAY.

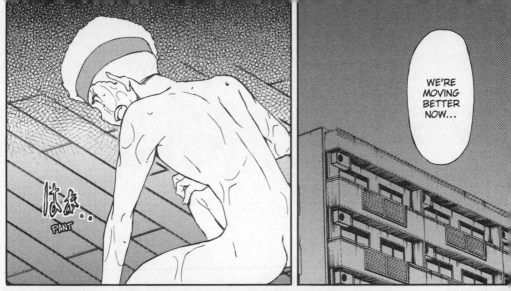

WE'RE MOVING BETTER NOW...

...BUT STILL... COMPARED TO CLAIRE...

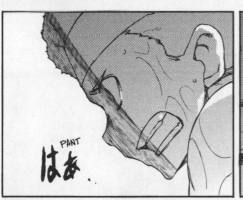

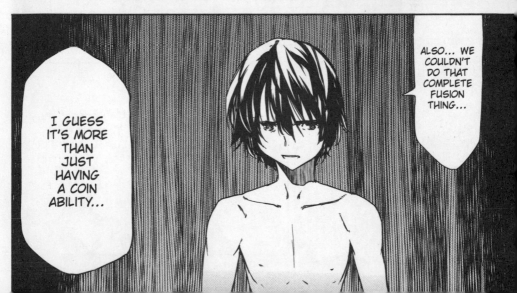

ALSO... WE COULDN'T DO THAT COMPLETE FUSION THING...

I GUESS IT'S MORE THAN JUST HAVING A COIN ABILITY...

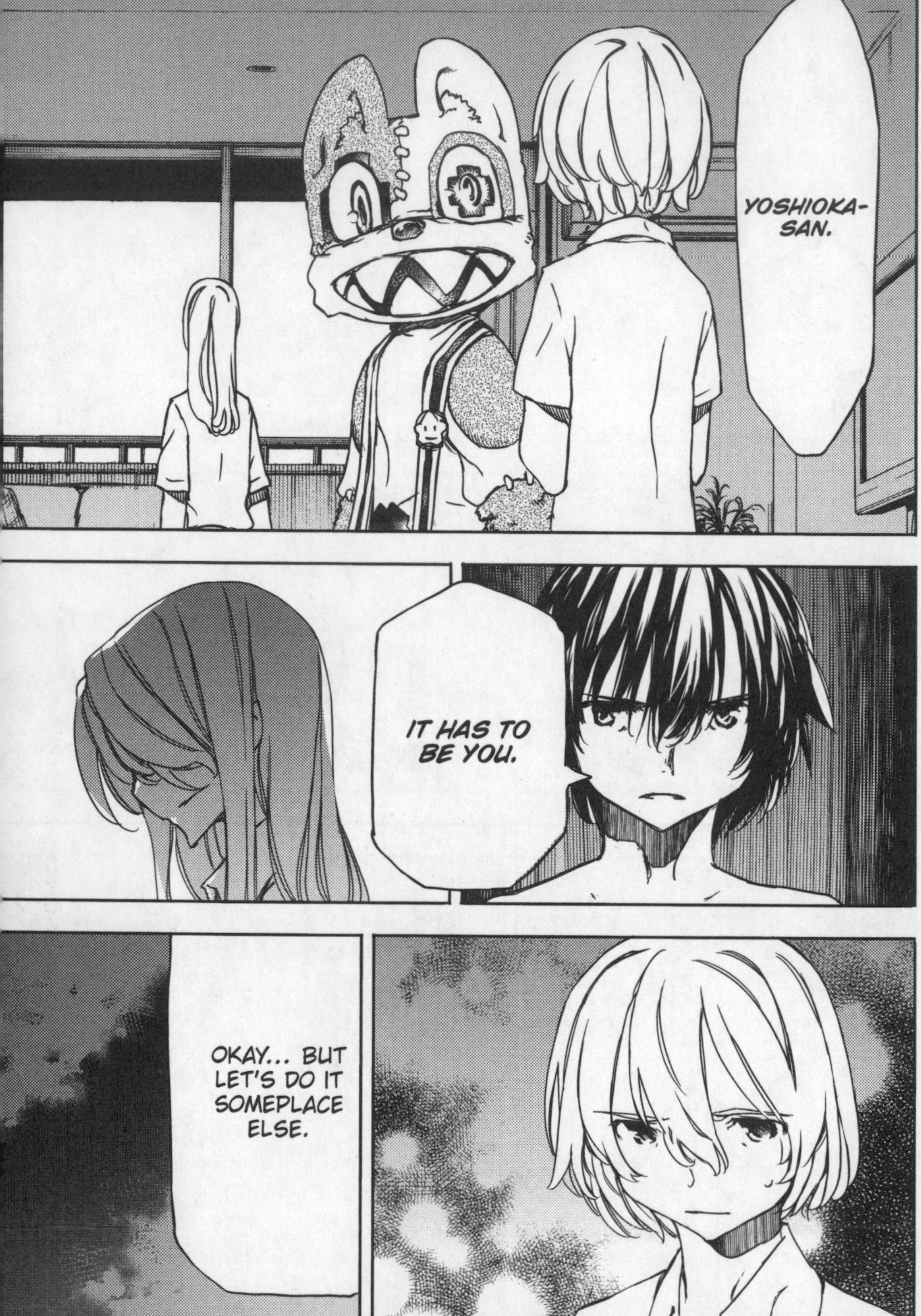
YOSHIOKA-SAN.
IT HAS TO BE YOU.
OKAY... BUT LET'S DO IT SOMEPLACE ELSE.

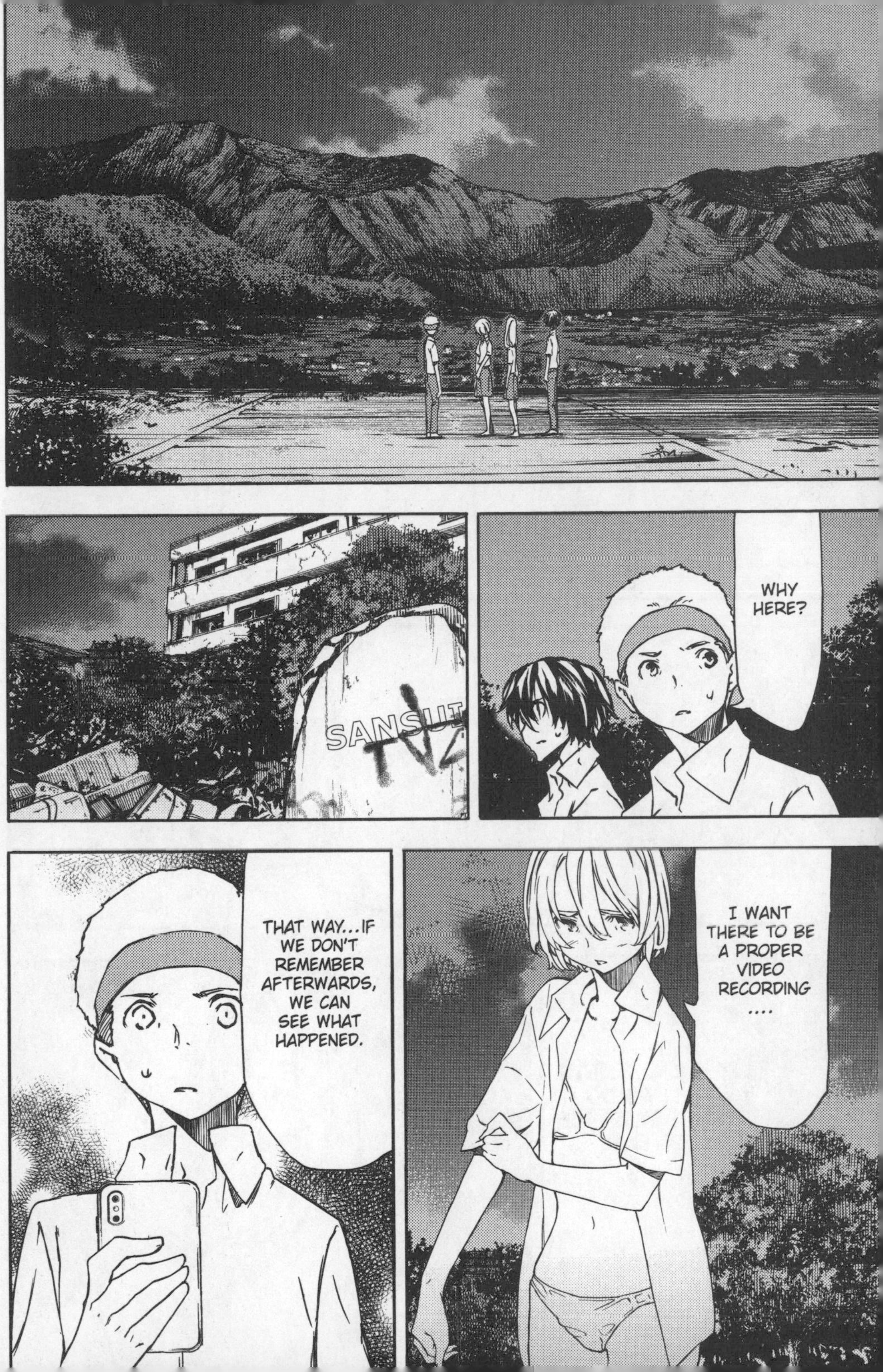
WHY HERE?
SANSUI
I WANT THERE TO BE A PROPER VIDEO RECORDING....
THAT WAY...IF WE DON'T REMEMBER AFTERWARDS, WE CAN SEE WHAT HAPPENED.

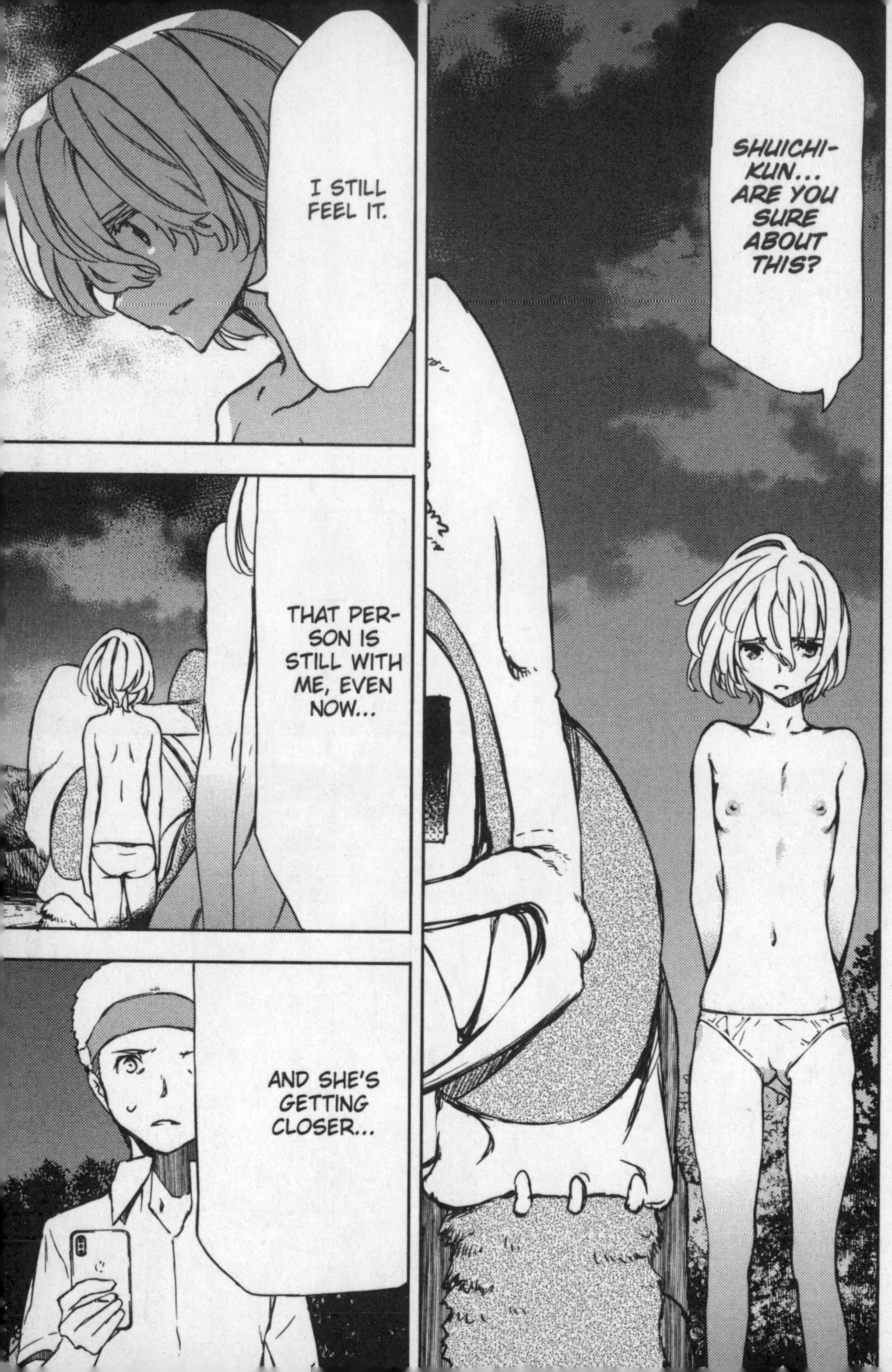
SHUICHI-KUN... ARE YOU SURE ABOUT THIS?
I STILL FEEL IT.
THAT PER-SON IS STILL WITH ME, EVEN NOW...
AND SHE'S GETTING CLOSER...

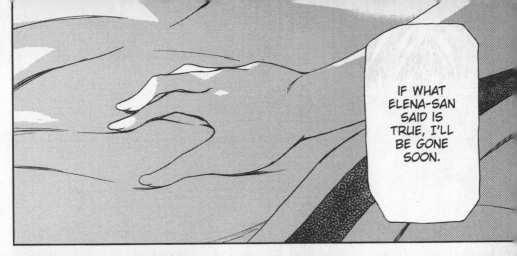

IF WHAT ELENA-SAN SAID IS TRUE, I'LL BE GONE SOON.

EVEN SO...

COMBINING WITH YOU MIGHT BE HARMFUL SOMEHOW...

...I WANT TO HELP YOU.

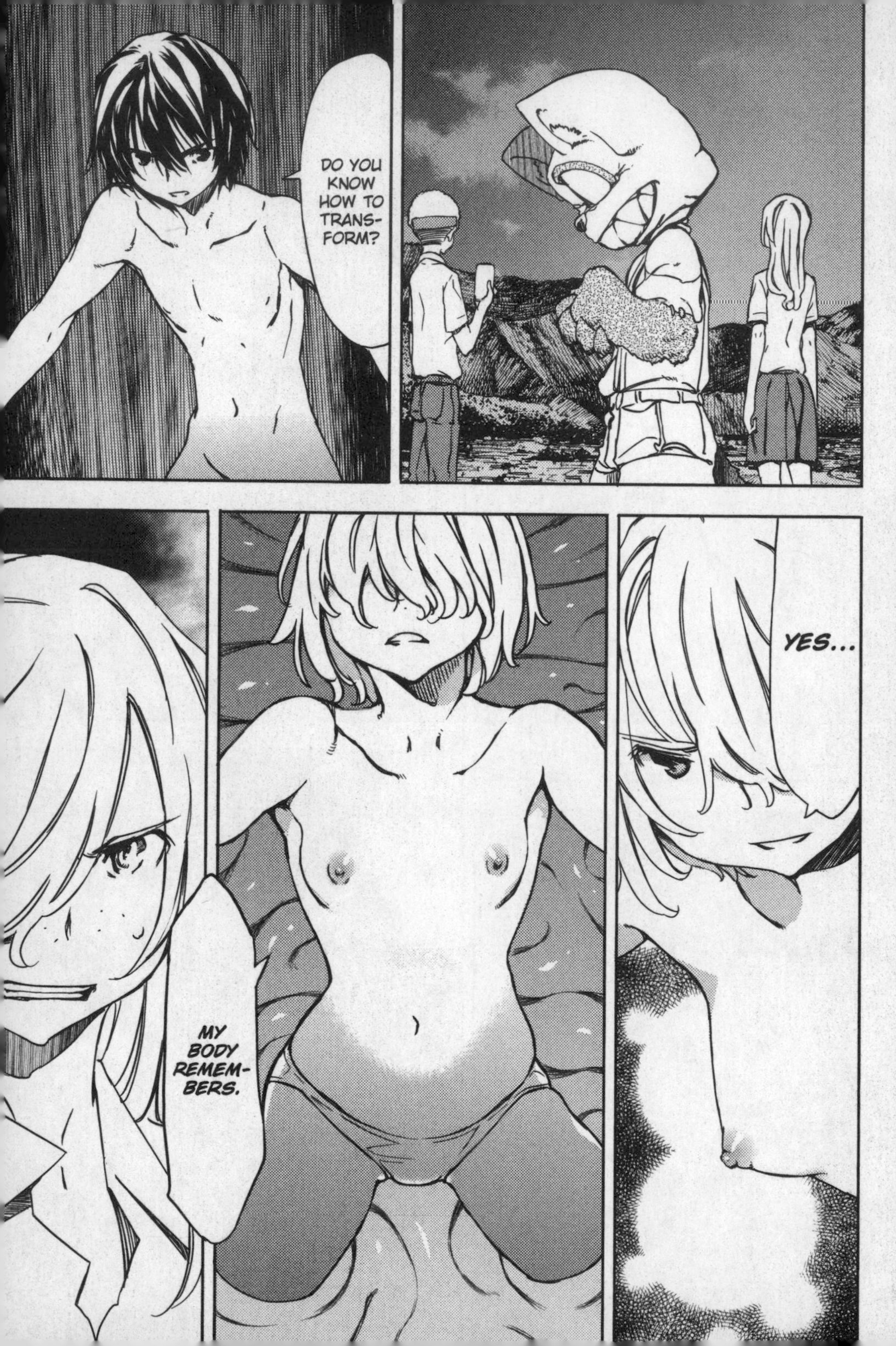
DO YOU KNOW HOW TO TRANS-FORM?
YES...
MY BODY REMEM-BERS.

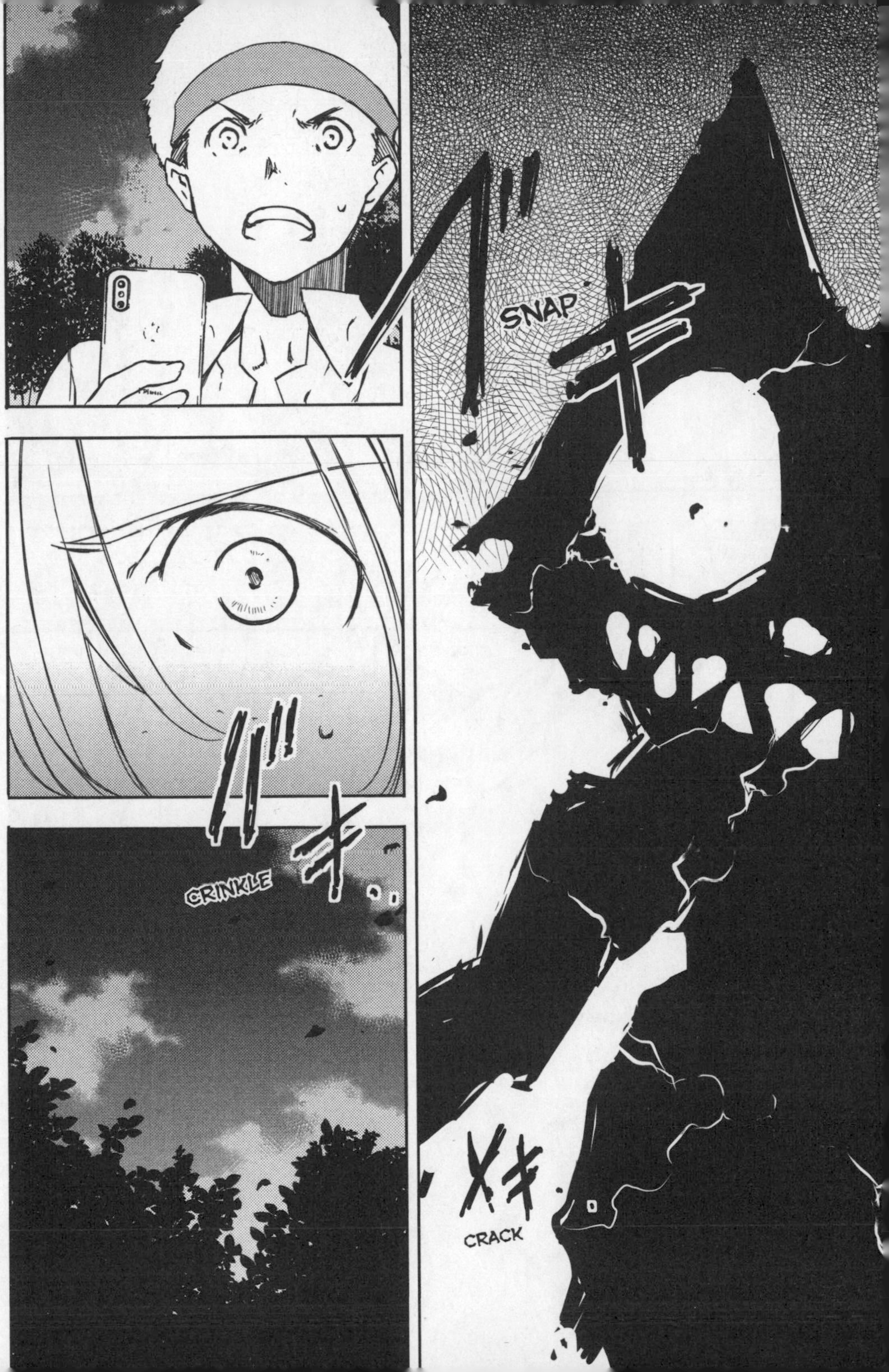
SNAP
CRACK
CRINKLE

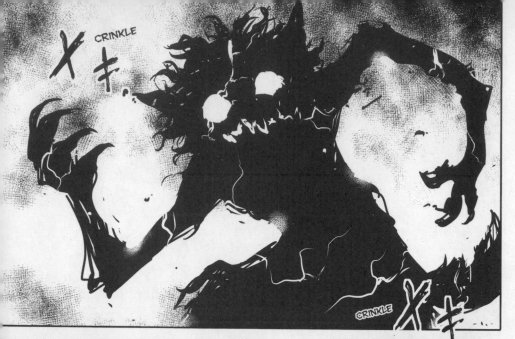

CRINKLE

CRINKLE

THIS IS
SHUICHI'S...

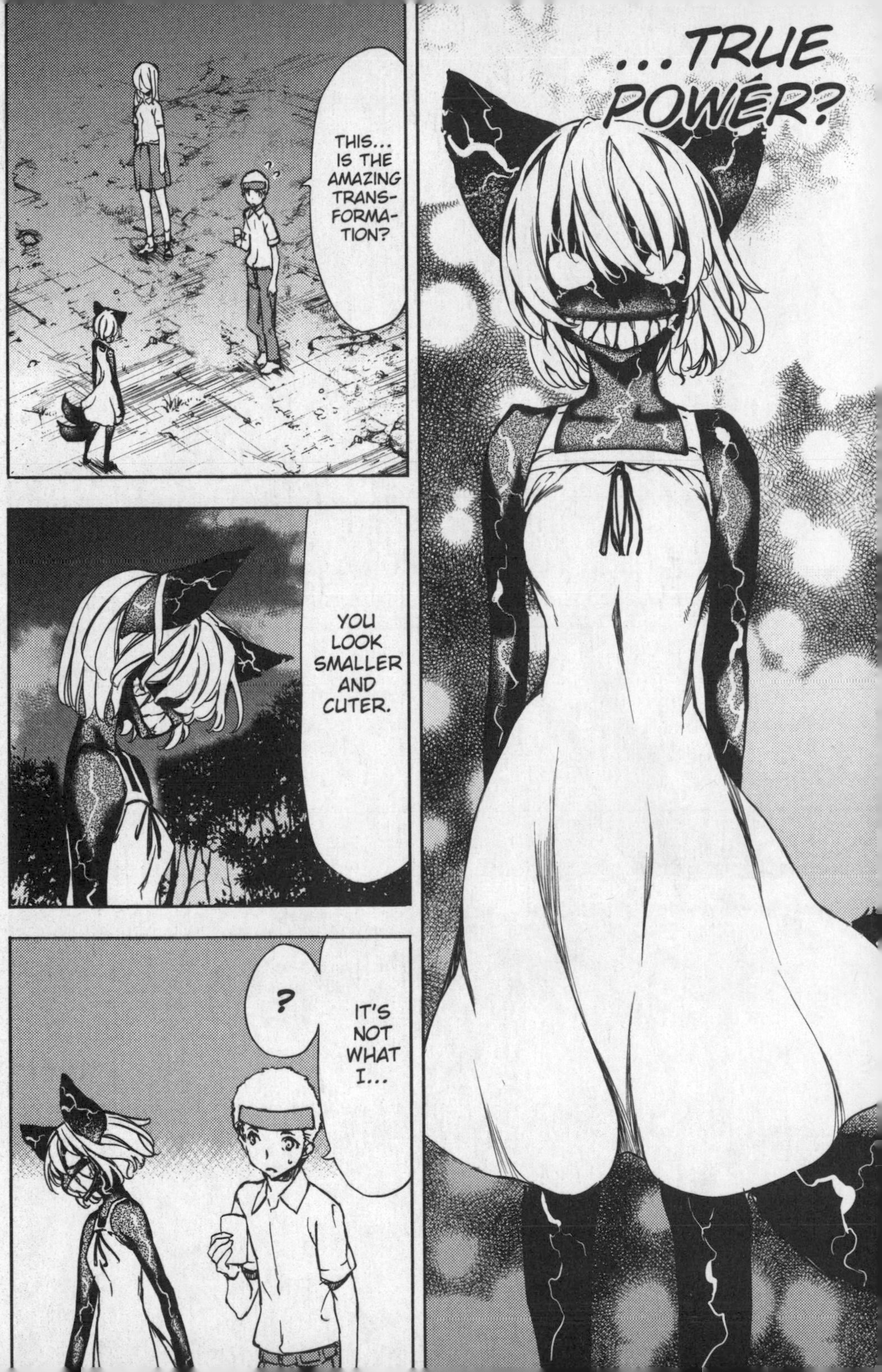
...TRUE POWER?
THIS... IS THE AMAZING TRANSFORMATION?
YOU LOOK SMALLER AND CUTER.
IT'S NOT WHAT I...
?

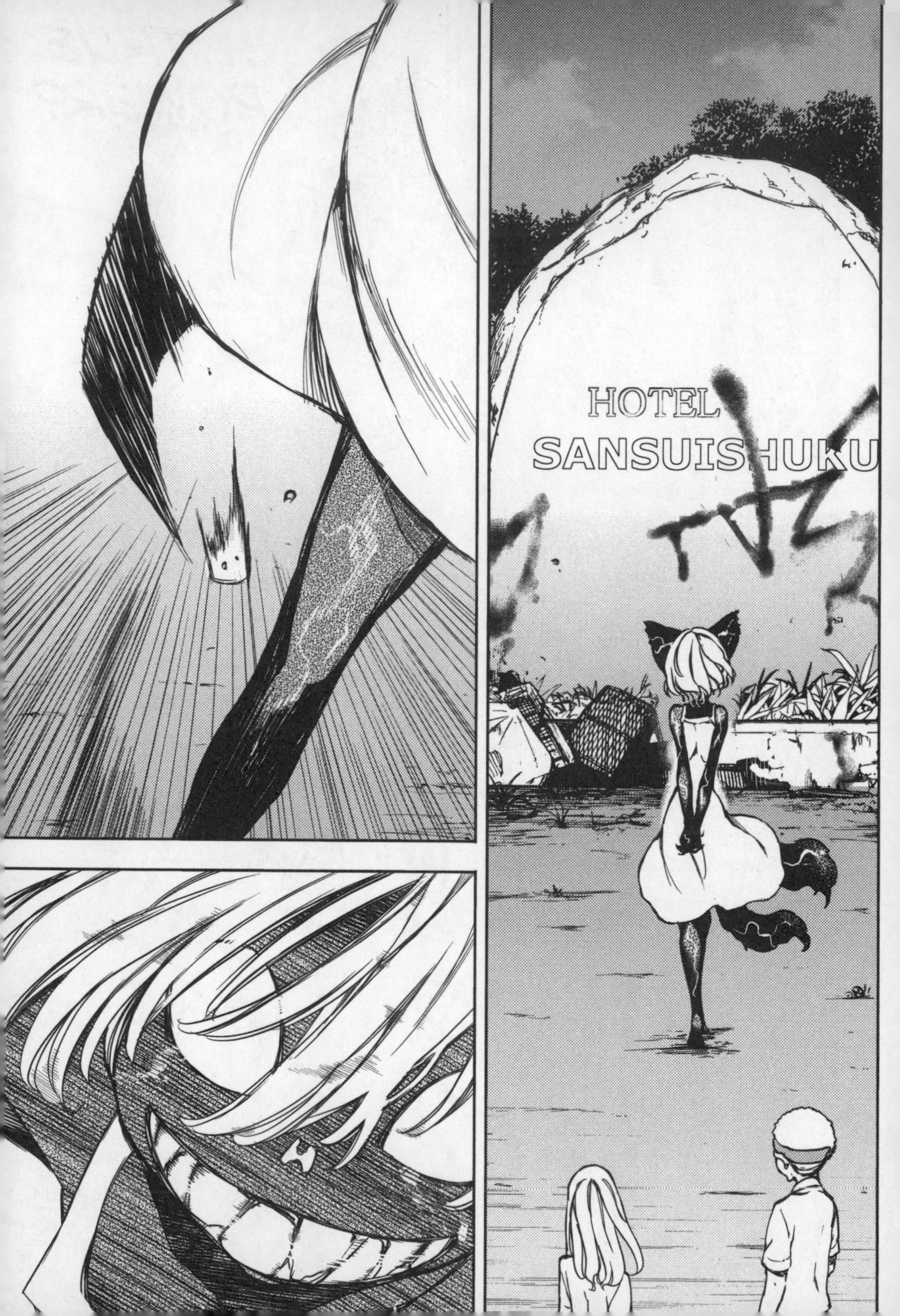
HOTEL
SANSUISHUKU

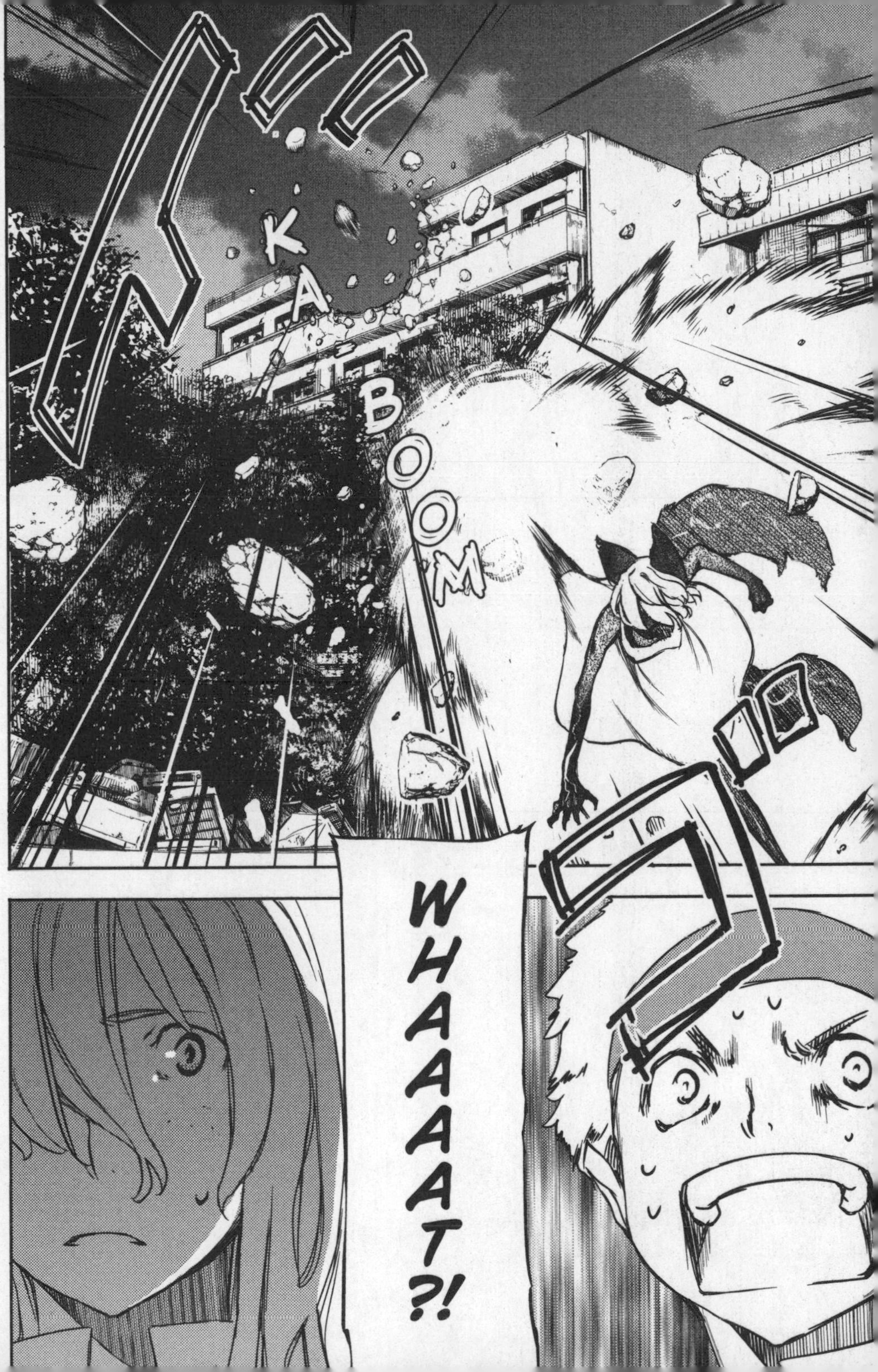
KABOOM
WHAAAAT?!

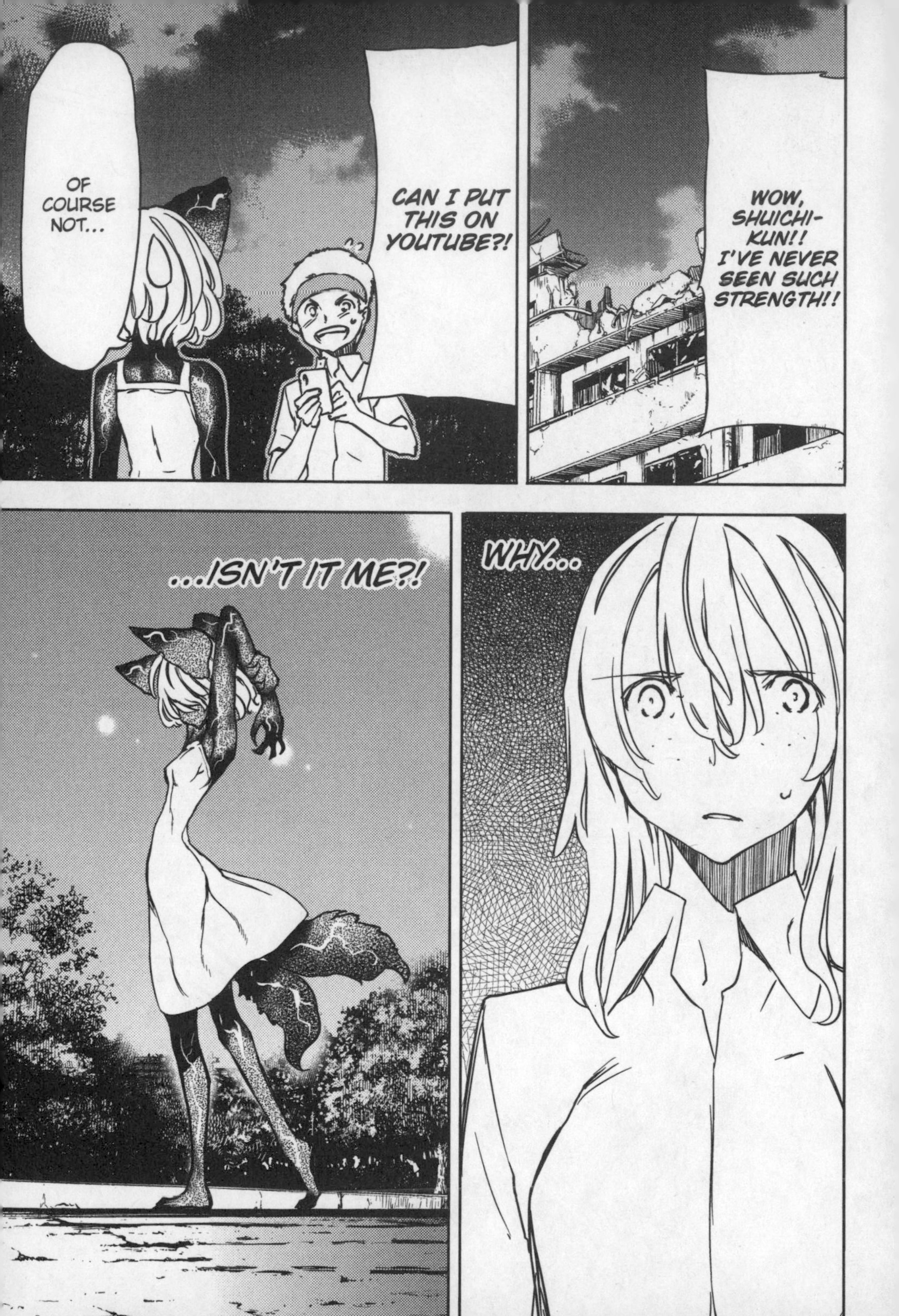
WOW, SHUICHI-KUN!! I'VE NEVER SEEN SUCH STRENGTH!!
CAN I PUT THIS ON YOUTUBE?!
OF COURSE NOT...
WHY...
...ISN'T IT ME?!

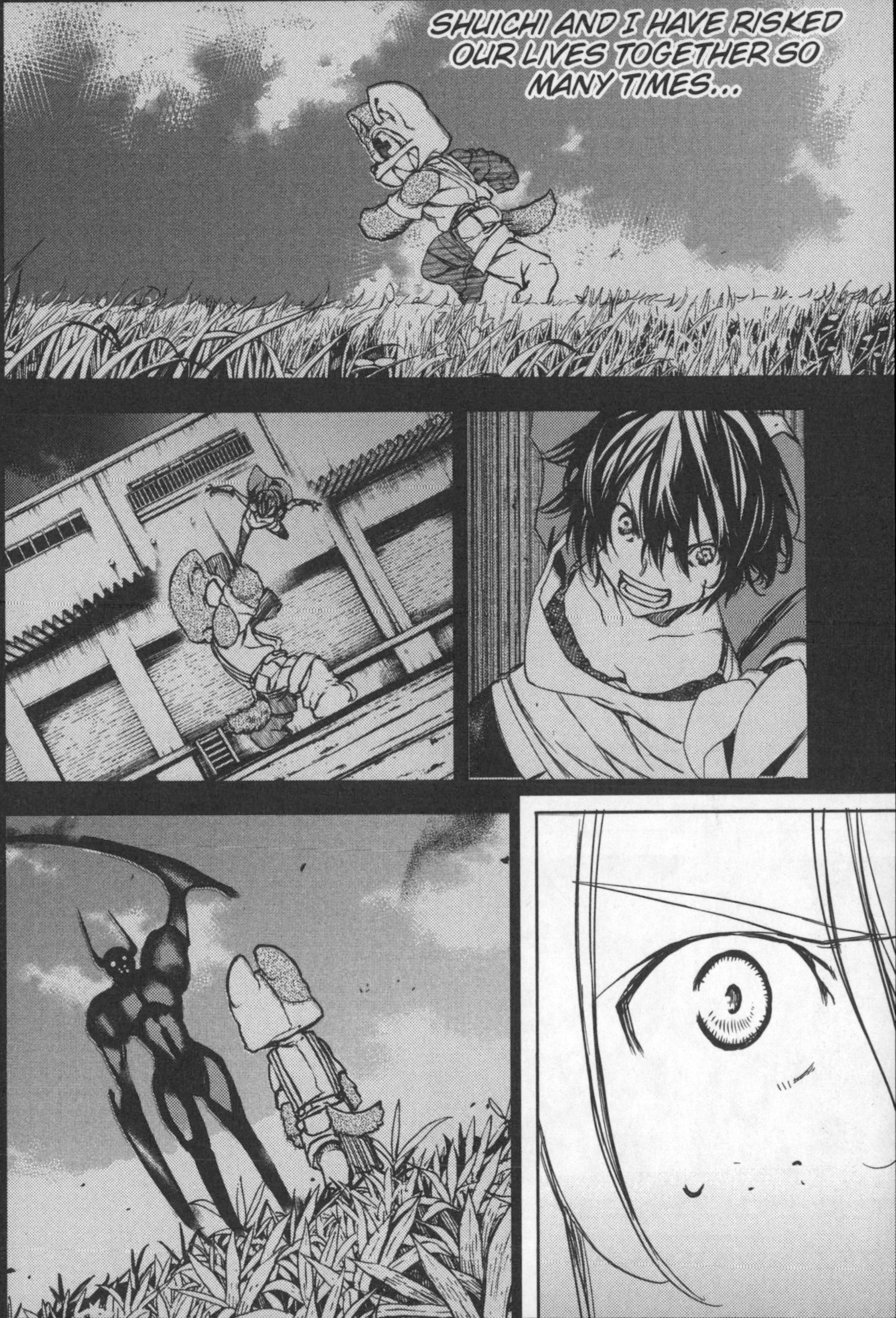
SHUICHI AND I HAVE RISKED OUR LIVES TOGETHER SO MANY TIMES...

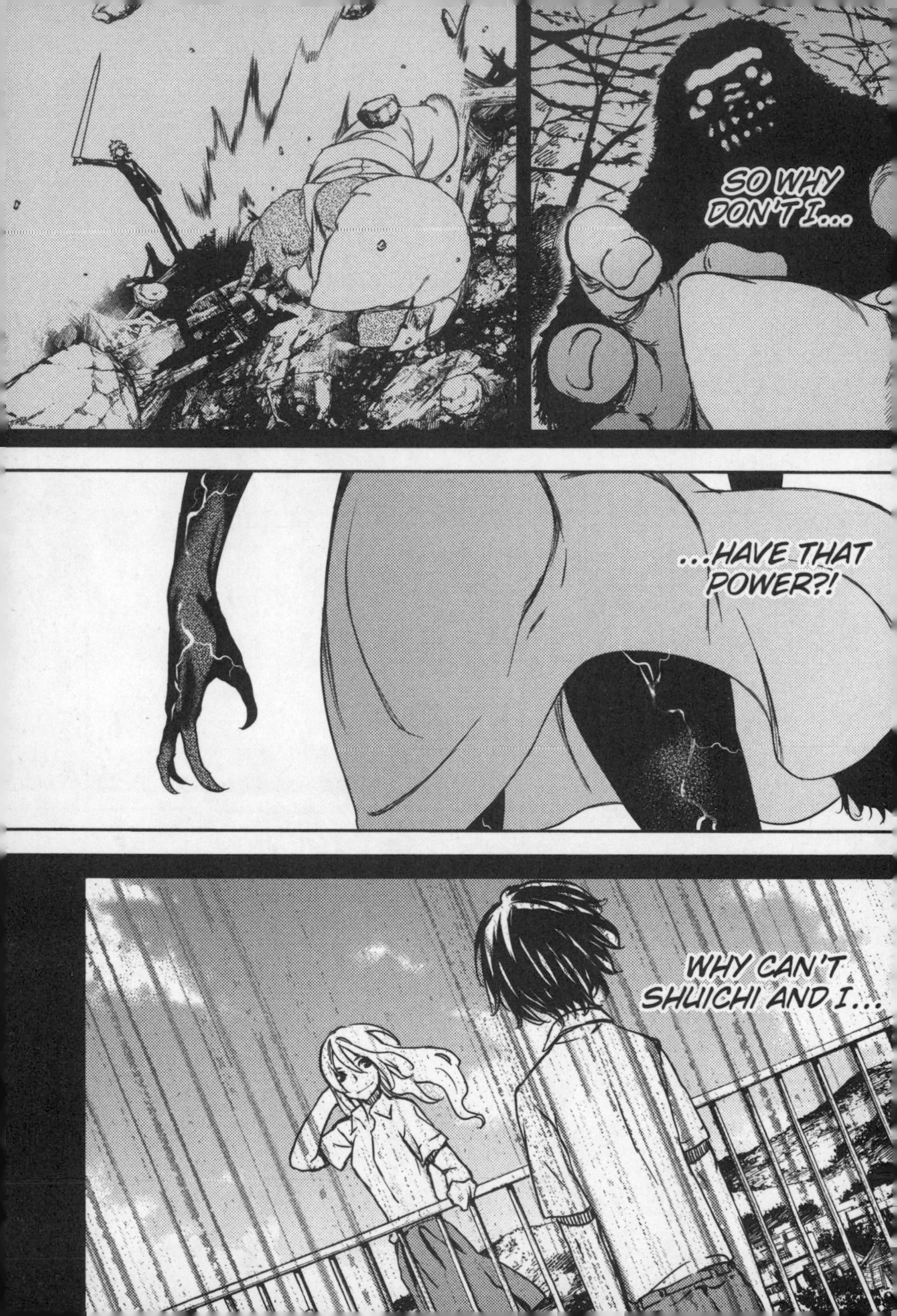
SO WHY DON'T I...
...HAVE THAT POWER?!
WHY CAN'T SHUICHI AND I...

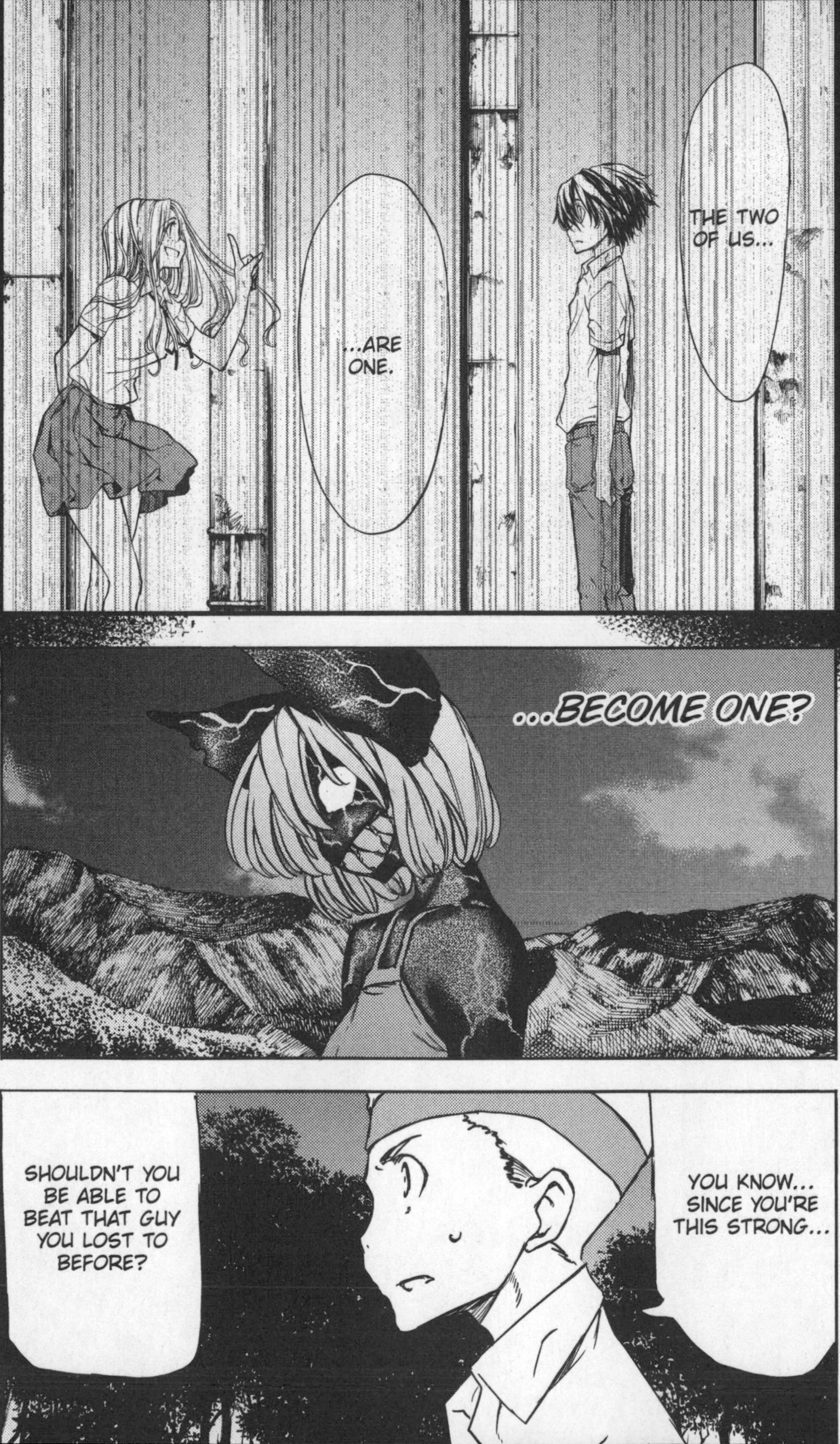
THE TWO OF US...
...ARE ONE.
...BECOME ONE?
YOU KNOW... SINCE YOU'RE THIS STRONG...
SHOULDN'T YOU BE ABLE TO BEAT THAT GUY YOU LOST TO BEFORE?

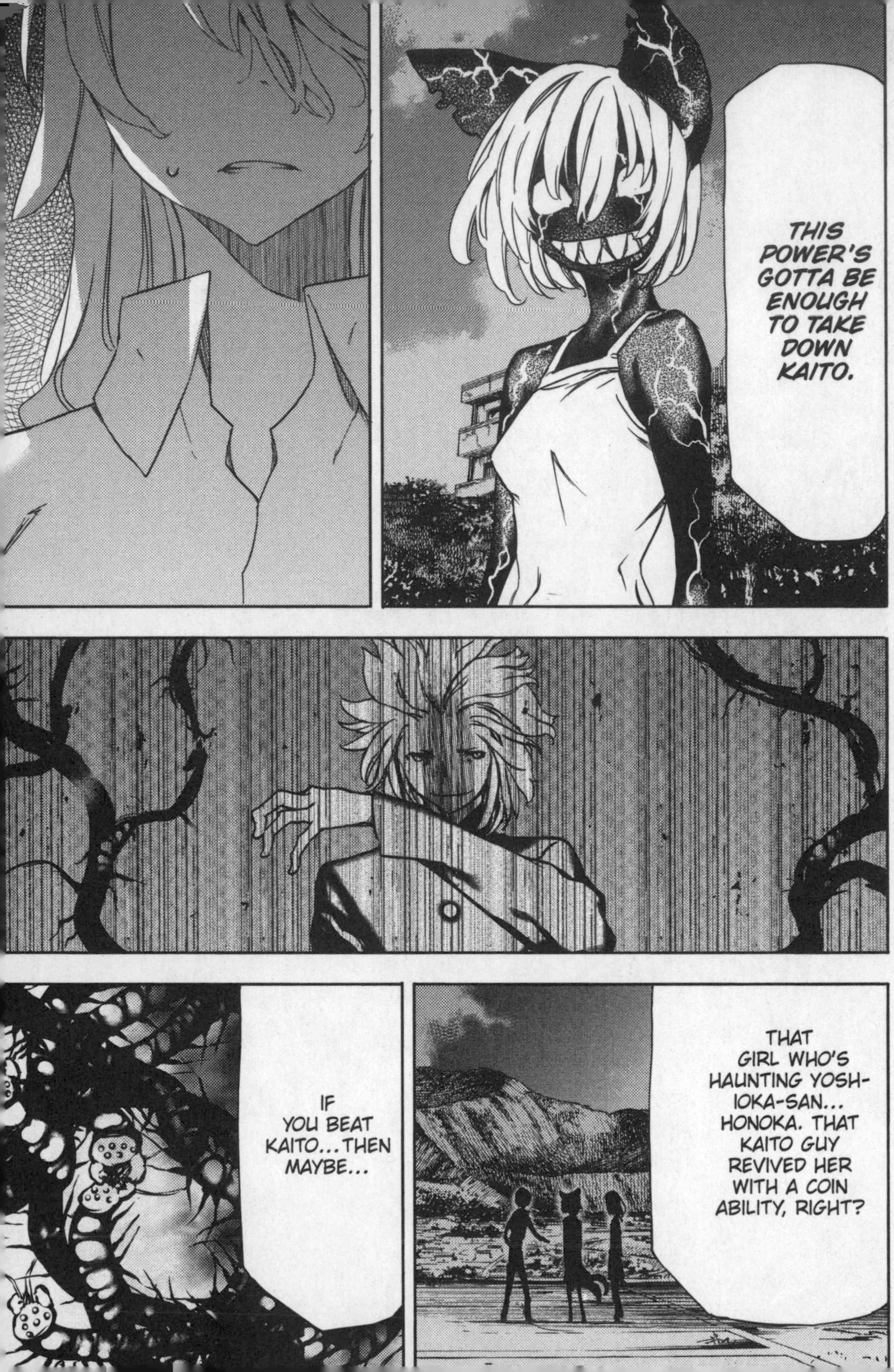
THIS POWER'S GOTTA BE ENOUGH TO TAKE DOWN KAITO.
THAT GIRL WHO'S HAUNTING YOSH-IOKA-SAN... HONOKA. THAT KAITO GUY REVIVED HER WITH A COIN ABILITY, RIGHT?
IF YOU BEAT KAITO... THEN MAYBE...

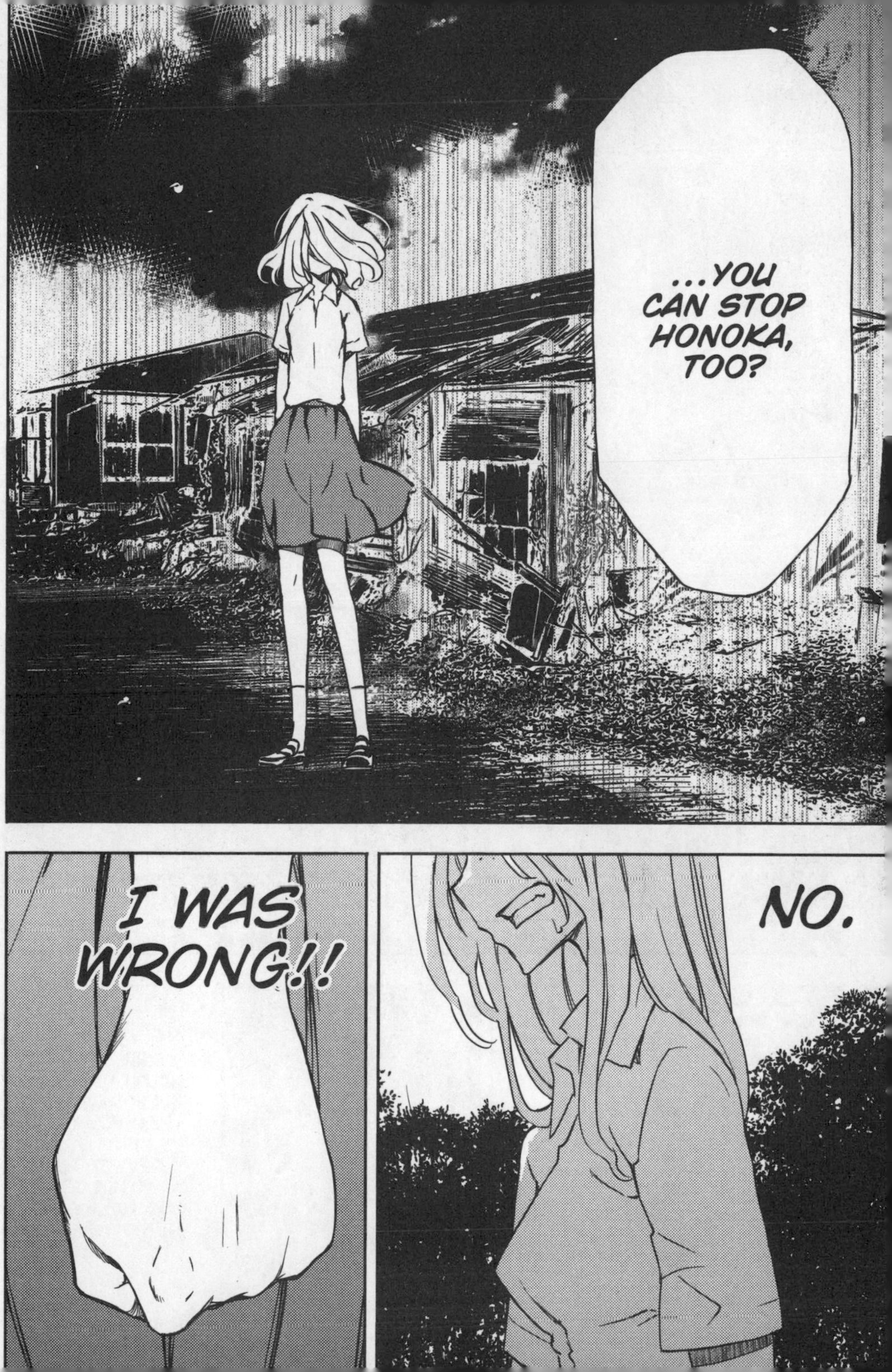
...YOU CAN STOP HONOKA, TOO?
NO.
I WAS WRONG!!

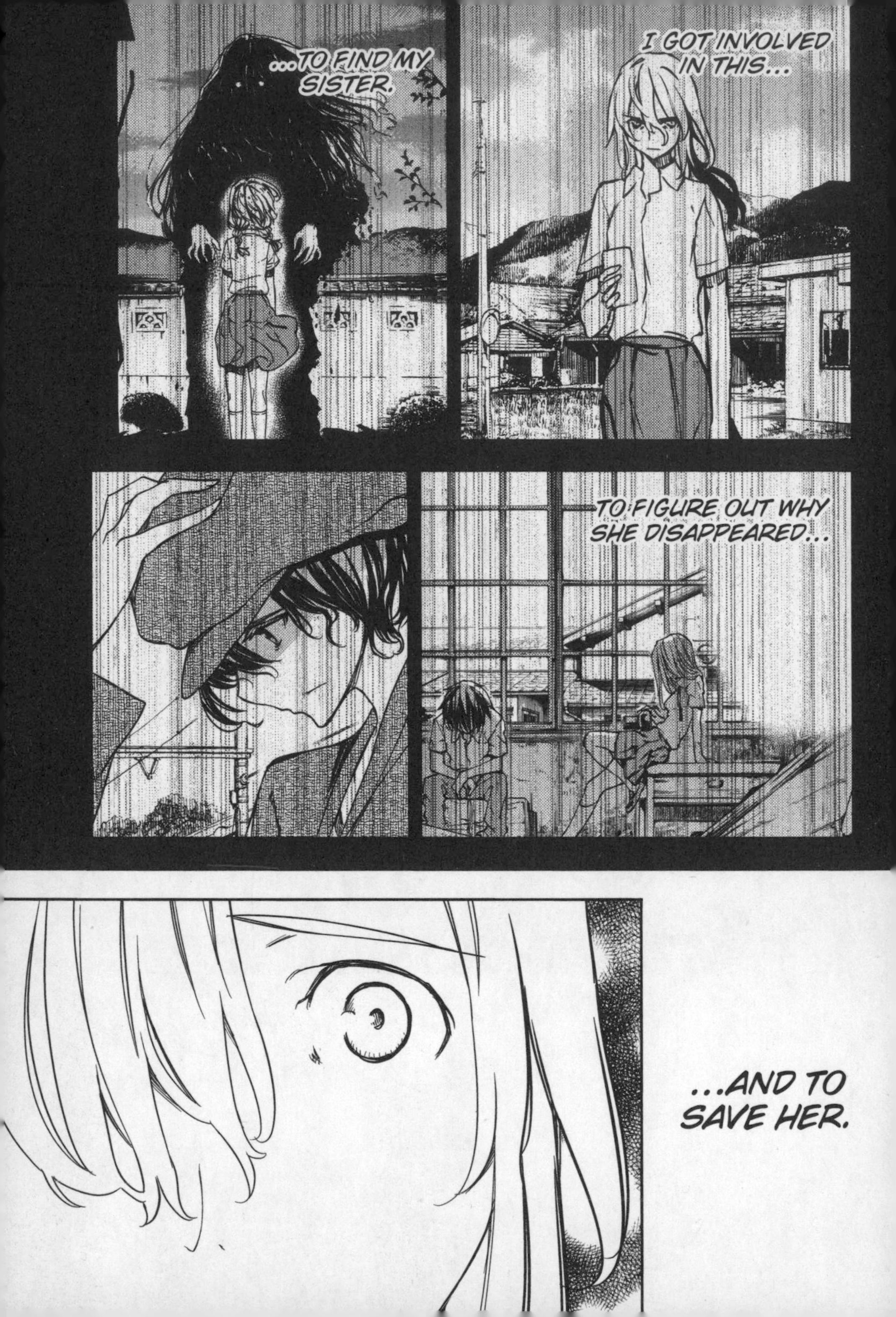
I GOT INVOLVED IN THIS...
...TO FIND MY SISTER.
TO FIGURE OUT WHY SHE DISAPPEARED...
...AND TO SAVE HER.

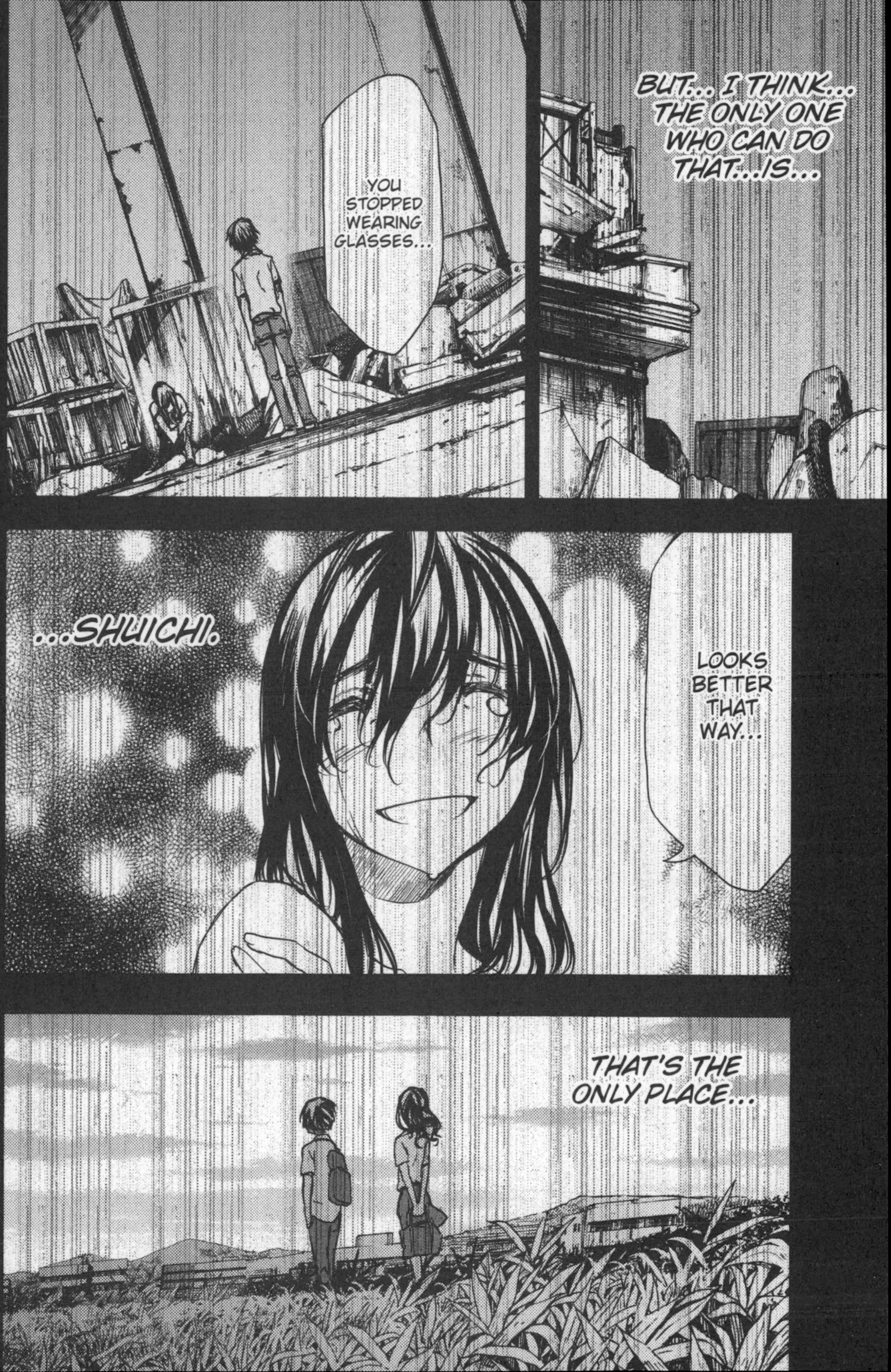
BUT... I THINK... THE ONLY ONE WHO CAN DO THAT...IS...
YOU STOPPED WEARING GLASSES...
...SHUICHI.
LOOKS BETTER THAT WAY...
THAT'S THE ONLY PLACE...

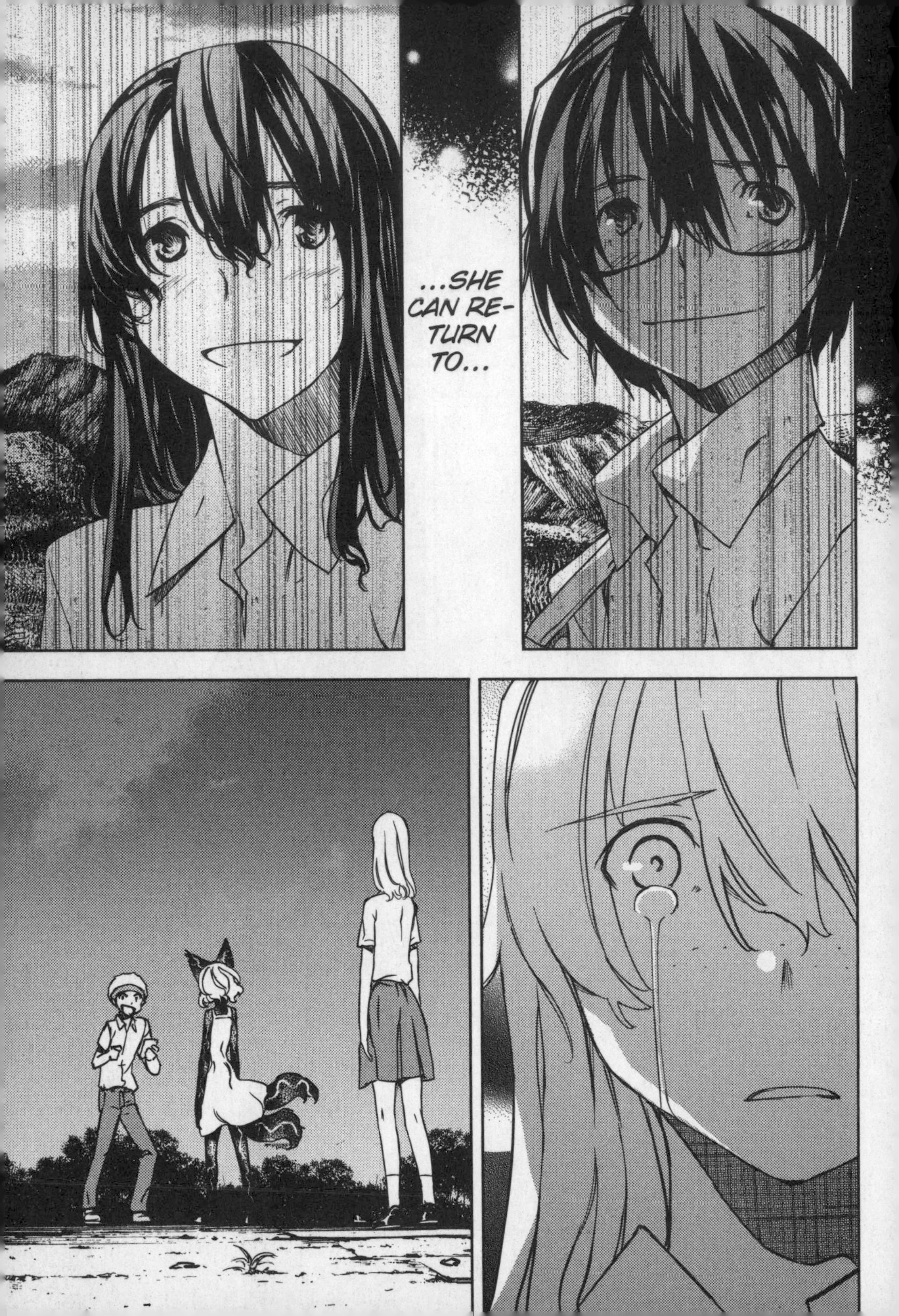
...SHE CAN RE- TURN TO...

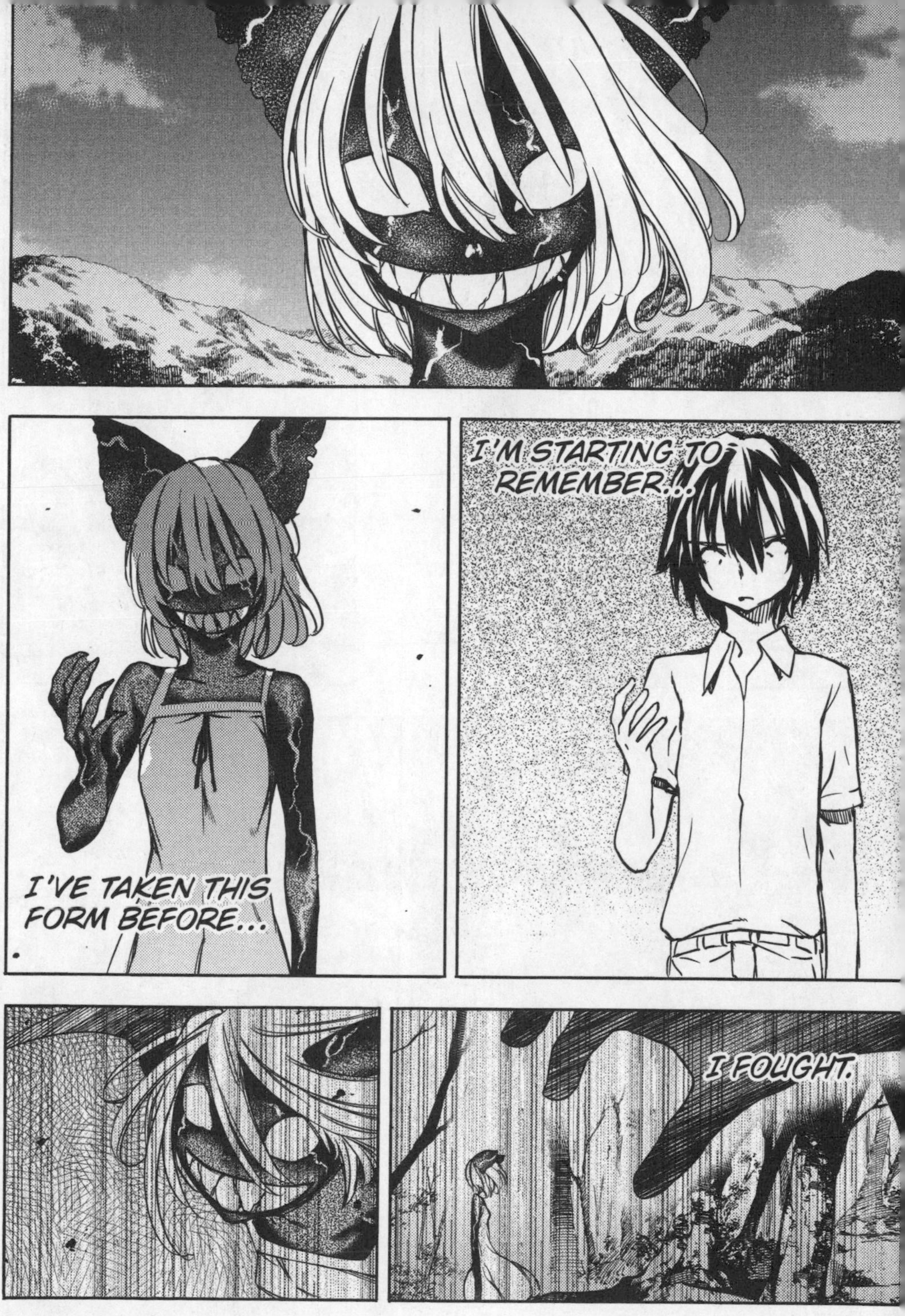
I'M STARTING TO REMEMBER...
I'VE TAKEN THIS FORM BEFORE...
I FOUGHT.

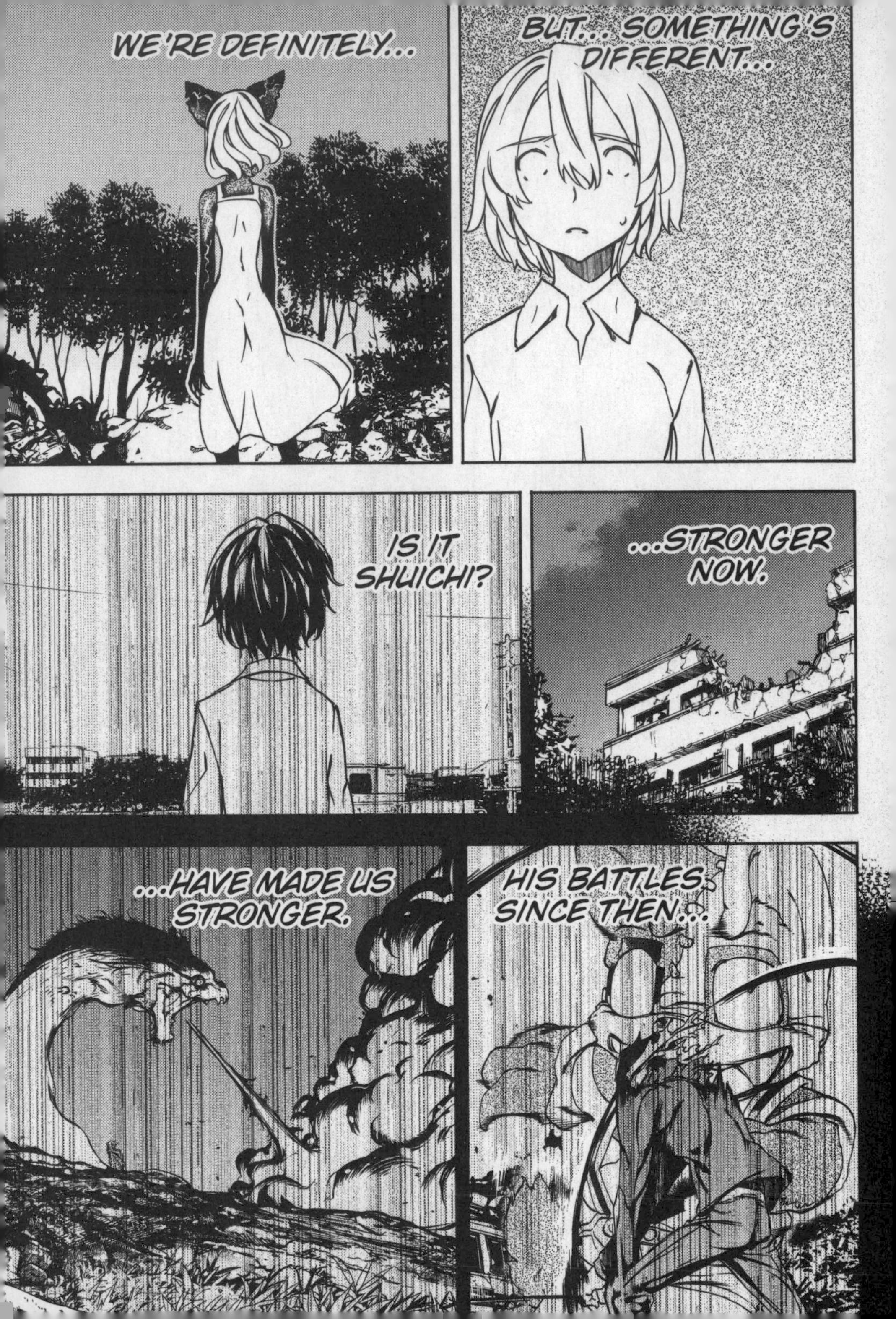
BUT... SOMETHING'S DIFFERENT...
WE'RE DEFINITELY...
...STRONGER NOW.
IS IT SHUICHI?
HIS BATTLES SINCE THEN...
...HAVE MADE US STRONGER.

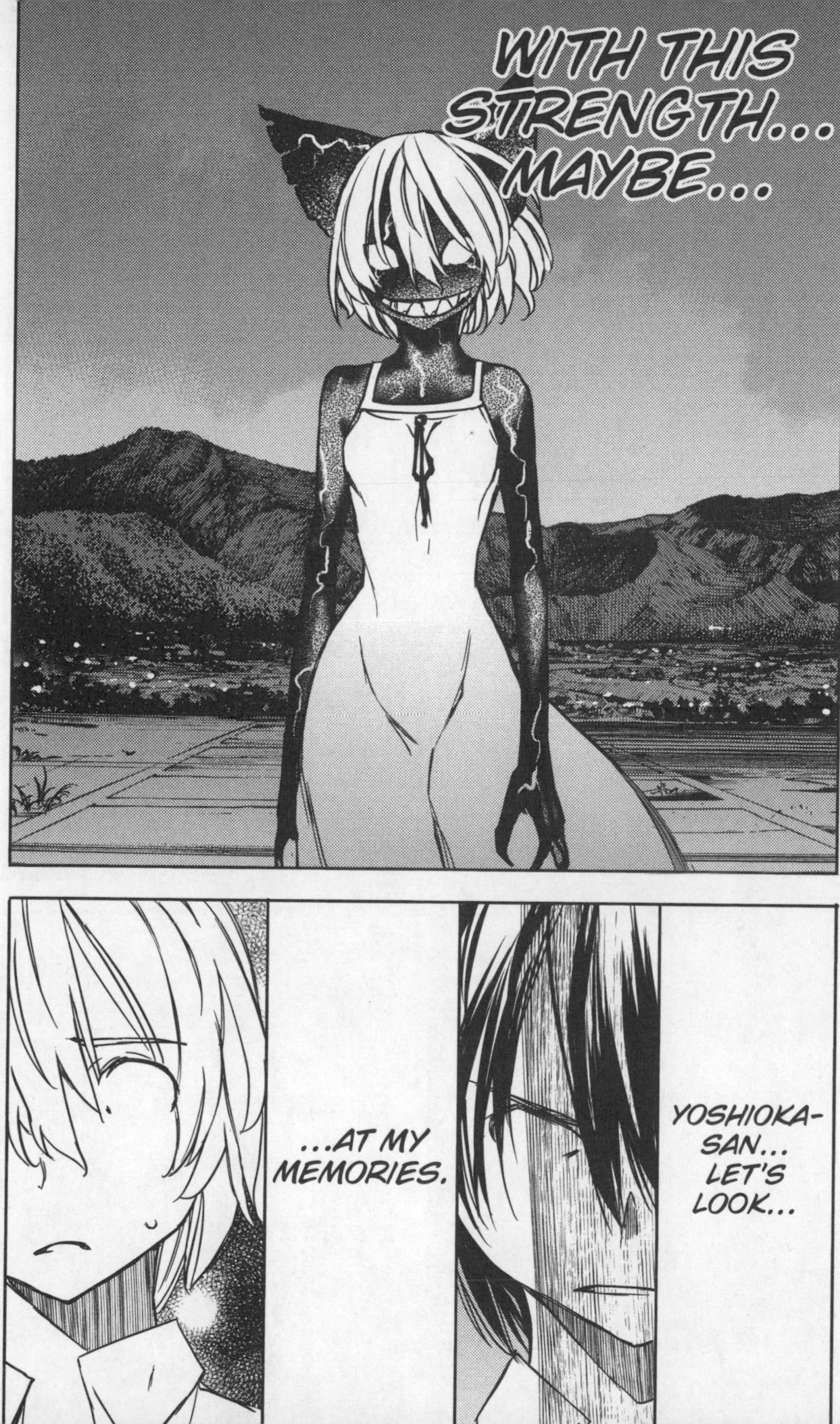
WITH THIS STRENGTH... MAYBE...
YOSHIOKA-SAN... LET'S LOOK...
...AT MY MEMORIES.

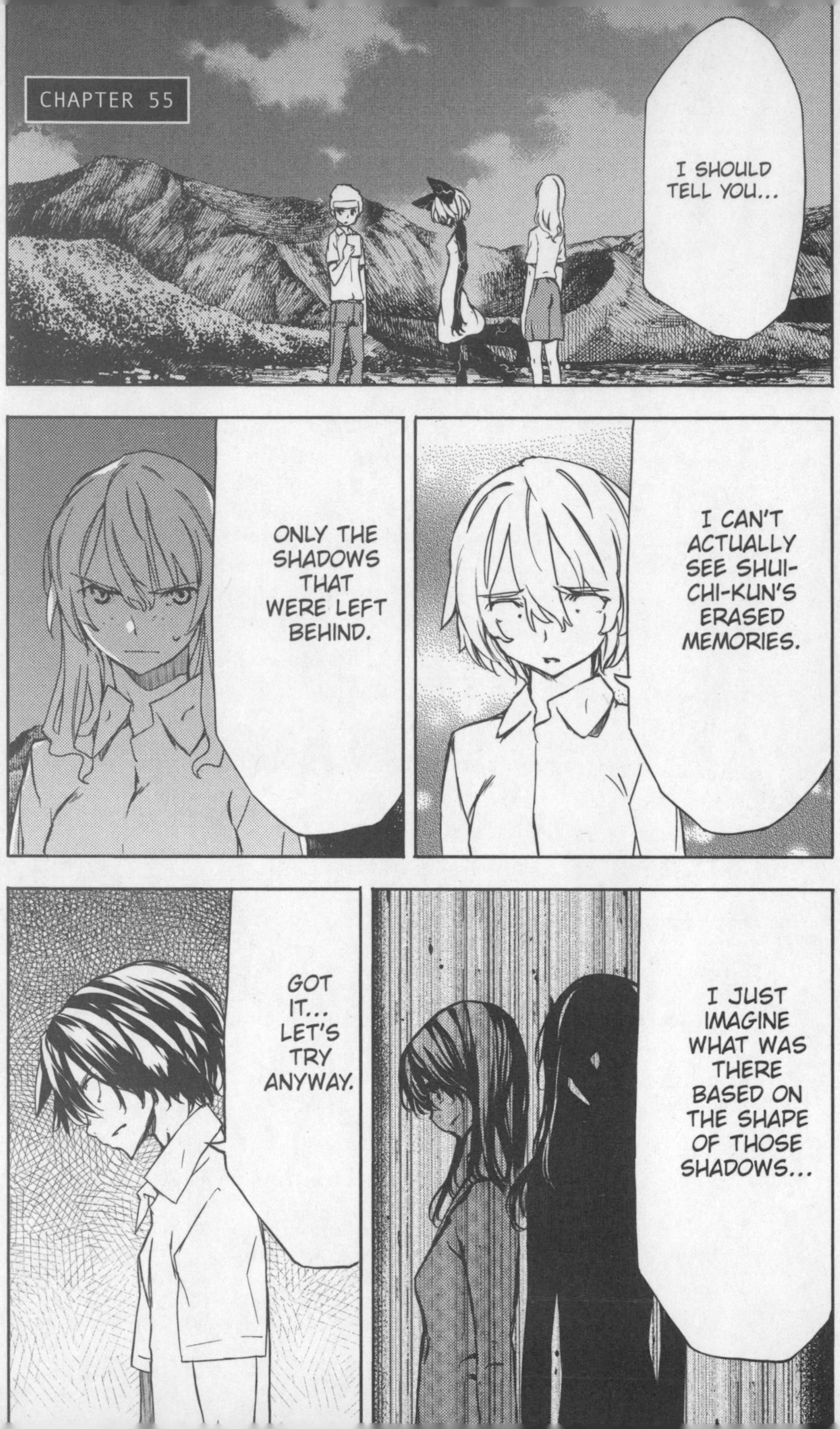
CHAPTER 55
I SHOULD TELL YOU...
I CAN'T ACTUALLY SEE SHUI-CHI-KUN'S ERASED MEMORIES.
ONLY THE SHADOWS THAT WERE LEFT BEHIND.
I JUST IMAGINE WHAT WAS THERE BASED ON THE SHAPE OF THOSE SHADOWS...
GOT IT... LET'S TRY ANYWAY.

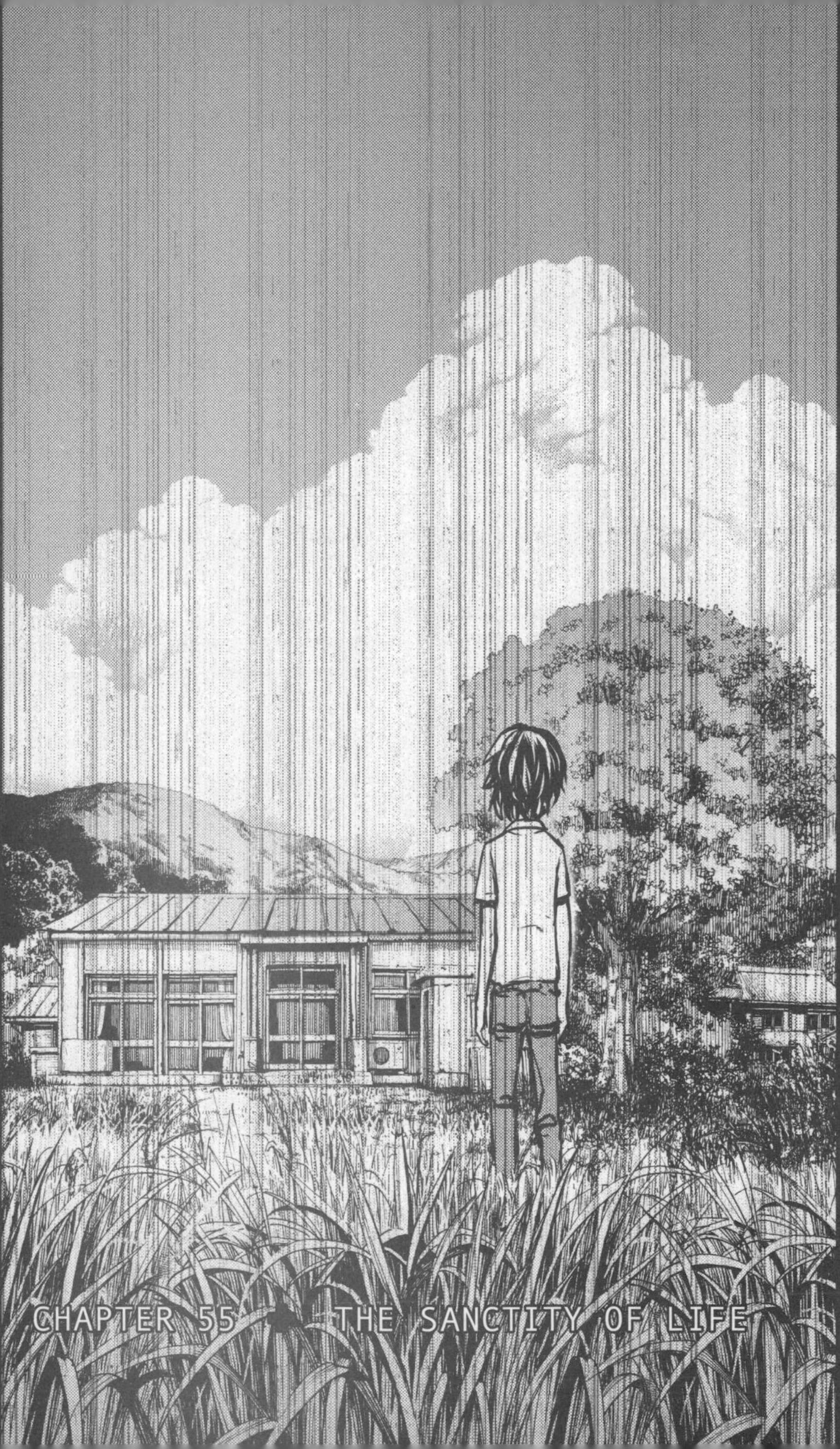
CHAPTER 55 THE SANCTITY OF LIFE

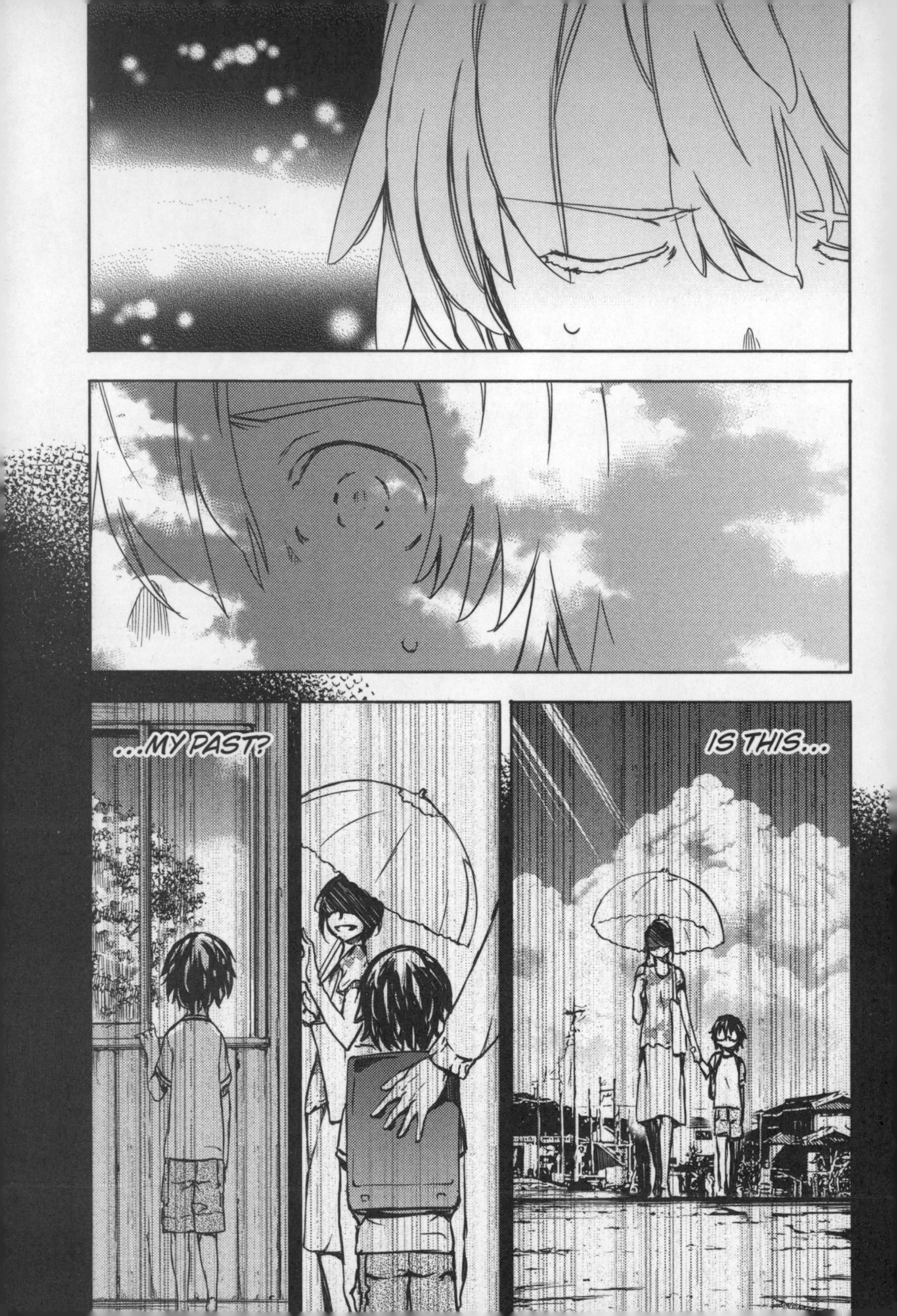
IS THIS...
...MY PAST?

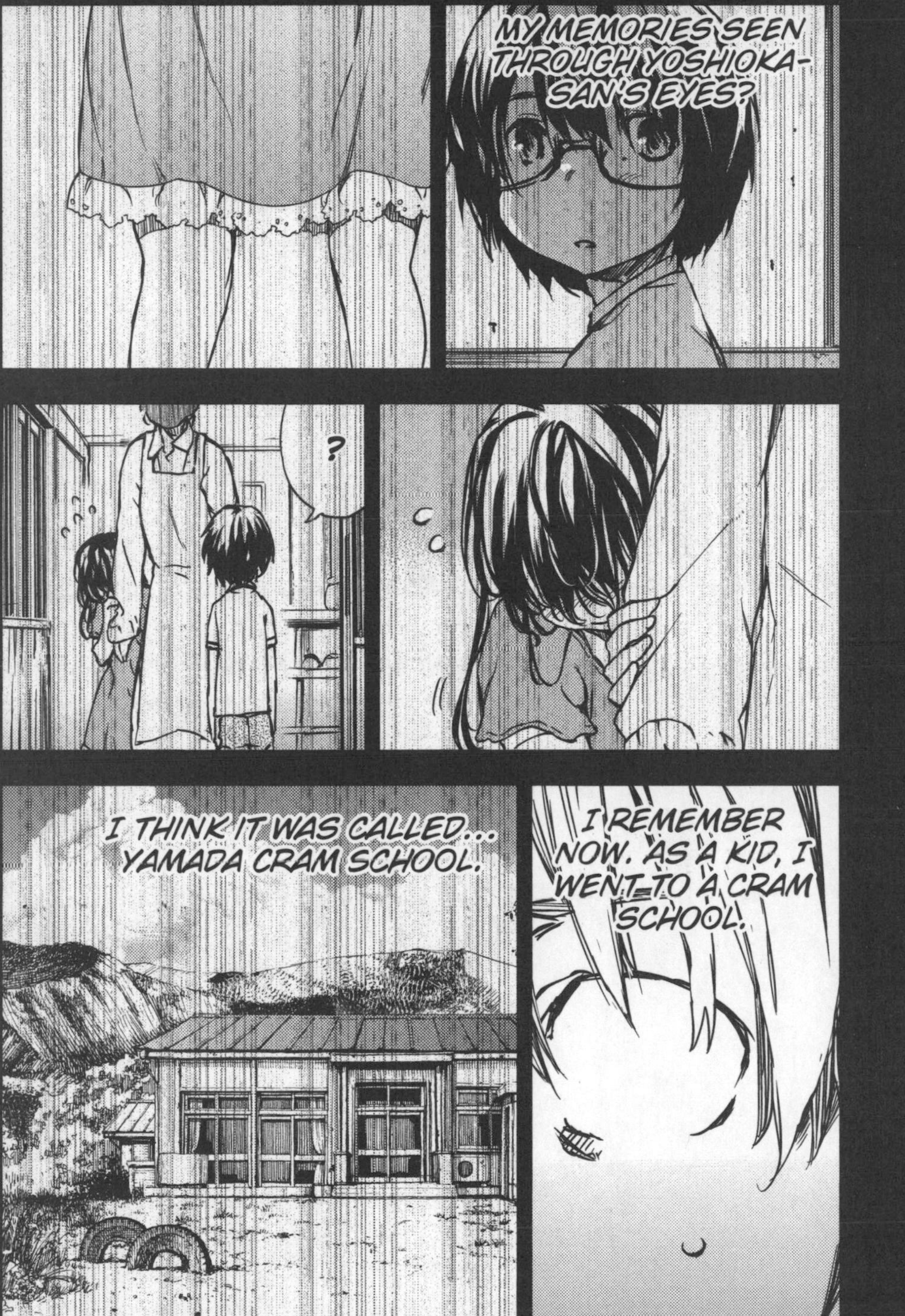
MY MEMORIES SEEN THROUGH YOSHIOKA-SAN'S EYES?
?
I REMEMBER NOW. AS A KID, I WENT TO A CRAM SCHOOL.
I THINK IT WAS CALLED... YAMADA CRAM SCHOOL.

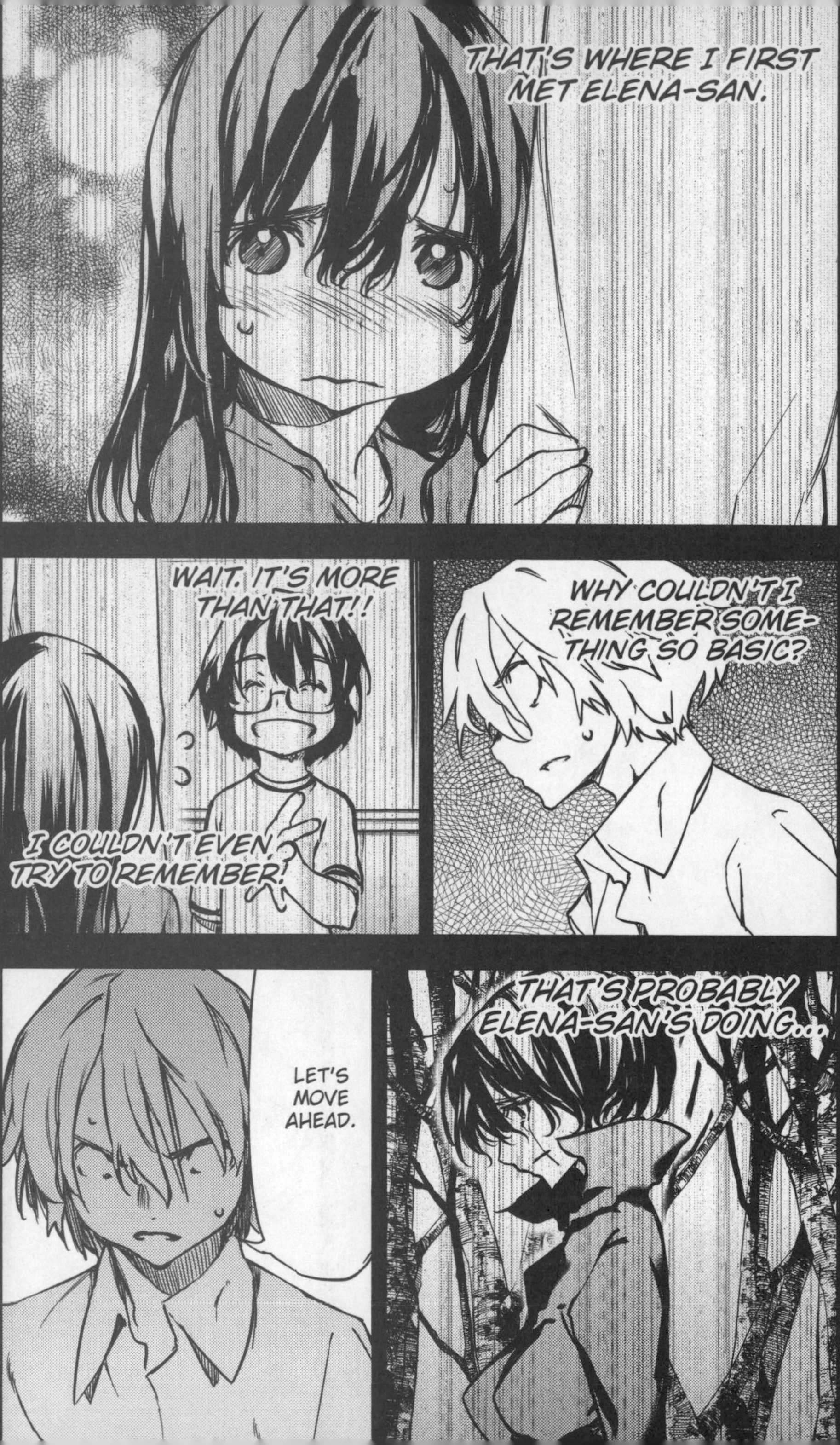
THAT'S WHERE I FIRST MET ELENA-SAN.
WHY COULDN'T I REMEMBER SOME-THING SO BASIC?
WAIT. IT'S MORE THAN THAT!!
I COULDN'T EVEN TRY TO REMEMBER!
THAT'S PROBABLY ELENA-SAN'S DOING...
LET'S MOVE AHEAD.

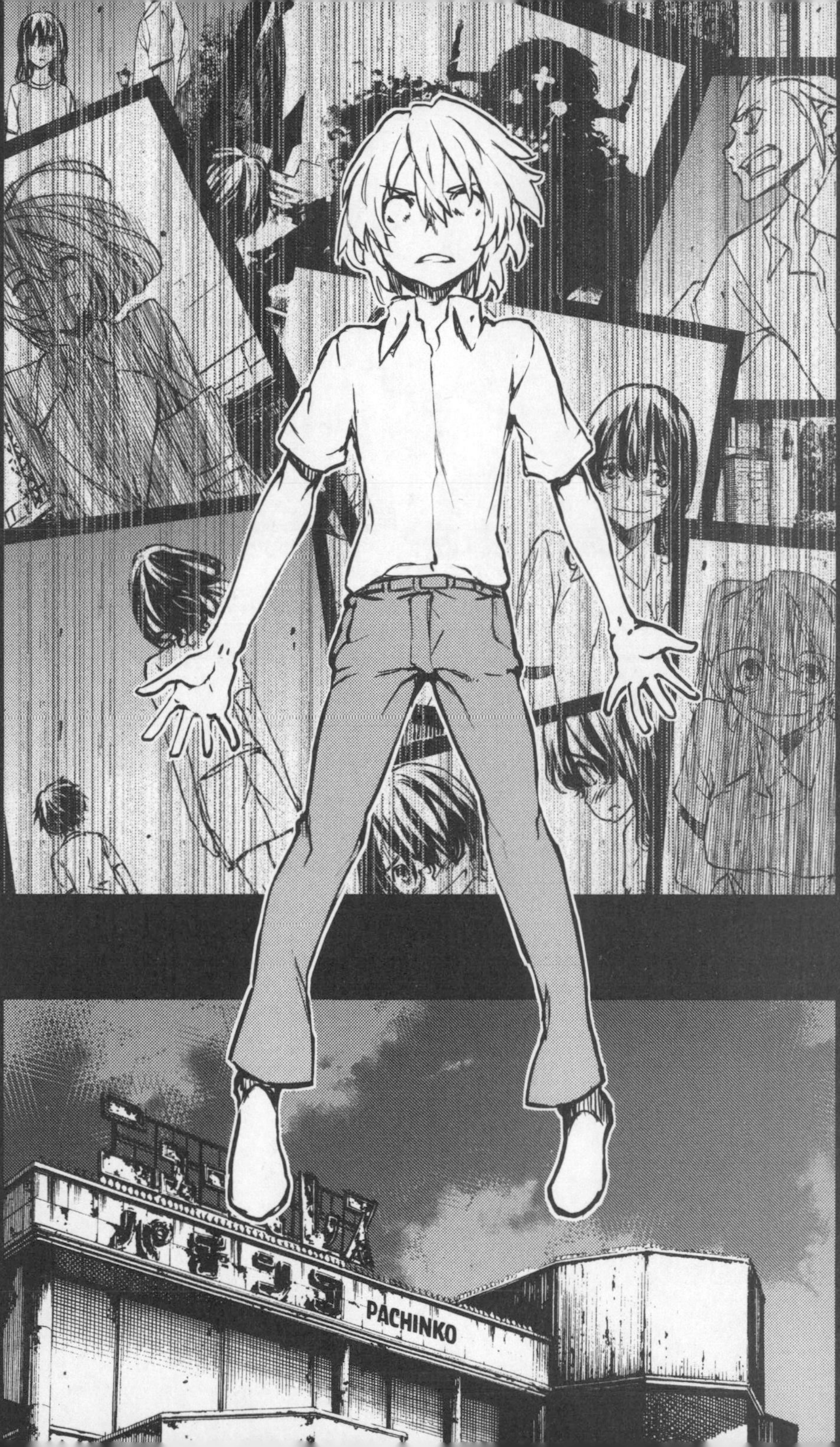
PACHINKO

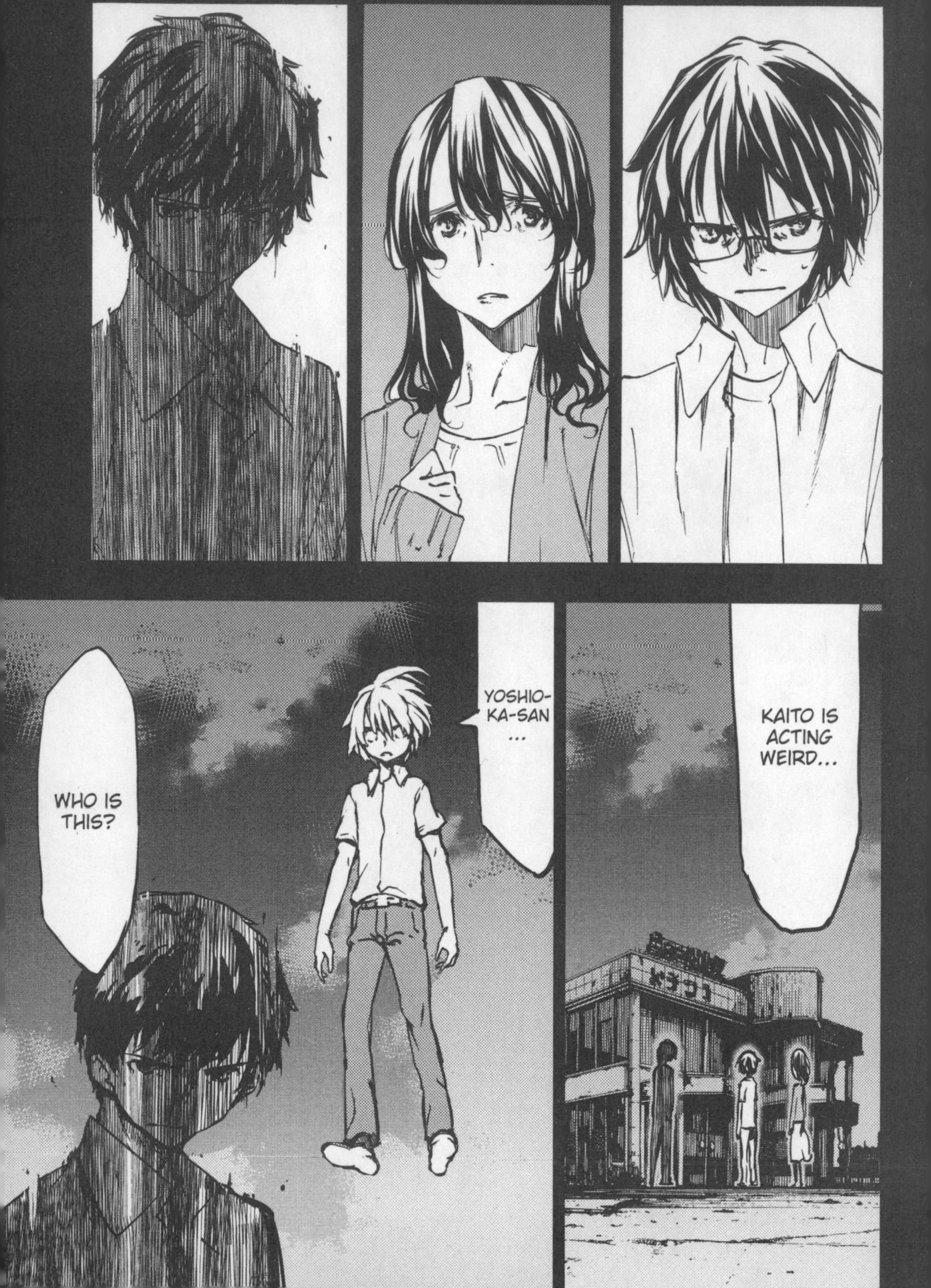
KAITO IS ACTING WEIRD...
YOSHIO-KA-SAN ...
WHO IS THIS?

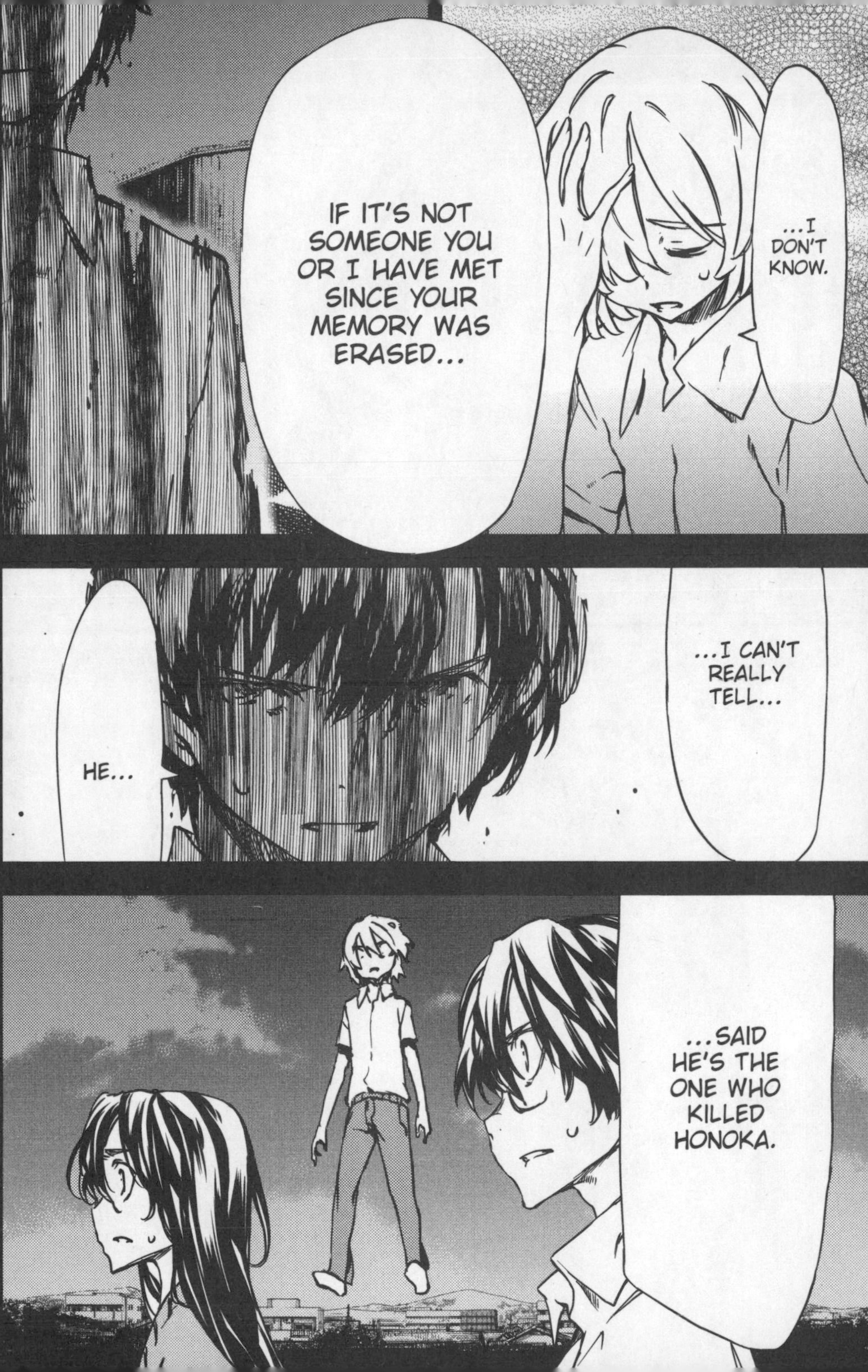
...I DON'T KNOW.
IF IT'S NOT SOMEONE YOU OR I HAVE MET SINCE YOUR MEMORY WAS ERASED...
...I CAN'T REALLY TELL...
HE...
...SAID HE'S THE ONE WHO KILLED HONOKA.

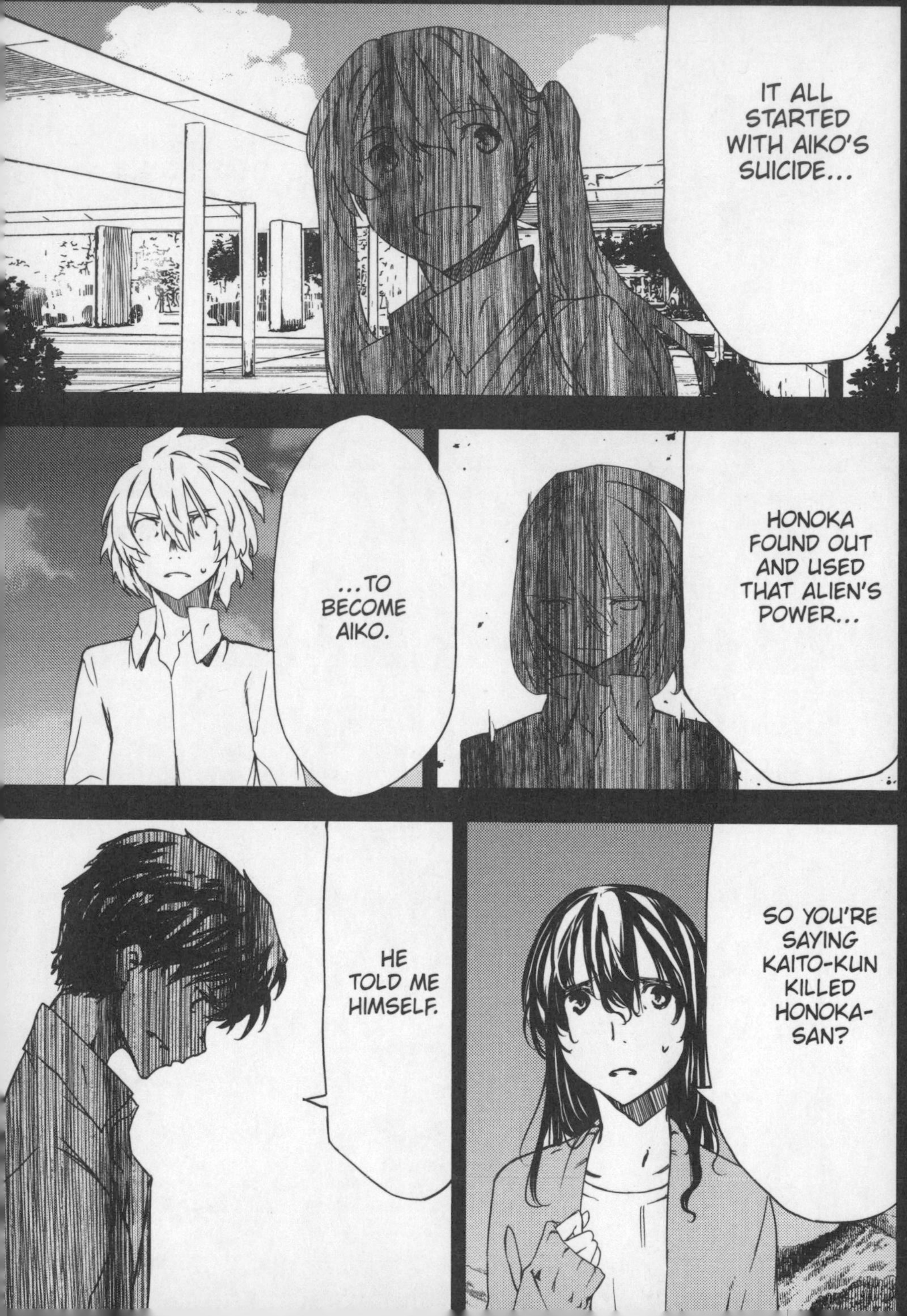
IT ALL STARTED WITH AIKO'S SUICIDE...
HONOKA FOUND OUT AND USED THAT ALIEN'S POWER...
...TO BECOME AIKO.
SO YOU'RE SAYING KAITO-KUN KILLED HONOKA-SAN?
HE TOLD ME HIMSELF.

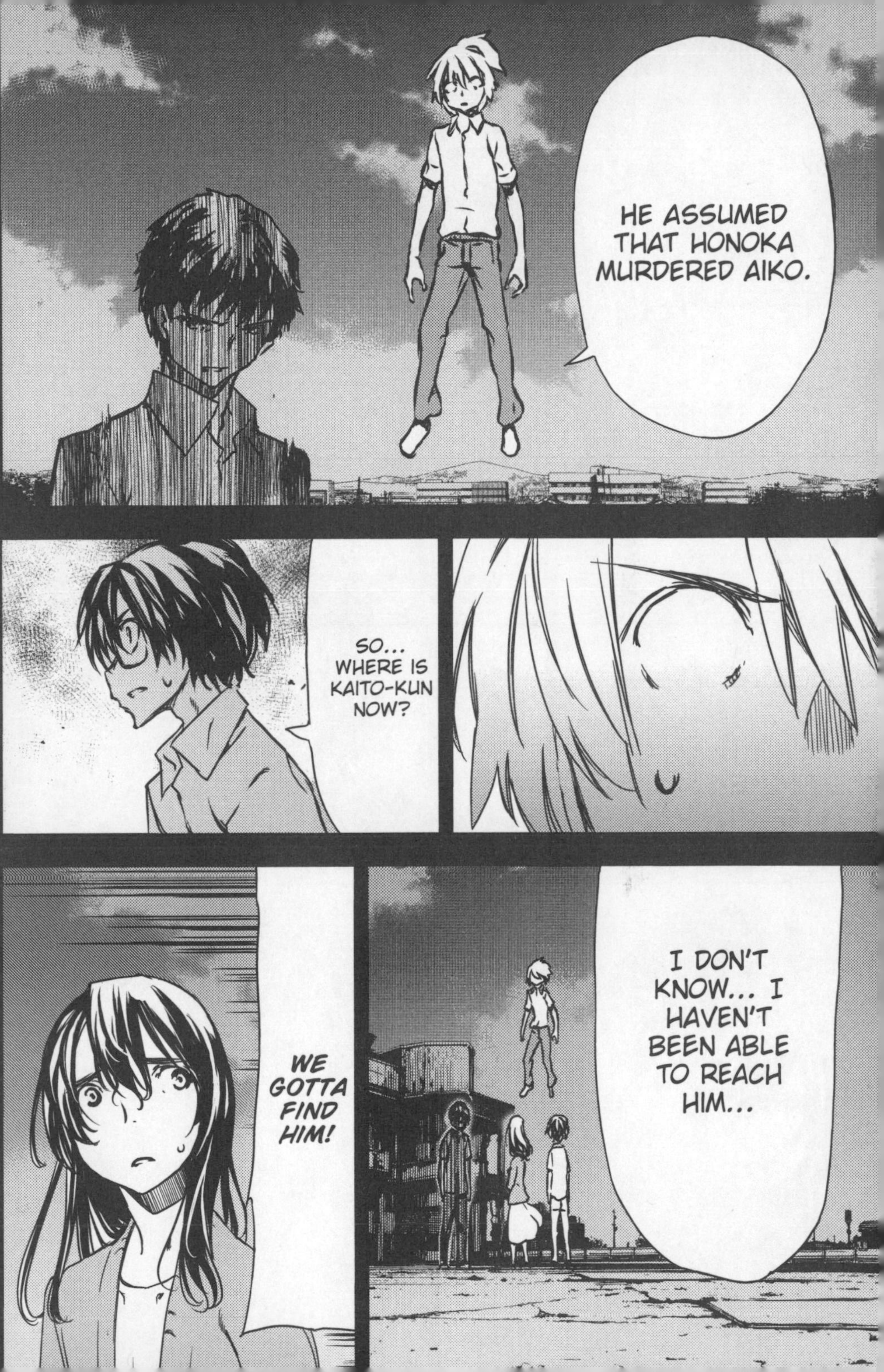
HE ASSUMED THAT HONOKA MURDERED AIKO.
SO... WHERE IS KAITO-KUN NOW?
I DON'T KNOW... I HAVEN'T BEEN ABLE TO REACH HIM...
WE GOTTA FIND HIM!

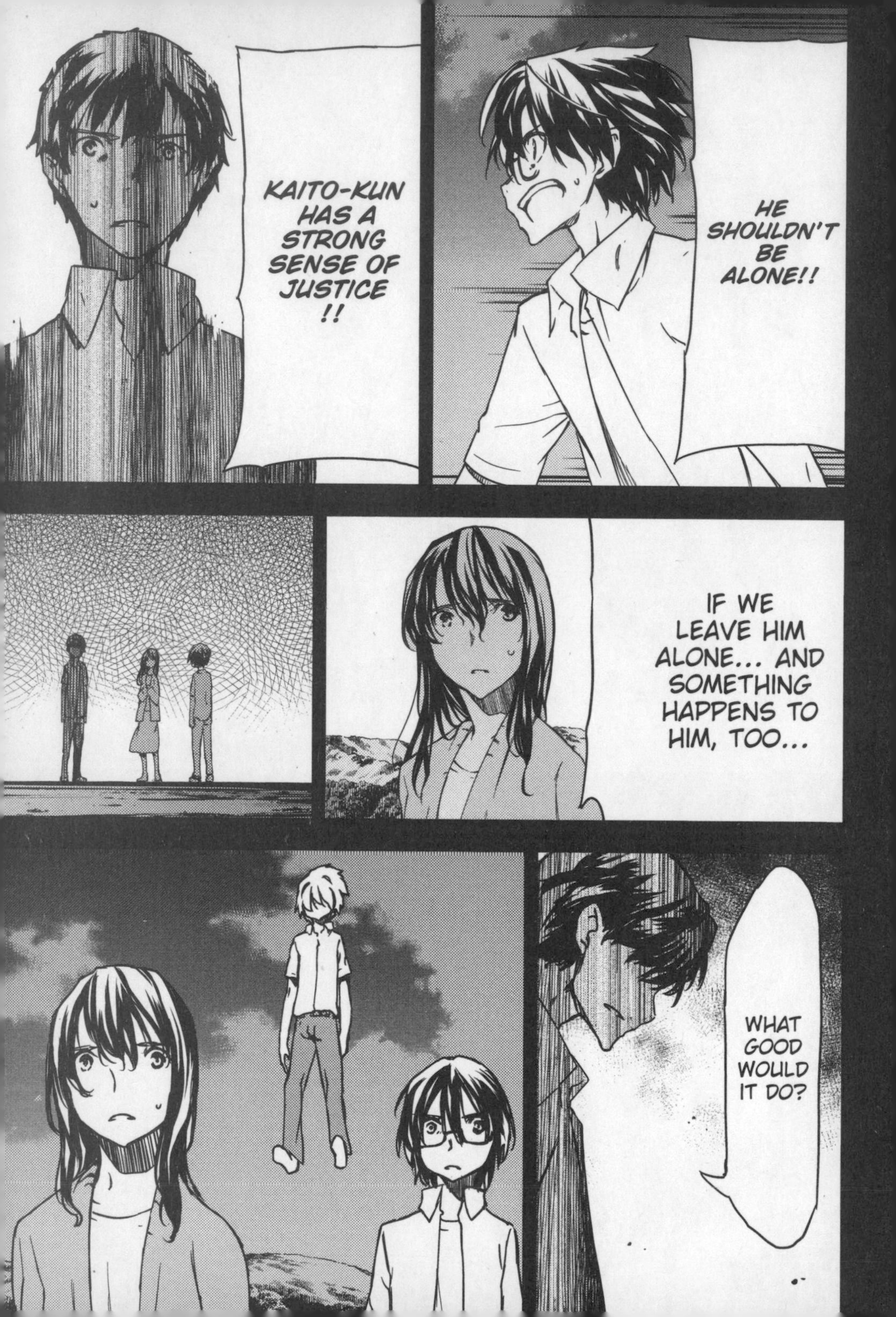
HE SHOULDN'T BE ALONE!!
KAITO-KUN HAS A STRONG SENSE OF JUSTICE!!
IF WE LEAVE HIM ALONE... AND SOMETHING HAPPENS TO HIM, TOO...
WHAT GOOD WOULD IT DO?

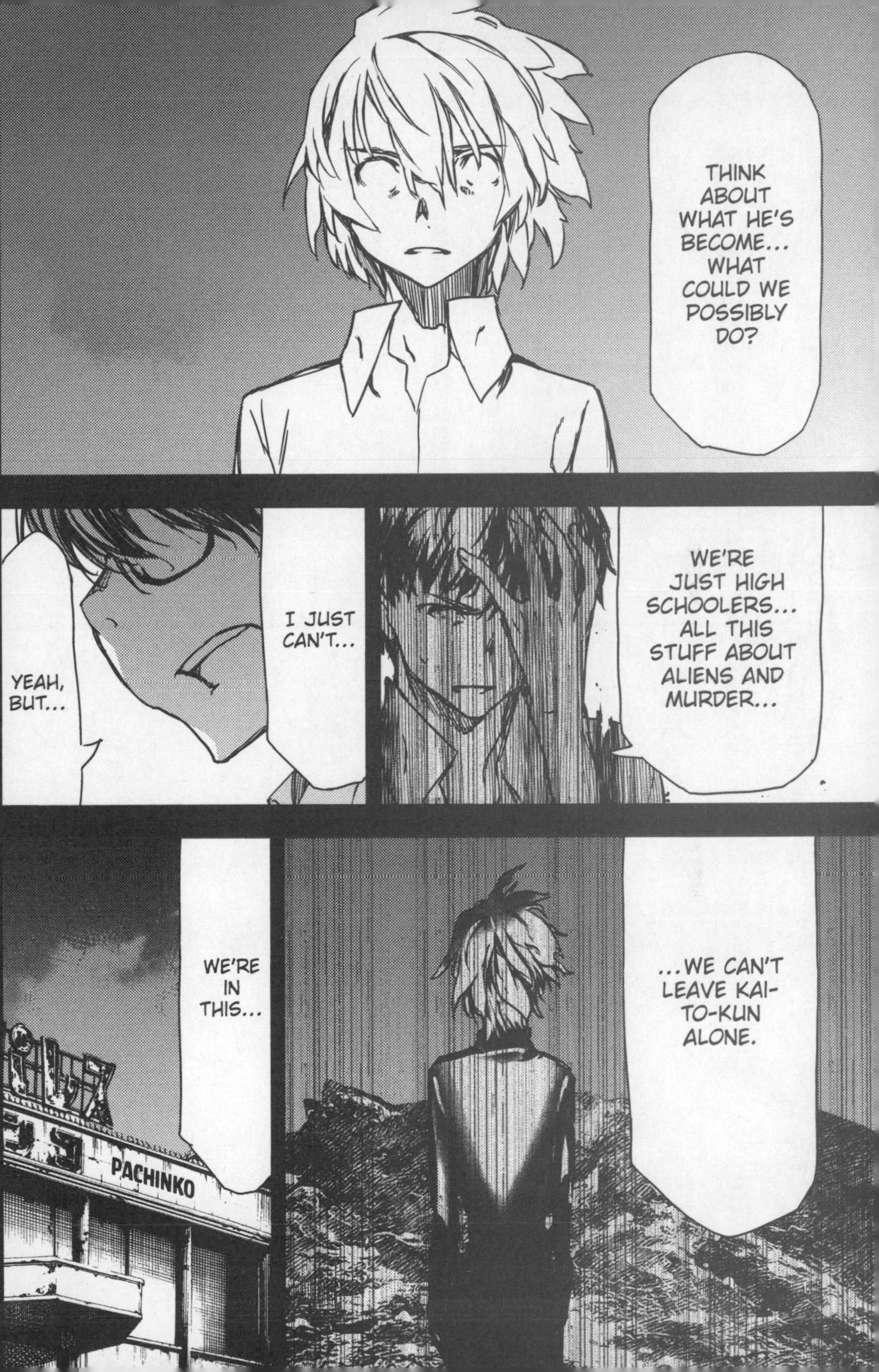
THINK ABOUT WHAT HE'S BECOME... WHAT COULD WE POSSIBLY DO?
WE'RE JUST HIGH SCHOOLERS... ALL THIS STUFF ABOUT ALIENS AND MURDER...
I JUST CAN'T...
YEAH, BUT...
...WE CAN'T LEAVE KAI-TO-KUN ALONE.
WE'RE IN THIS...
PACHINKO

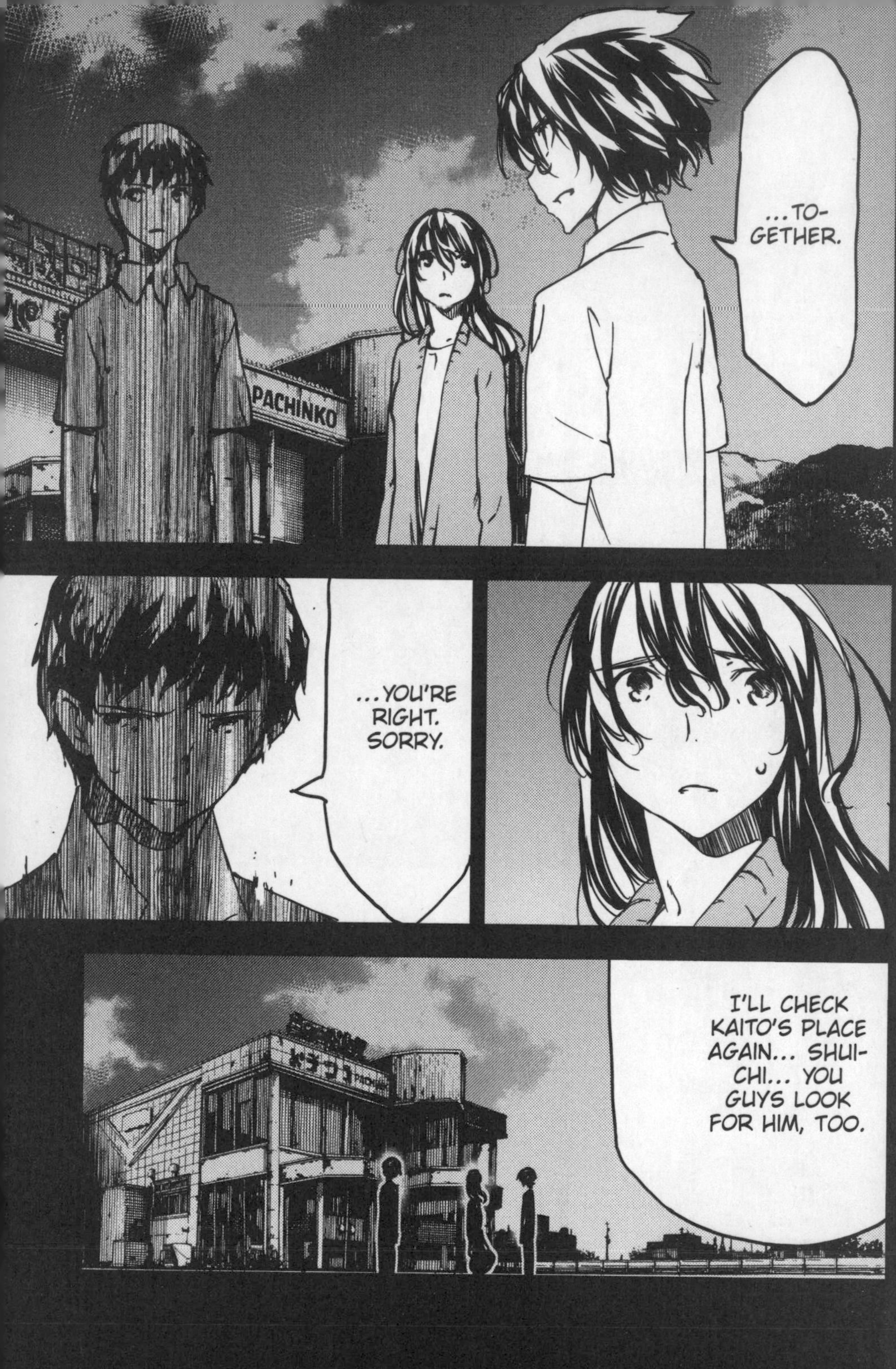
...TO-GETHER.
PACHINKO
...YOU'RE RIGHT. SORRY.
I'LL CHECK KAITO'S PLACE AGAIN... SHUI-CHI... YOU GUYS LOOK FOR HIM, TOO.

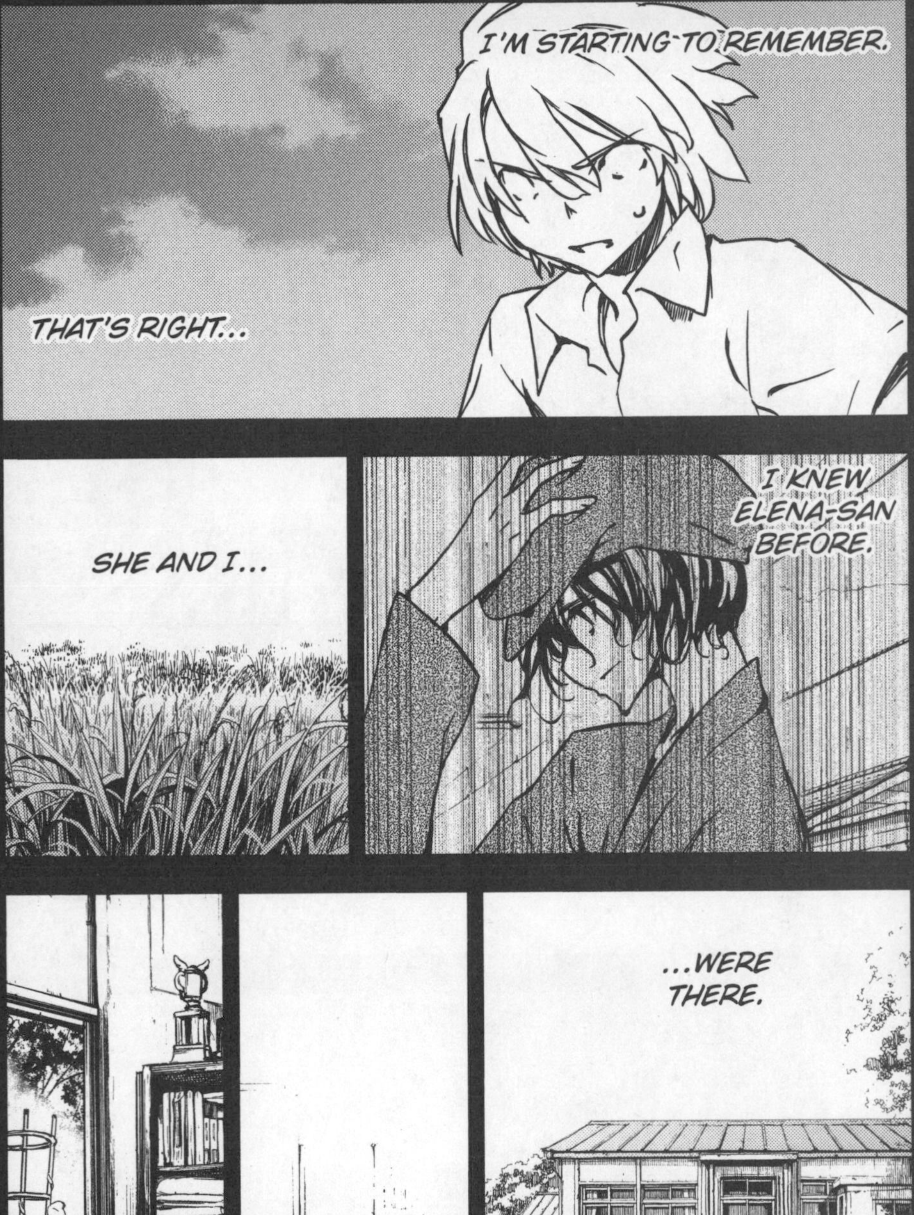
I'M STARTING TO REMEMBER.
THAT'S RIGHT...
I KNEW ELENA-SAN BEFORE.
SHE AND I...
...WERE THERE.

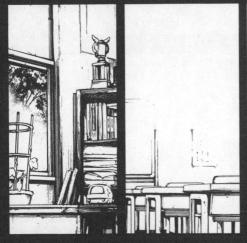

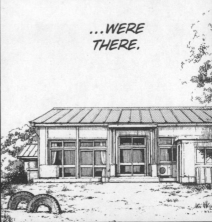

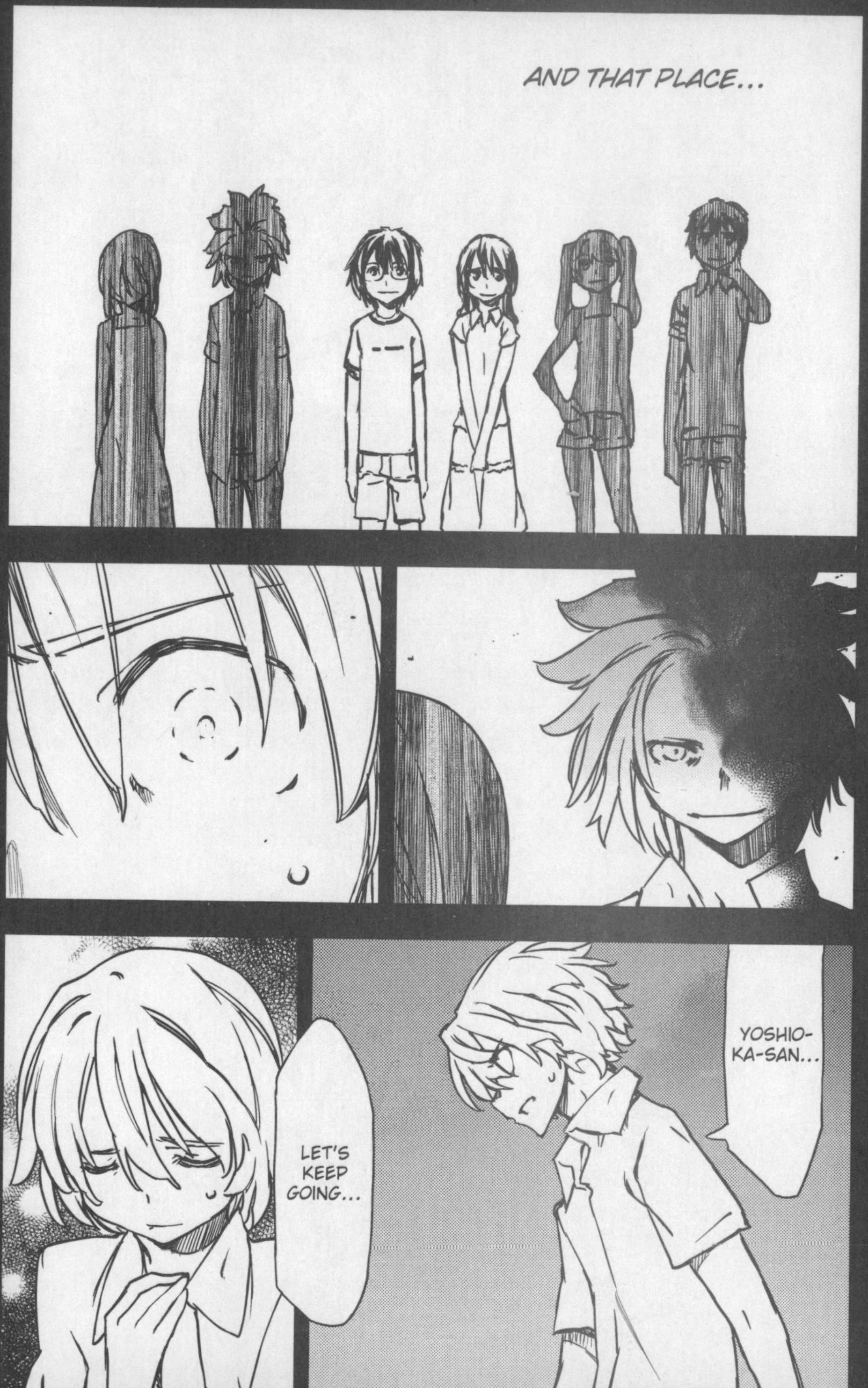
AND THAT PLACE...
YOSHIO-
KA-SAN...
LET'S
KEEP
GOING...

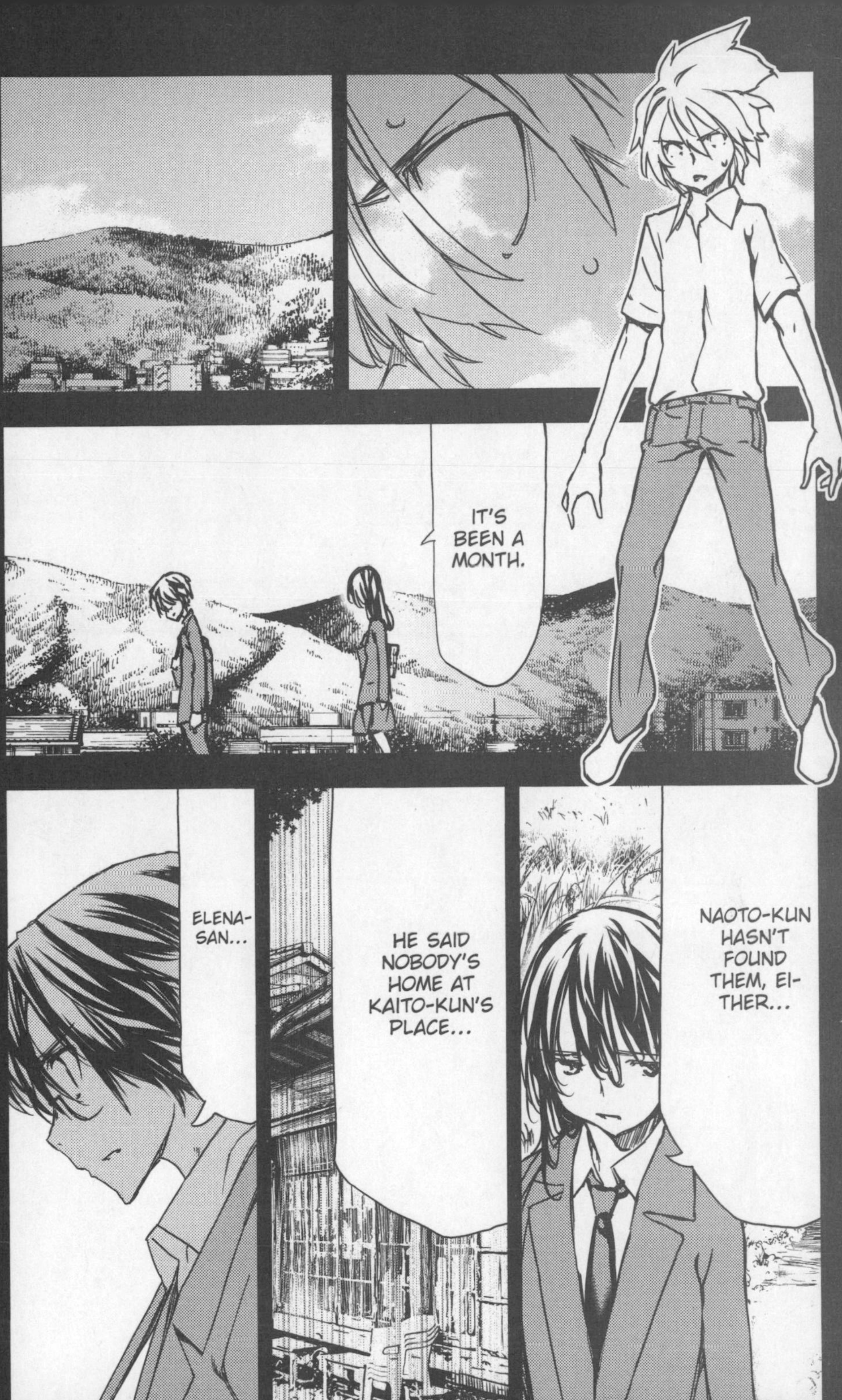
IT'S BEEN A MONTH.
NAOTO-KUN HASN'T FOUND THEM, EI-THER...
HE SAID NOBODY'S HOME AT KAITO-KUN'S PLACE...
ELENA-SAN...

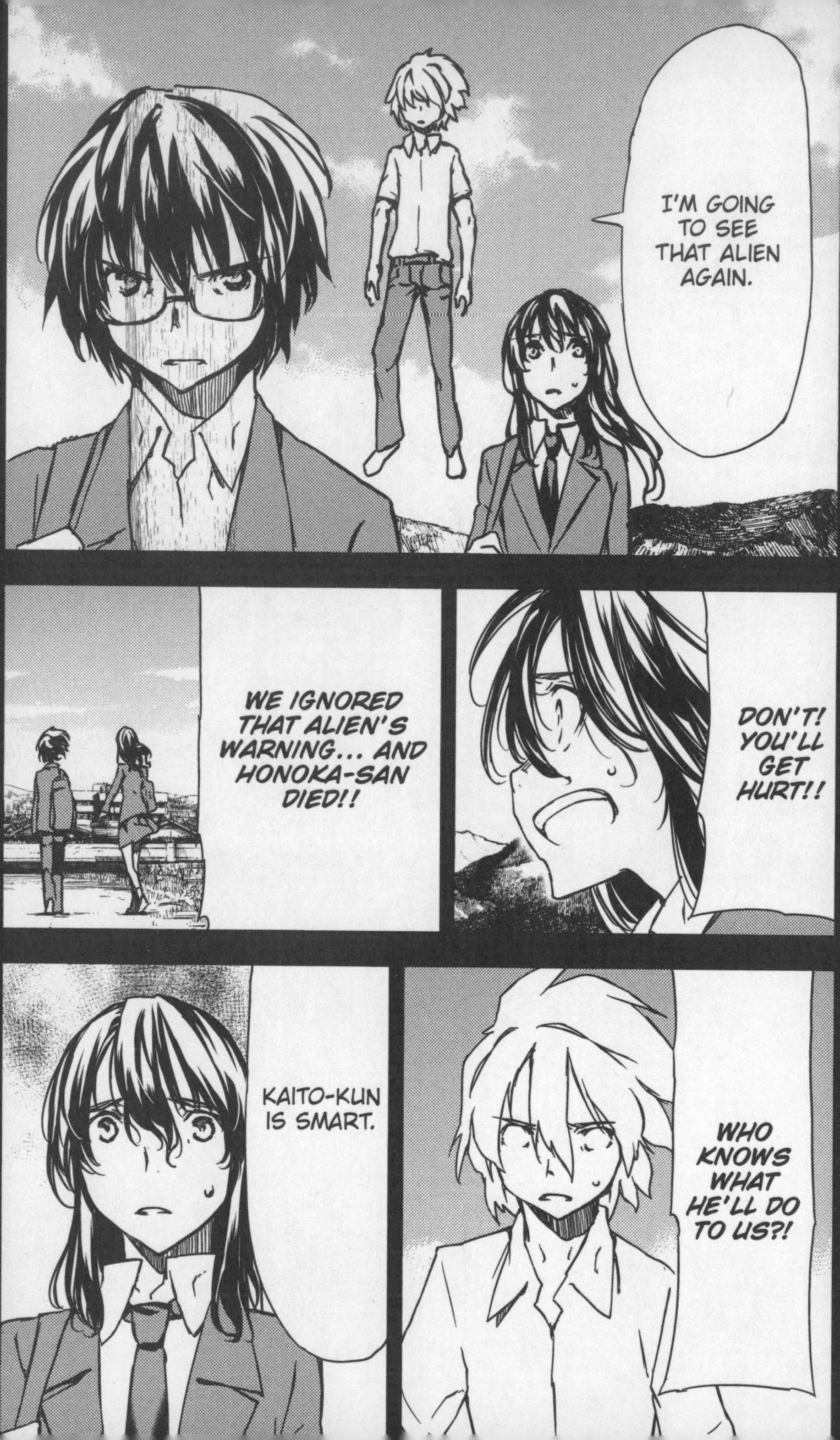
I'M GOING TO SEE THAT ALIEN AGAIN.
DON'T! YOU'LL GET HURT!!
WE IGNORED THAT ALIEN'S WARNING... AND HONOKA-SAN DIED!!
WHO KNOWS WHAT HE'LL DO TO US?!
KAITO-KUN IS SMART.

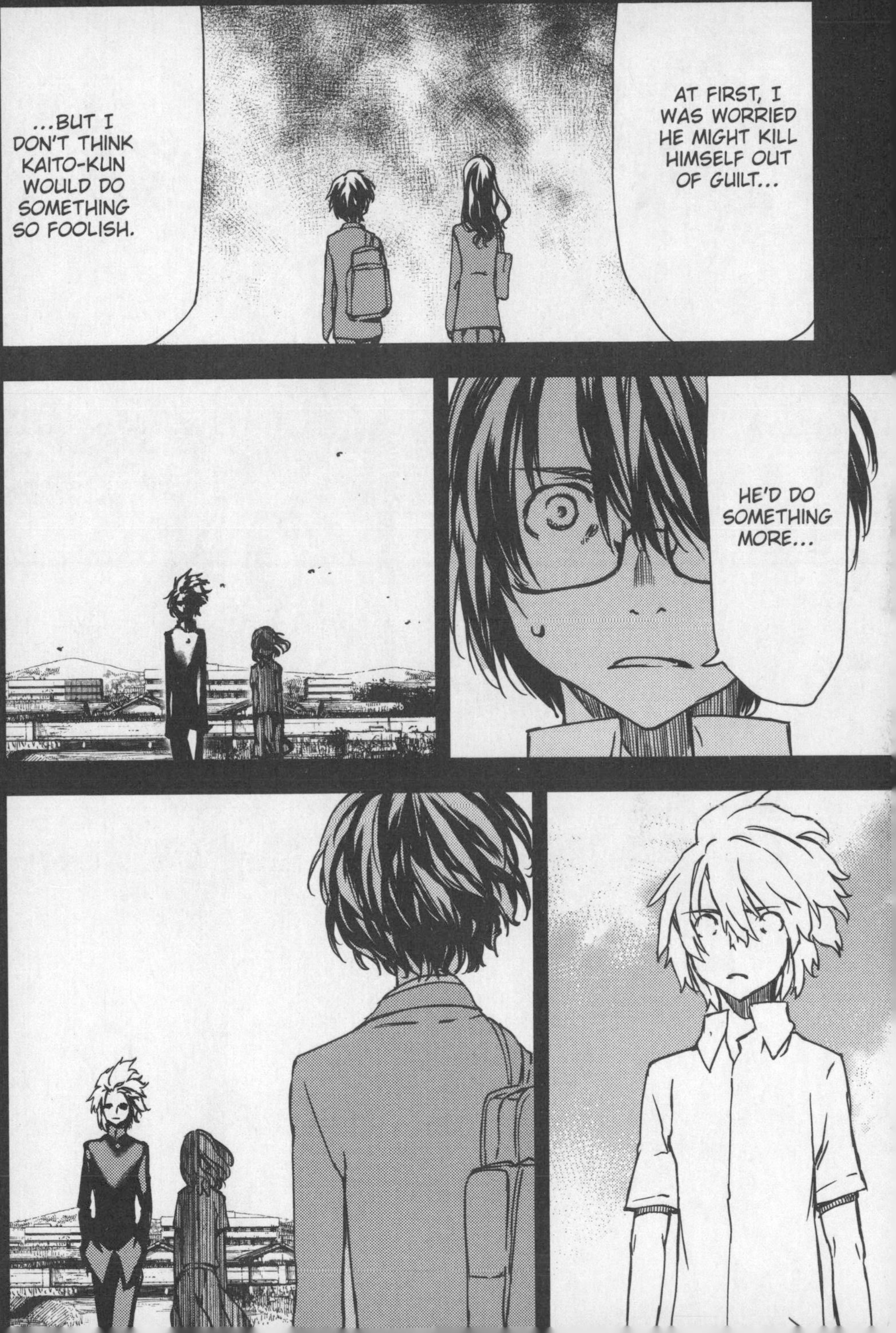
AT FIRST, I WAS WORRIED HE MIGHT KILL HIMSELF OUT OF GUILT...
...BUT I DON'T THINK KAITO-KUN WOULD DO SOMETHING SO FOOLISH.
HE'D DO SOMETHING MORE...

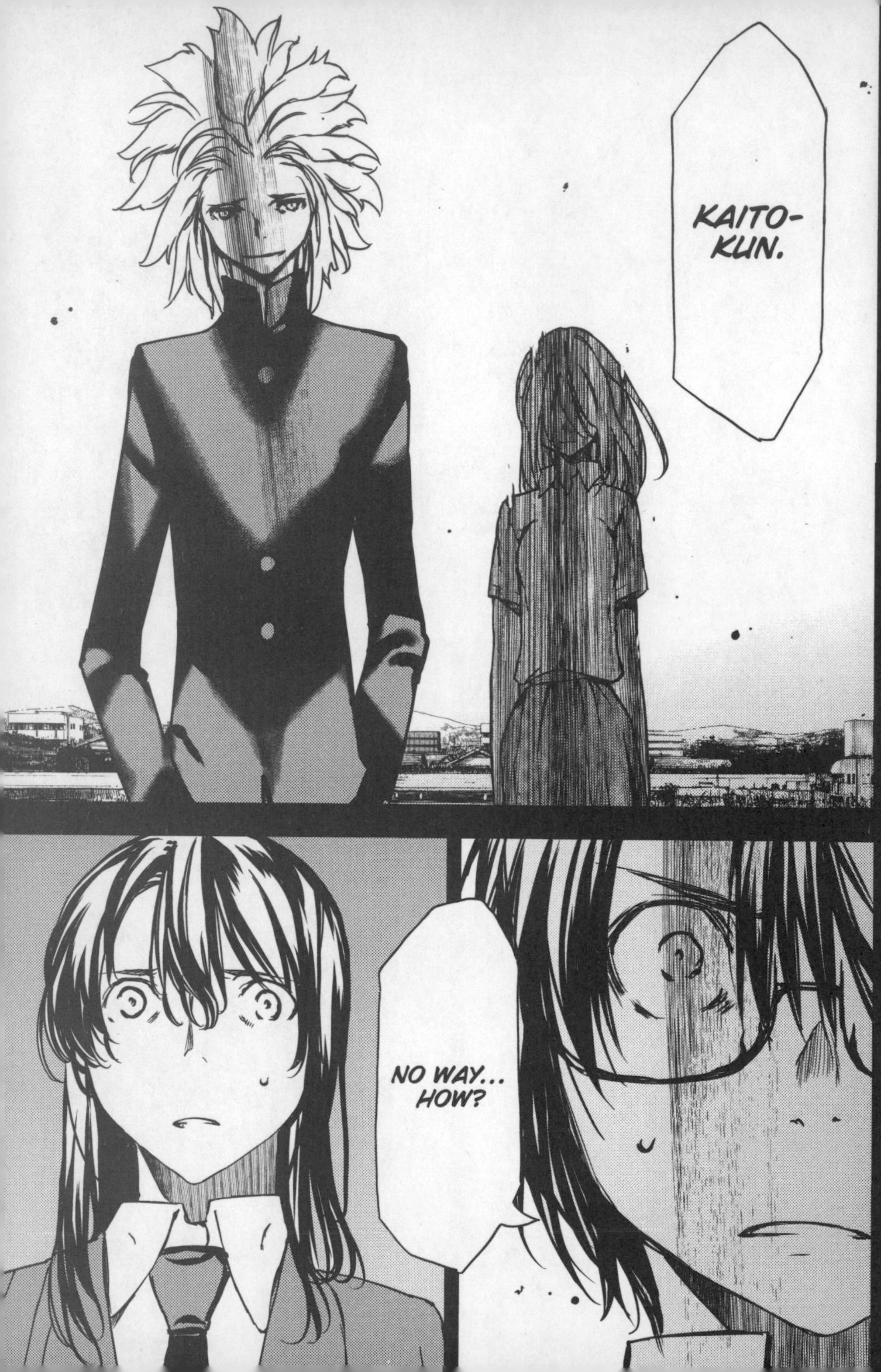
KAITO-KUN.
NO WAY... HOW?

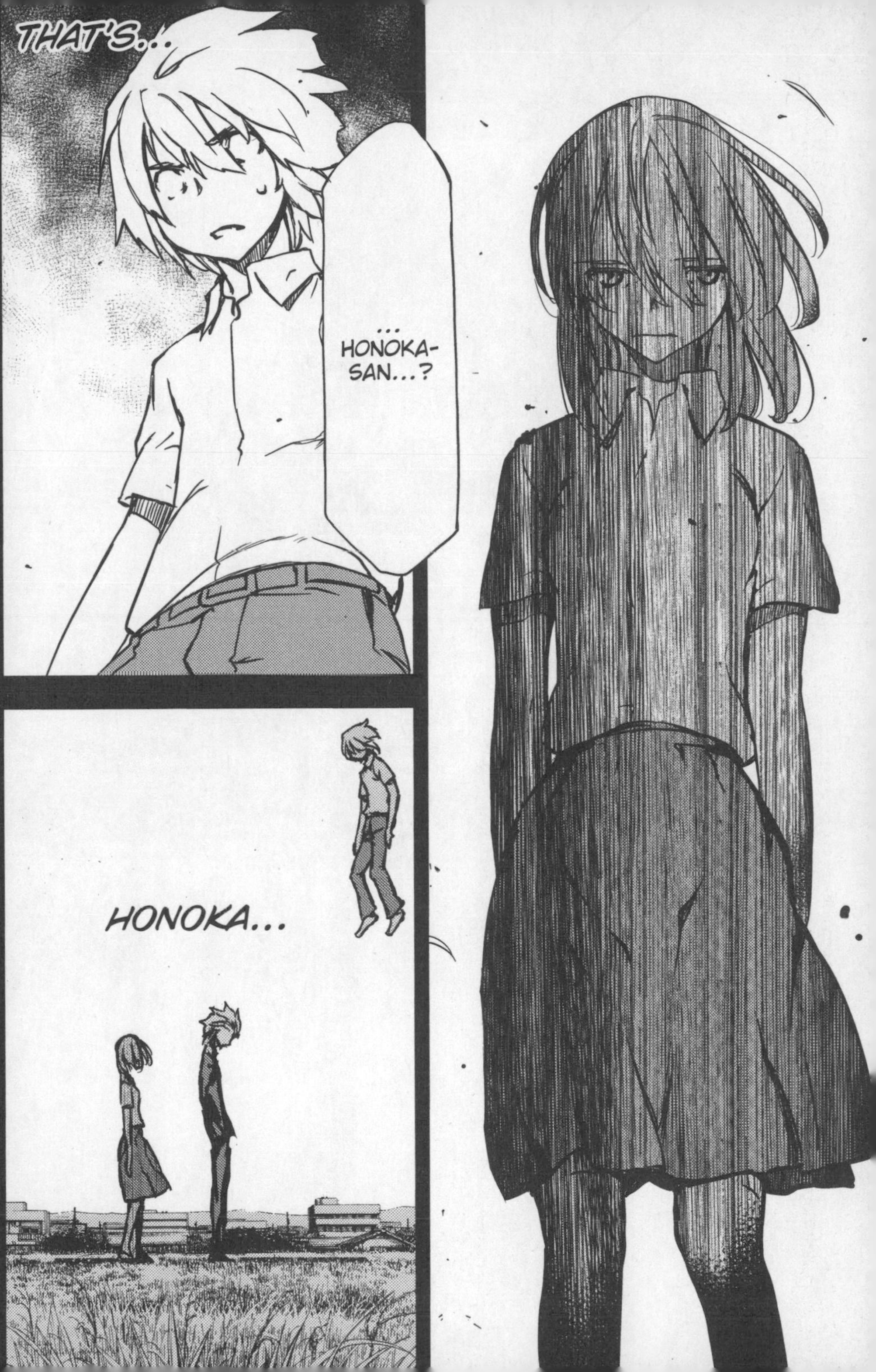
THAT'S...
... HONOKA-SAN...?
HONOKA...

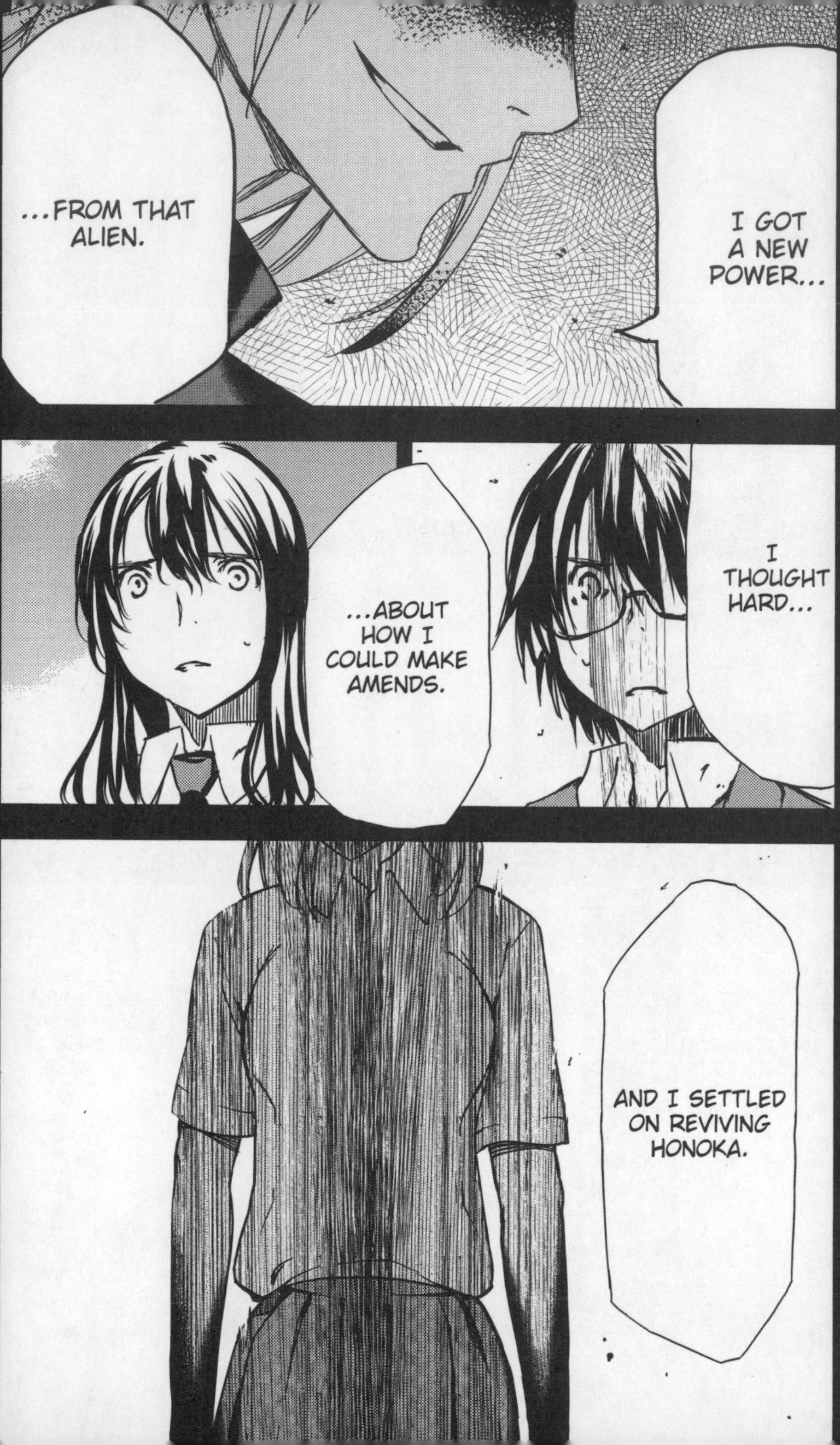
I GOT A NEW POWER...
...FROM THAT ALIEN.
I THOUGHT HARD...
...ABOUT HOW I COULD MAKE AMENDS.
AND I SETTLED ON REVIVING HONOKA.

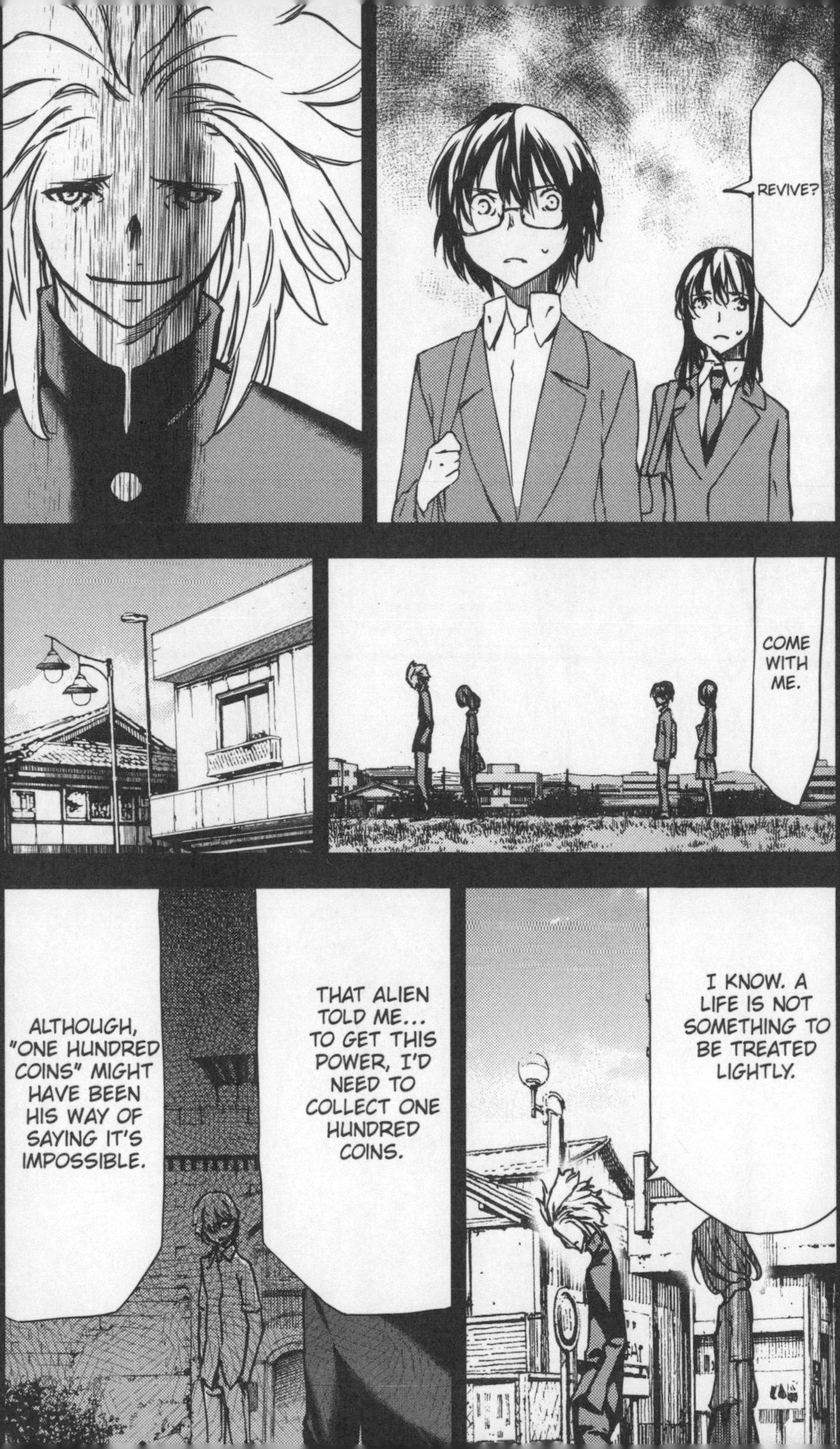
REVIVE?
COME WITH ME.
I KNOW. A LIFE IS NOT SOMETHING TO BE TREATED LIGHTLY.
THAT ALIEN TOLD ME... TO GET THIS POWER, I'D NEED TO COLLECT ONE HUNDRED COINS.
ALTHOUGH, "ONE HUNDRED COINS" MIGHT HAVE BEEN HIS WAY OF SAYING IT'S IMPOSSIBLE.

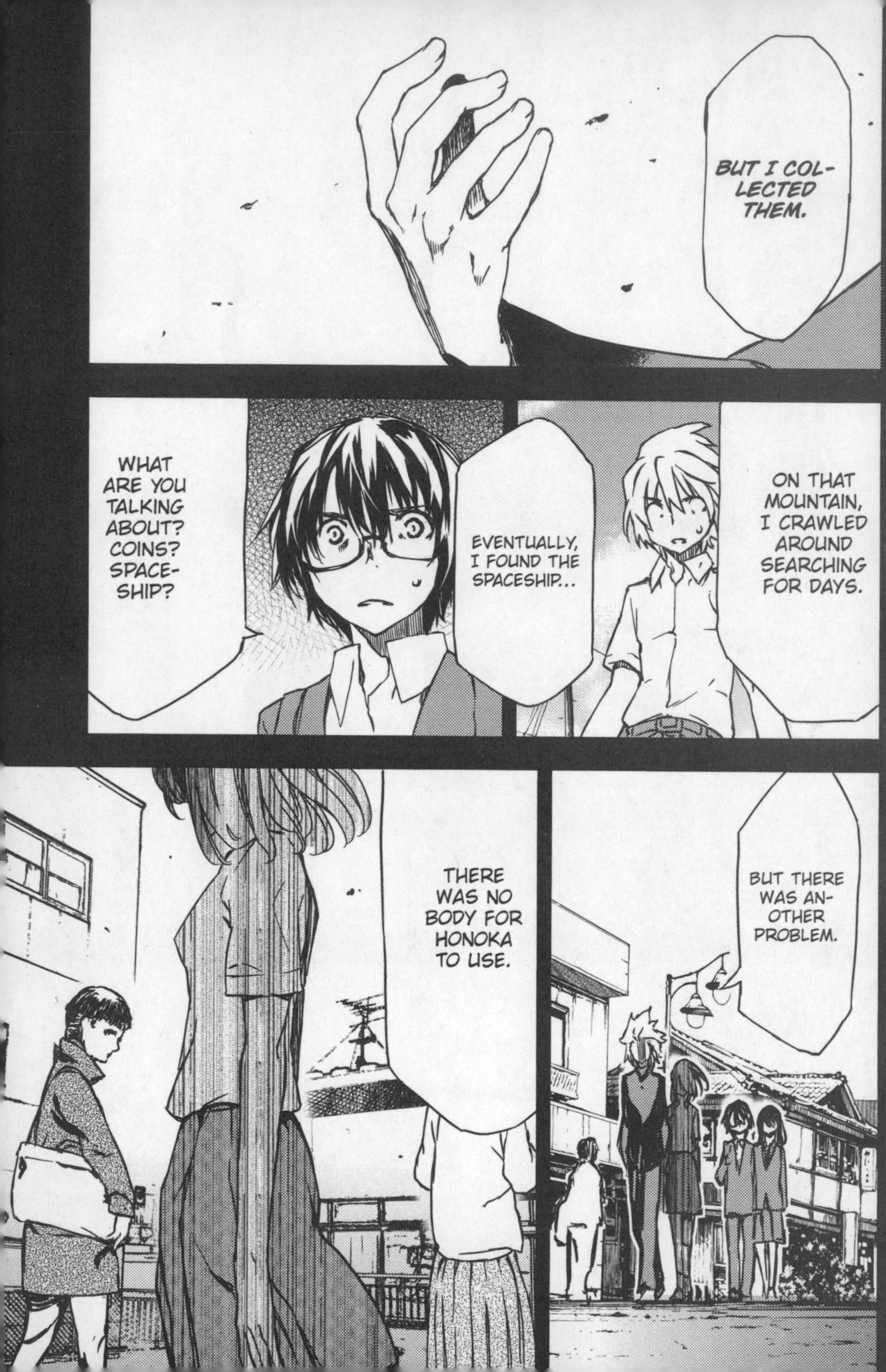
BUT I COLLECTED THEM.
ON THAT MOUNTAIN, I CRAWLED AROUND SEARCHING FOR DAYS.
EVENTUALLY, I FOUND THE SPACESHIP...
WHAT ARE YOU TALKING ABOUT? COINS? SPACESHIP?
BUT THERE WAS ANOTHER PROBLEM.
THERE WAS NO BODY FOR HONOKA TO USE.

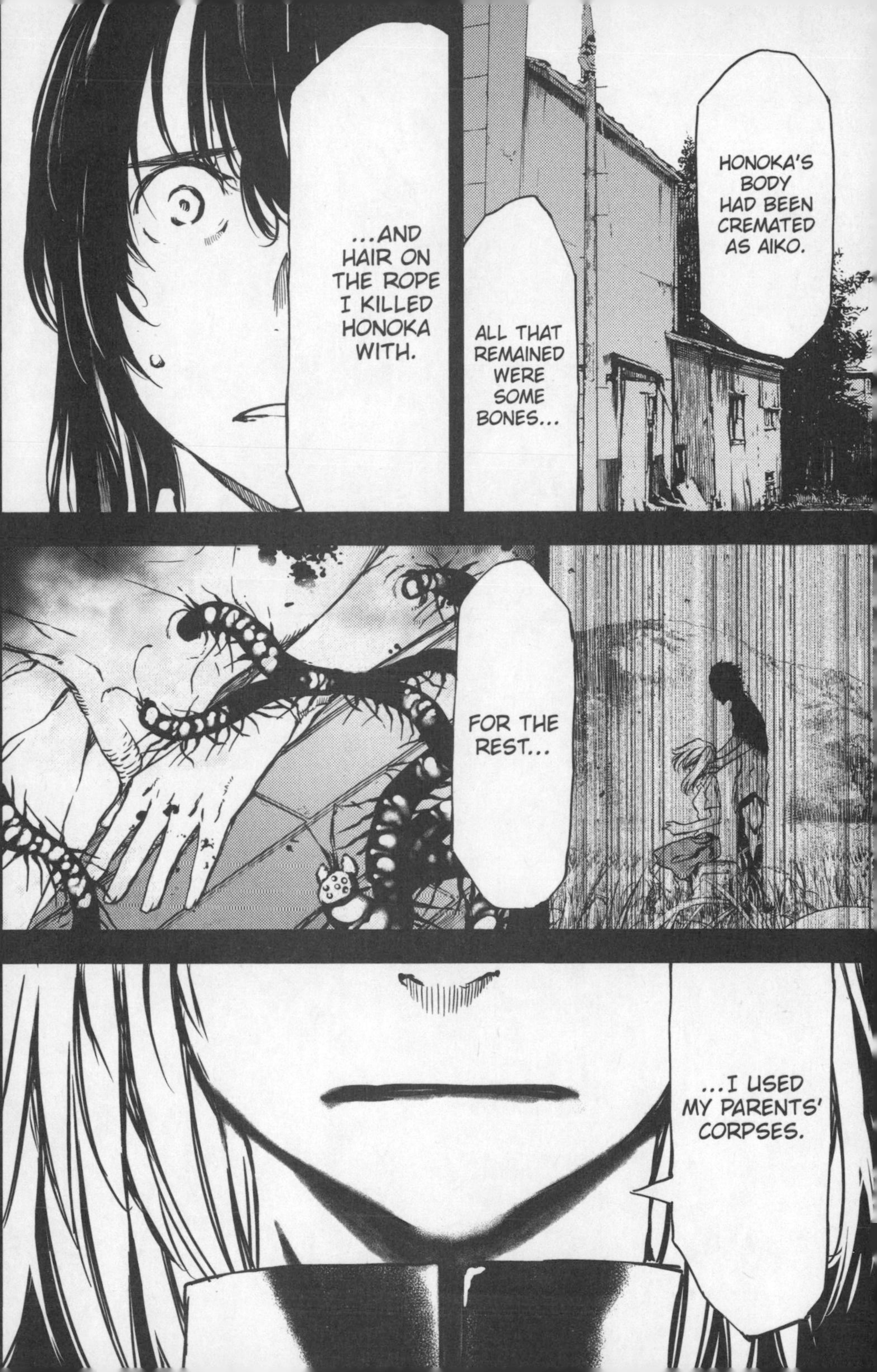
HONOKA'S BODY HAD BEEN CREMATED AS AIKO.
ALL THAT REMAINED WERE SOME BONES...
...AND HAIR ON THE ROPE I KILLED HONOKA WITH.
FOR THE REST...
...I USED MY PARENTS' CORPSES.

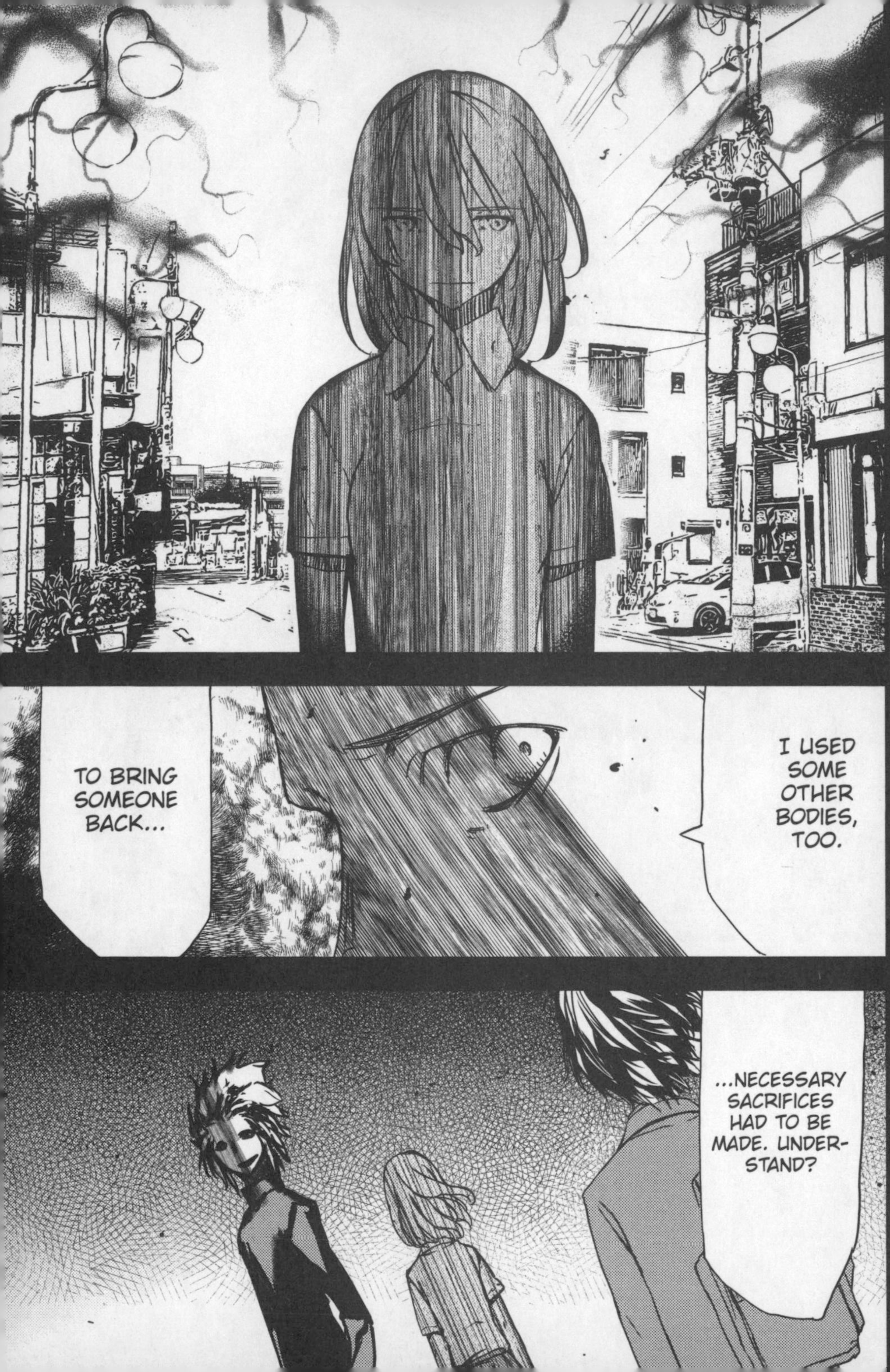
I USED SOME OTHER BODIES, TOO.
TO BRING SOMEONE BACK...
...NECESSARY SACRIFICES HAD TO BE MADE. UNDER-STAND?

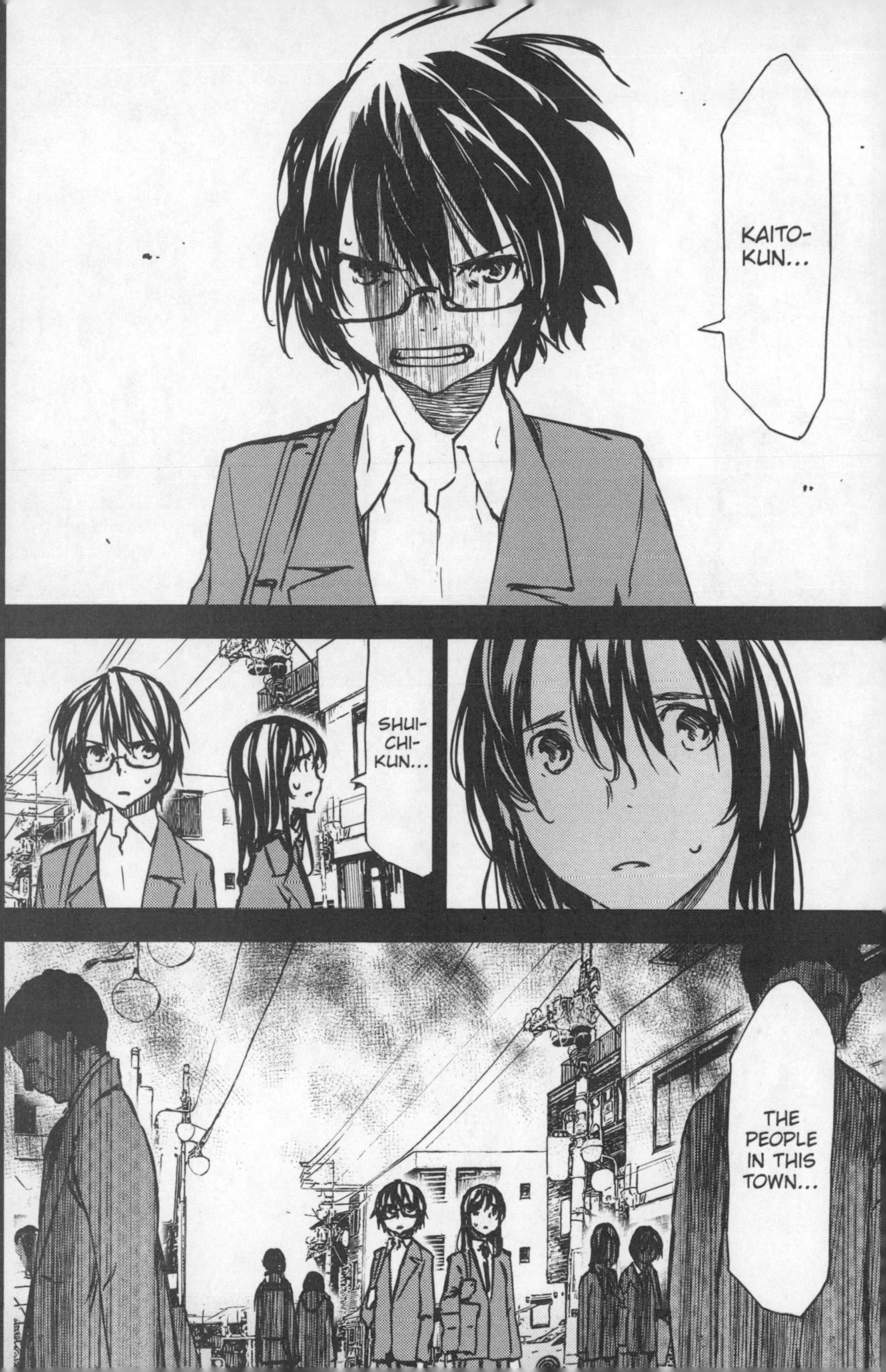
KAITO-KUN...
SHUI-CHI-KUN...
THE PEOPLE IN THIS TOWN...

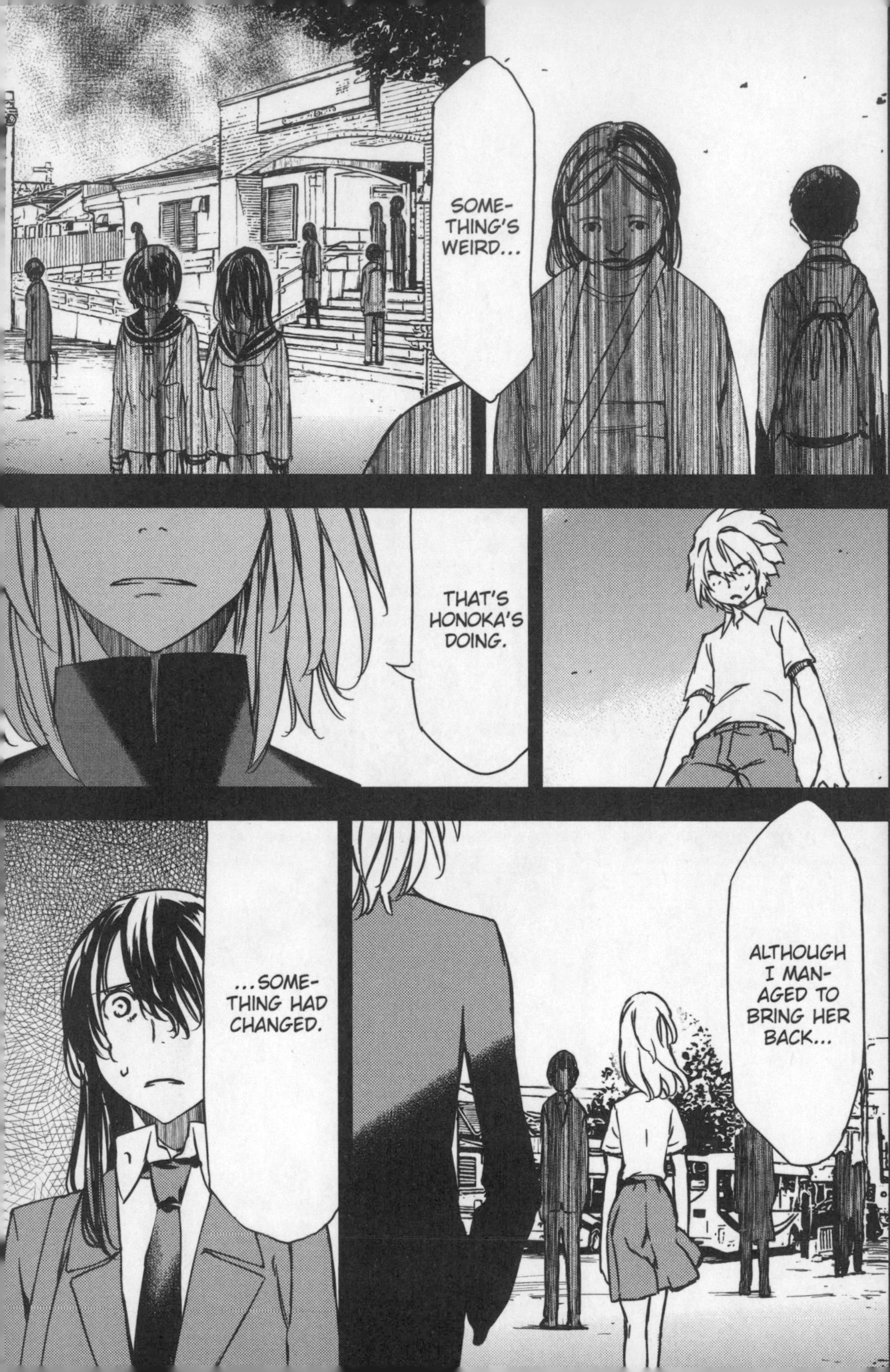
SOME-THING'S WEIRD...
THAT'S HONOKA'S DOING.
ALTHOUGH I MAN-AGED TO BRING HER BACK...
...SOME-THING HAD CHANGED.

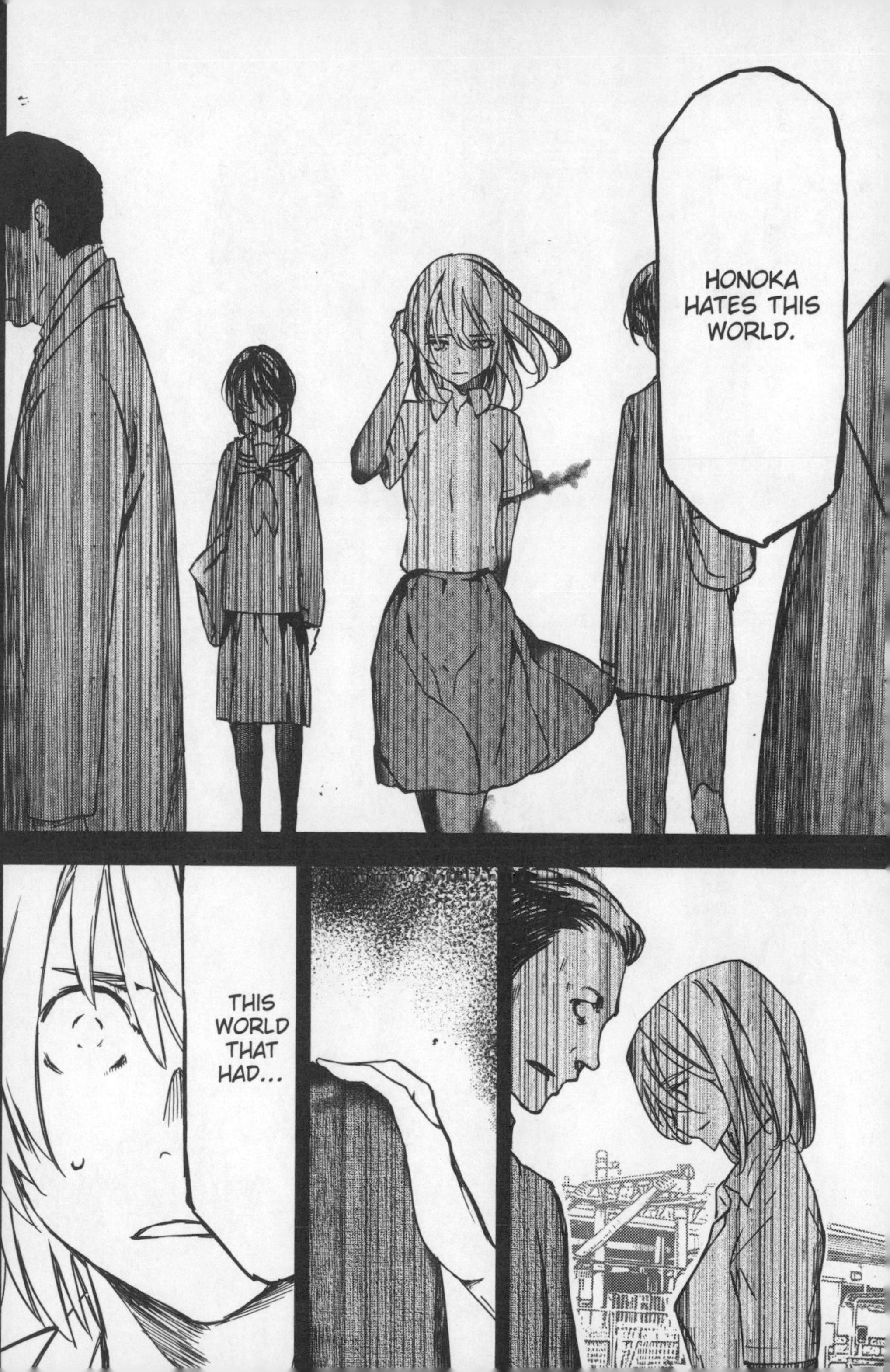
HONOKA HATES THIS WORLD.
THIS WORLD THAT HAD...

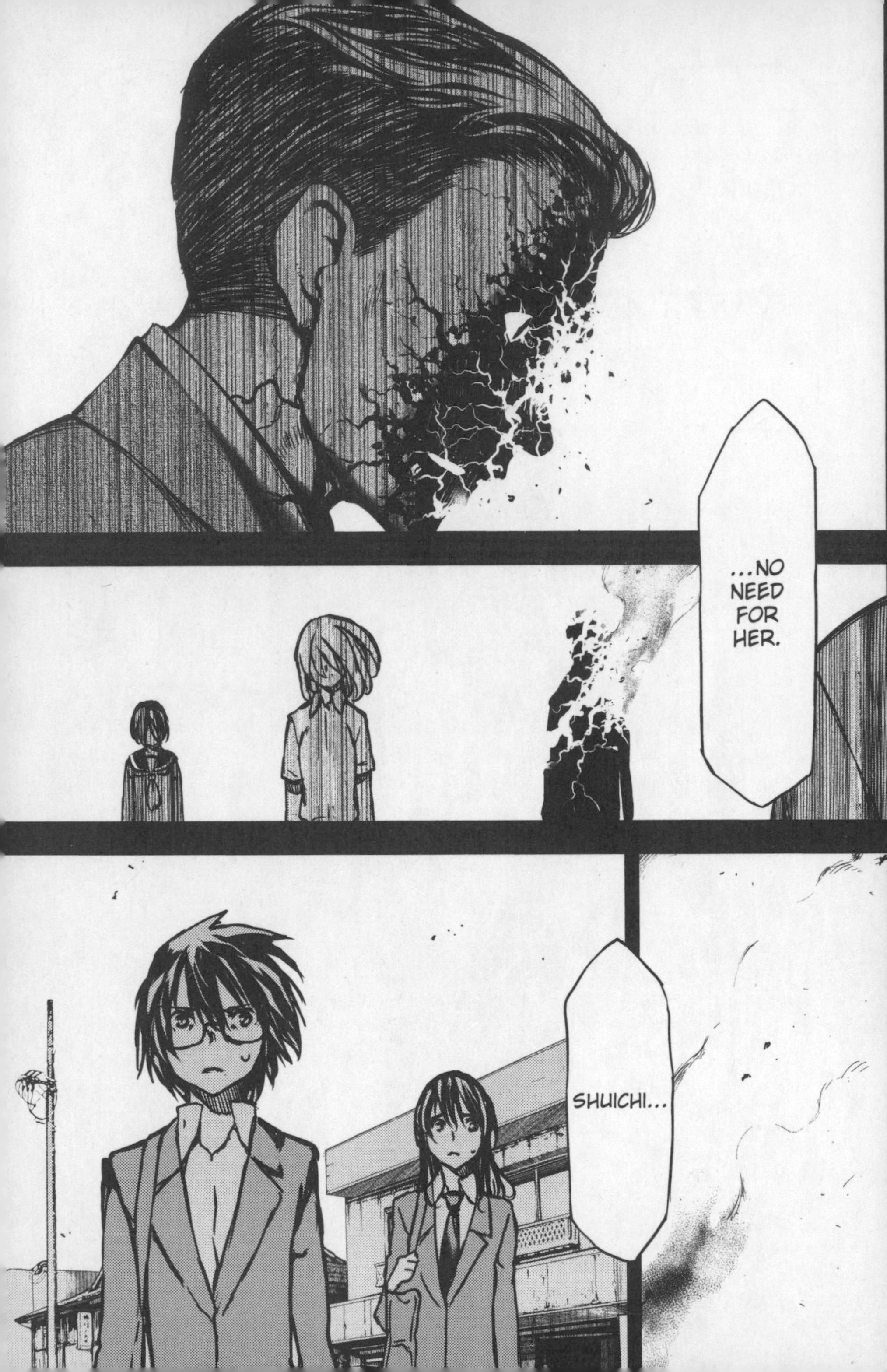
...NO NEED FOR HER.
SHUICHI...

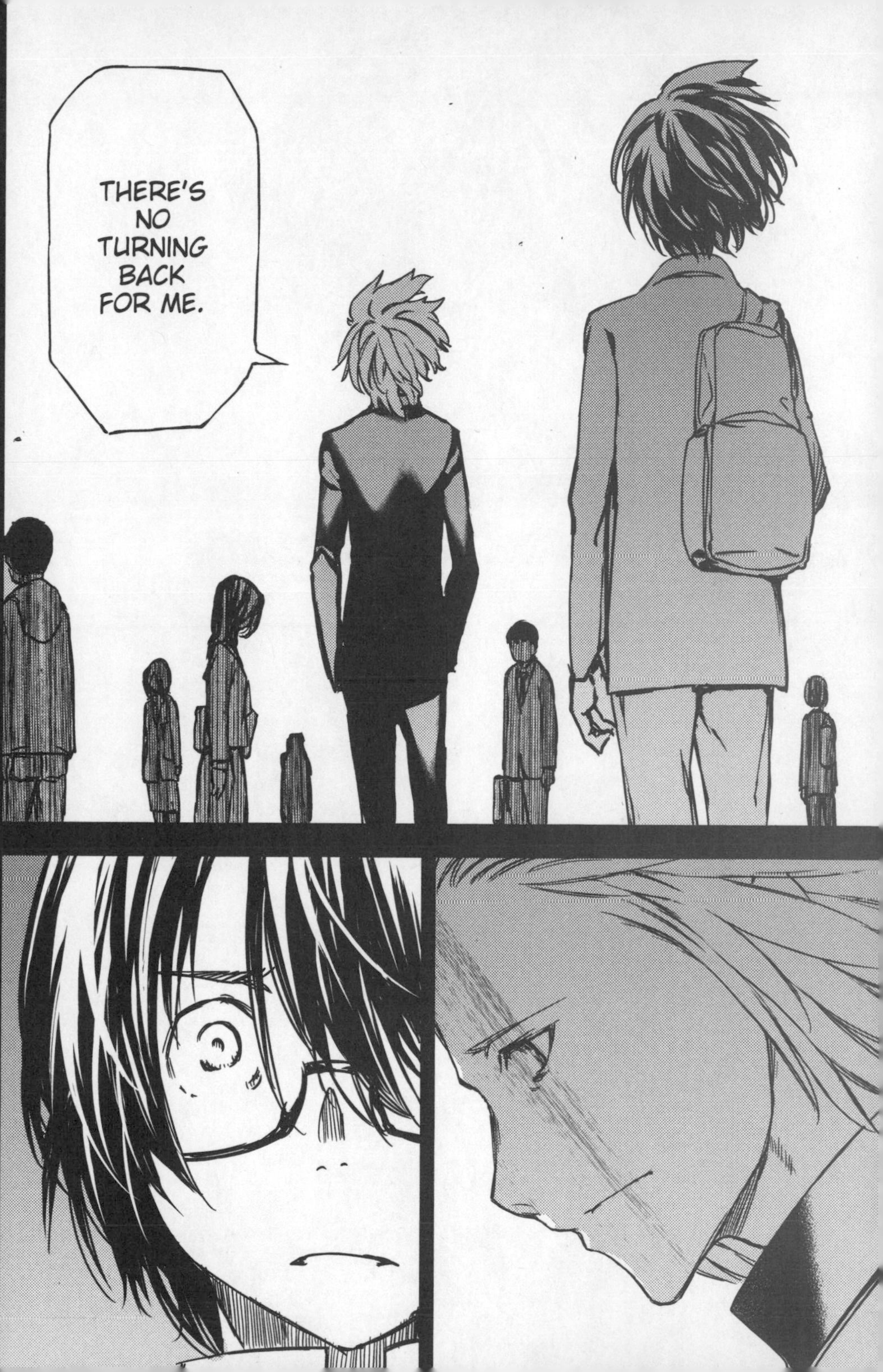
THERE'S NO TURNING BACK FOR ME.

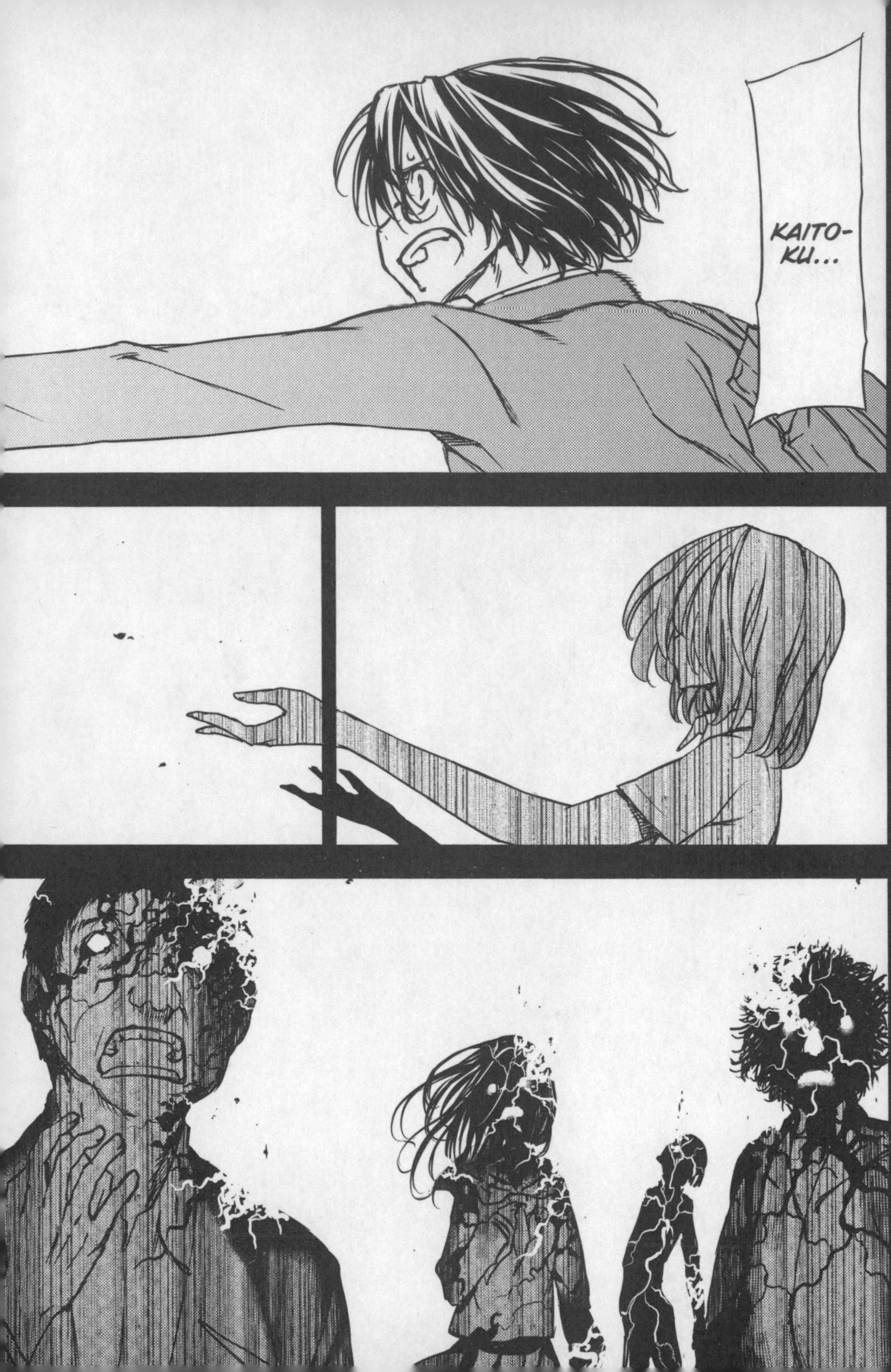
KAITO-
KU...

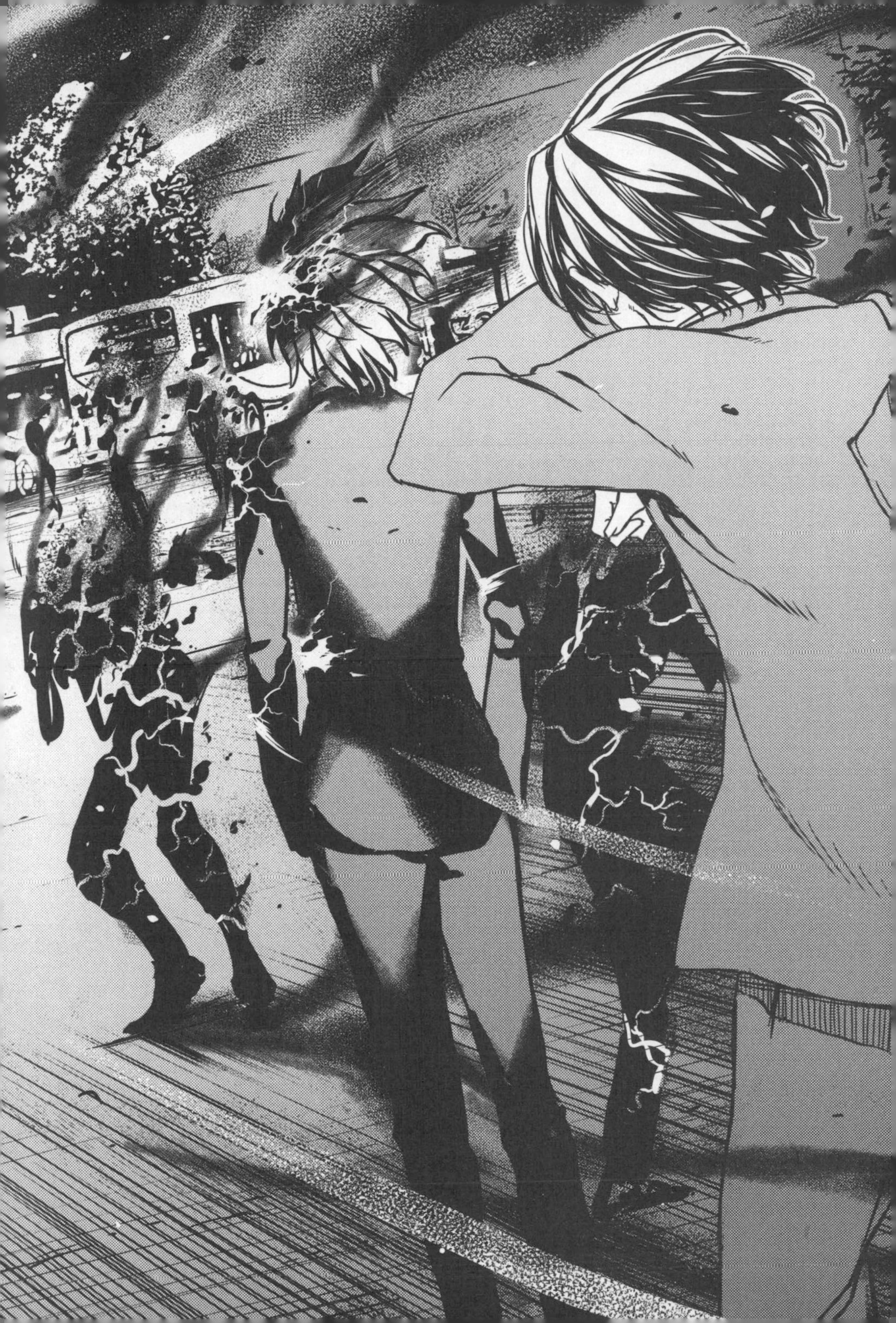

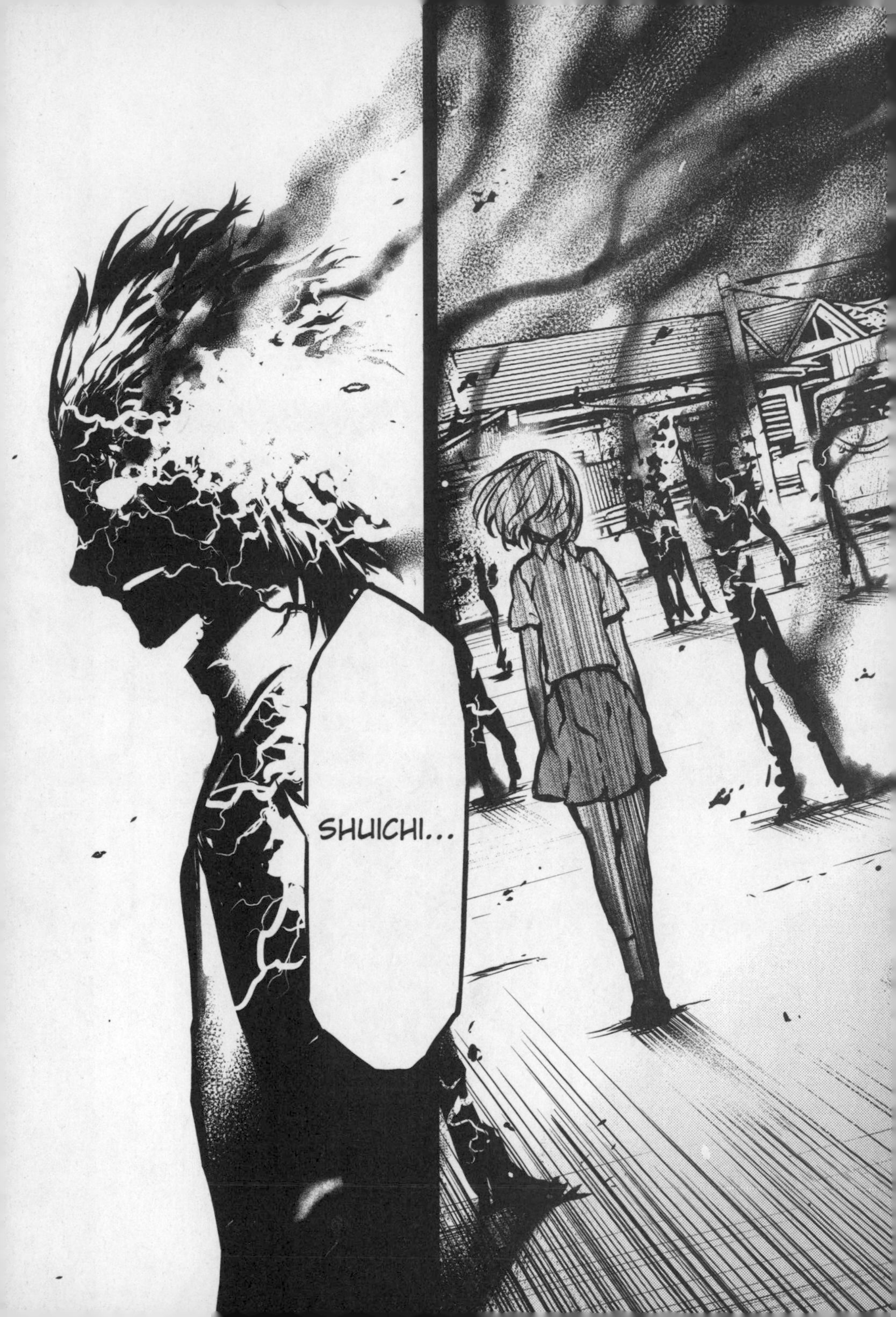
SHUICHI...

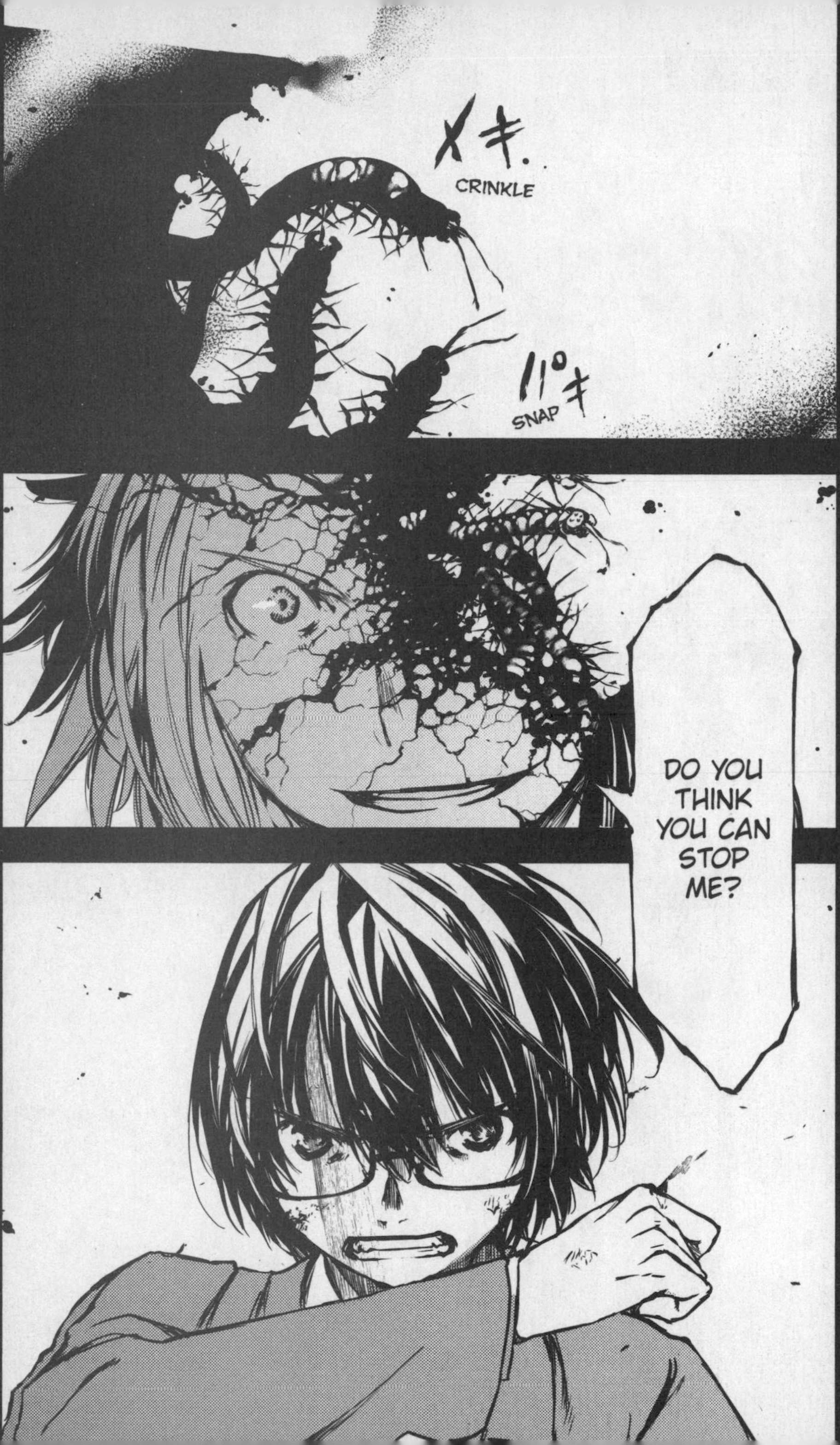
メキ
CRINKLE
パキ
SNAP
DO YOU THINK YOU CAN STOP ME?

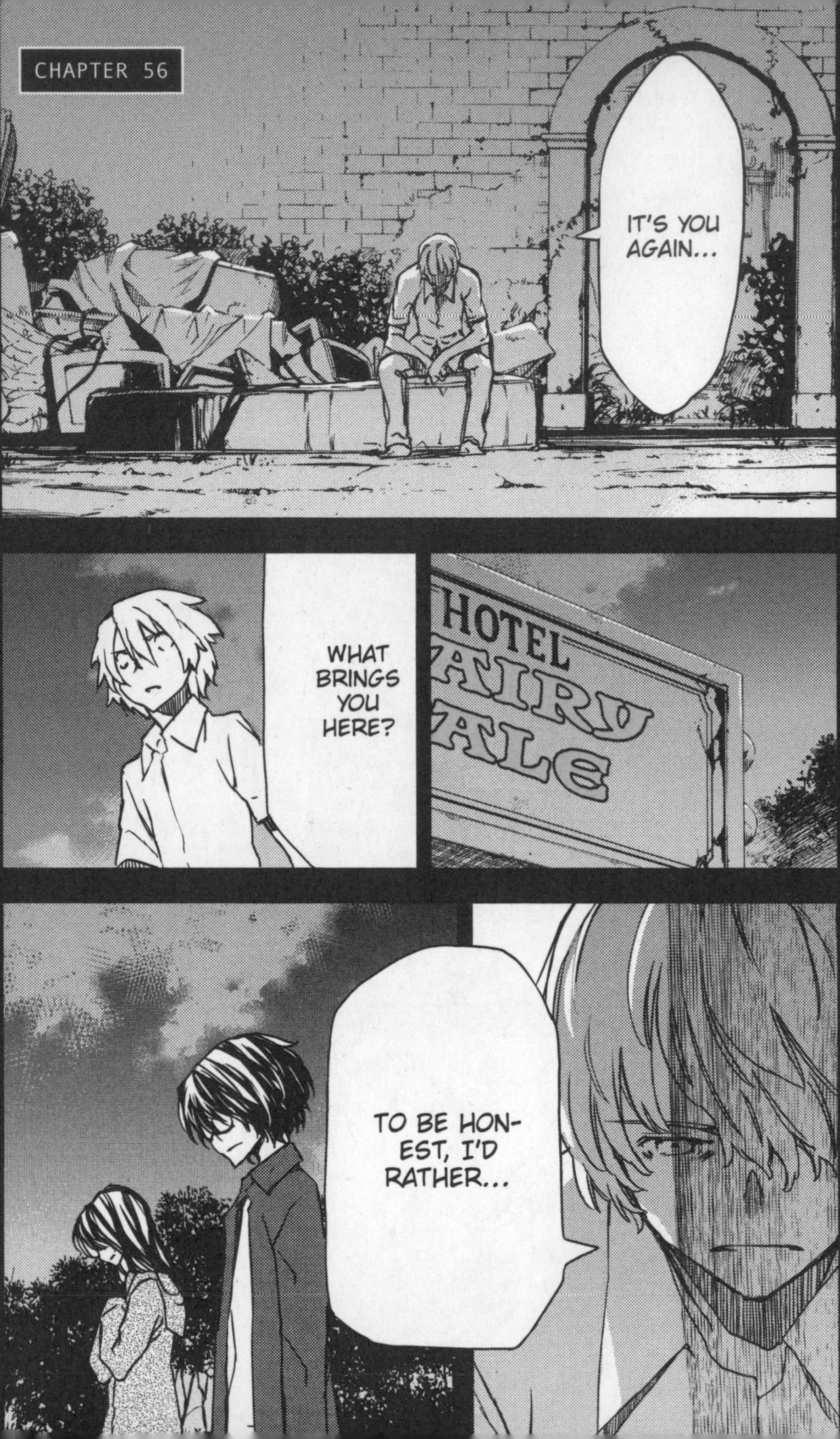
CHAPTER 56
IT'S YOU AGAIN...
HOTEL
WHAT BRINGS YOU HERE?
TO BE HON-EST, I'D RATHER...

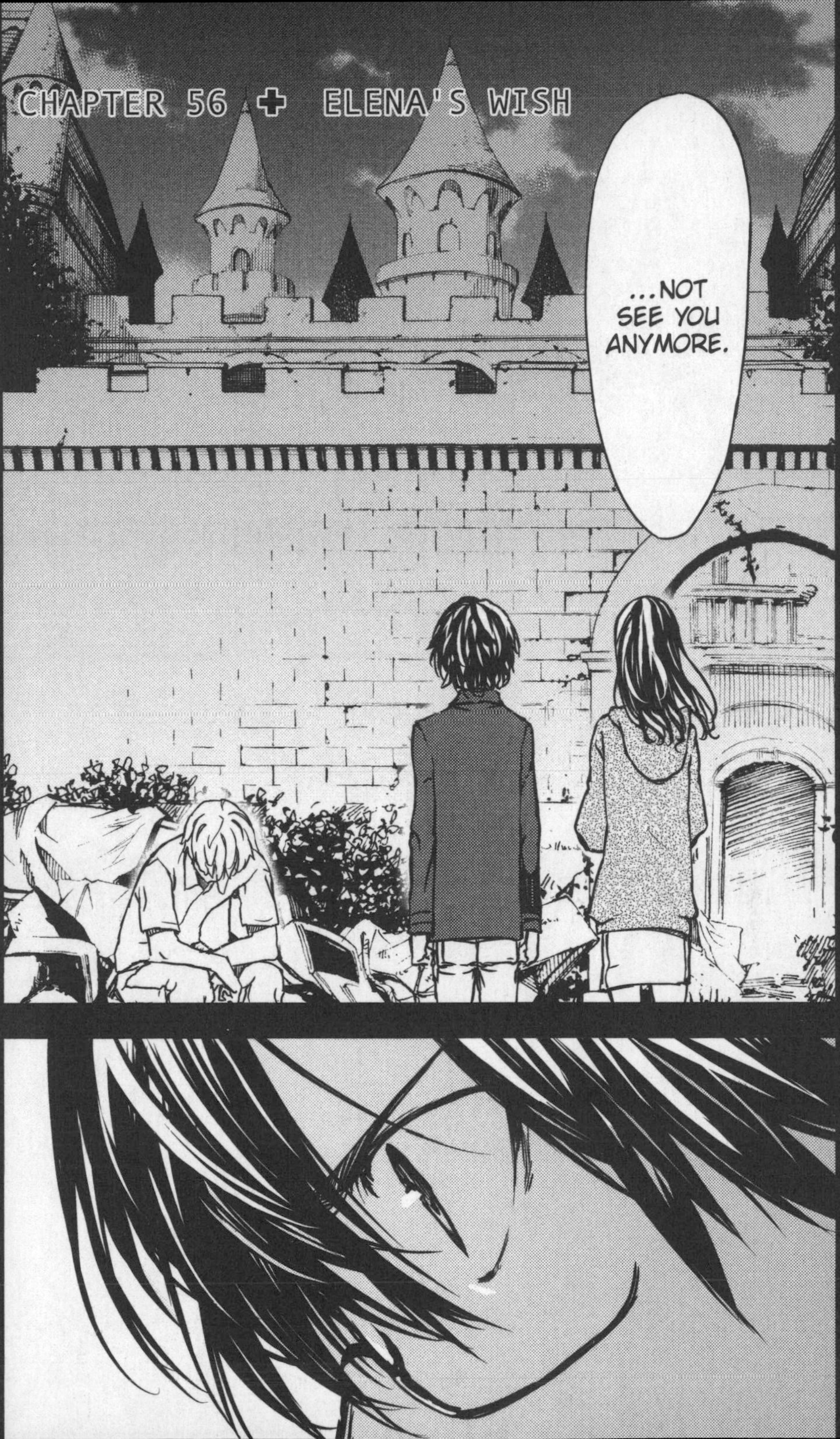
CHAPTER 56 + ELENA'S WISH
...NOT SEE YOU ANYMORE.

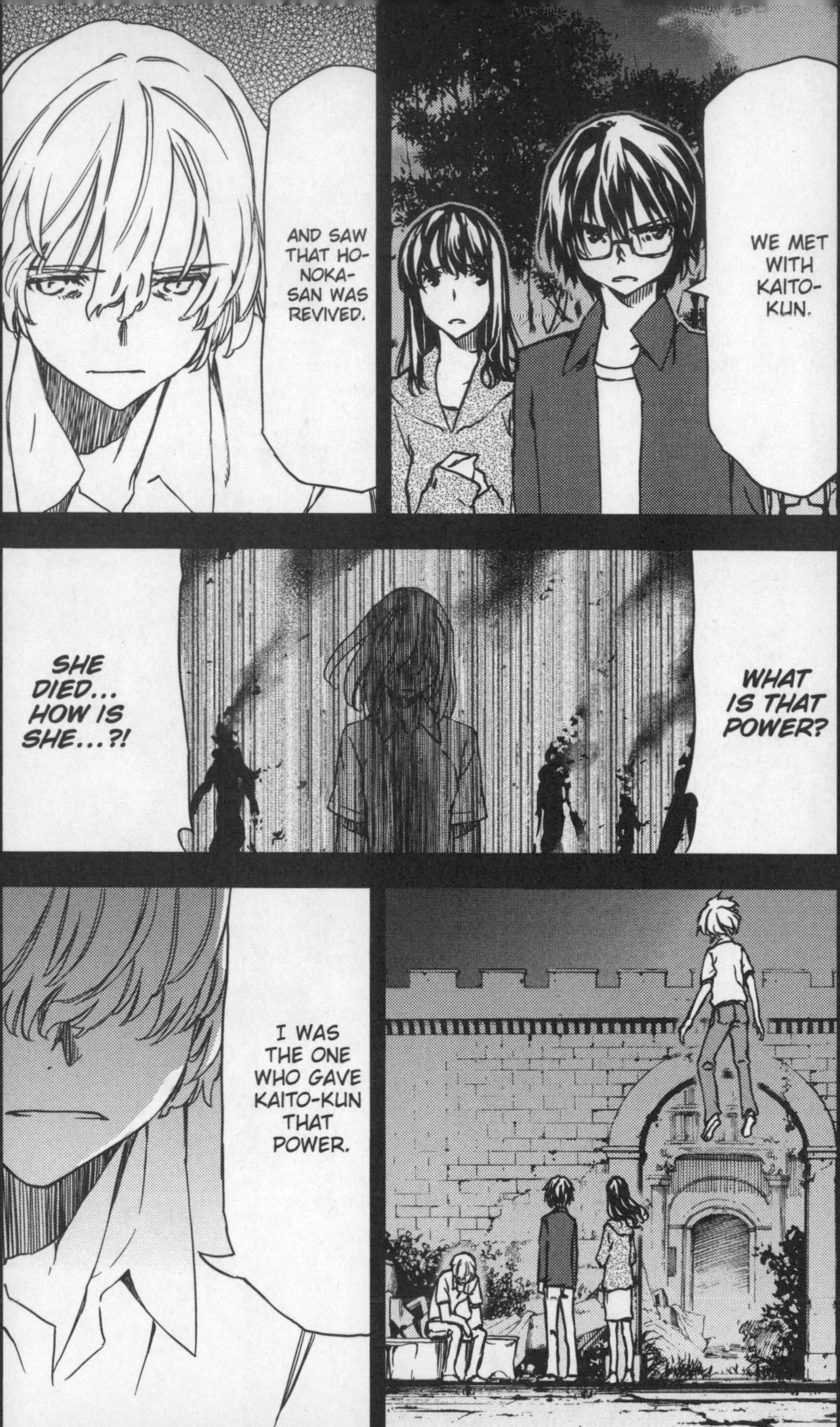
WE MET WITH KAITO-KUN.
AND SAW THAT HO-NOKA-SAN WAS REVIVED.
WHAT IS THAT POWER?
SHE DIED... HOW IS SHE...?!
I WAS THE ONE WHO GAVE KAITO-KUN THAT POWER.

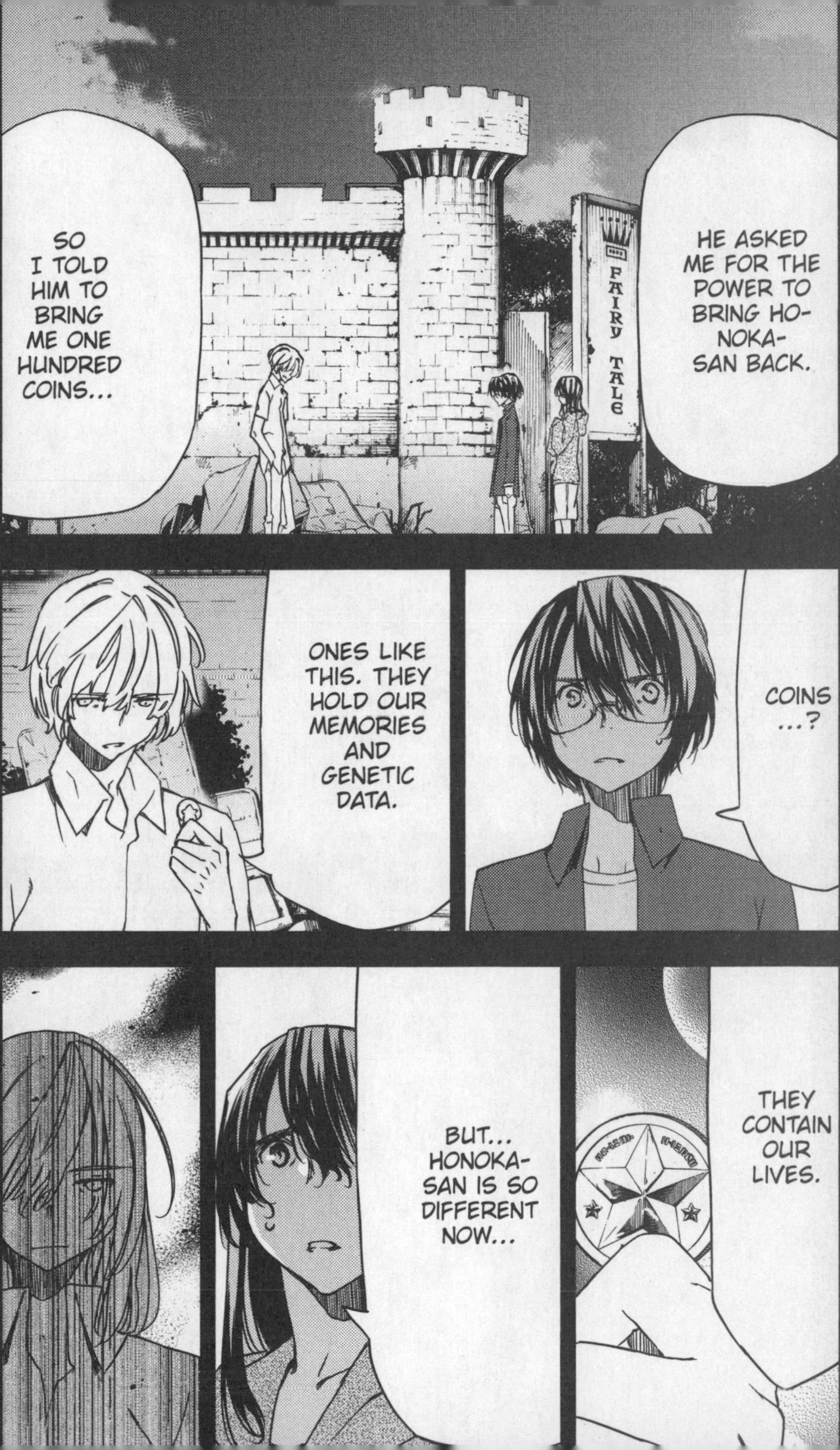
HE ASKED ME FOR THE POWER TO BRING HONOKA-SAN BACK.
FAIRY TALE
SO I TOLD HIM TO BRING ME ONE HUNDRED COINS...
COINS ...?
ONES LIKE THIS. THEY HOLD OUR MEMORIES AND GENETIC DATA.
THEY CONTAIN OUR LIVES.
BUT... HONOKA-SAN IS SO DIFFERENT NOW...

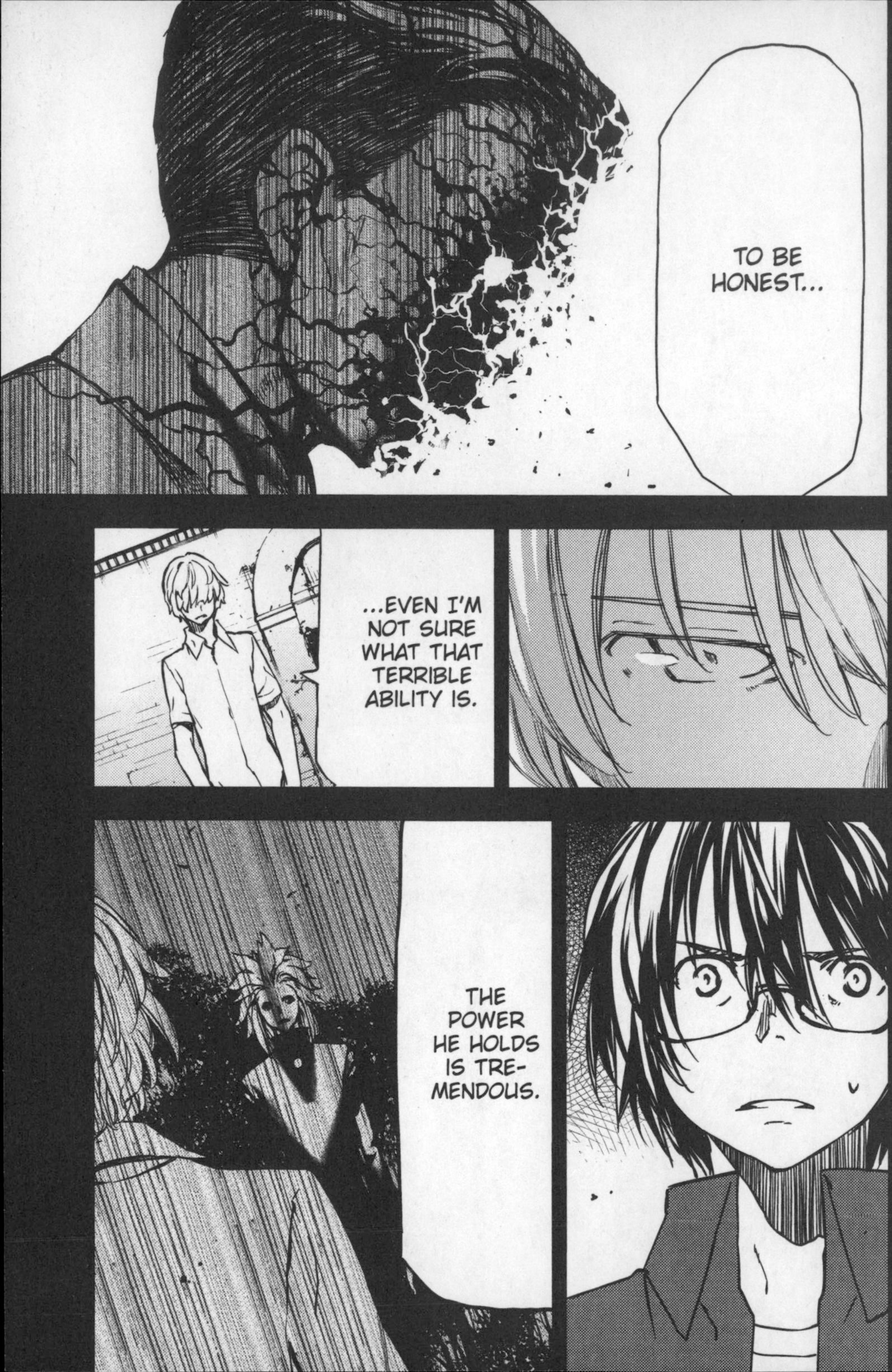
TO BE HONEST...
...EVEN I'M NOT SURE WHAT THAT TERRIBLE ABILITY IS.
THE POWER HE HOLDS IS TRE-MENDOUS.

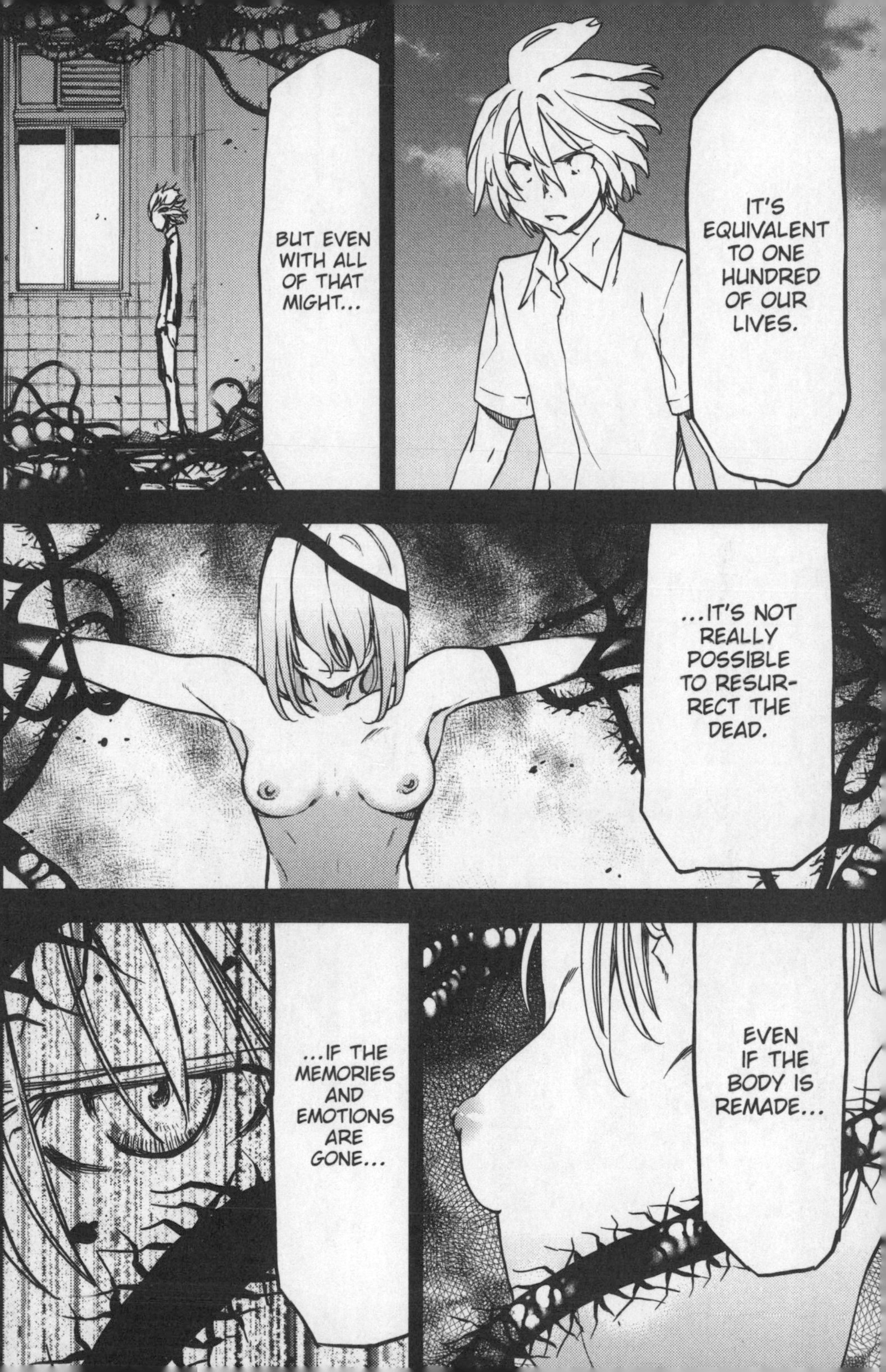
IT'S EQUIVALENT TO ONE HUNDRED OF OUR LIVES.
BUT EVEN WITH ALL OF THAT MIGHT...
...IT'S NOT REALLY POSSIBLE TO RESURRECT THE DEAD.
EVEN IF THE BODY IS REMADE...
...IF THE MEMORIES AND EMOTIONS ARE GONE...

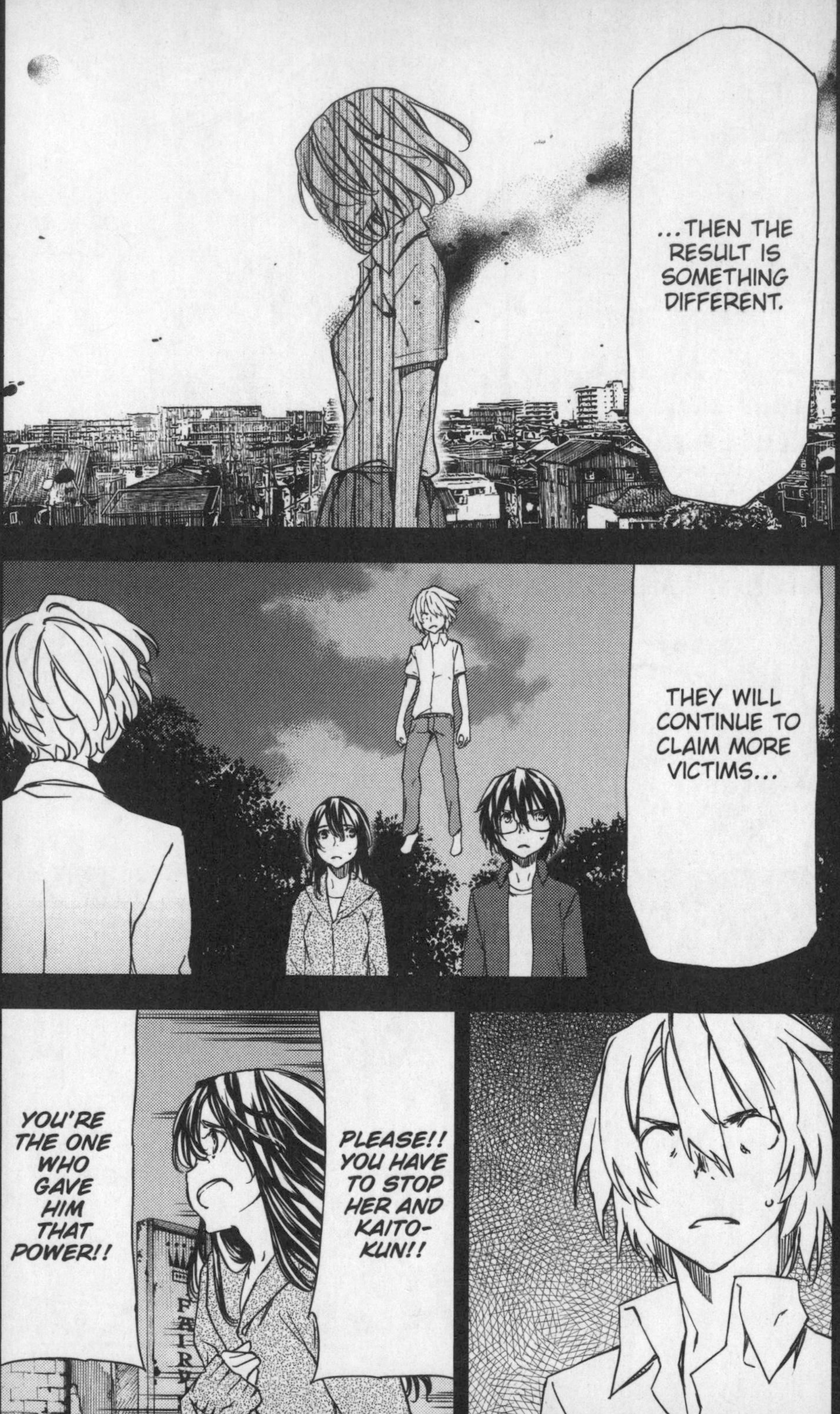
...THEN THE RESULT IS SOMETHING DIFFERENT.
THEY WILL CONTINUE TO CLAIM MORE VICTIMS...
PLEASE!! YOU HAVE TO STOP HER AND KAITO-KUN!!
YOU'RE THE ONE WHO GAVE HIM THAT POWER!!

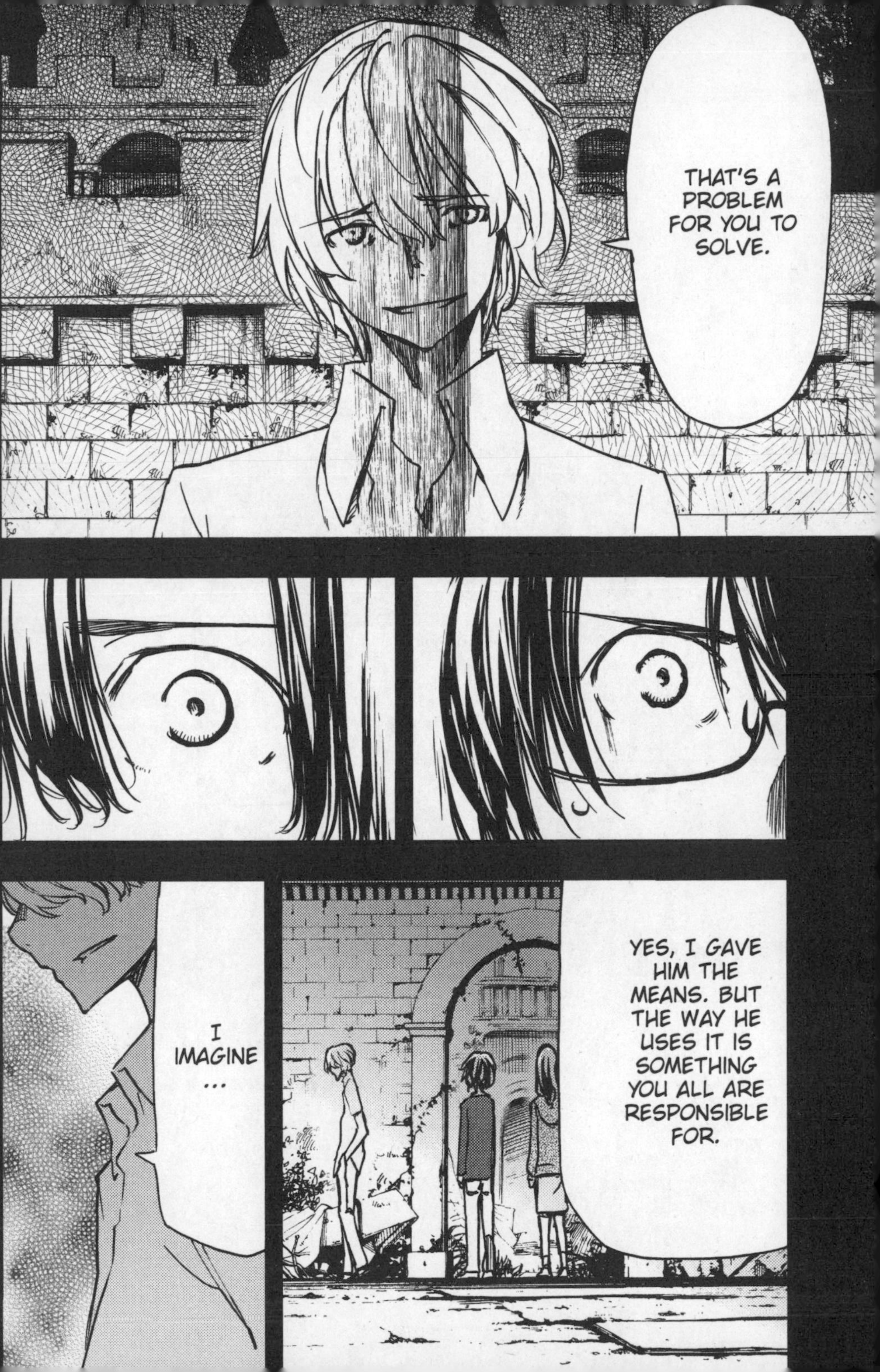
THAT'S A PROBLEM FOR YOU TO SOLVE.
YES, I GAVE HIM THE MEANS. BUT THE WAY HE USES IT IS SOMETHING YOU ALL ARE RESPONSIBLE FOR.
I IMAGINE ...

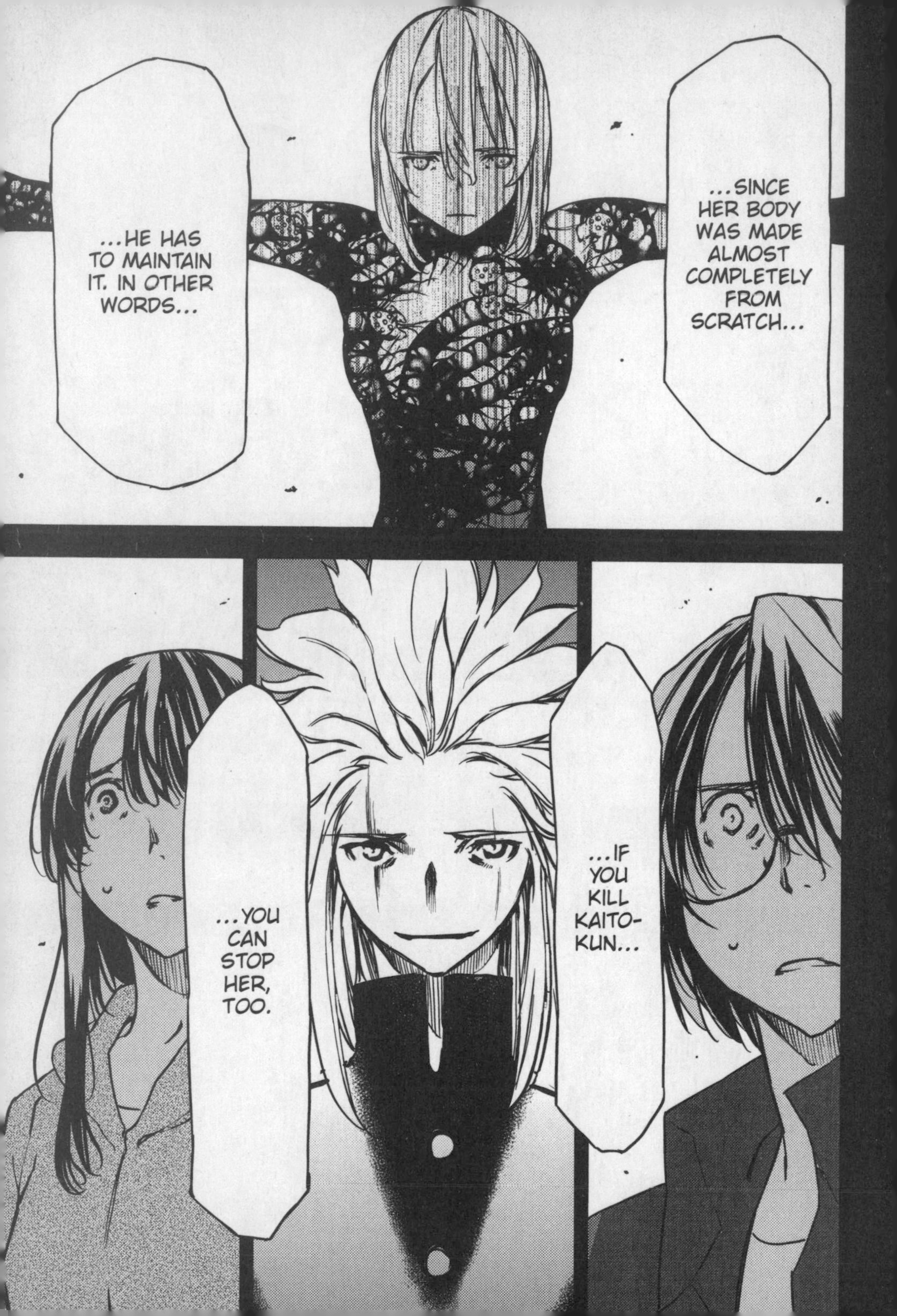
...SINCE HER BODY WAS MADE ALMOST COMPLETELY FROM SCRATCH...
...HE HAS TO MAINTAIN IT. IN OTHER WORDS...
...IF YOU KILL KAITO-KUN...
...YOU CAN STOP HER, TOO.

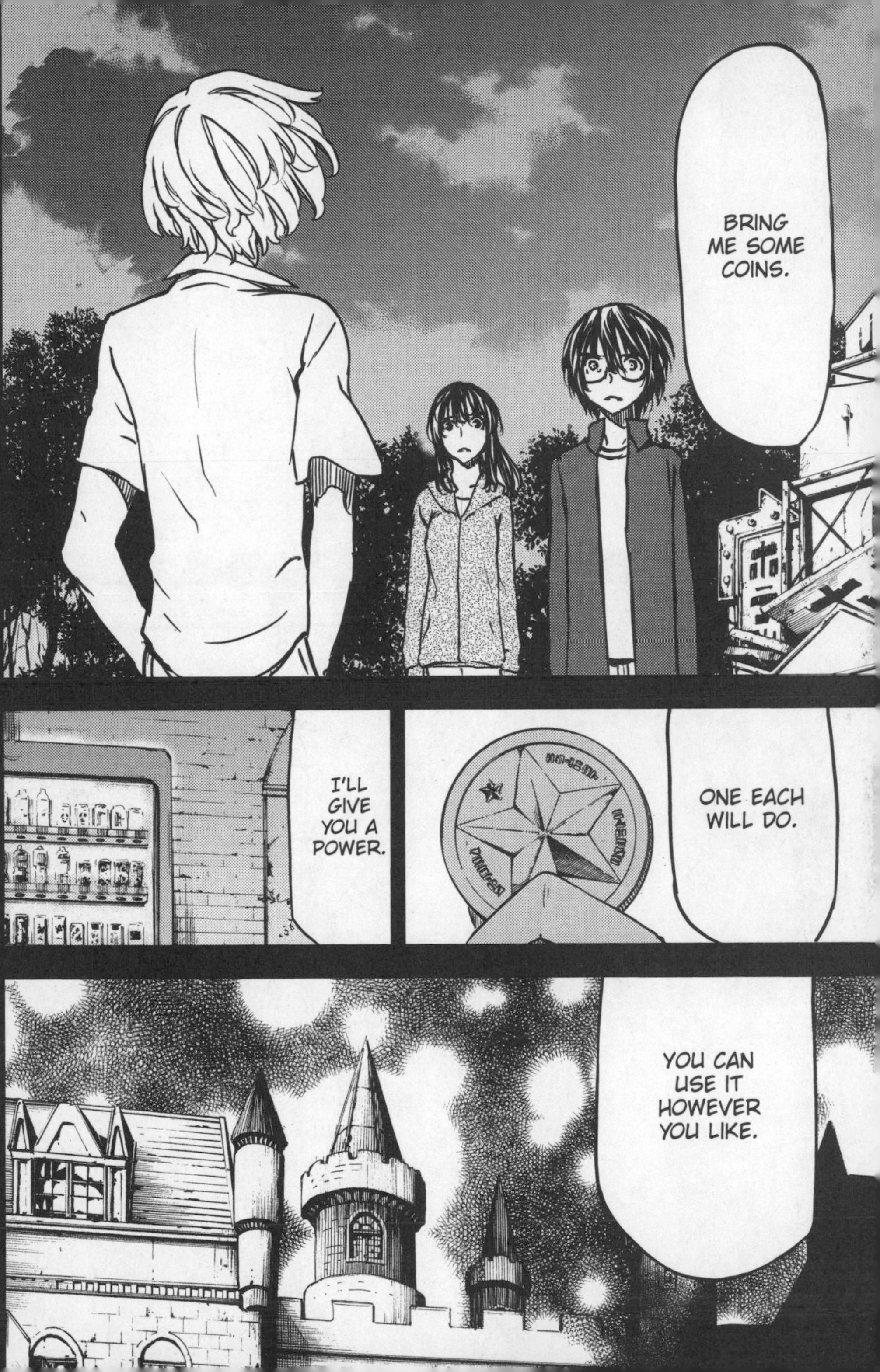
BRING ME SOME COINS.
ONE EACH WILL DO.
I'LL GIVE YOU A POWER.
YOU CAN USE IT HOWEVER YOU LIKE.

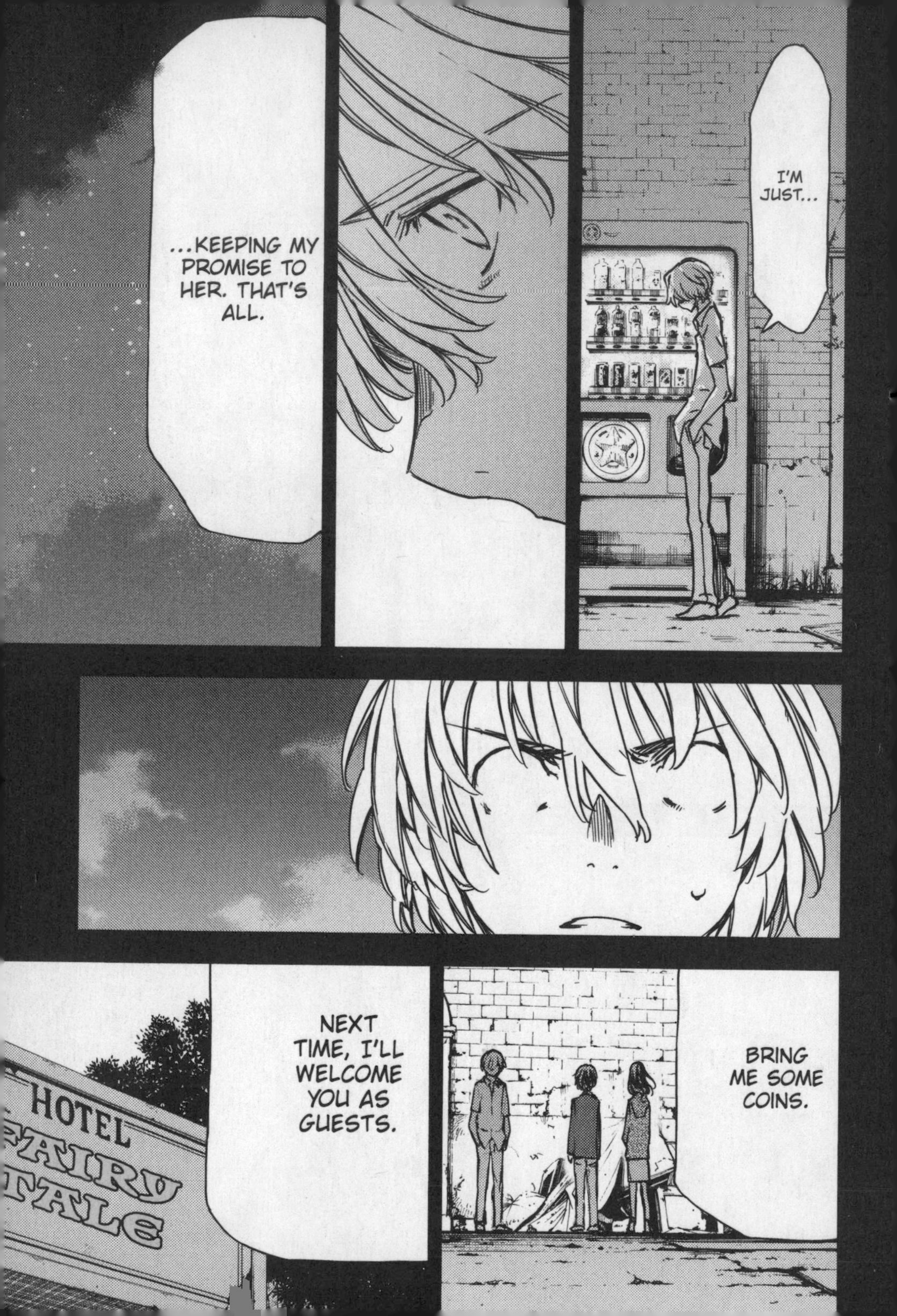
I'M JUST...
...KEEPING MY PROMISE TO HER. THAT'S ALL.
BRING ME SOME COINS.
NEXT TIME, I'LL WELCOME YOU AS GUESTS.
HOTEL

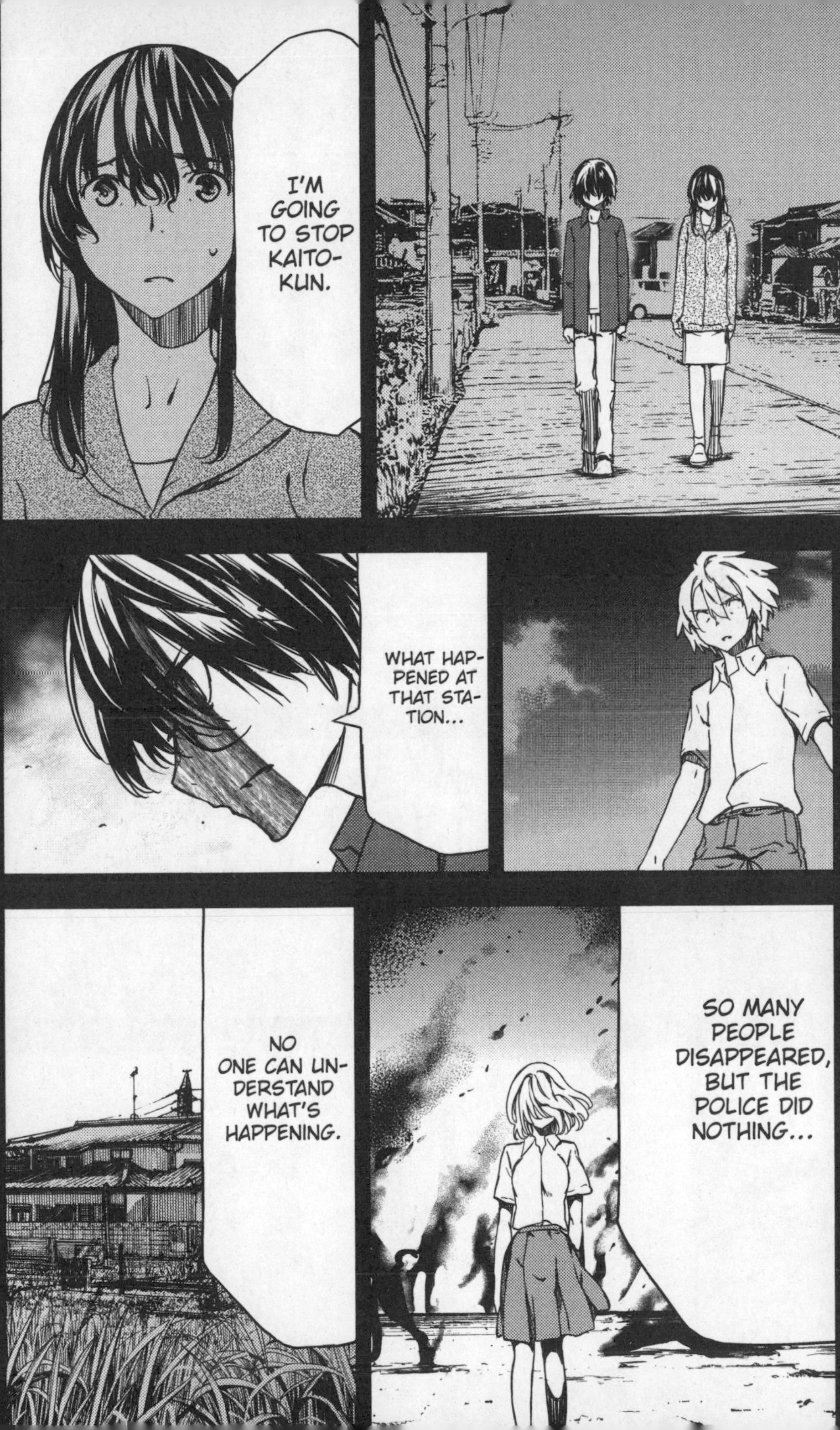
I'M GOING TO STOP KAITO-KUN.
WHAT HAPPENED AT THAT STATION...
SO MANY PEOPLE DISAPPEARED, BUT THE POLICE DID NOTHING...
NO ONE CAN UNDERSTAND WHAT'S HAPPENING.

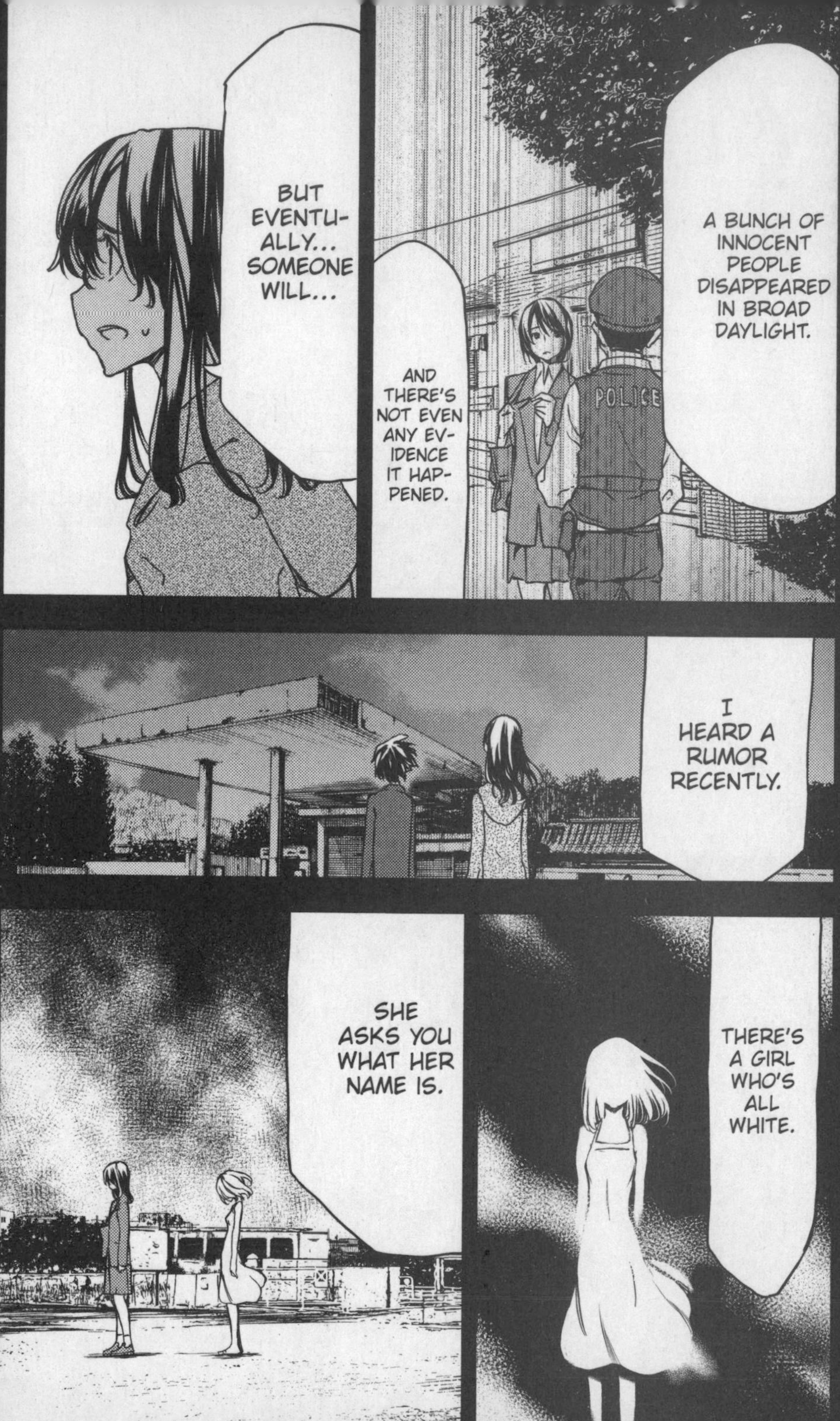
A BUNCH OF INNOCENT PEOPLE DISAPPEARED IN BROAD DAYLIGHT.
AND THERE'S NOT EVEN ANY EVIDENCE IT HAPPENED.
BUT EVENTUALLY... SOMEONE WILL...
I HEARD A RUMOR RECENTLY.
THERE'S A GIRL WHO'S ALL WHITE.
SHE ASKS YOU WHAT HER NAME IS.

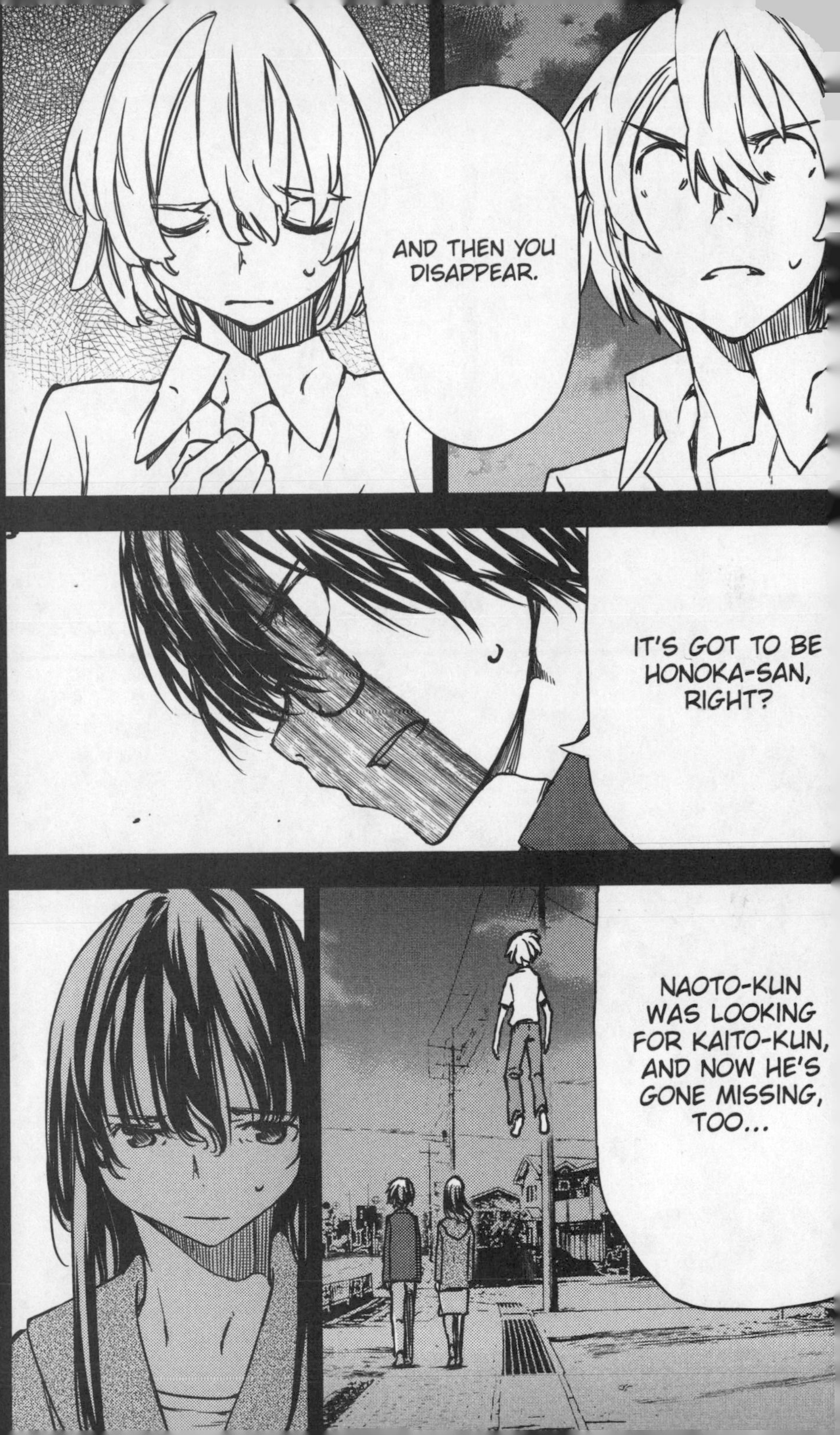
AND THEN YOU DISAPPEAR.
IT'S GOT TO BE HONOKA-SAN, RIGHT?
NAOTO-KUN WAS LOOKING FOR KAITO-KUN, AND NOW HE'S GONE MISSING, TOO...

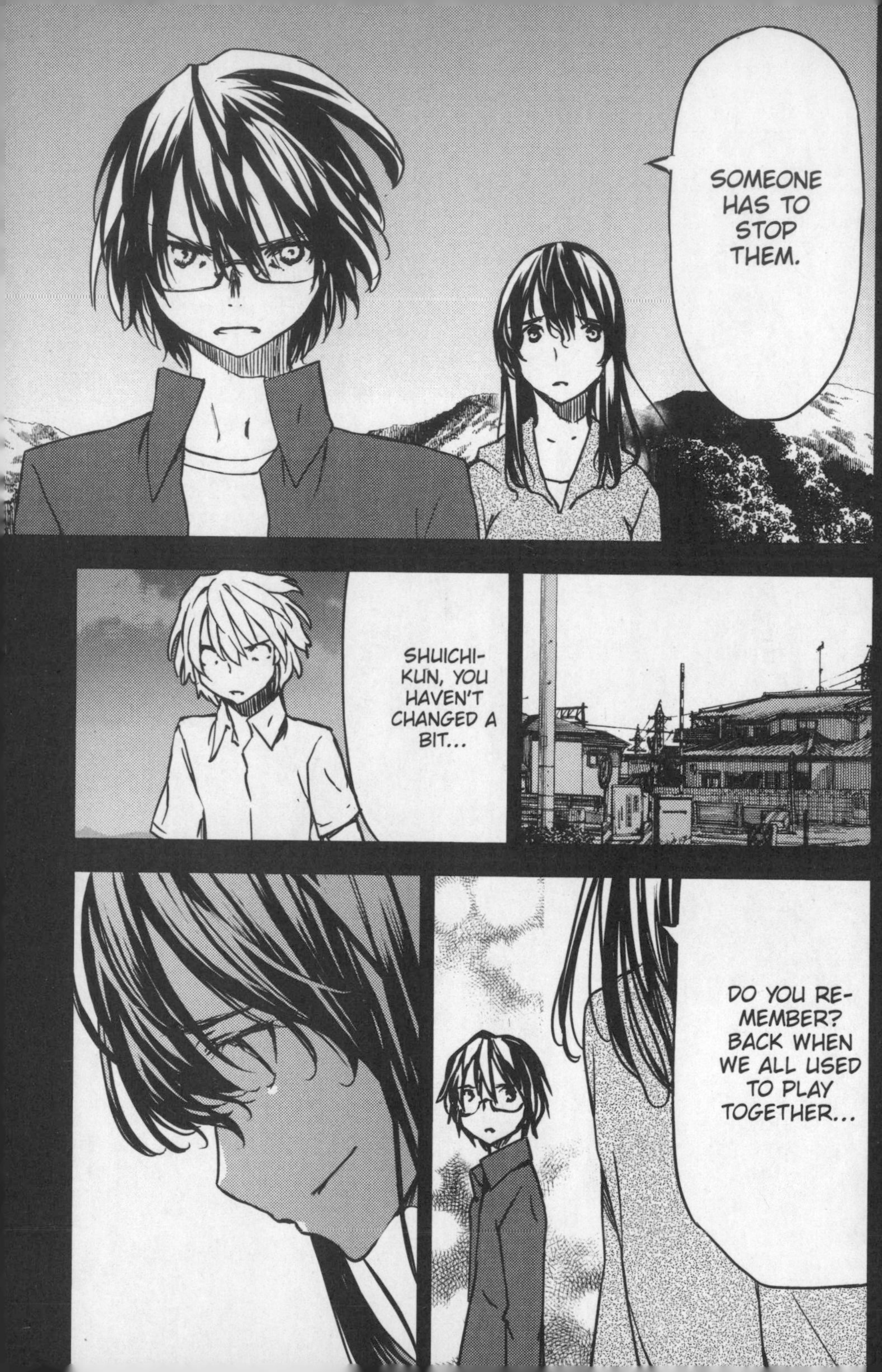
SOMEONE HAS TO STOP THEM.
SHUICHI-KUN, YOU HAVEN'T CHANGED A BIT...
DO YOU RE-MEMBER? BACK WHEN WE ALL USED TO PLAY TOGETHER...

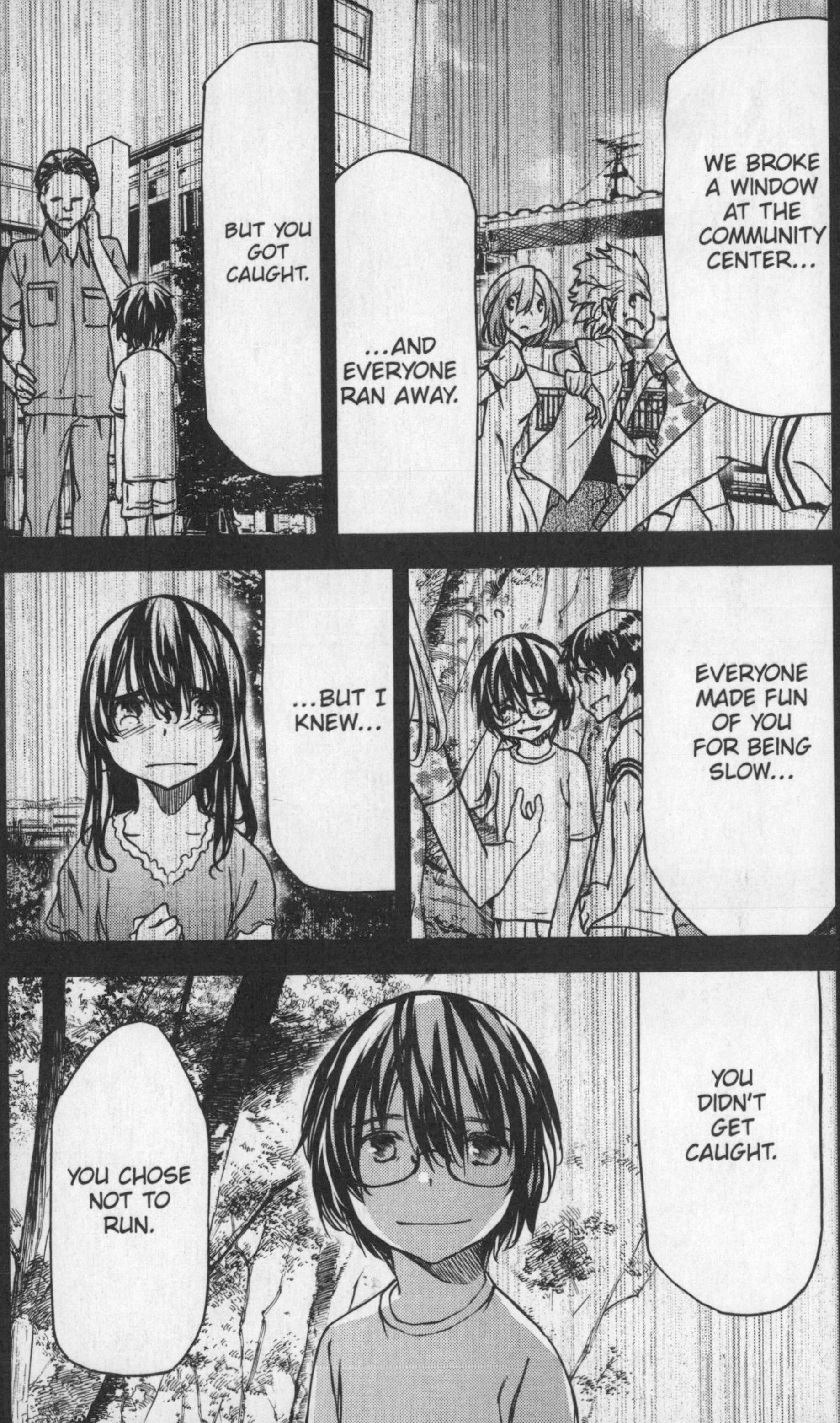
WE BROKE A WINDOW AT THE COMMUNITY CENTER...
...AND EVERYONE RAN AWAY.
BUT YOU GOT CAUGHT.
EVERYONE MADE FUN OF YOU FOR BEING SLOW...
...BUT I KNEW...
YOU DIDN'T GET CAUGHT.
YOU CHOSE NOT TO RUN.

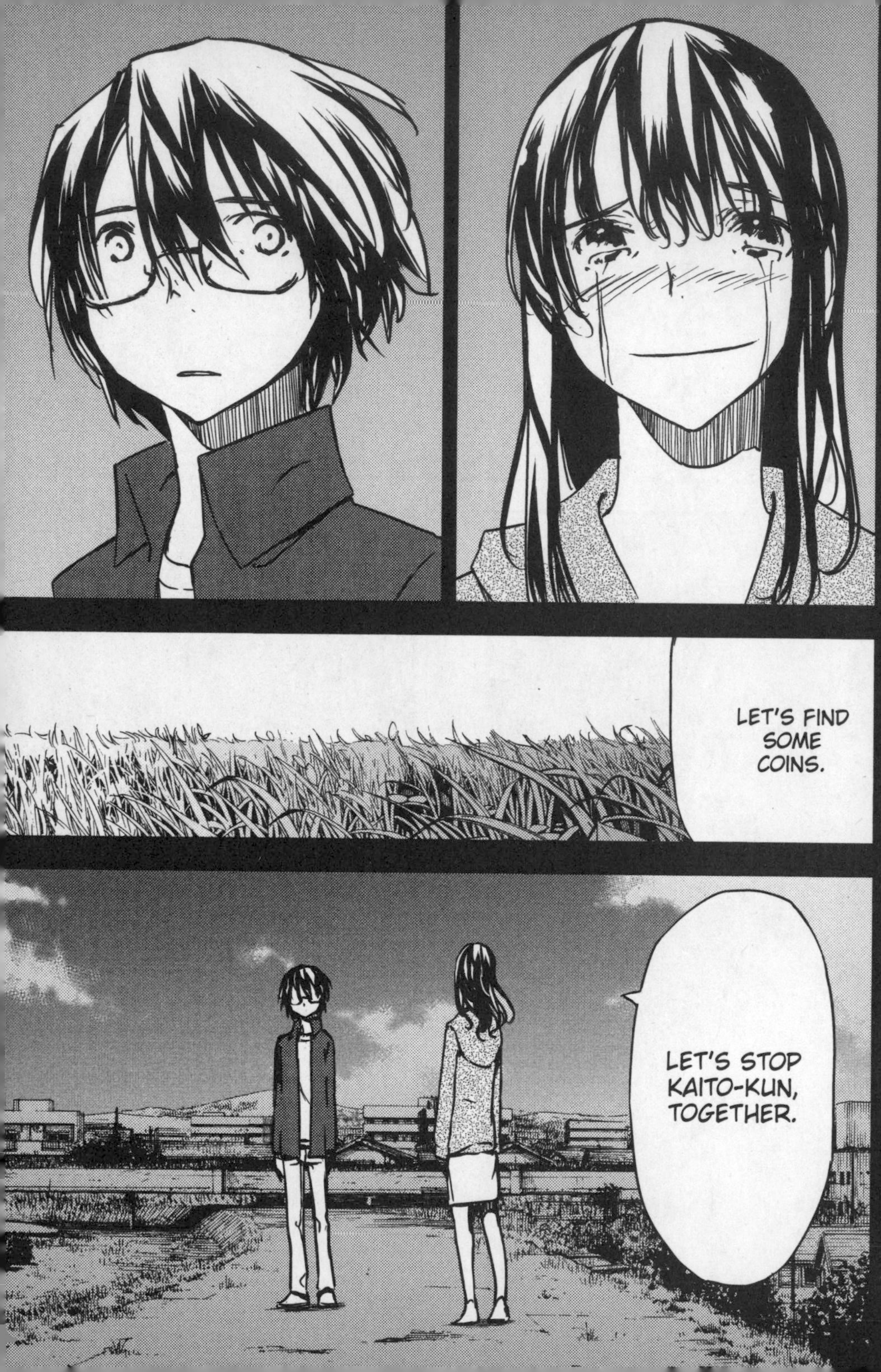
LET'S FIND SOME COINS.
LET'S STOP KAITO-KUN, TOGETHER.

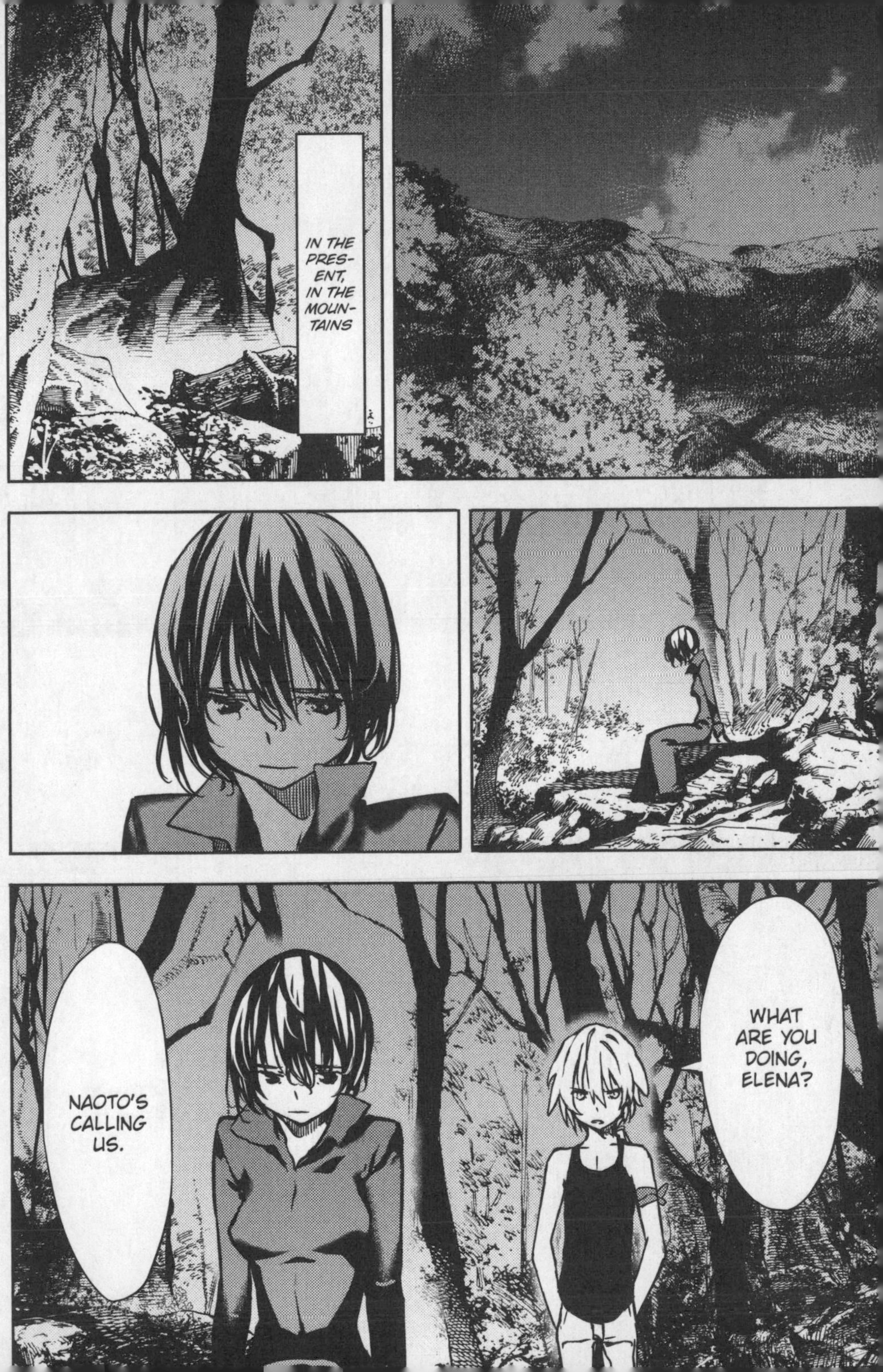
IN THE PRESENT, IN THE MOUNTAINS
WHAT ARE YOU DOING, ELENA?
NAOTO'S CALLING US.

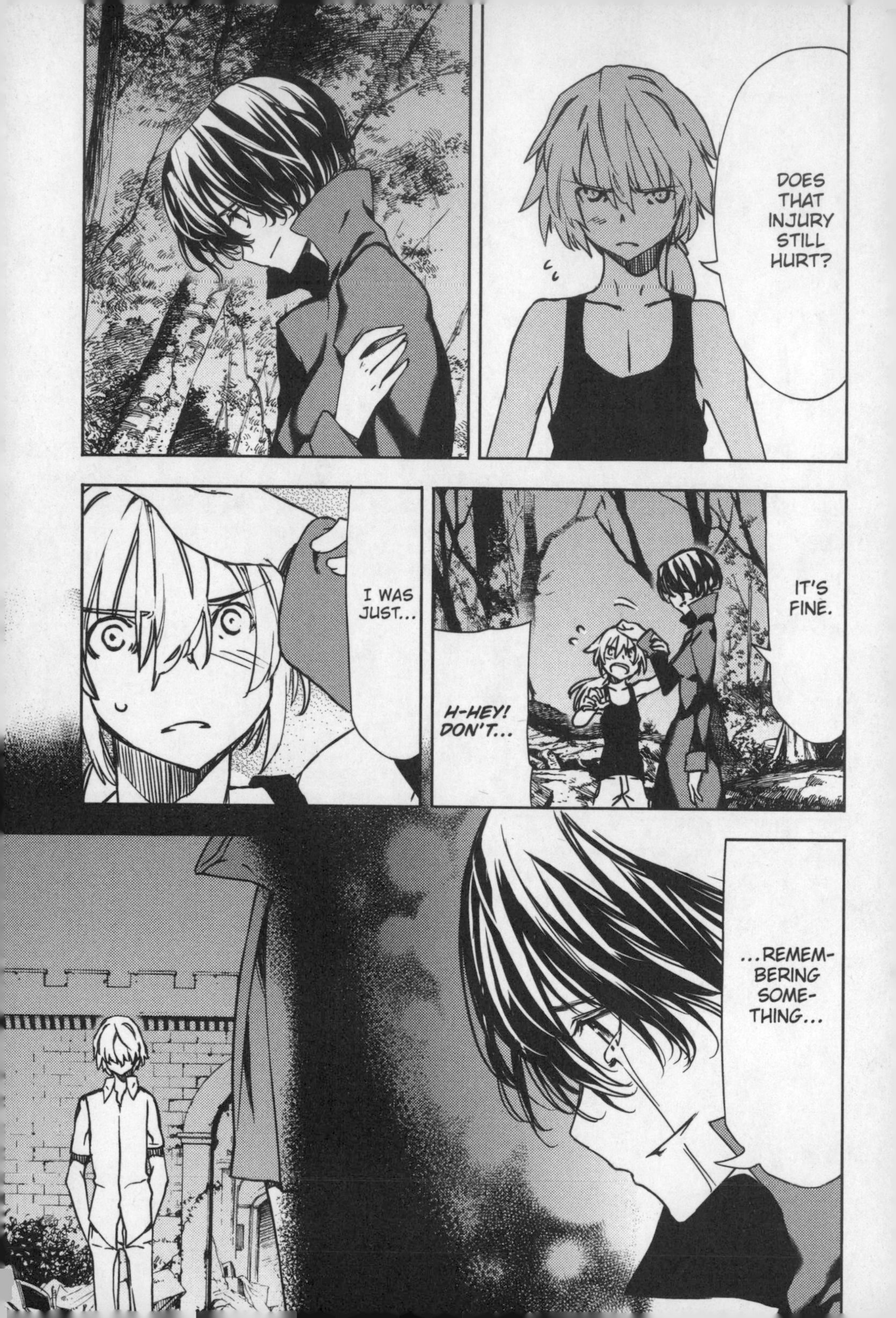
DOES THAT INJURY STILL HURT?
IT'S FINE.
H-HEY! DON'T...
I WAS JUST...
...REMEMBERING SOMETHING...

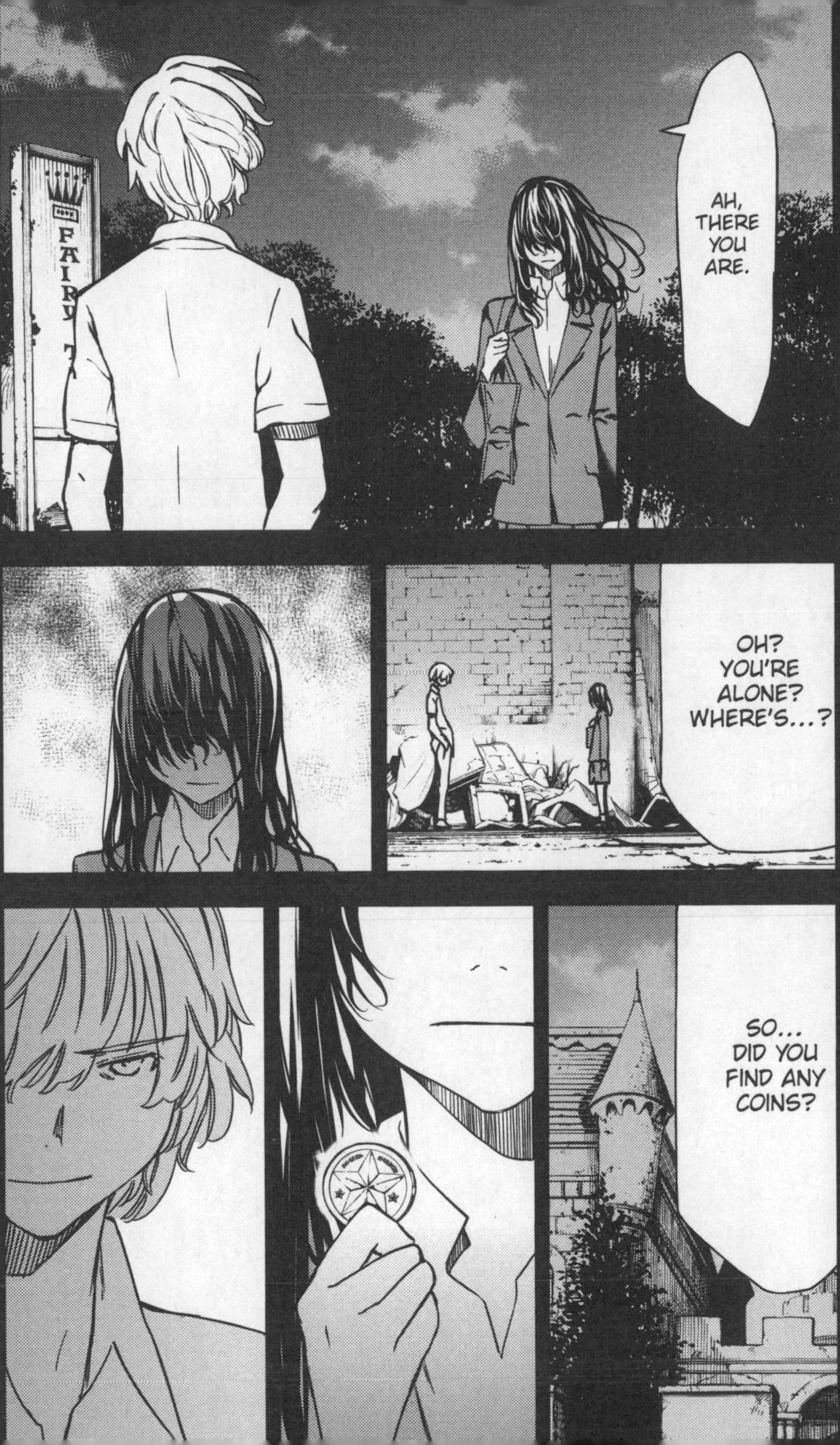
AH, THERE YOU ARE.
FAIRY
OH? YOU'RE ALONE? WHERE'S...?
SO... DID YOU FIND ANY COINS?

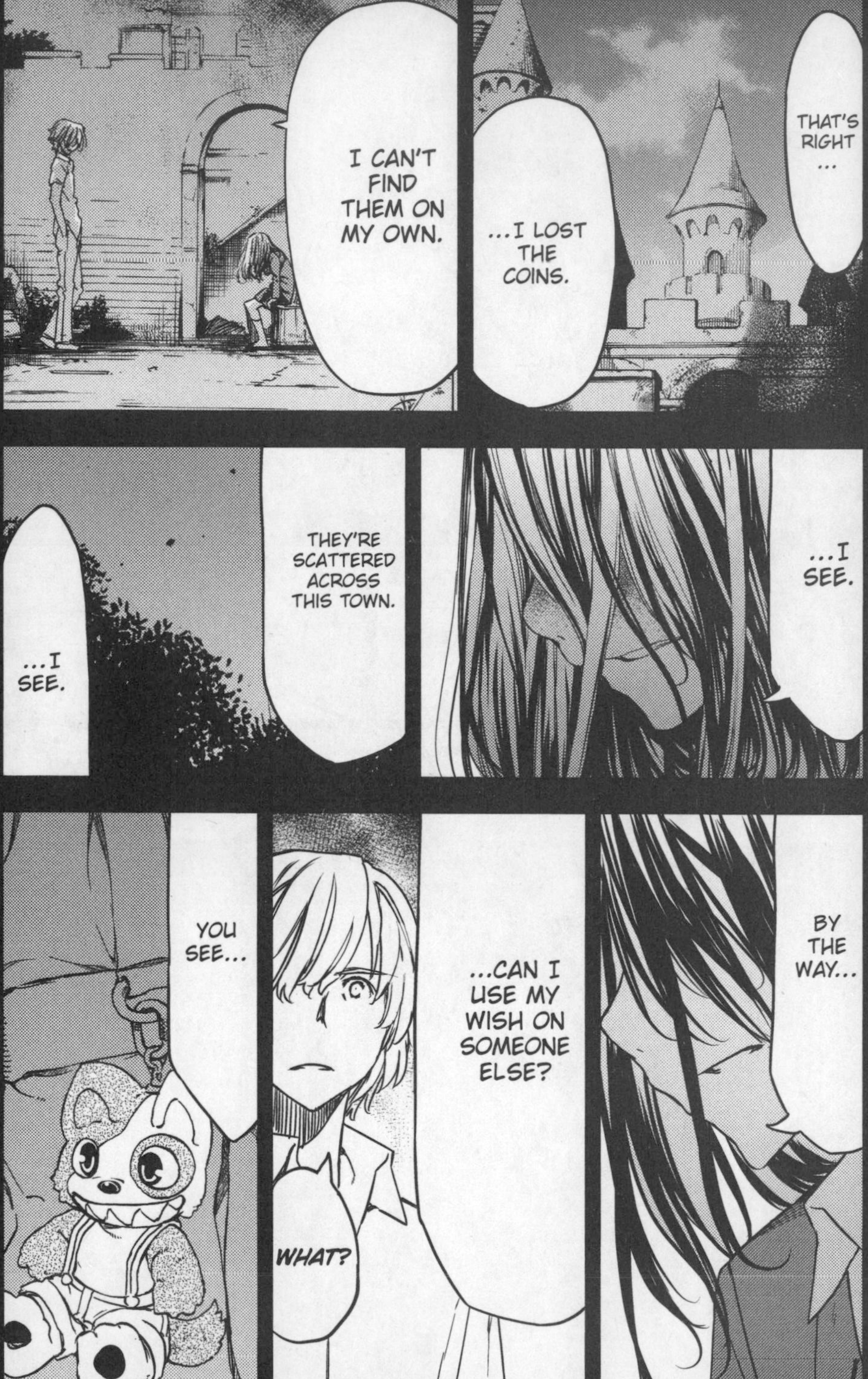
THAT'S RIGHT ...
...I LOST THE COINS.
I CAN'T FIND THEM ON MY OWN.
...I SEE.
THEY'RE SCATTERED ACROSS THIS TOWN.
...I SEE.
BY THE WAY...
...CAN I USE MY WISH ON SOMEONE ELSE?
WHAT?
YOU SEE...

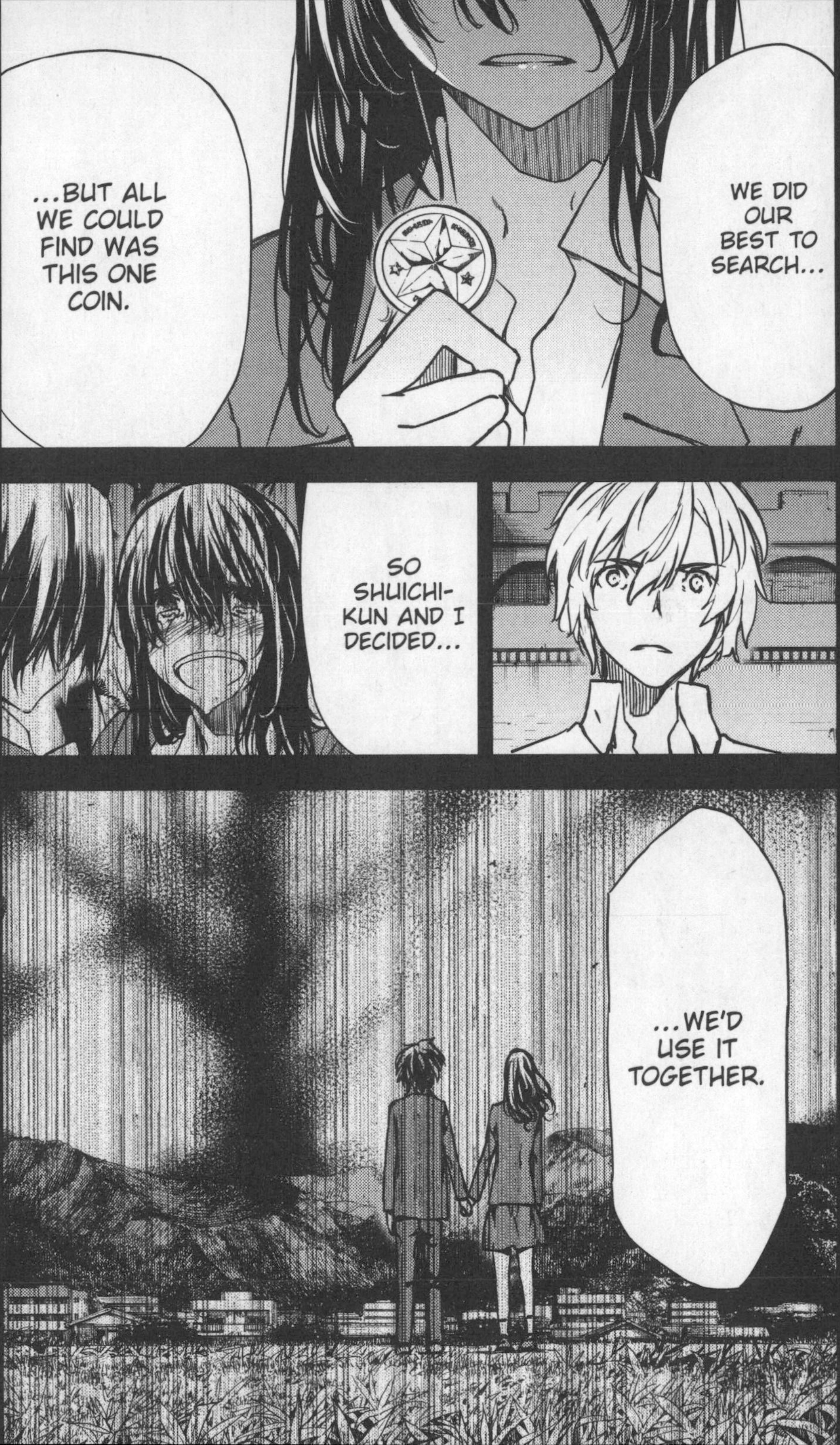
WE DID OUR BEST TO SEARCH...
...BUT ALL WE COULD FIND WAS THIS ONE COIN.
SO SHUICHI-KUN AND I DECIDED...
...WE'D USE IT TOGETHER.

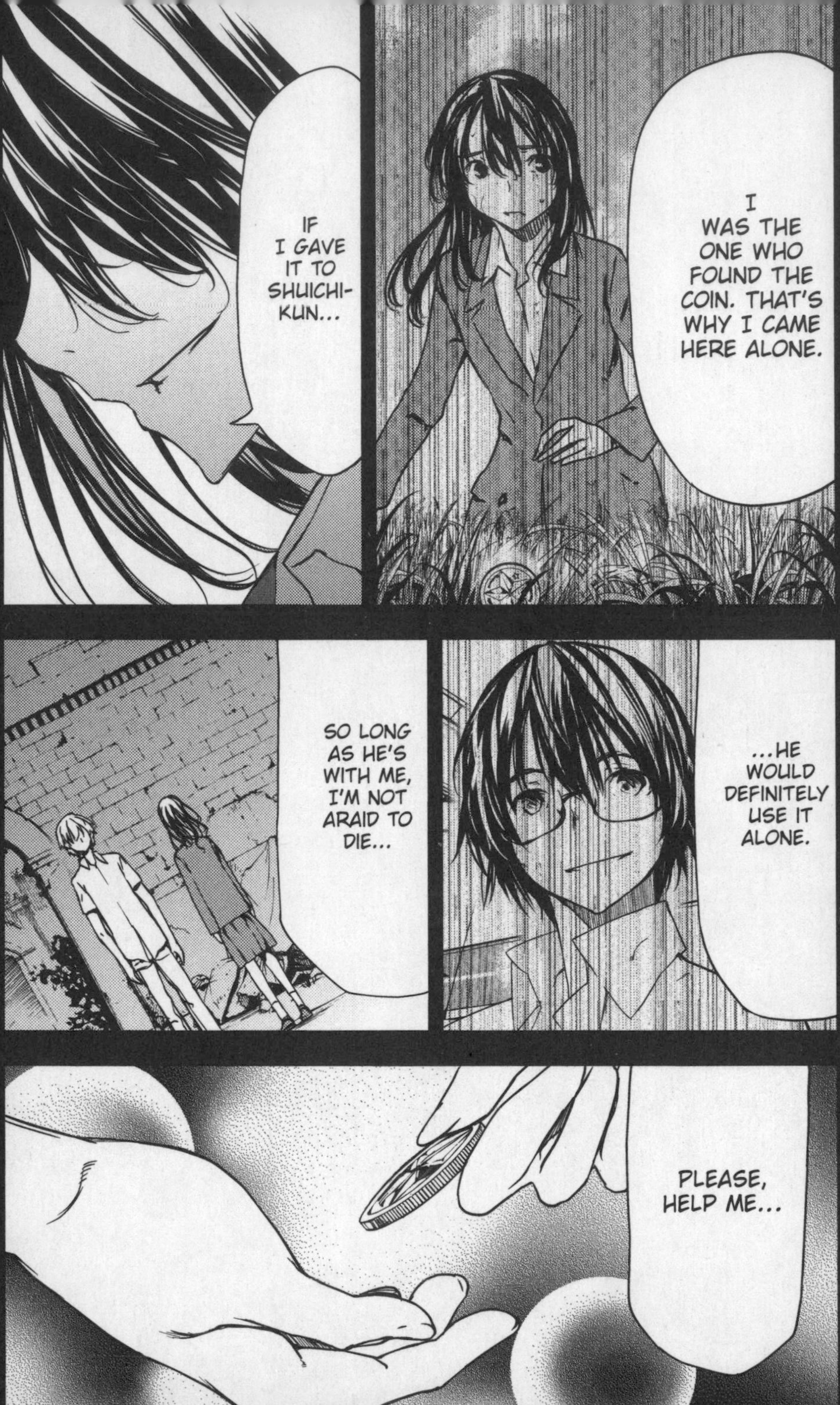
I WAS THE ONE WHO FOUND THE COIN. THAT'S WHY I CAME HERE ALONE.
IF I GAVE IT TO SHUICHI-KUN...
...HE WOULD DEFINITELY USE IT ALONE.
SO LONG AS HE'S WITH ME, I'M NOT ARAID TO DIE...
PLEASE, HELP ME...

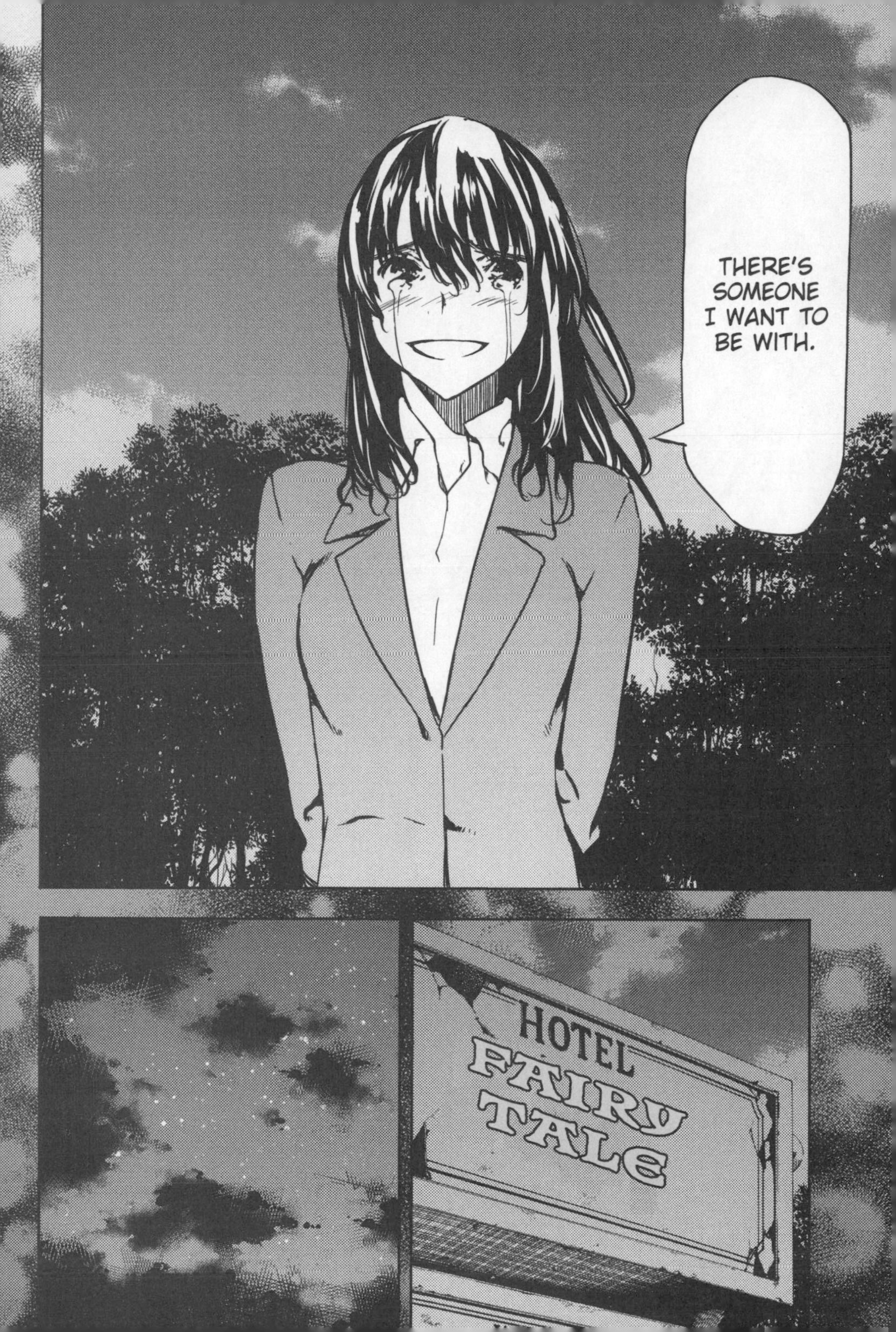
THERE'S SOMEONE I WANT TO BE WITH.
HOTEL FAIRY TALE

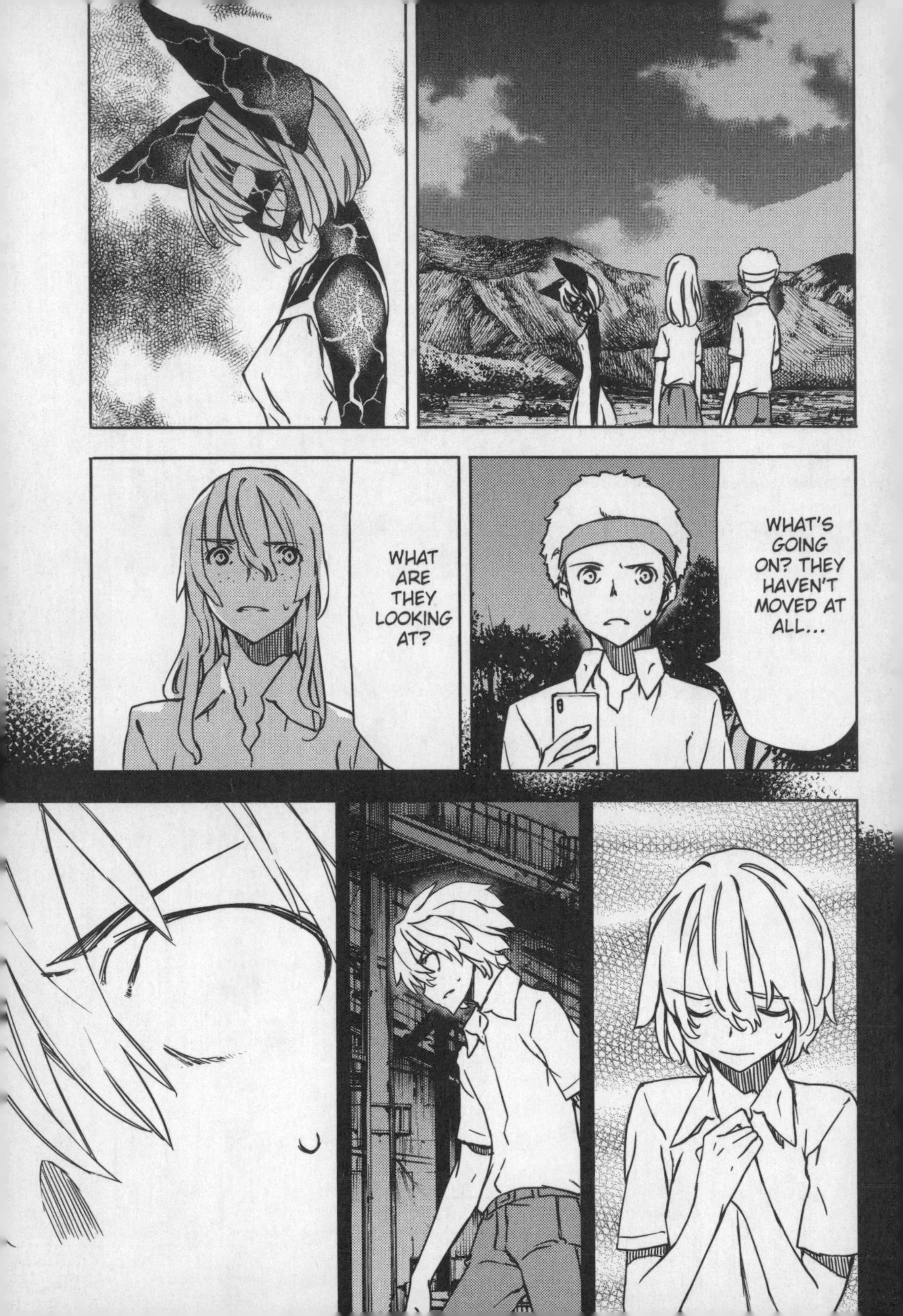
WHAT'S GOING ON? THEY HAVEN'T MOVED AT ALL...
WHAT ARE THEY LOOKING AT?

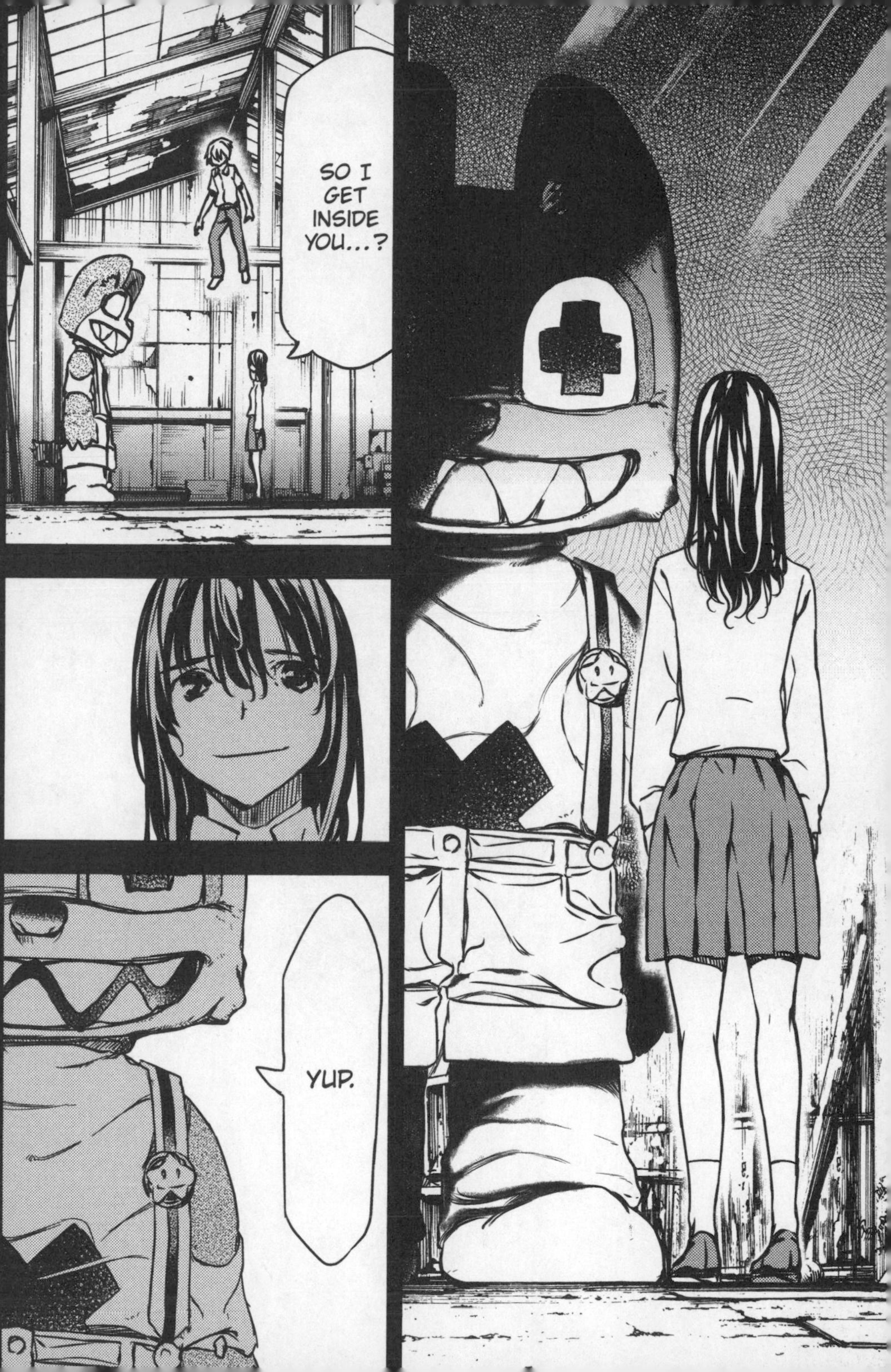
SO I GET INSIDE YOU...?
YUP.

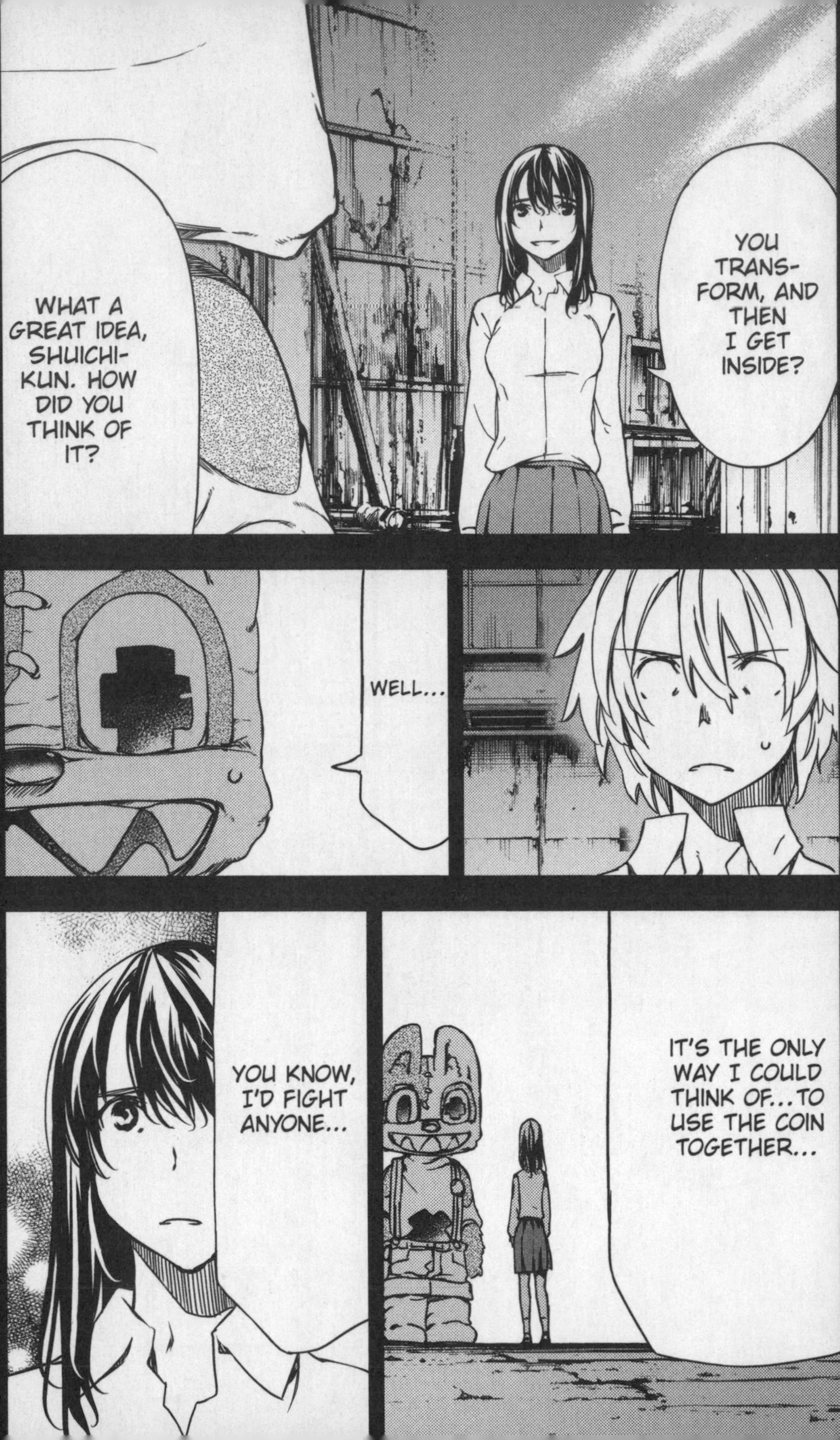
YOU TRANS-FORM, AND THEN I GET INSIDE?
WHAT A GREAT IDEA, SHUICHI-KUN. HOW DID YOU THINK OF IT?
WELL...
IT'S THE ONLY WAY I COULD THINK OF...TO USE THE COIN TOGETHER...
YOU KNOW, I'D FIGHT ANYONE...

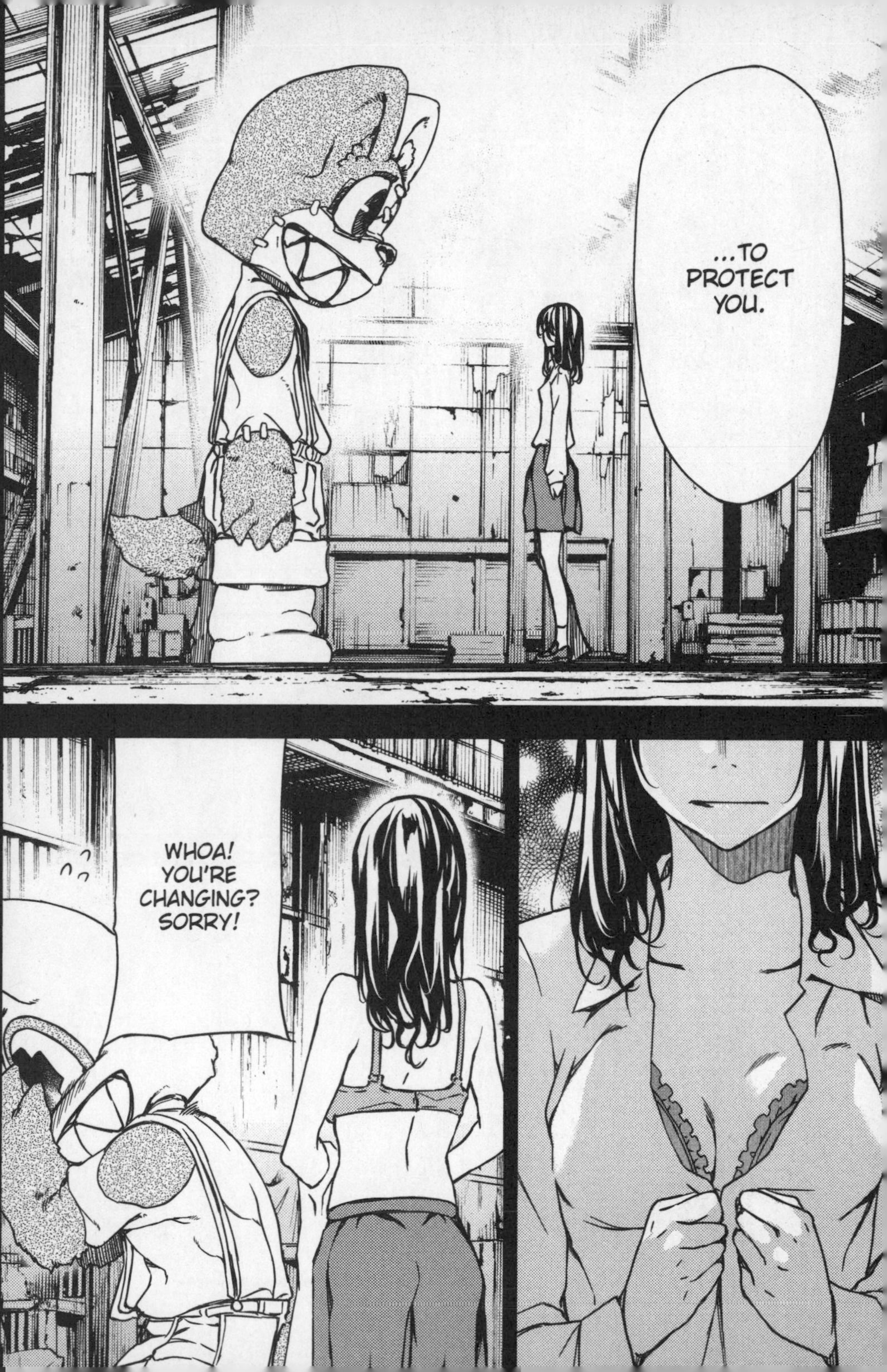
...TO PROTECT YOU.
WHOA! YOU'RE CHANGING? SORRY!

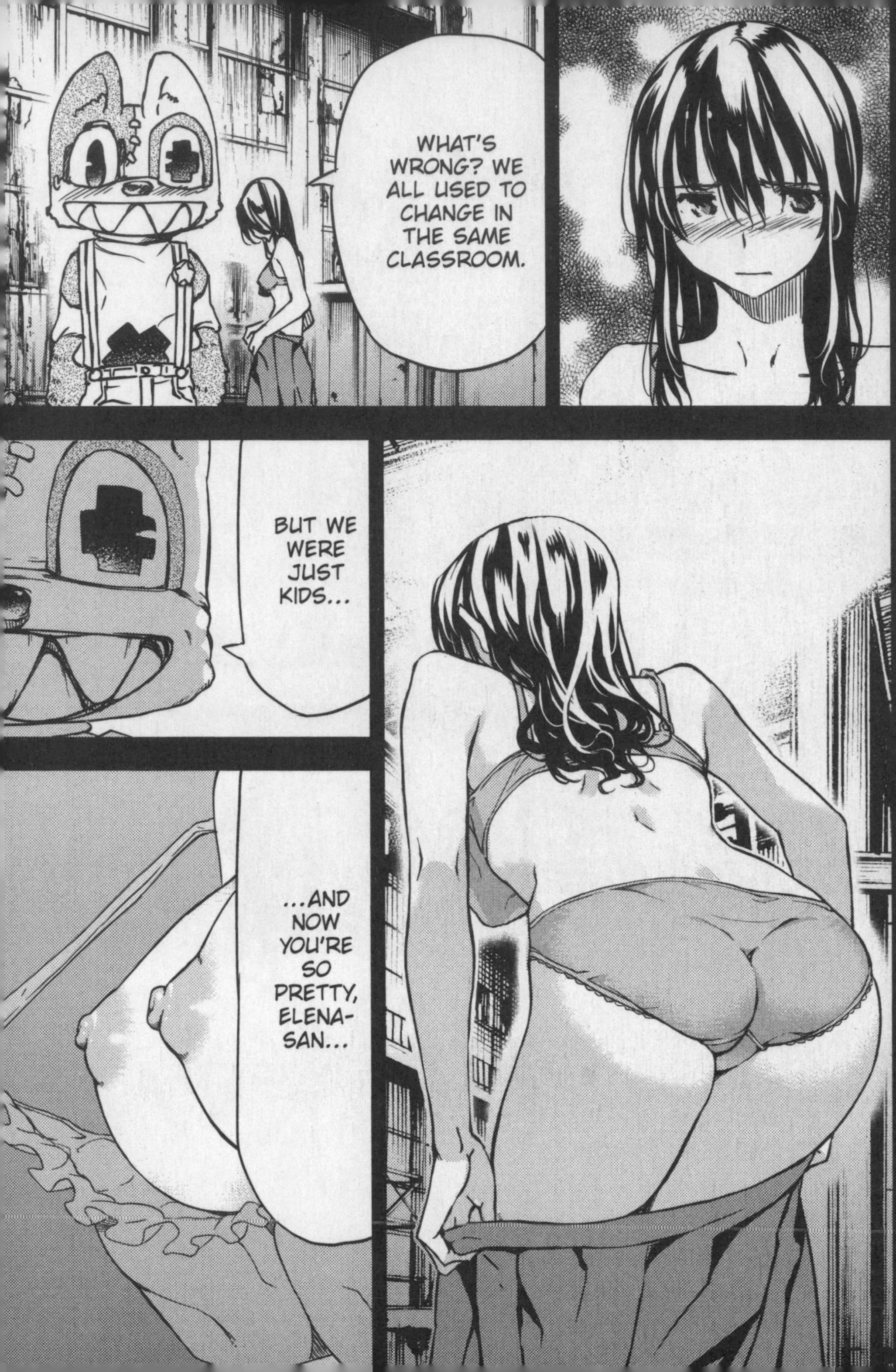
WHAT'S WRONG? WE ALL USED TO CHANGE IN THE SAME CLASSROOM.
BUT WE WERE JUST KIDS...
...AND NOW YOU'RE SO PRETTY, ELENA-SAN...

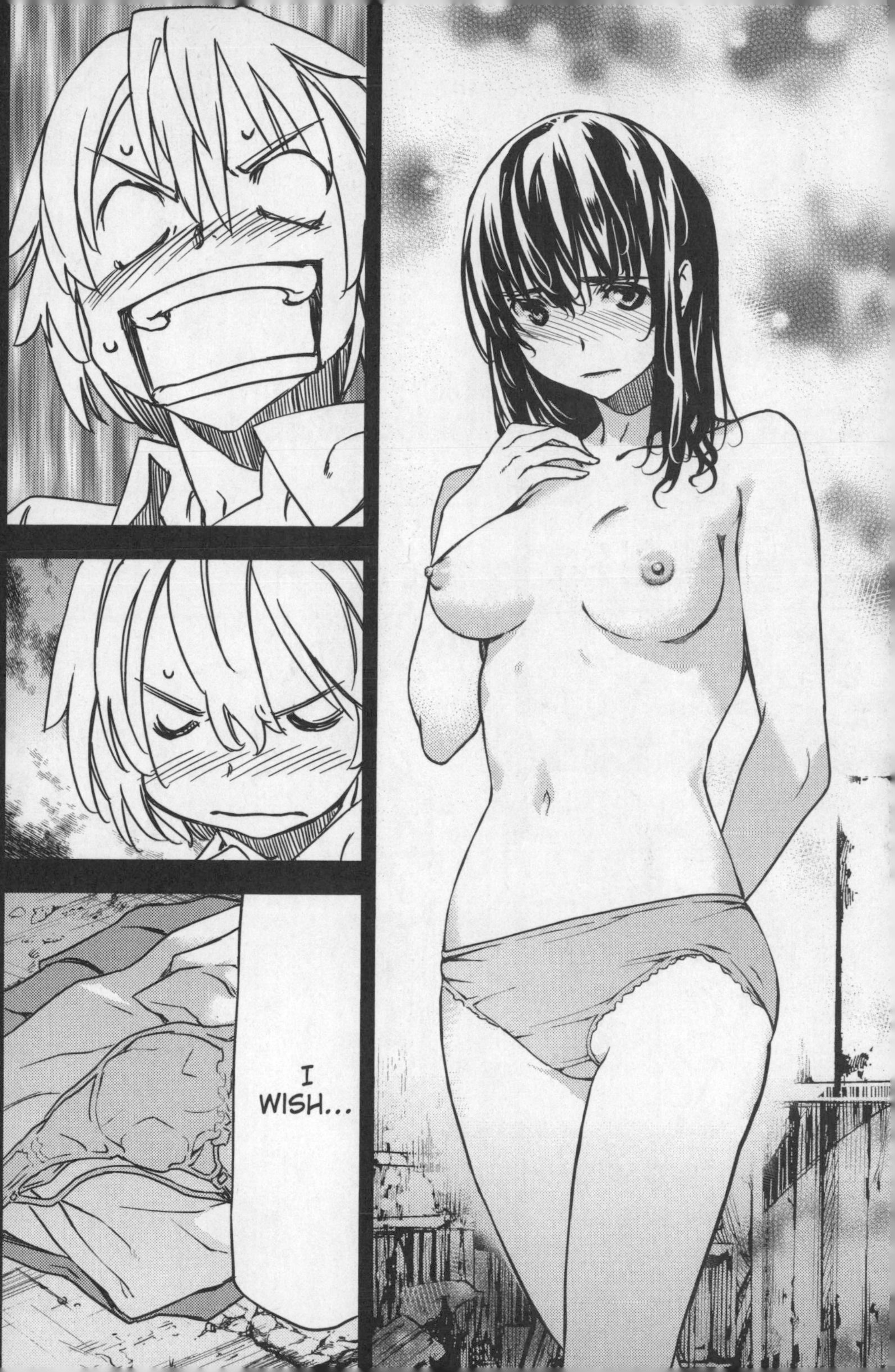
I WISH...

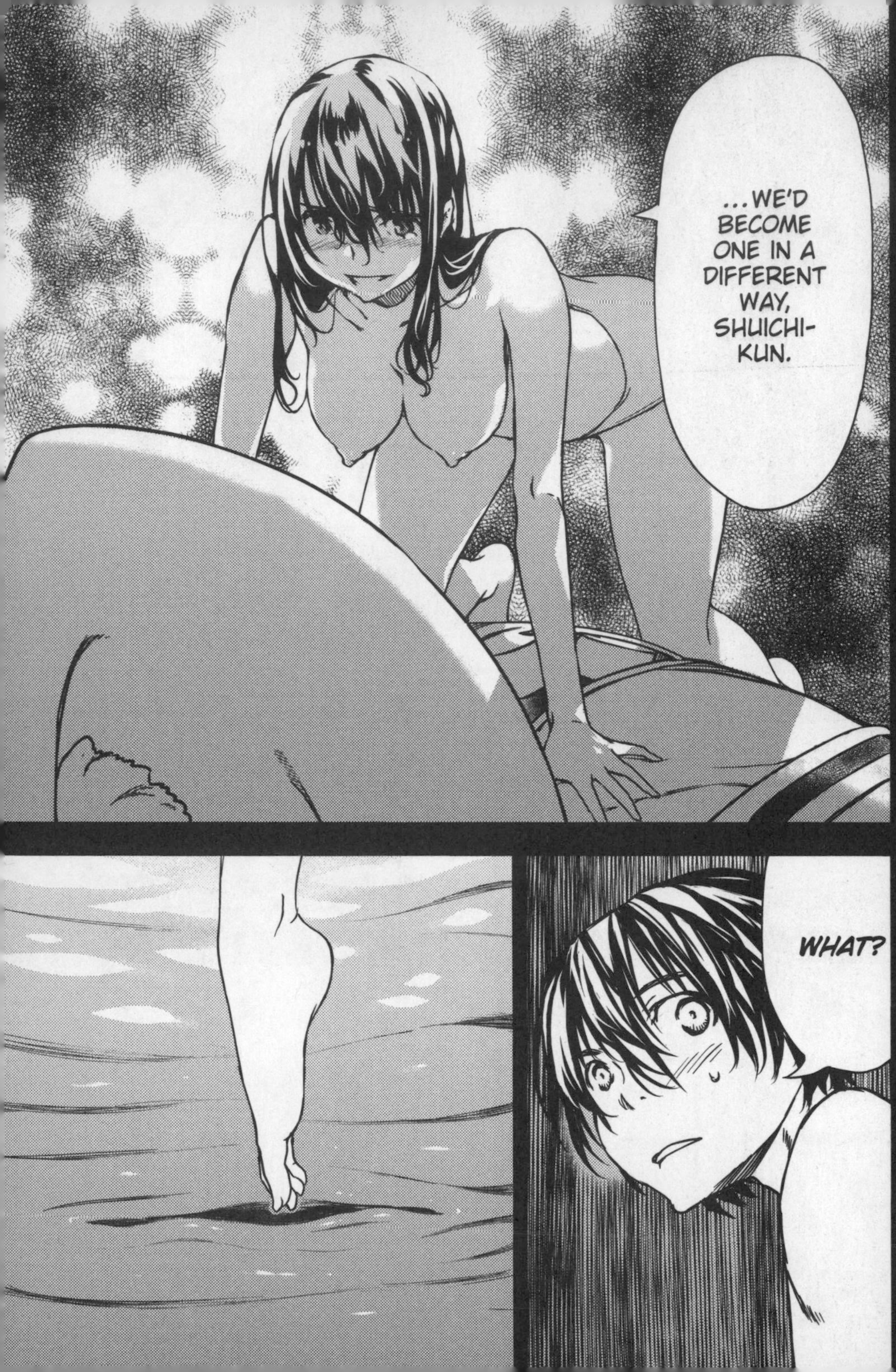
...WE'D BECOME ONE IN A DIFFERENT WAY, SHUICHI-KUN.
WHAT?

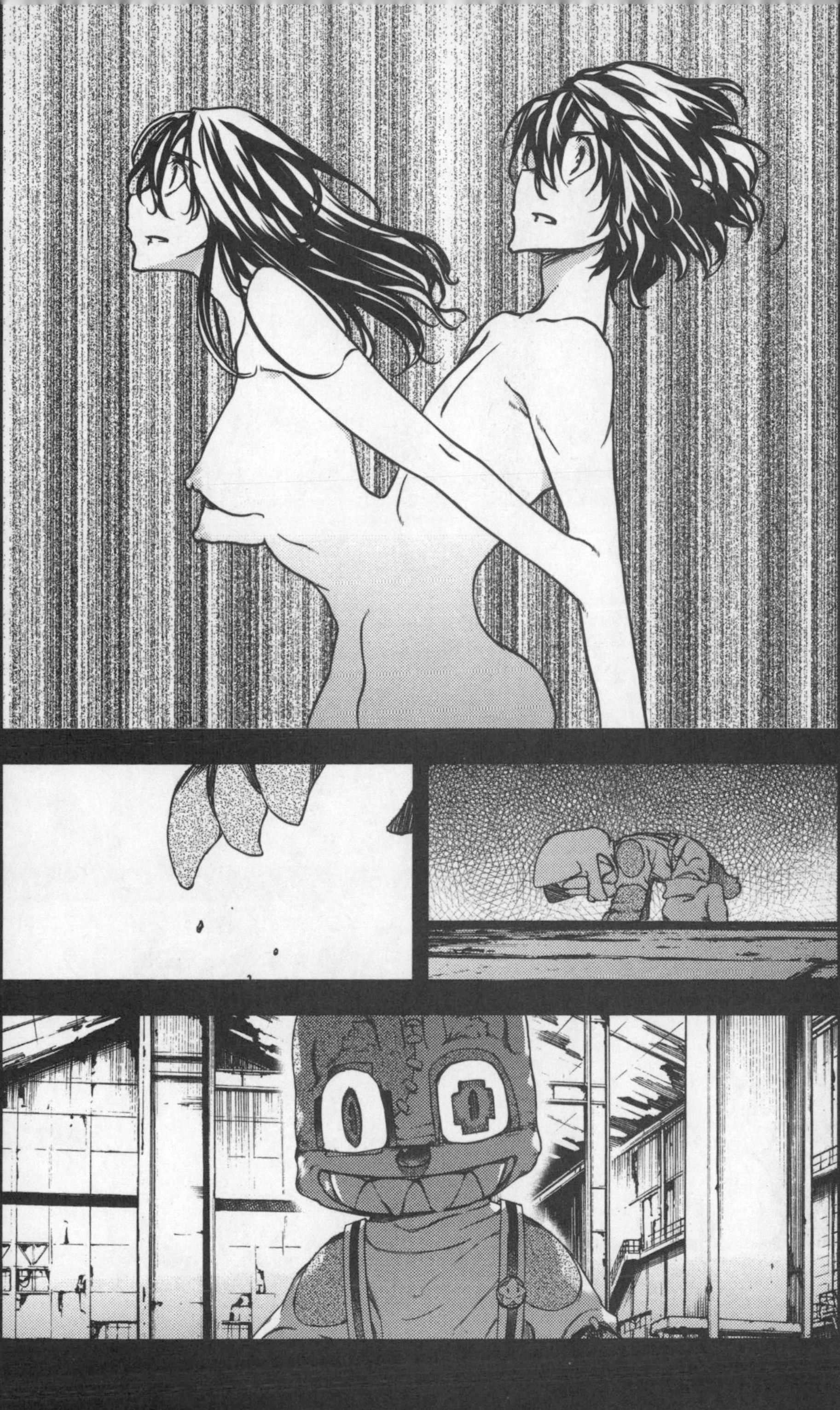

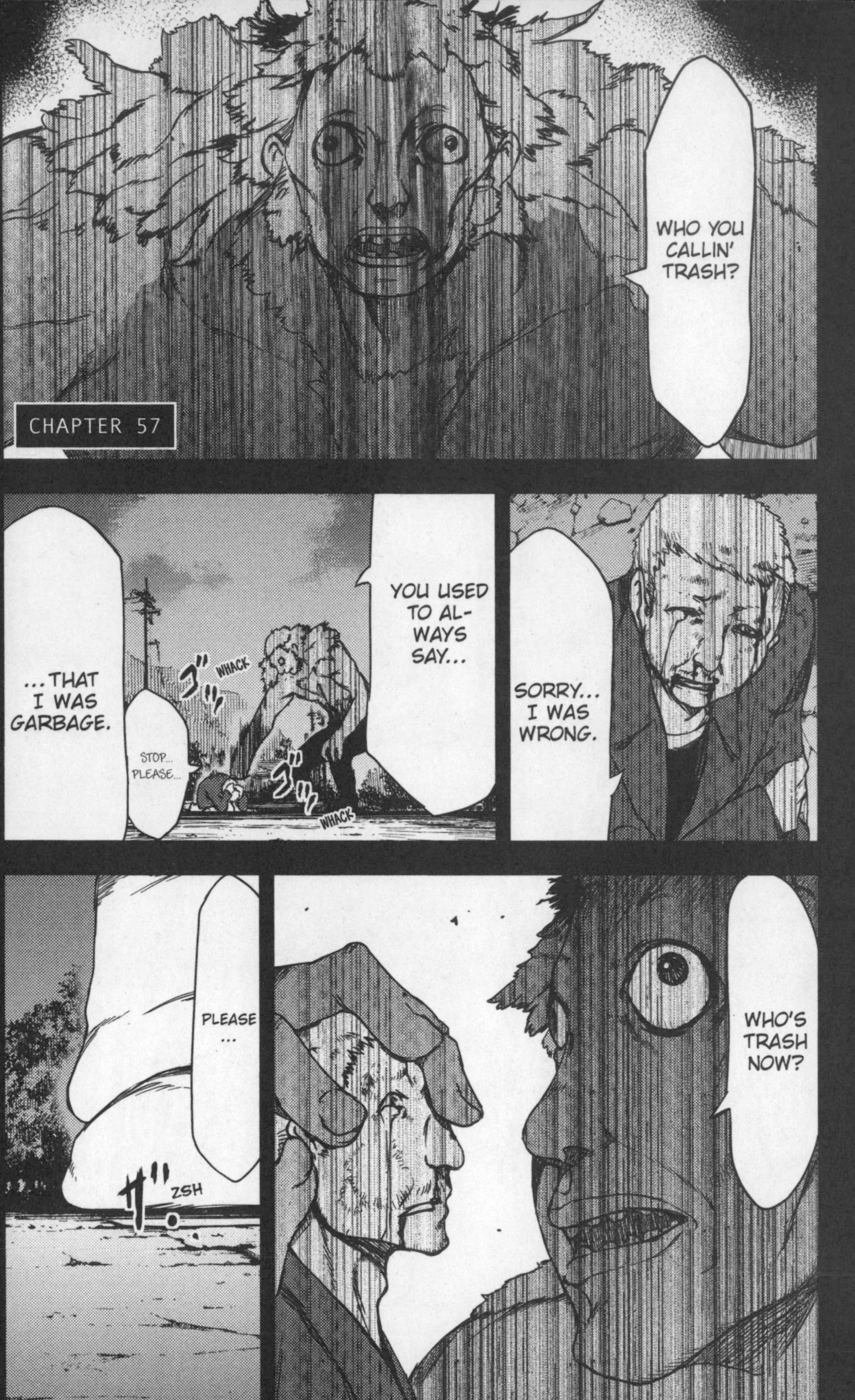
WHO YOU CALLIN' TRASH?
CHAPTER 57
SORRY... I WAS WRONG.
YOU USED TO AL- WAYS SAY...
WHACK
...THAT I WAS GARBAGE.
STOP... PLEASE...
WHACK
WHO'S TRASH NOW?
PLEASE ...
ZSH

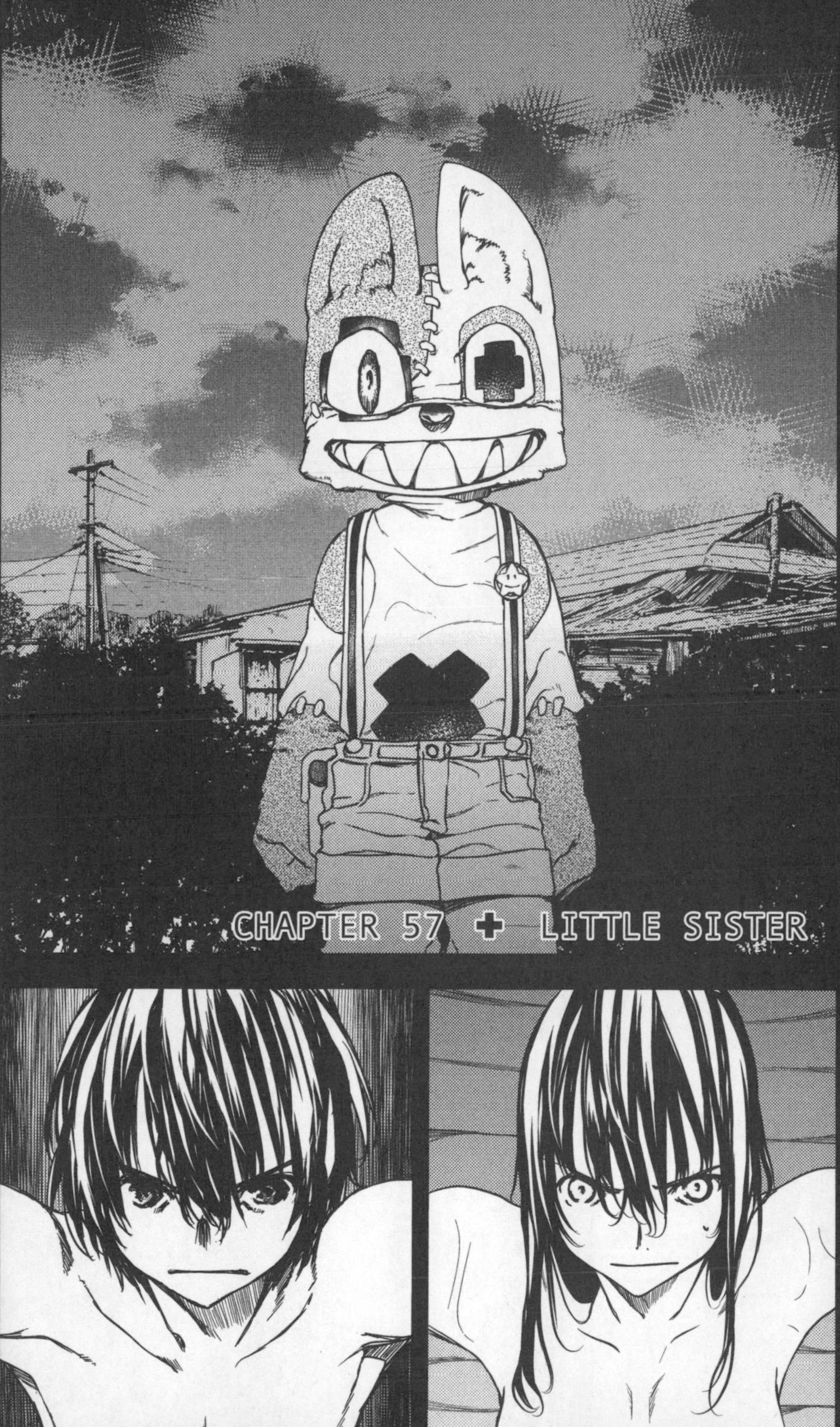
CHAPTER 57 + LITTLE SISTER

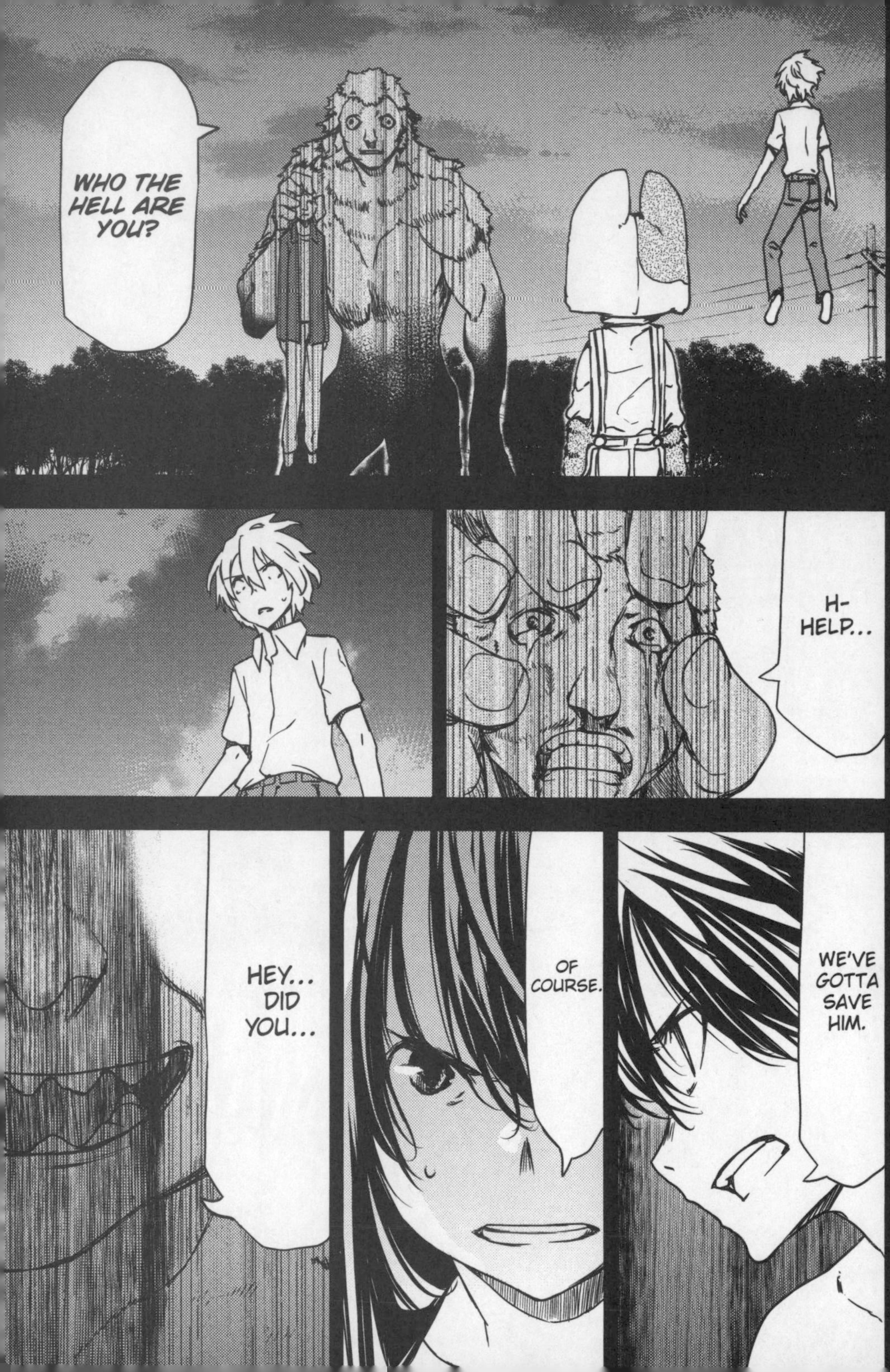
WHO THE HELL ARE YOU?
H- HELP...
WE'VE GOTTA SAVE HIM.
OF COURSE.
HEY... DID YOU...

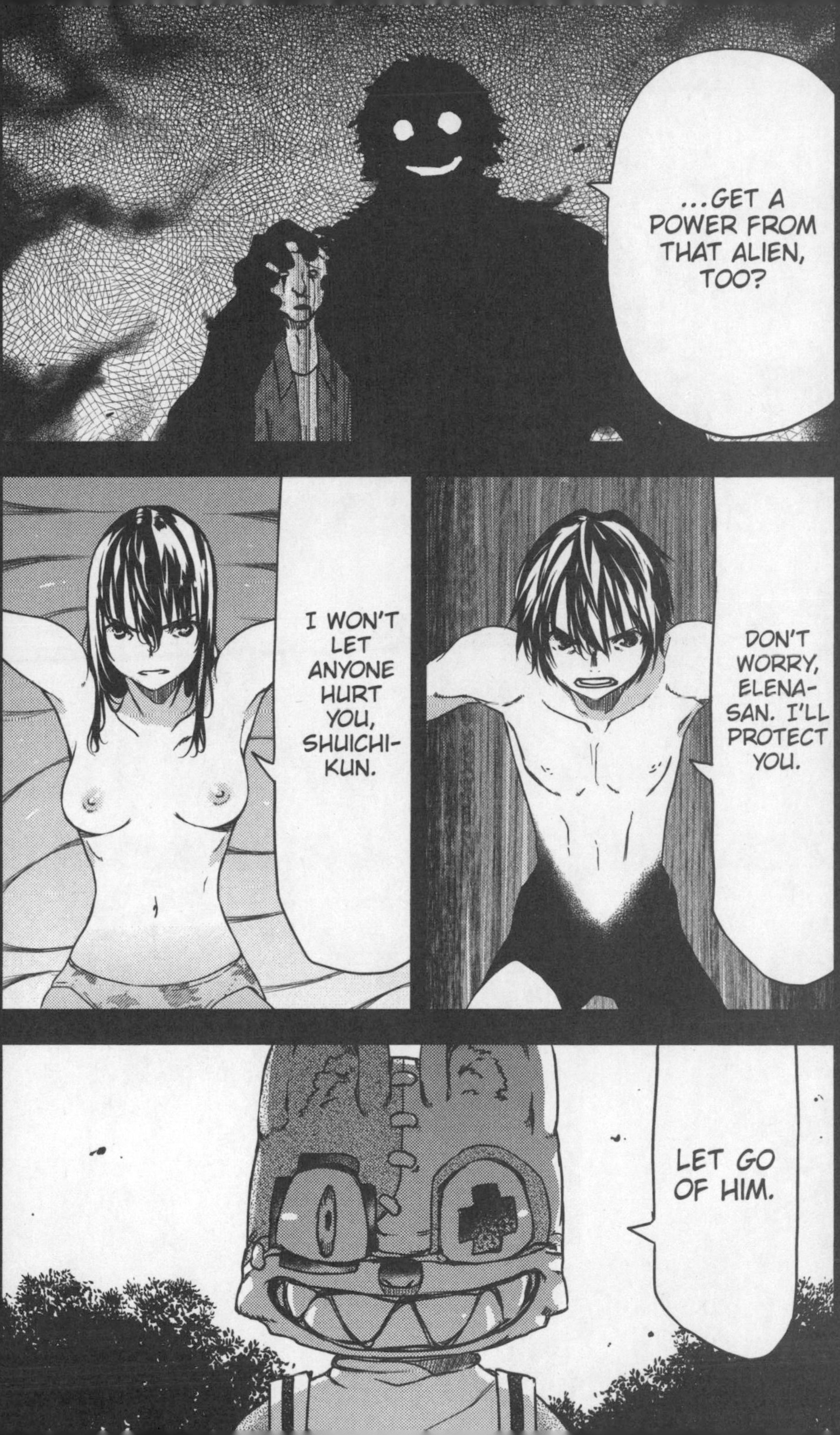
...GET A POWER FROM THAT ALIEN, TOO?
DON'T WORRY, ELENA-SAN. I'LL PROTECT YOU.
I WON'T LET ANYONE HURT YOU, SHUICHI-KUN.
LET GO OF HIM.

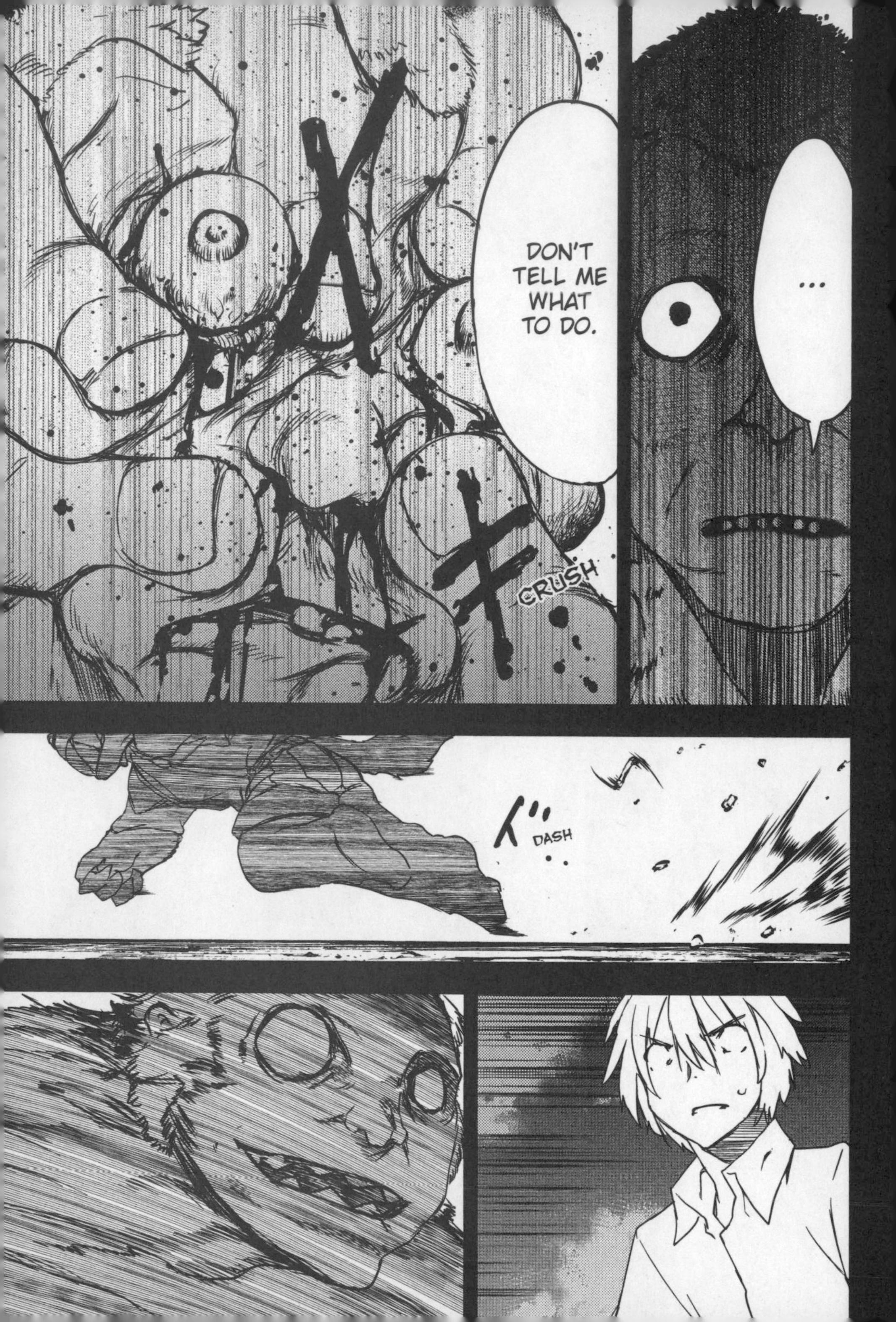
...
DON'T TELL ME WHAT TO DO.
CRUSH
ド
DASH

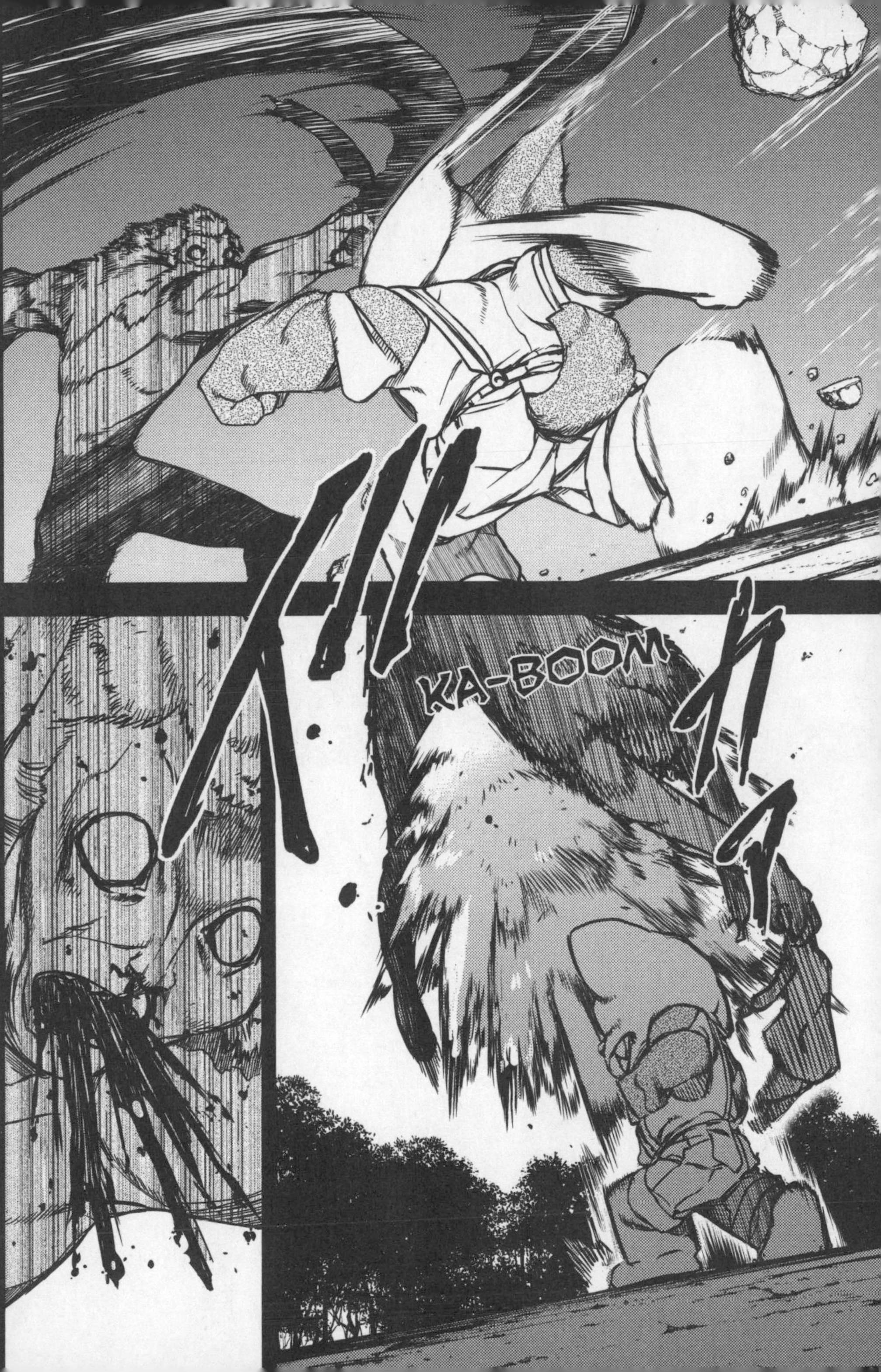
KA-BOOM

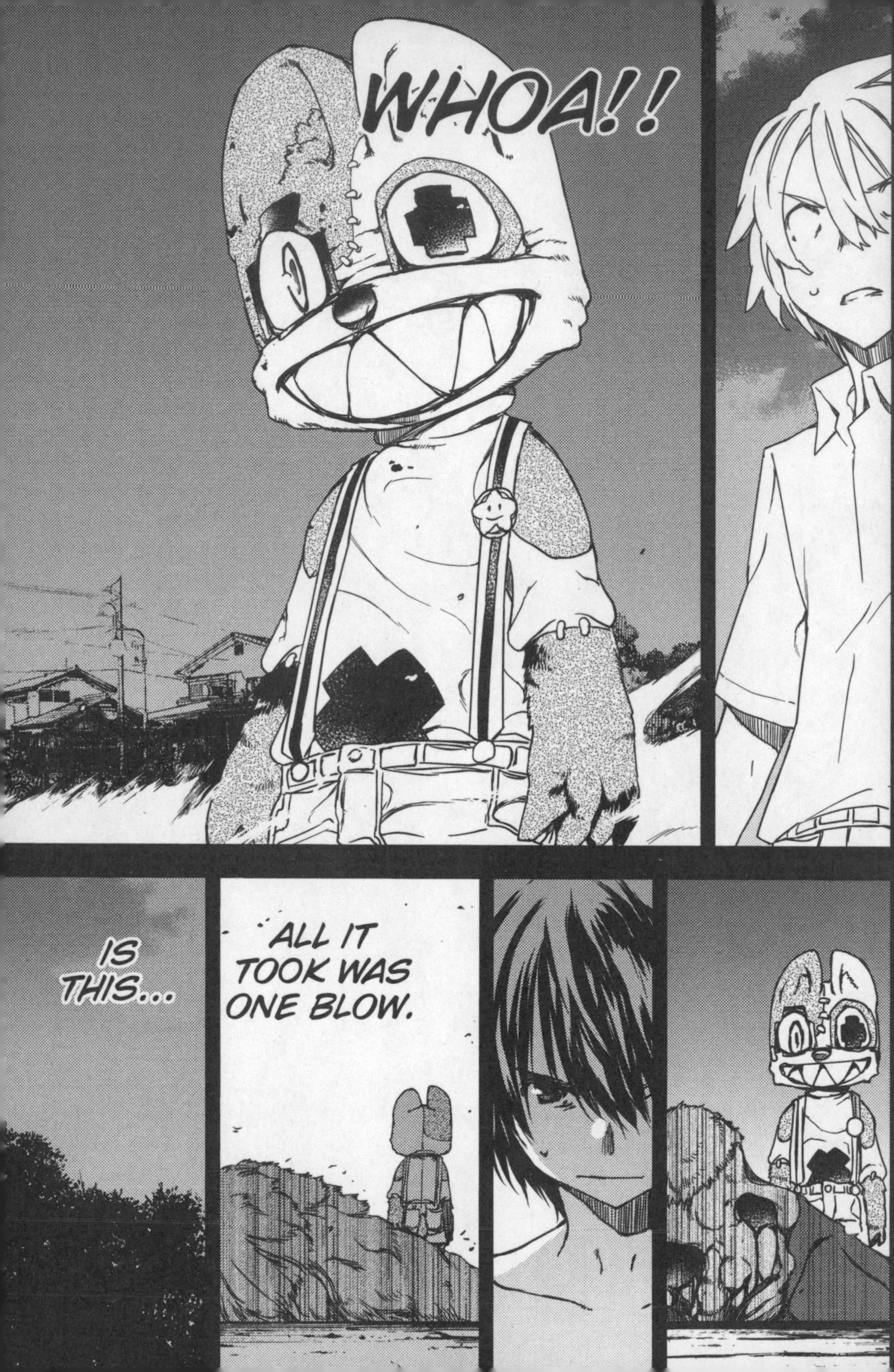
WHOA!!
ALL IT TOOK WAS ONE BLOW.
IS THIS...

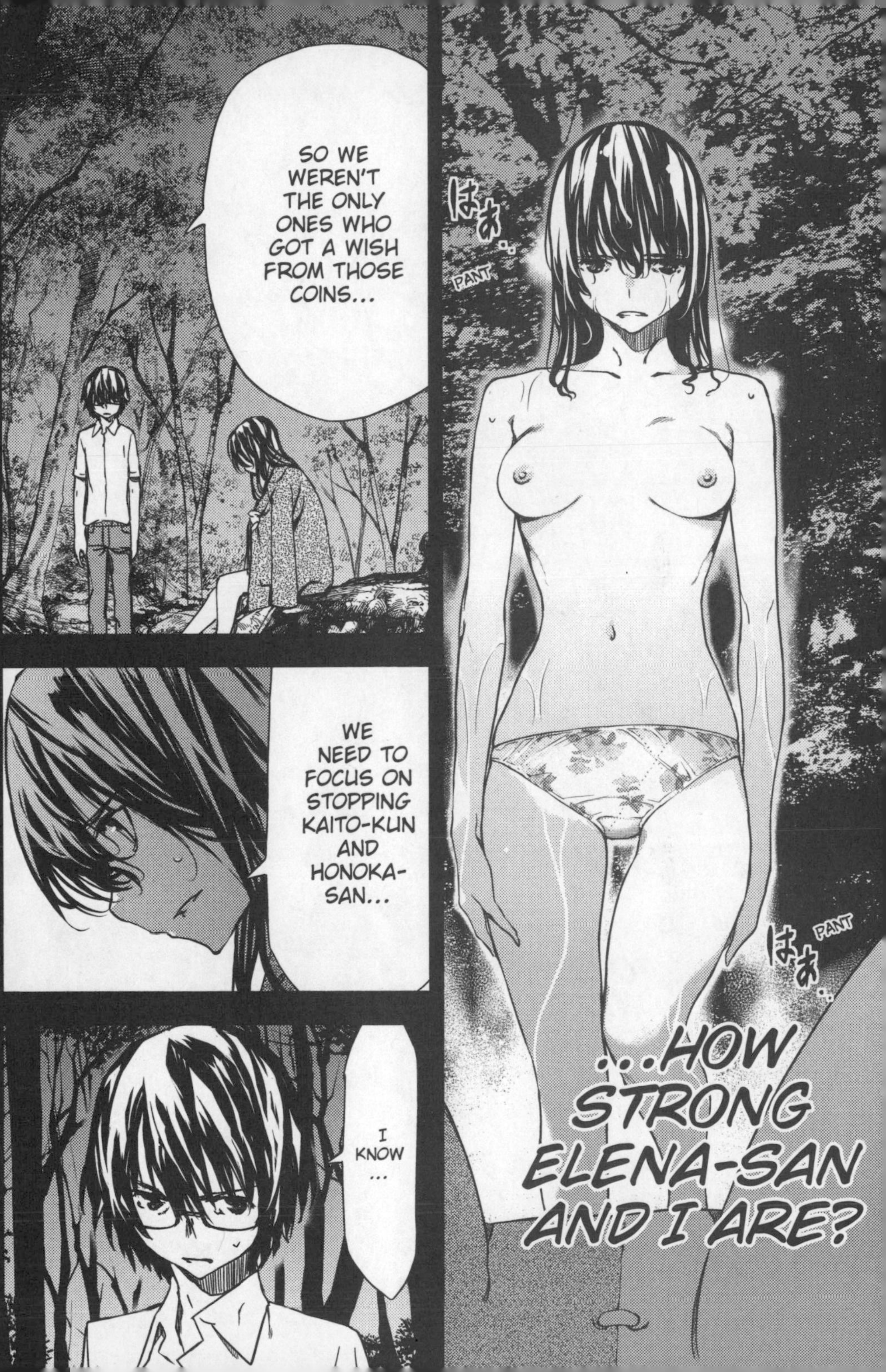
はぁ..
PANT
はぁ..
PANT
...HOW STRONG ELENA-SAN AND I ARE?
SO WE WEREN'T THE ONLY ONES WHO GOT A WISH FROM THOSE COINS...
WE NEED TO FOCUS ON STOPPING KAITO-KUN AND HONOKA-SAN...
I KNOW ...

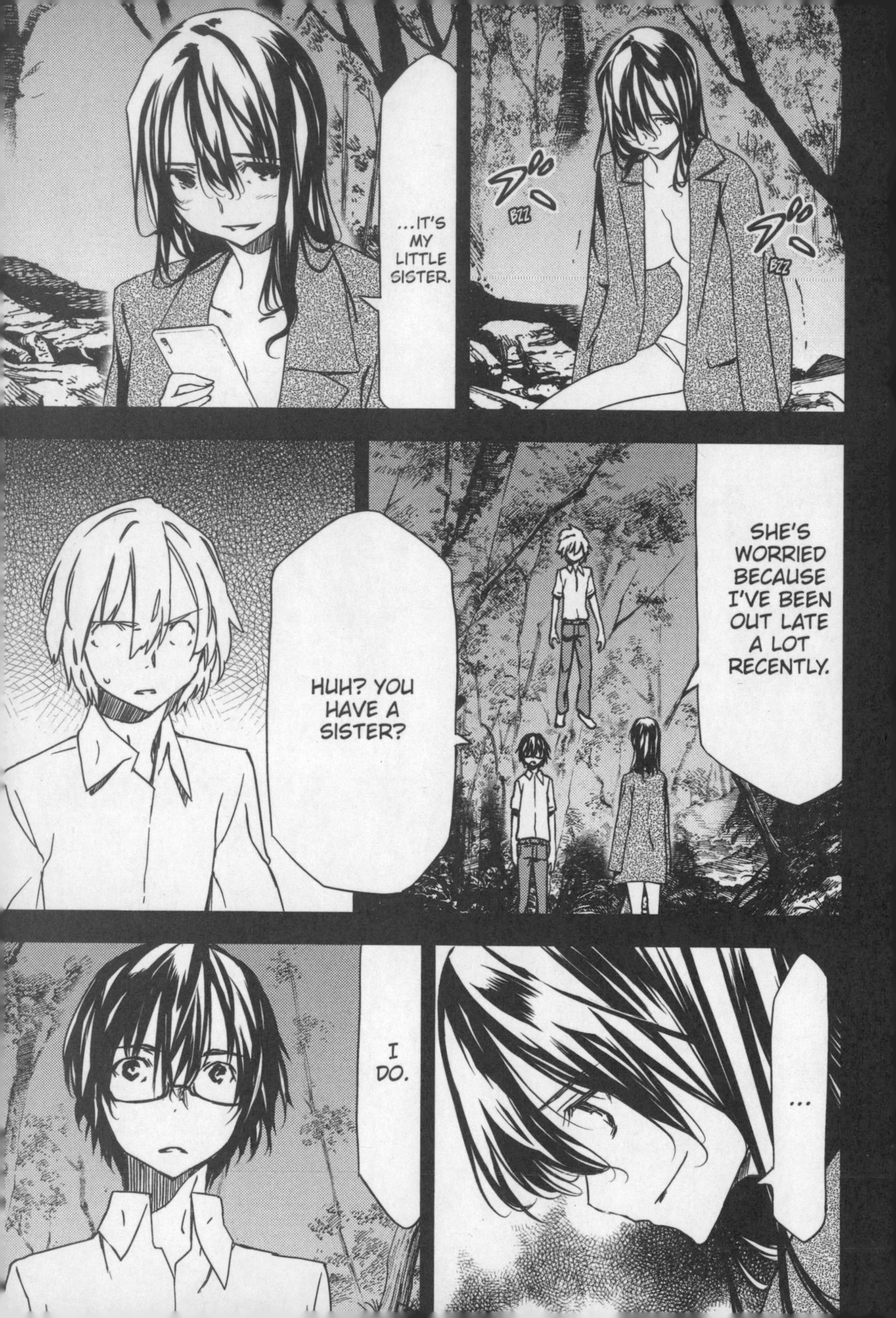
BZZ
BZZ
...IT'S MY LITTLE SISTER.
SHE'S WORRIED BECAUSE I'VE BEEN OUT LATE A LOT RECENTLY.
HUH? YOU HAVE A SISTER?
...
I DO.

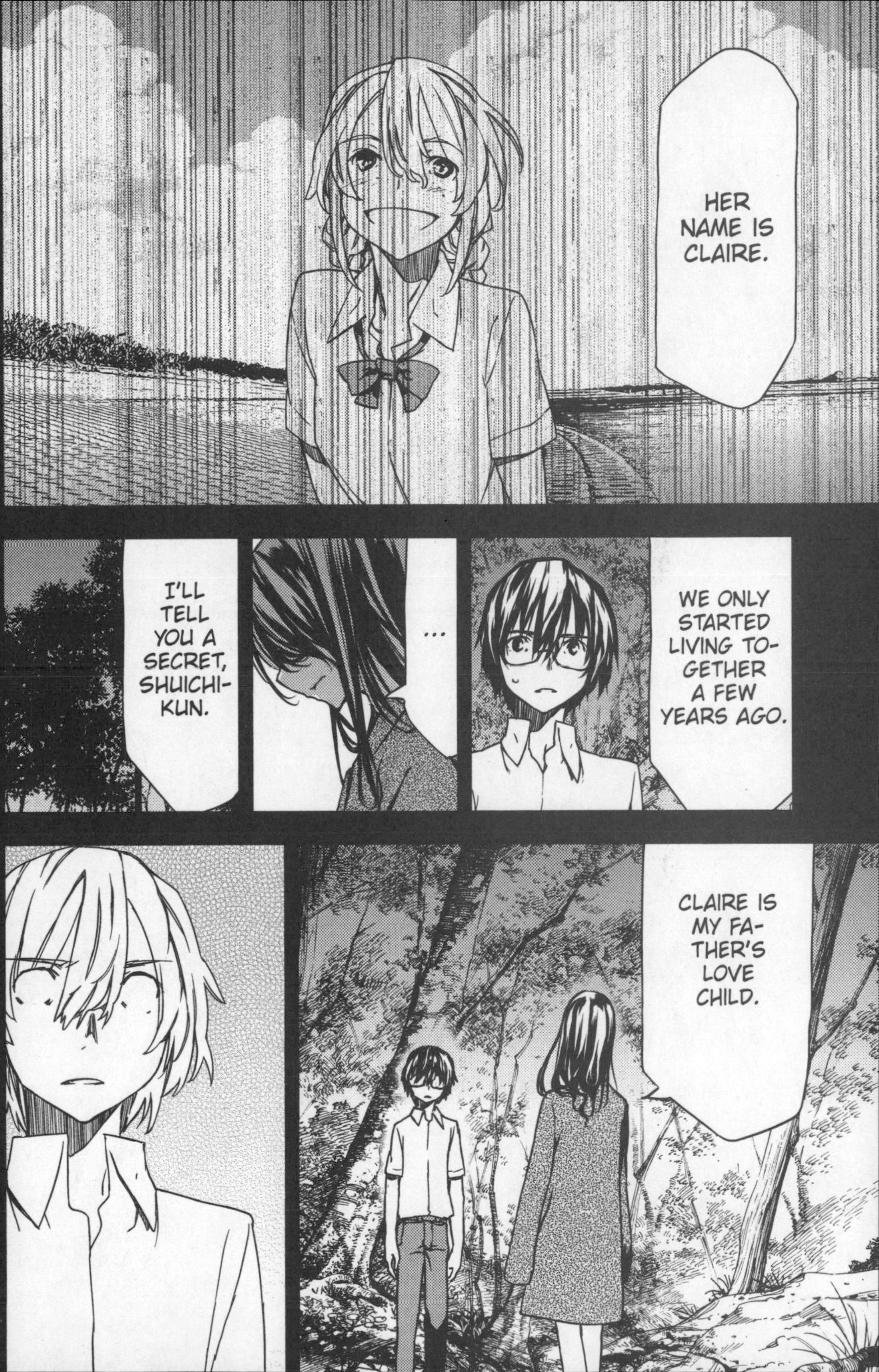
HER NAME IS CLAIRE.
WE ONLY STARTED LIVING TO-GETHER A FEW YEARS AGO.
...
I'LL TELL YOU A SECRET, SHUICHI-KUN.
CLAIRE IS MY FA-THER'S LOVE CHILD.

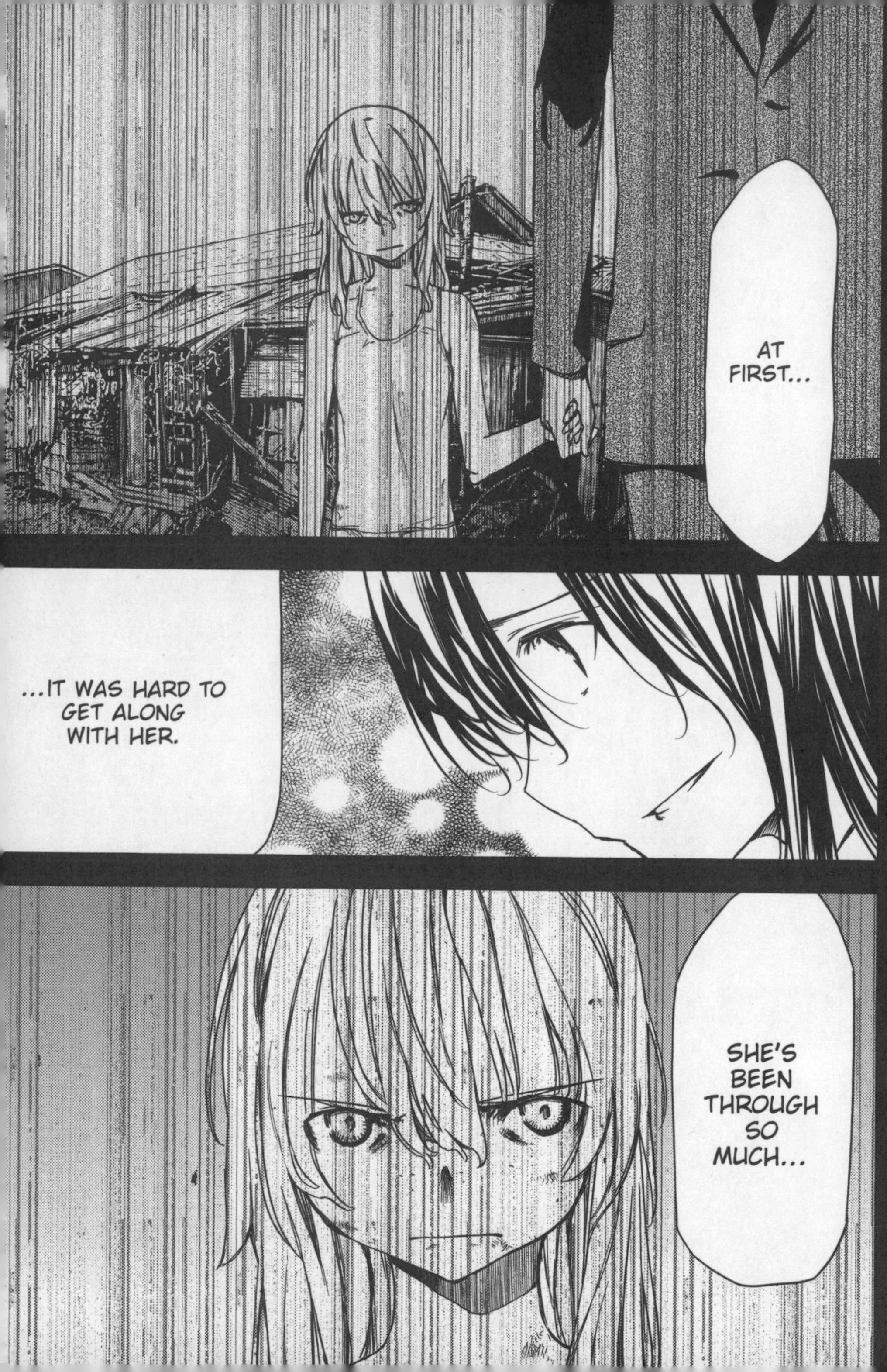
AT FIRST...
...IT WAS HARD TO GET ALONG WITH HER.
SHE'S BEEN THROUGH SO MUCH...

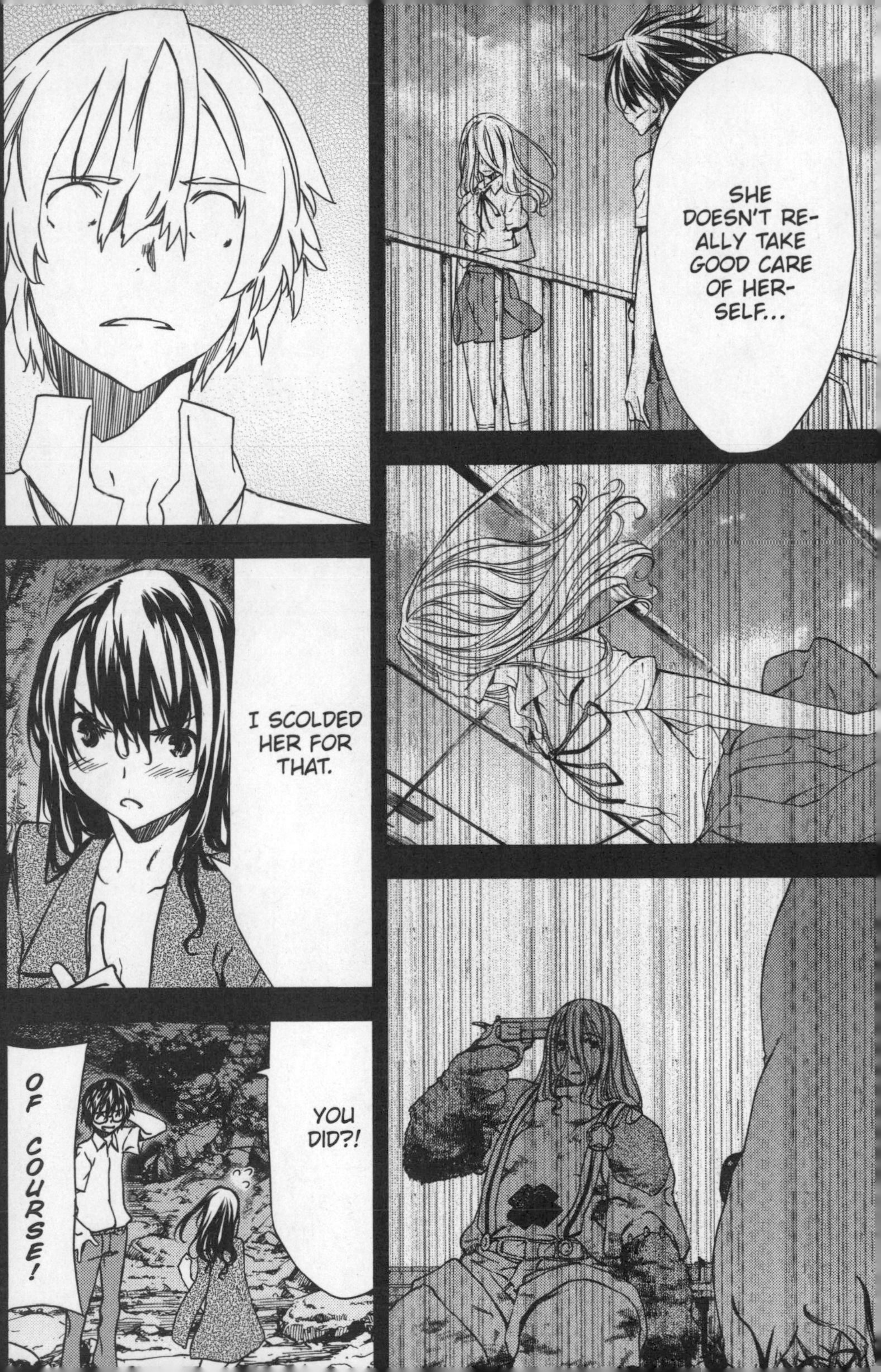
SHE DOESN'T RE-ALLY TAKE GOOD CARE OF HER-SELF...
I SCOLDED HER FOR THAT.
YOU DID?!
OF COURSE!

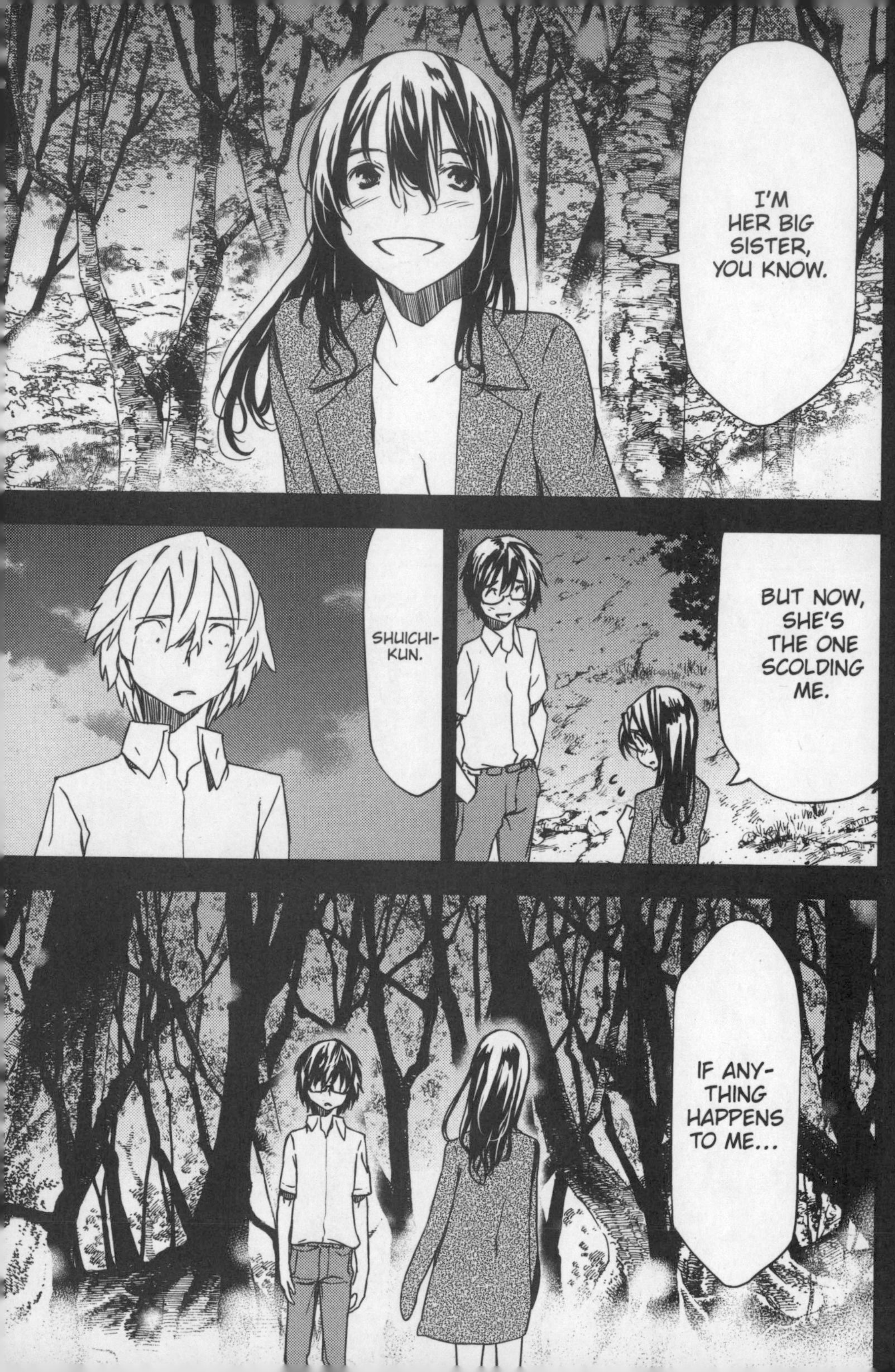
I'M HER BIG SISTER, YOU KNOW.
BUT NOW, SHE'S THE ONE SCOLDING ME.
SHUICHI-KUN.
IF ANY-THING HAPPENS TO ME...

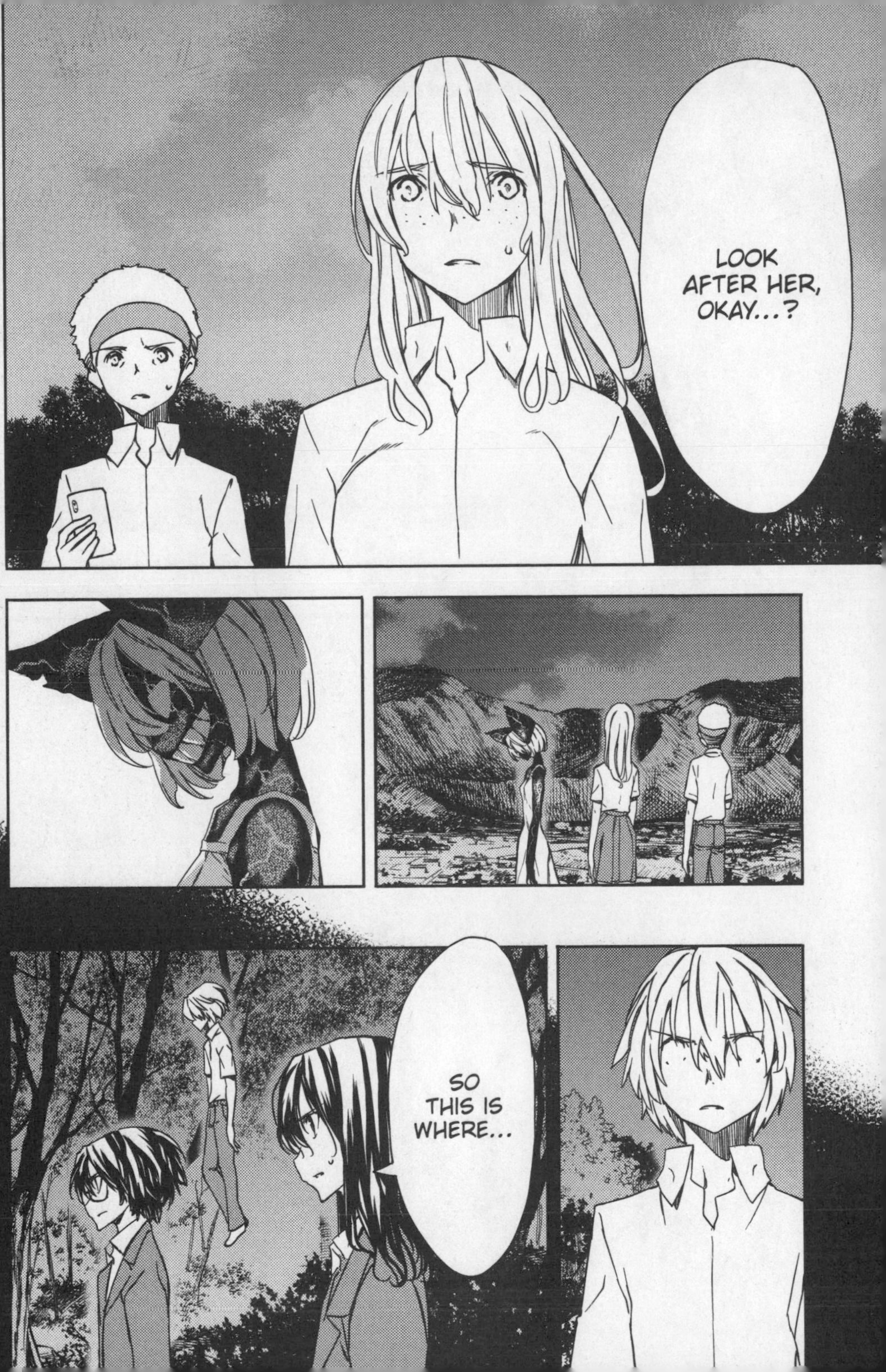
LOOK AFTER HER, OKAY...?
SO THIS IS WHERE...

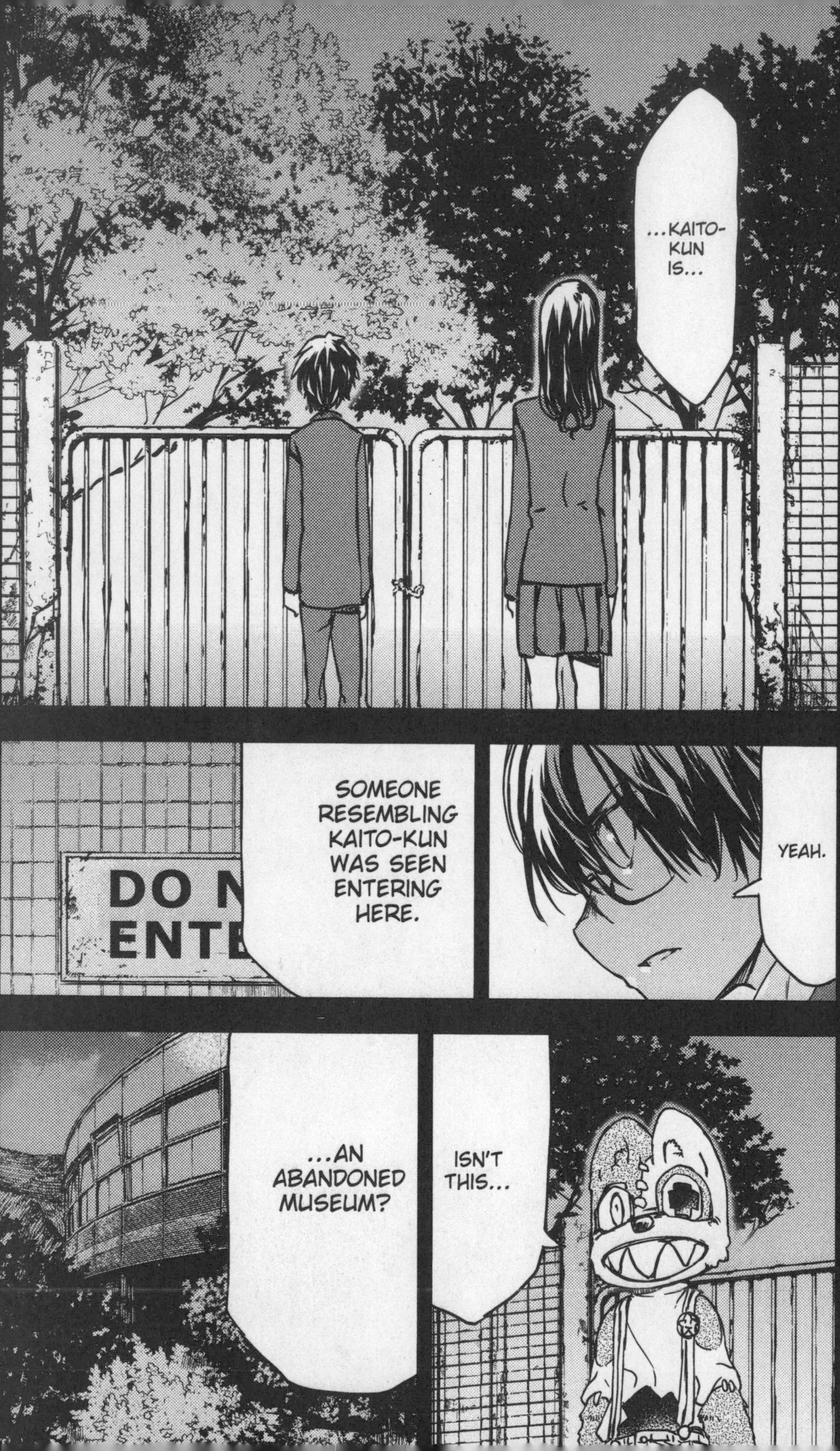
...KAITO-KUN IS...
YEAH.
SOMEONE RESEMBLING KAITO-KUN WAS SEEN ENTERING HERE.
DO N
ENTE
ISN'T THIS...
...AN ABANDONED MUSEUM?

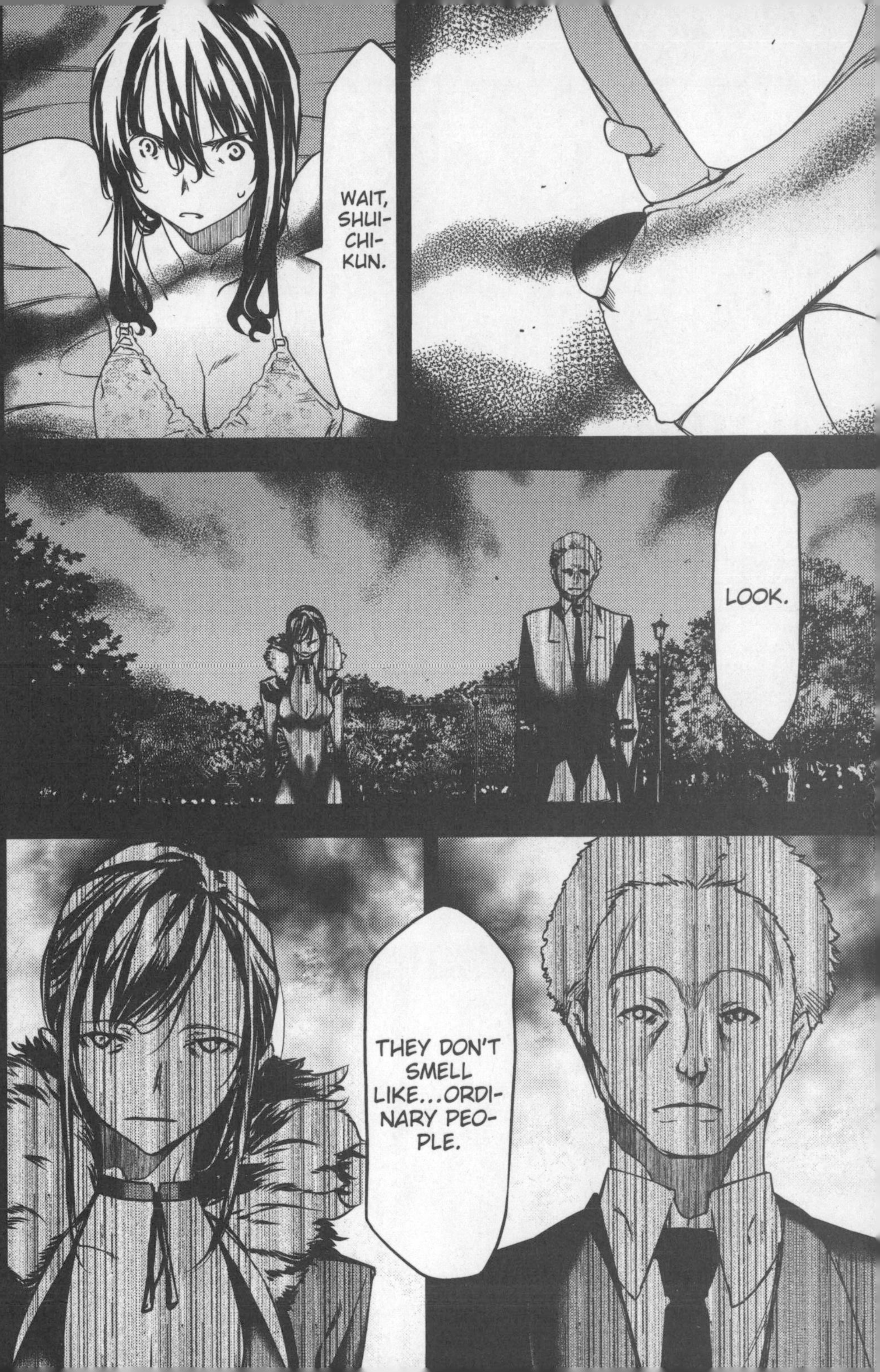
WAIT, SHUICHI-KUN.
LOOK.
THEY DON'T SMELL LIKE...ORDINARY PEOPLE.

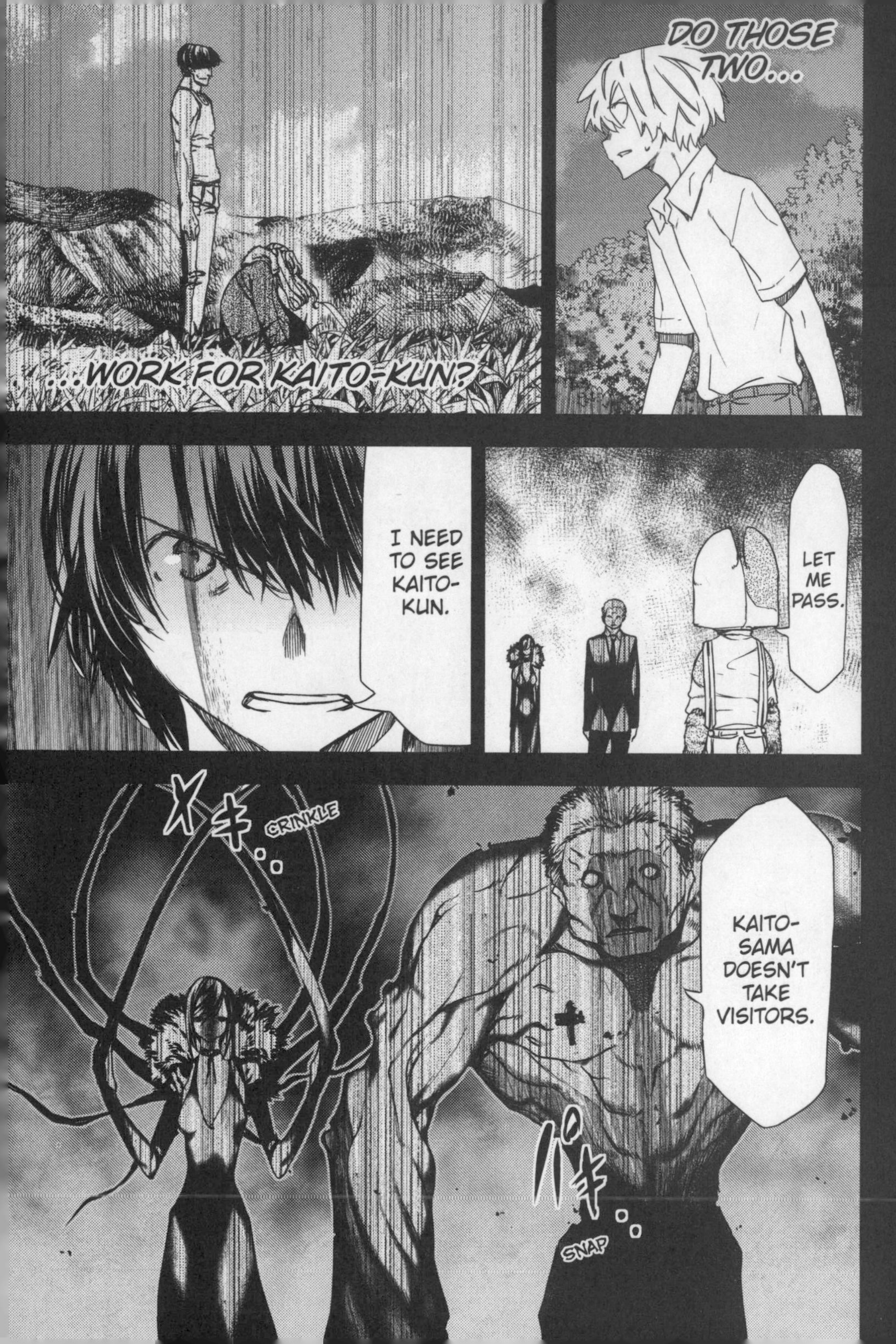
DO THOSE TWO...
...WORK FOR KAITO-KUN?
LET ME PASS.
I NEED TO SEE KAITO-KUN.
KAITO-SAMA DOESN'T TAKE VISITORS.
メキ
CRINKLE
パキ
SNAP

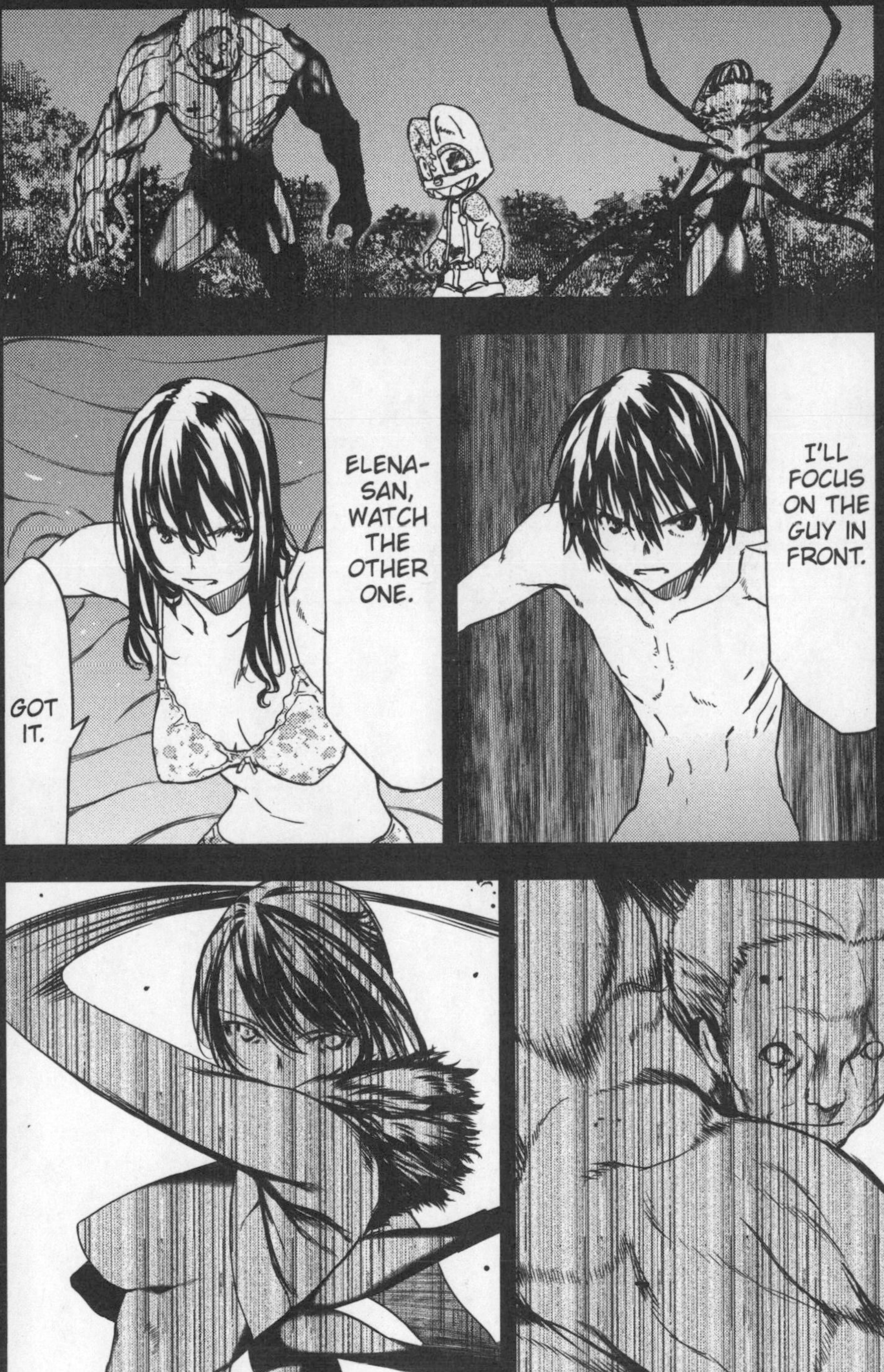
I'LL FOCUS ON THE GUY IN FRONT.
ELENA-SAN, WATCH THE OTHER ONE.
GOT IT.

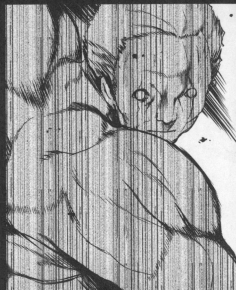

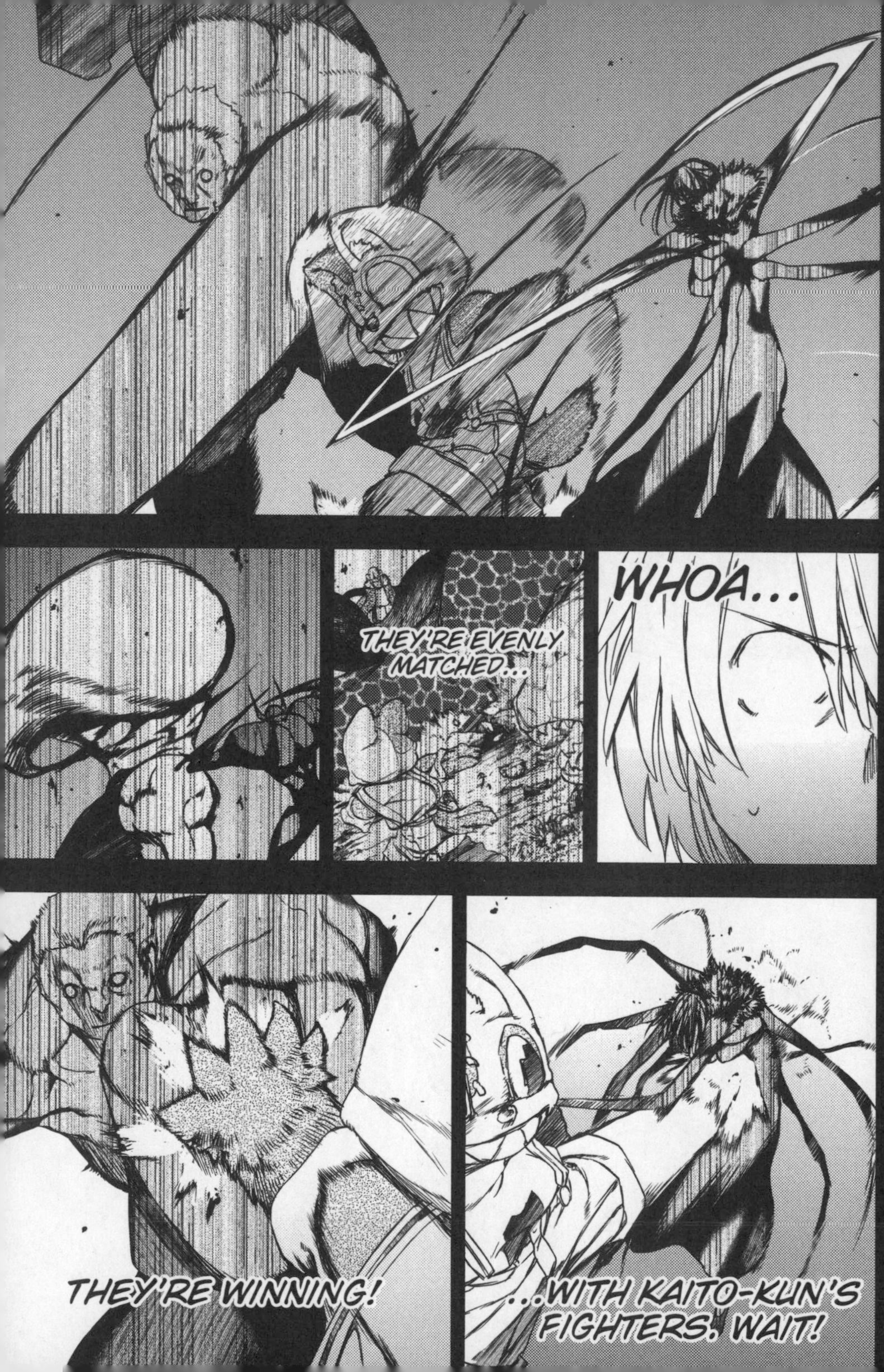
WHOA...
THEY'RE EVENLY MATCHED...
...WITH KAITO-KUN'S FIGHTERS. WAIT!
THEY'RE WINNING!

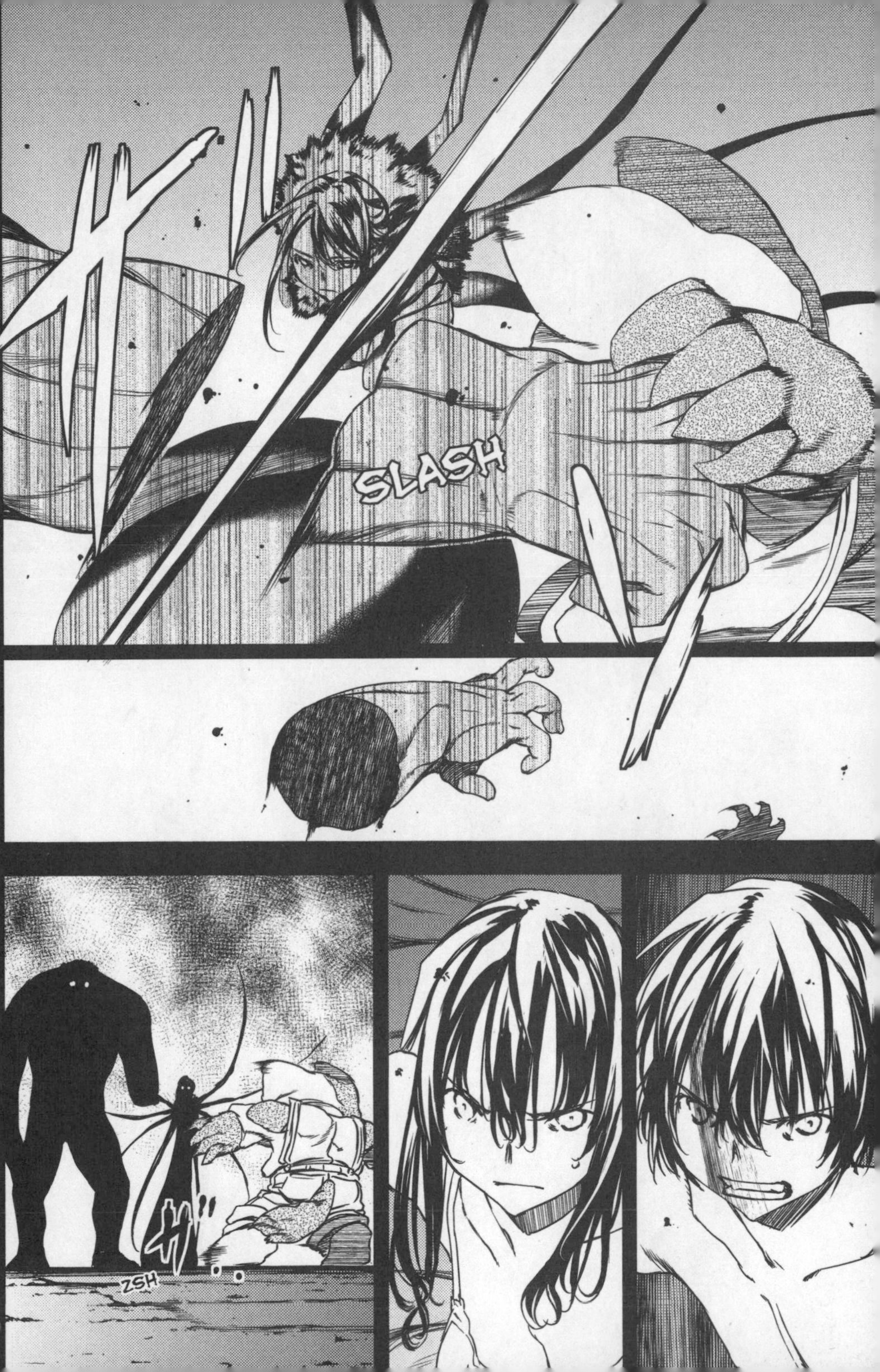
SLASH
ZSH

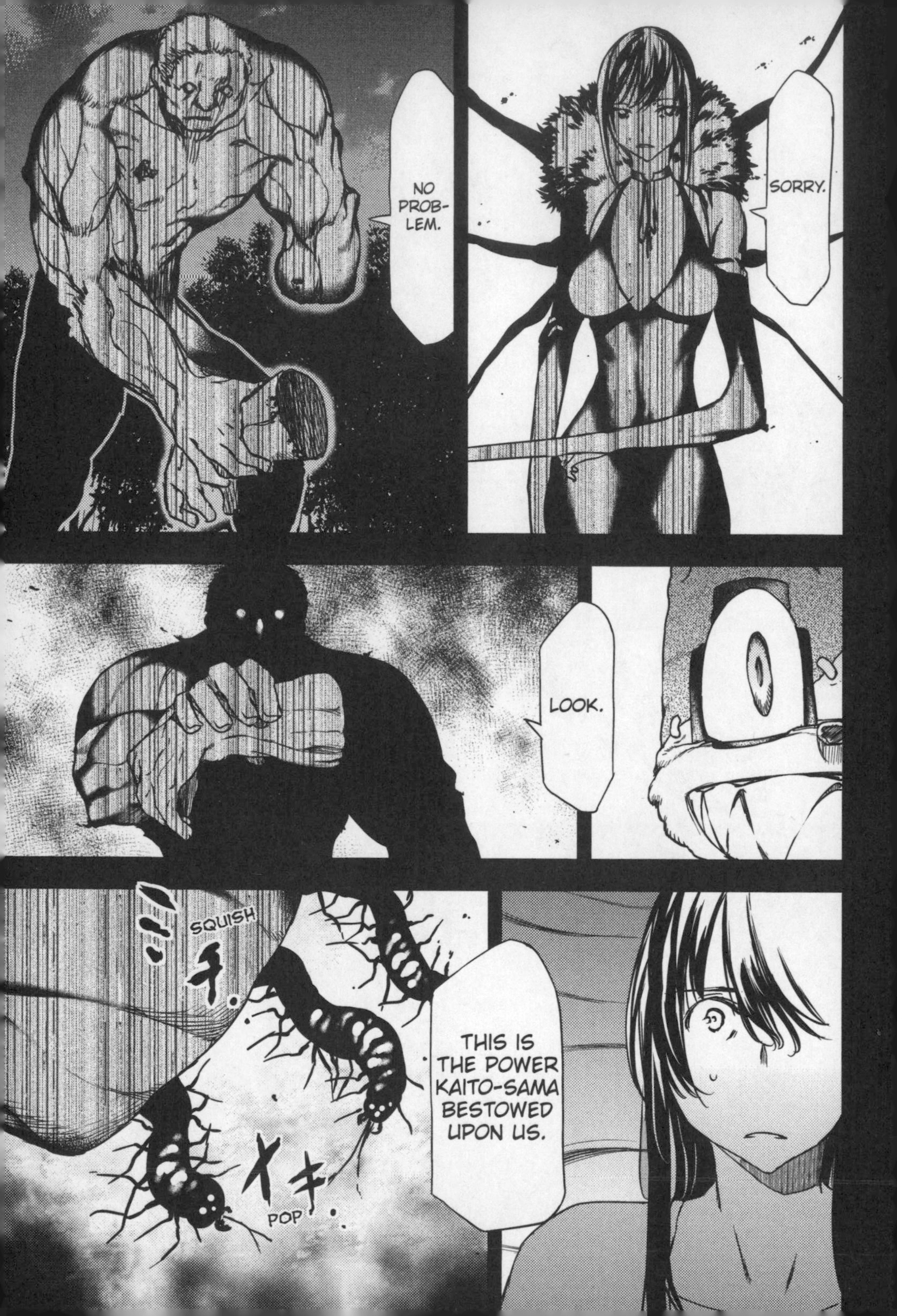
SORRY.
NO PROB-LEM.
LOOK.
THIS IS THE POWER KAITO-SAMA BESTOWED UPON US.
ぐちゅ
SQUISH
メキ
POP

KAITO-SAMA MADE MY BODY IMMORTAL.

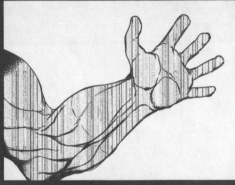

I OWE EVERYTHING TO HIM.

STILL... IT DOESN'T LOOK LIKE... WE HAVE MUCH CHANCE IN THIS FIGHT.

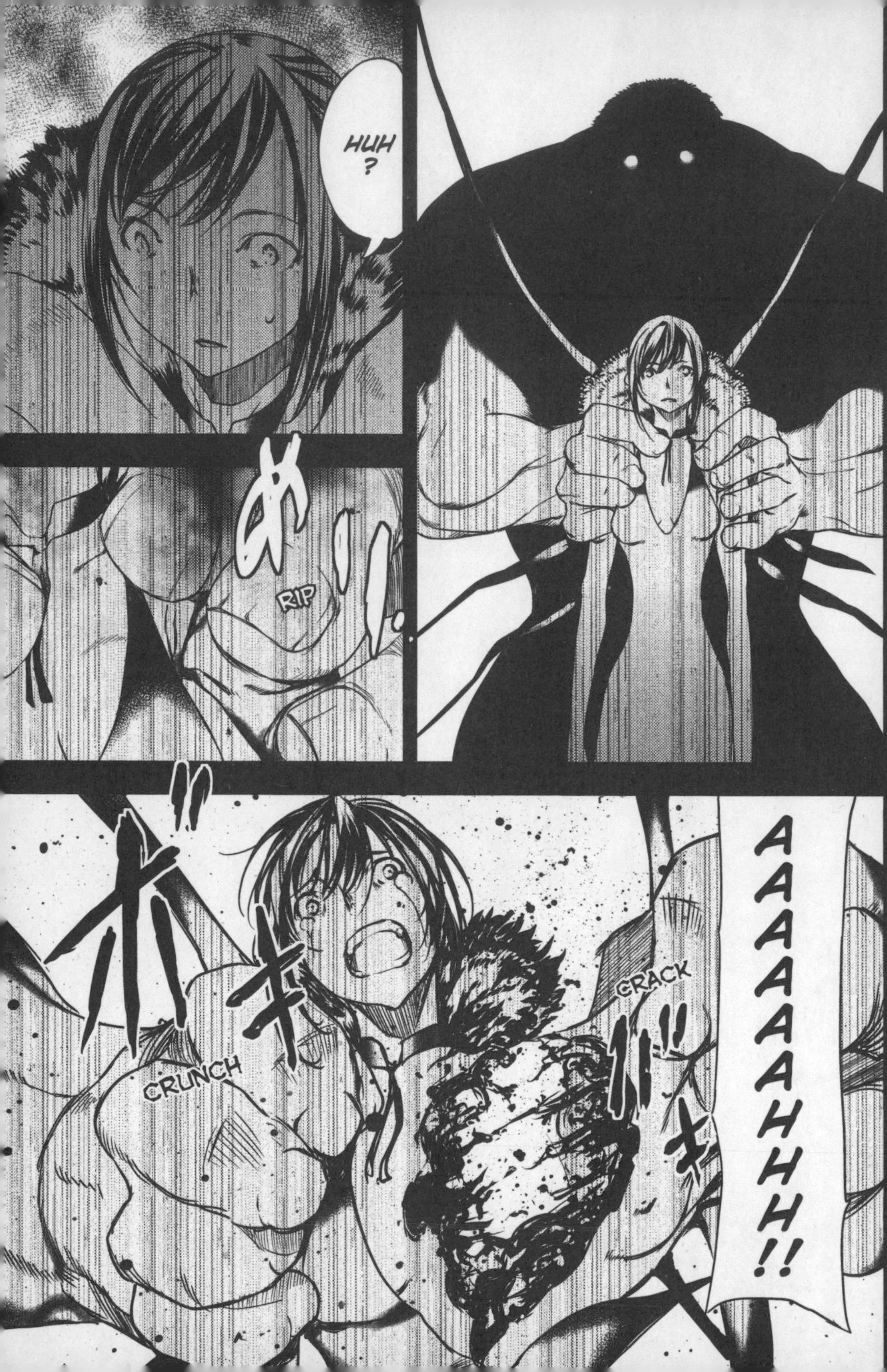
HUH ?
RIP
AAAAAAHHH!!
CRACK
CRUNCH

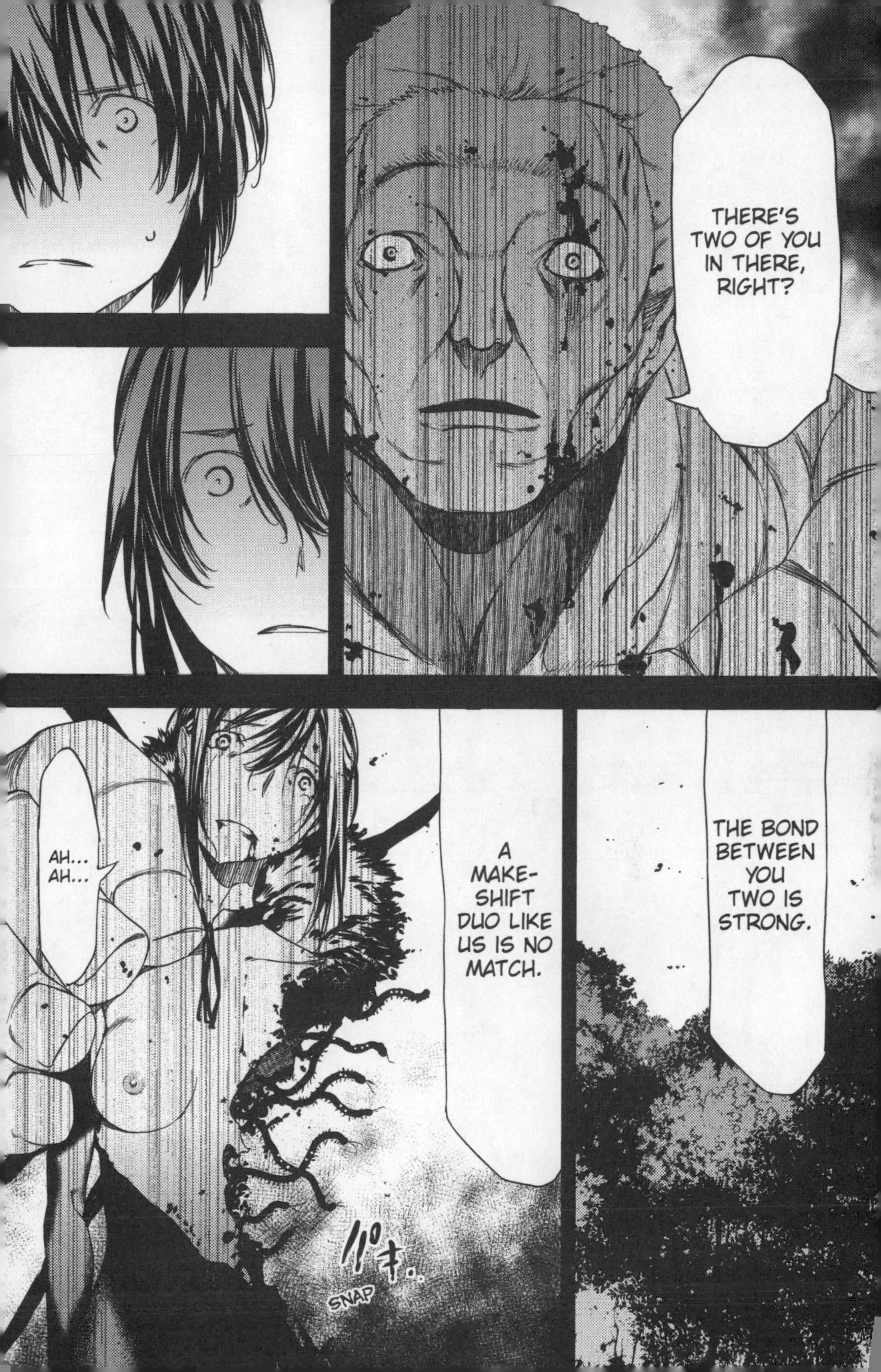
THERE'S TWO OF YOU IN THERE, RIGHT?
THE BOND BETWEEN YOU TWO IS STRONG.
A MAKE-SHIFT DUO LIKE US IS NO MATCH.
AH... AH...
パキ。
SNAP

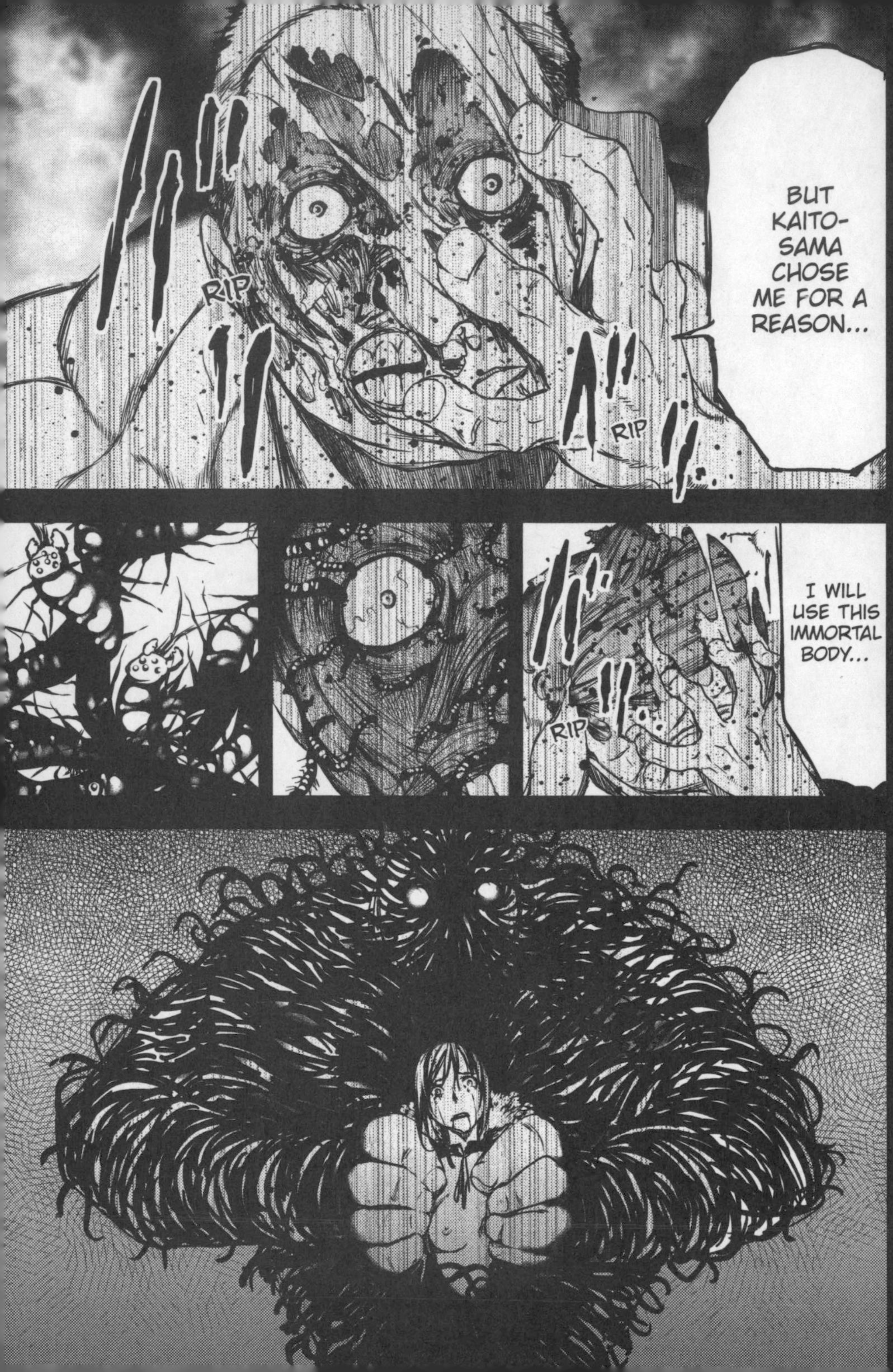

BUT KAITO-SAMA CHOSE ME FOR A REASON...
RIP
RIP
I WILL USE THIS IMMORTAL BODY...
RIP

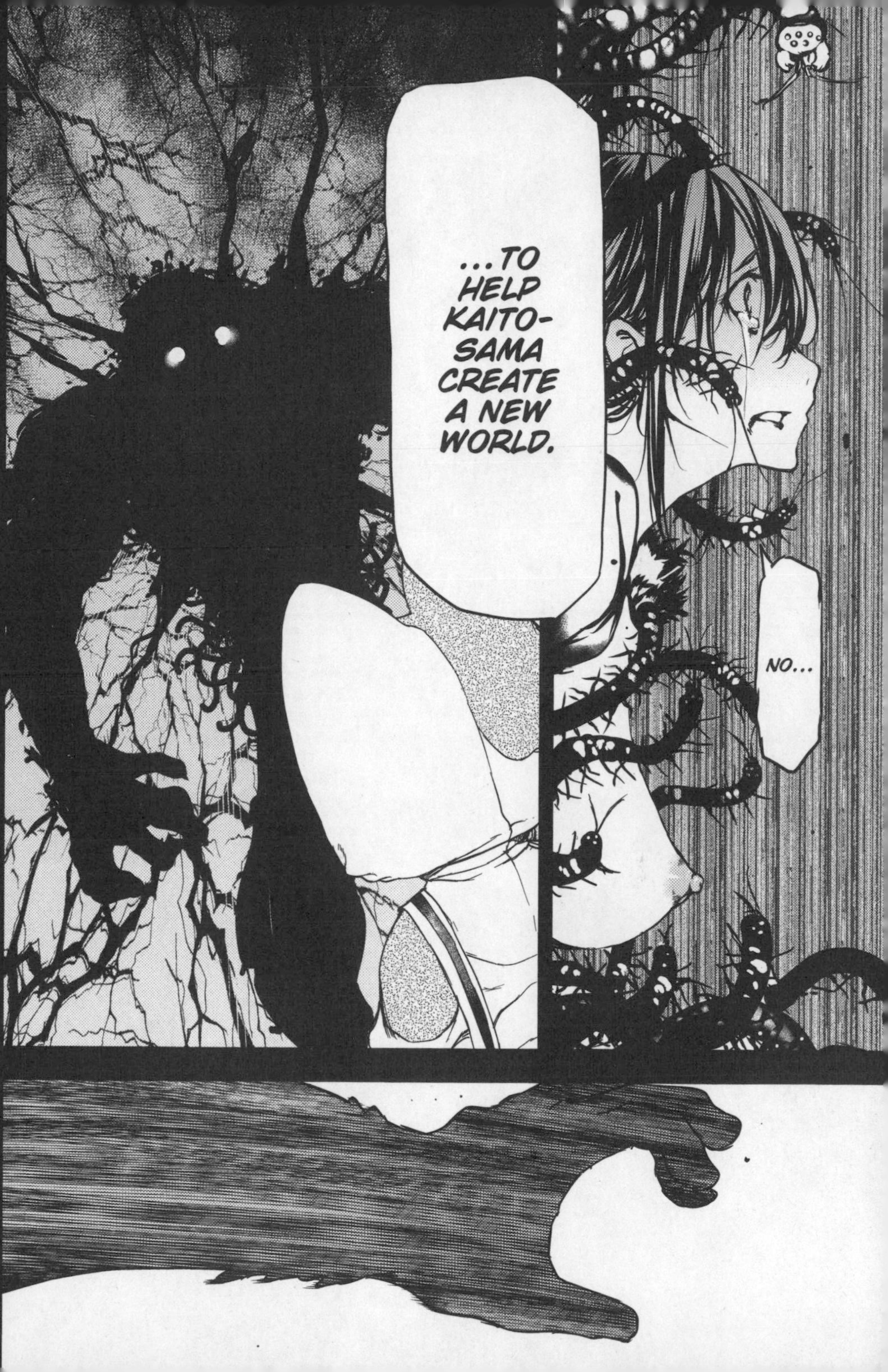

...TO HELP KAITO-SAMA CREATE A NEW WORLD.
NO...

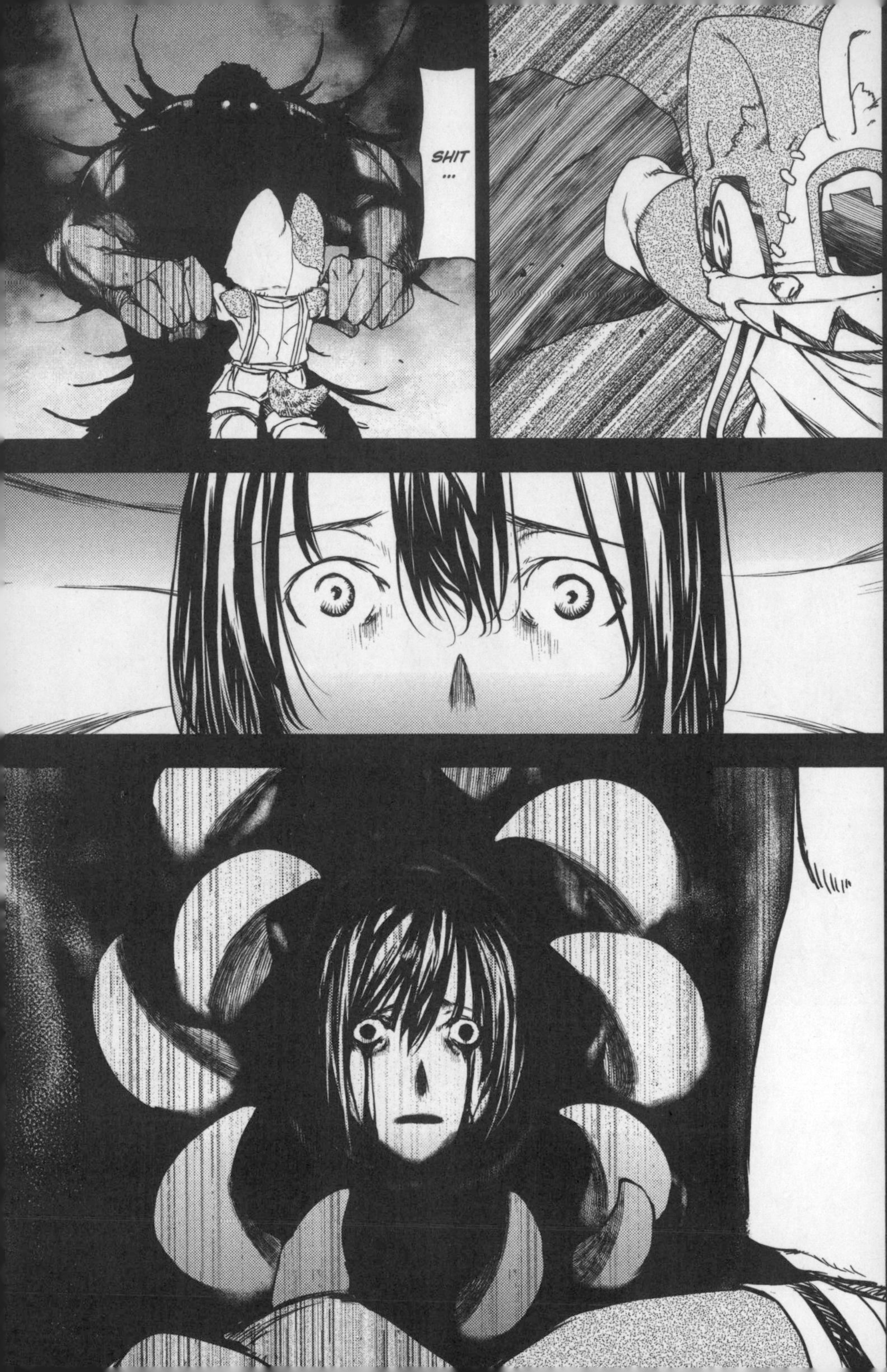
SHIT
...

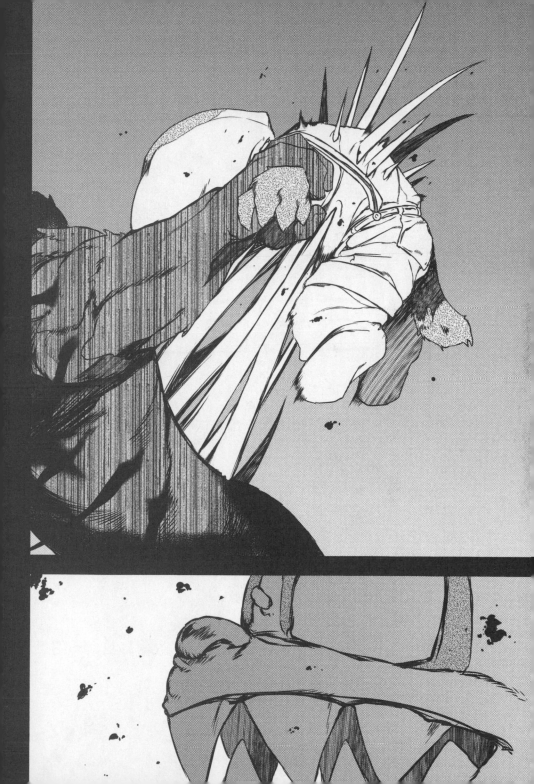

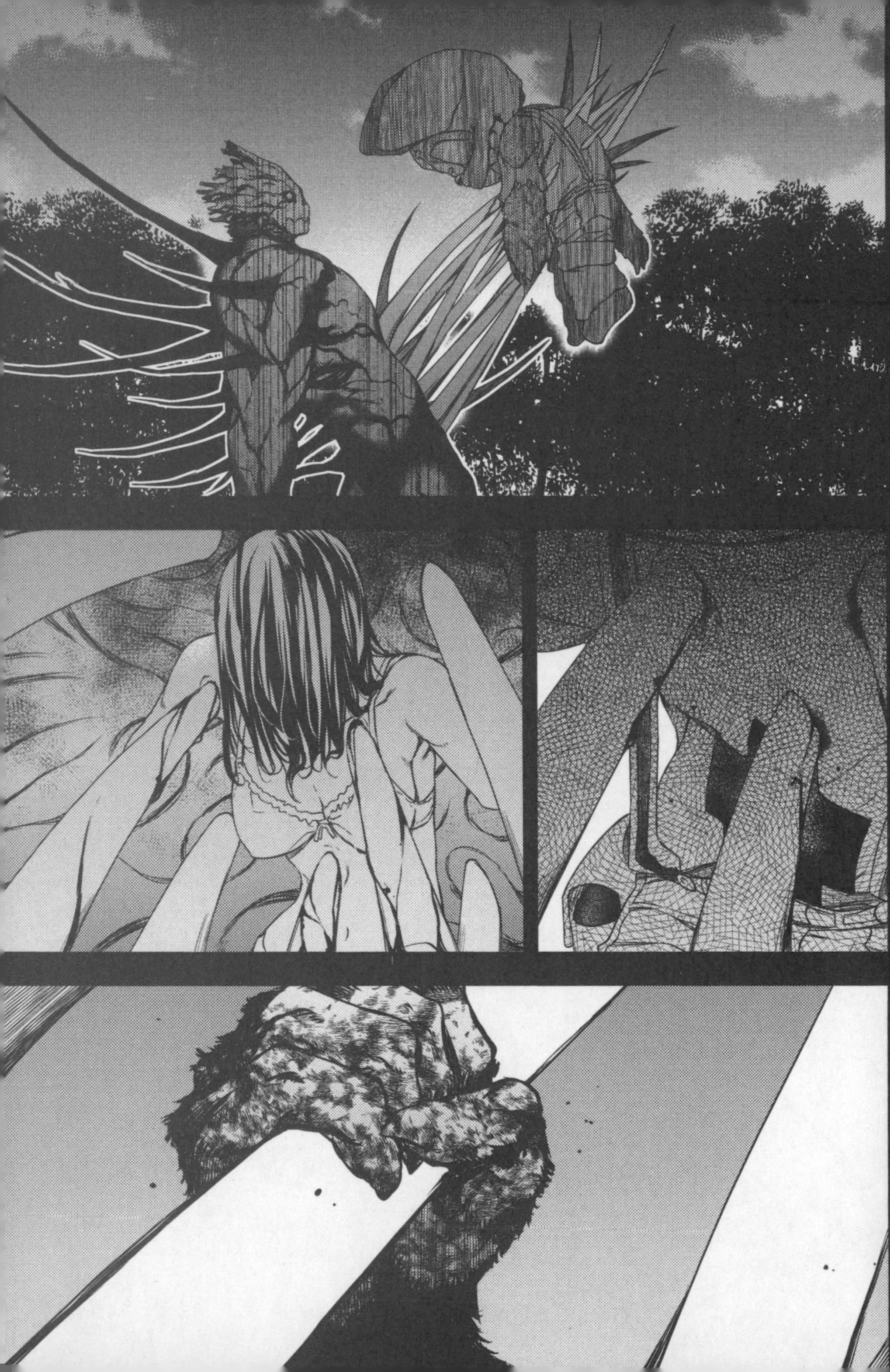

AAARRGH!!

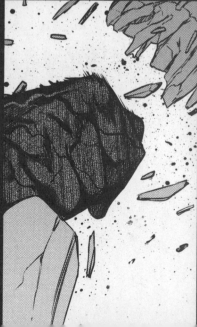

SNAP

CRACK

WHAT'S
GOING
ON...?

WHAT'S
THIS?

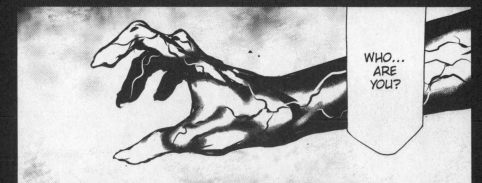

WHO...
ARE
YOU?

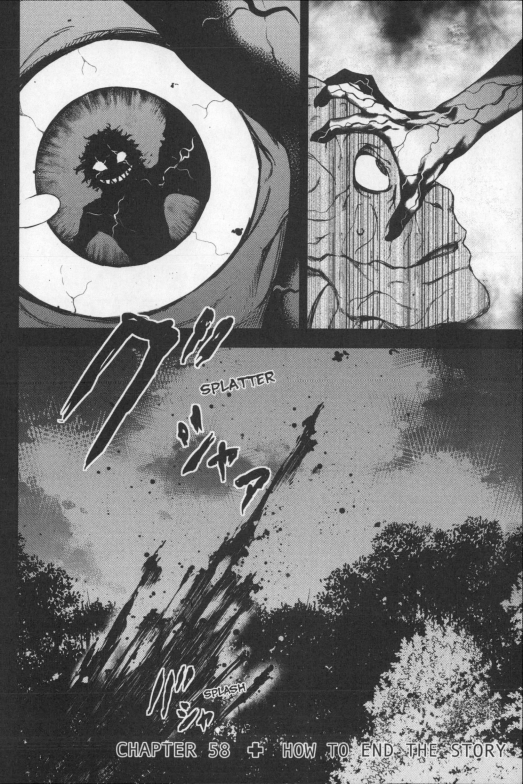

SPLATTER

SPLASH

CHAPTER 58 ✛ HOW TO END THE STORY

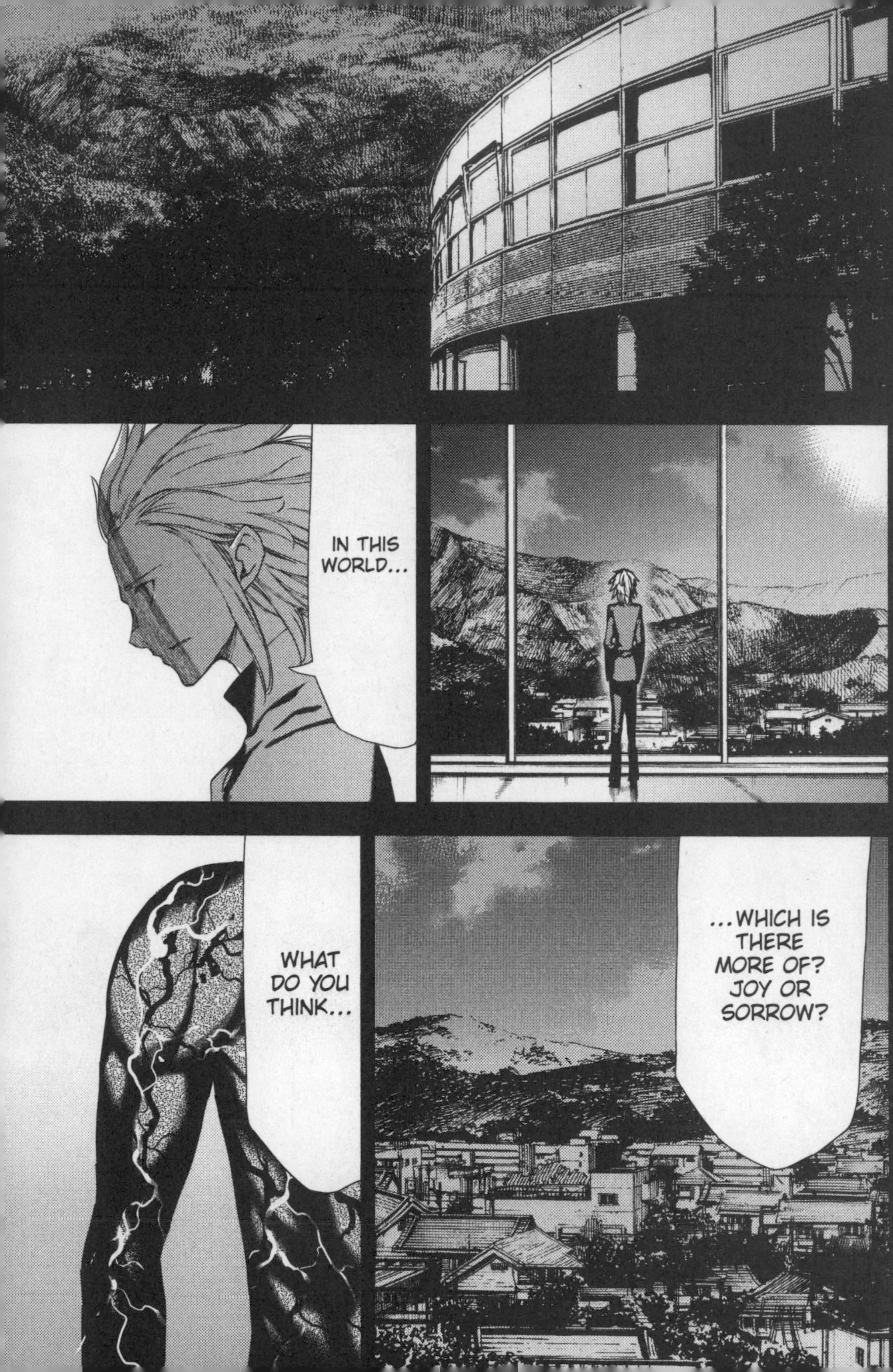
IN THIS WORLD...
...WHICH IS THERE MORE OF? JOY OR SORROW?
WHAT DO YOU THINK...

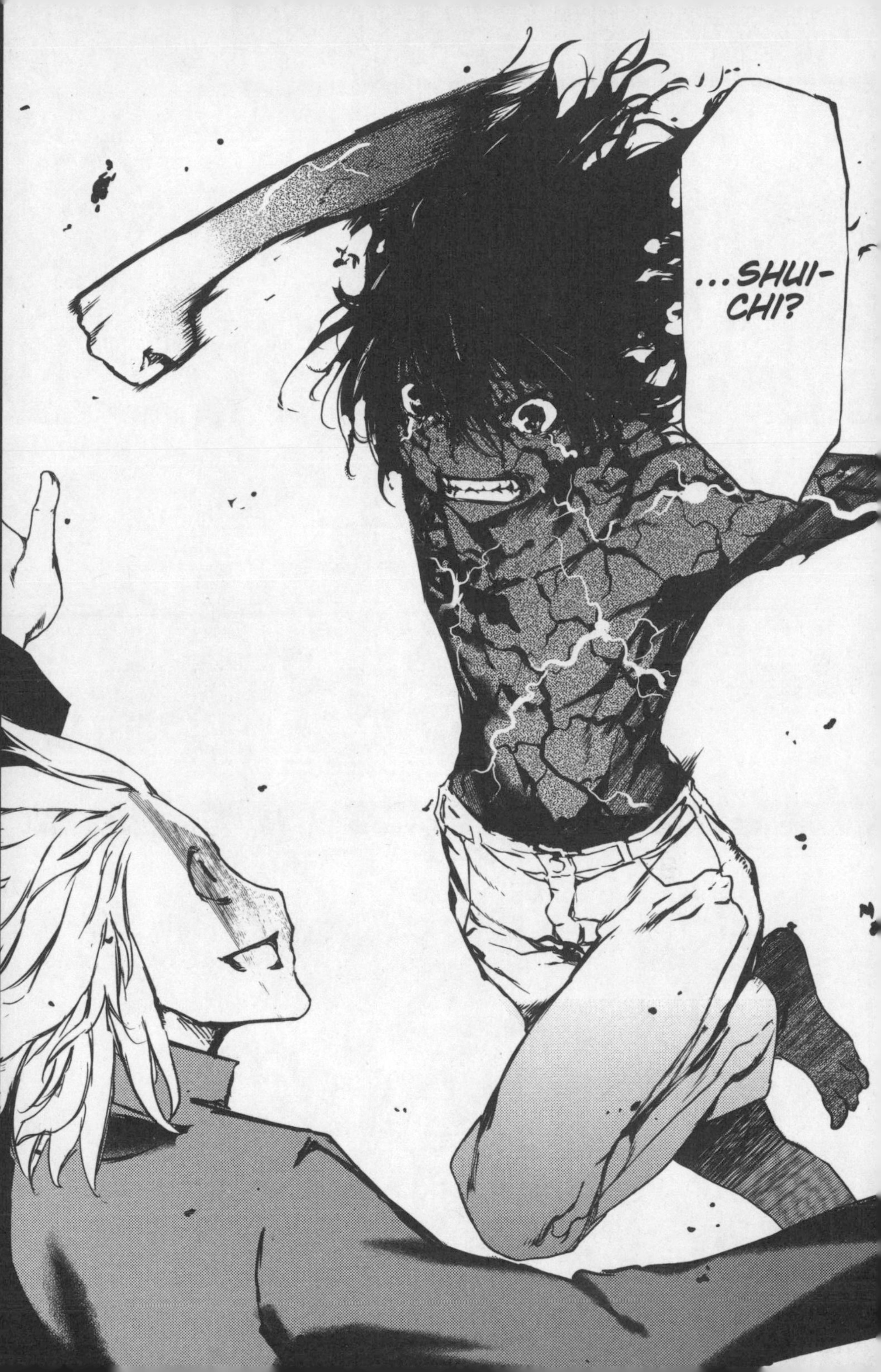
...SHUI-
CHI?

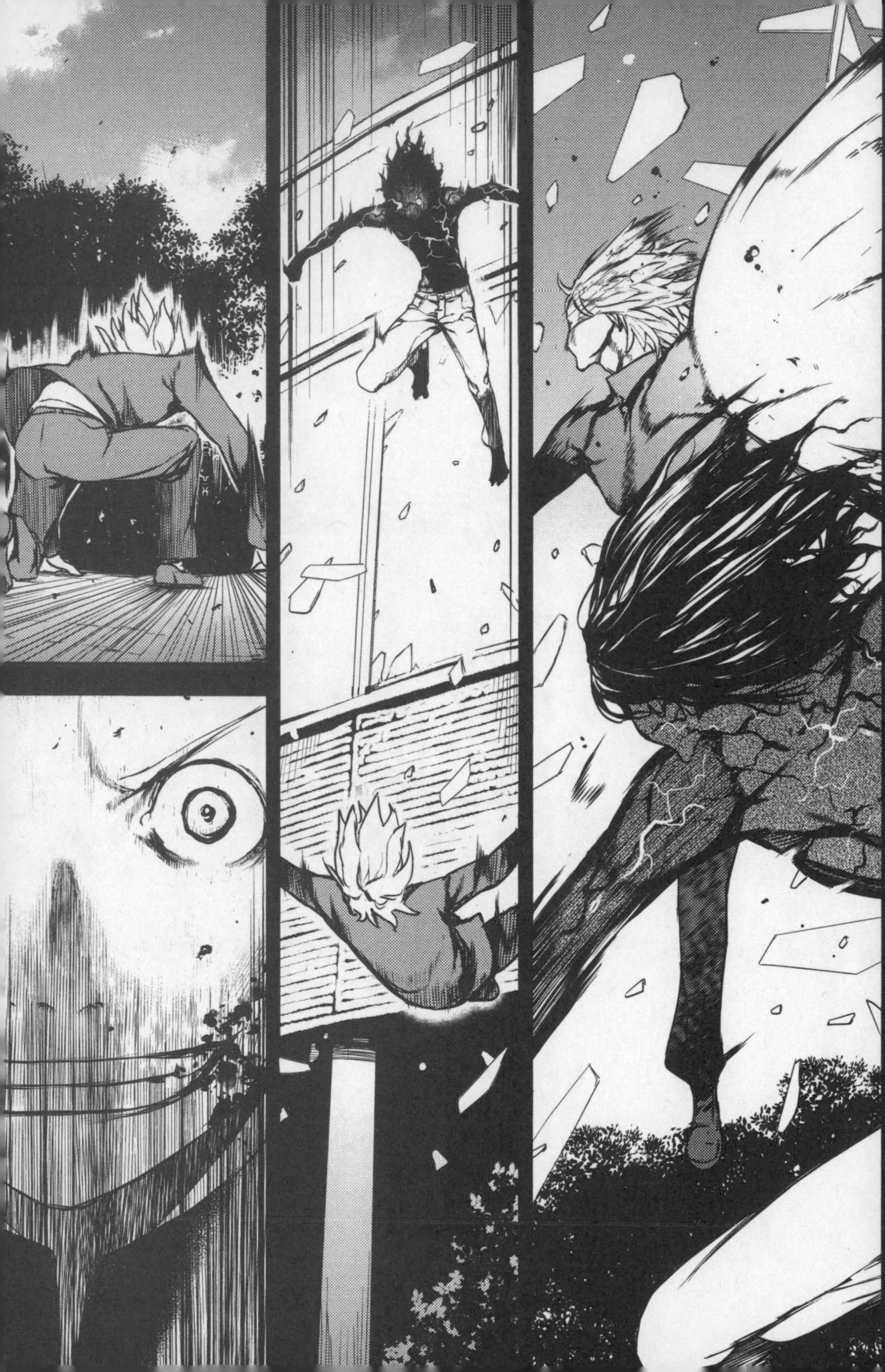

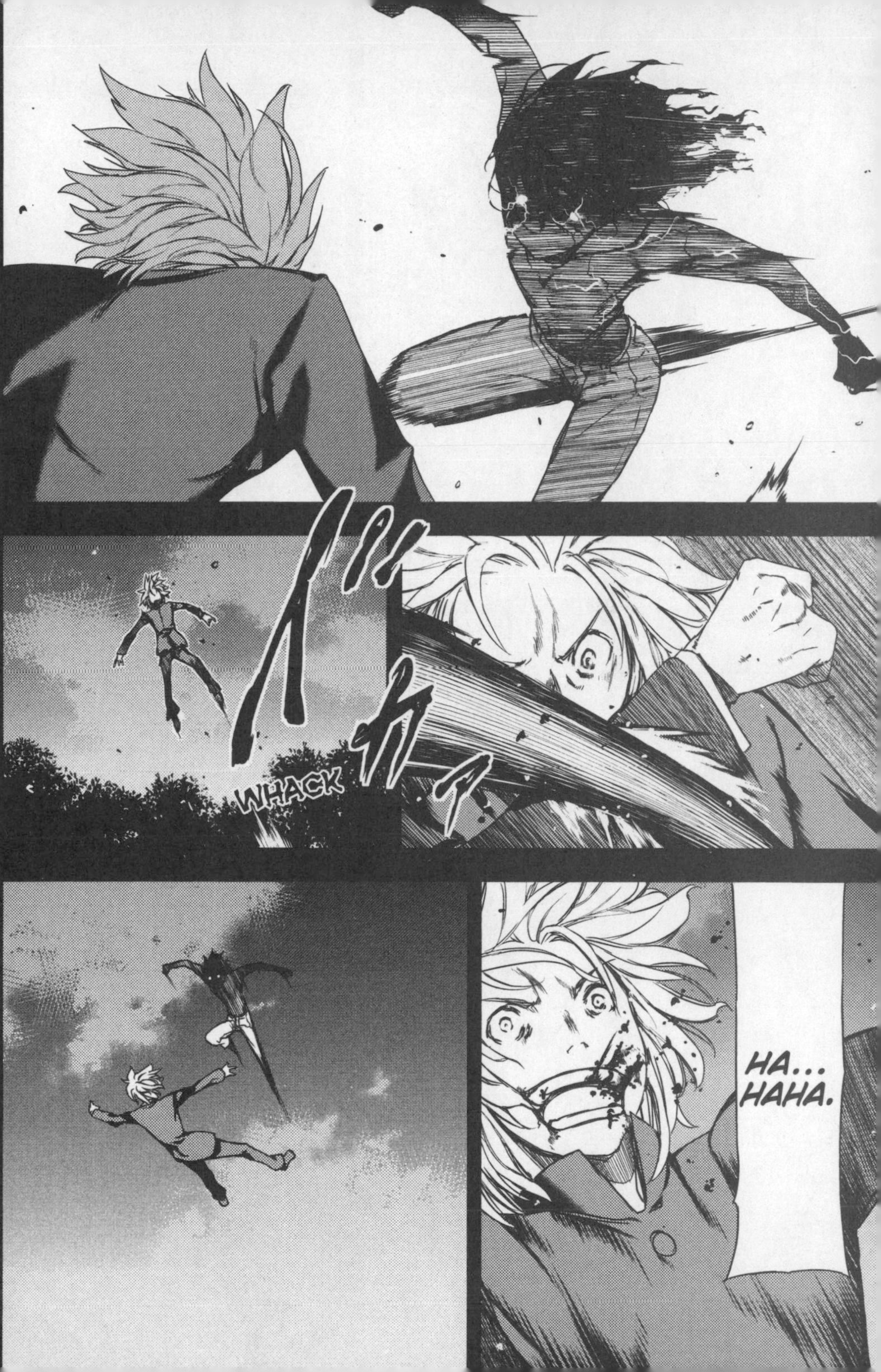
WHACK
HA... HAHA.

...THIS
IS
YOUR
POWER.

SO,
SHUICHI...

THUD

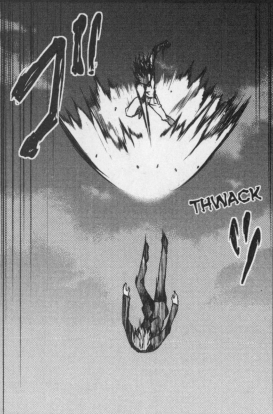

THWACK

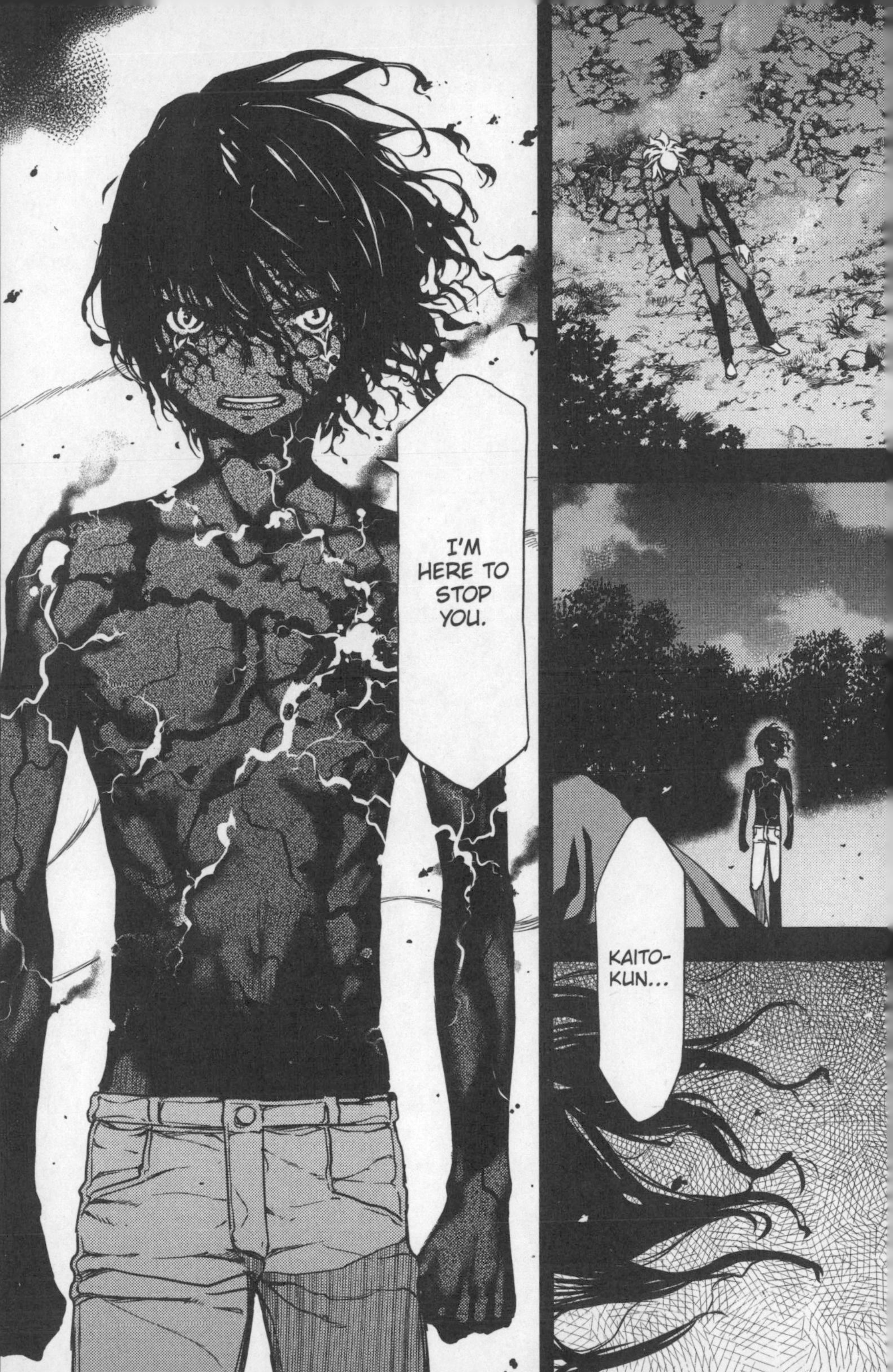
KAITO-KUN...
I'M HERE TO STOP YOU.

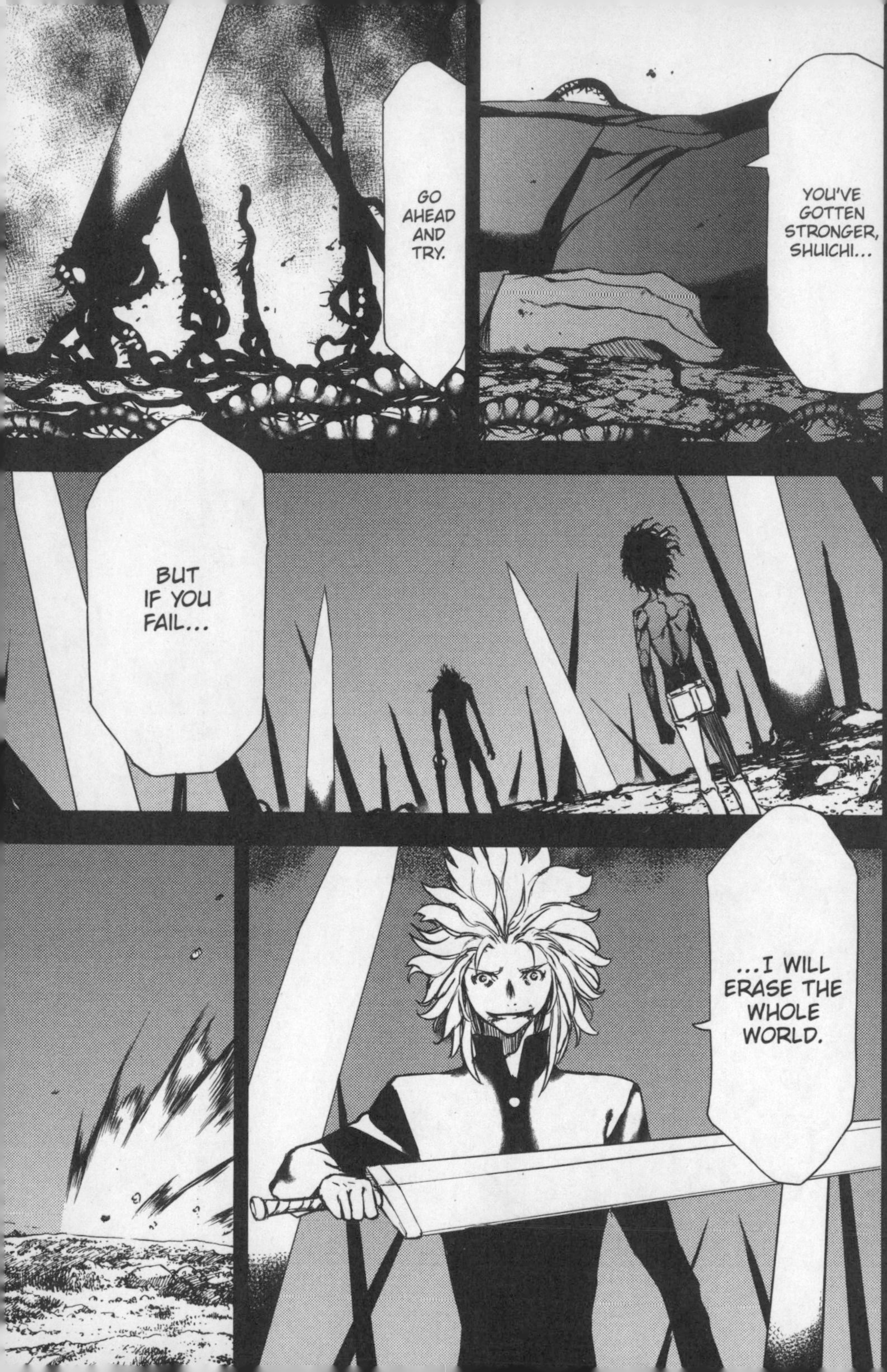
YOU'VE GOTTEN STRONGER, SHUICHI...
GO AHEAD AND TRY.
BUT IF YOU FAIL...
...I WILL ERASE THE WHOLE WORLD.

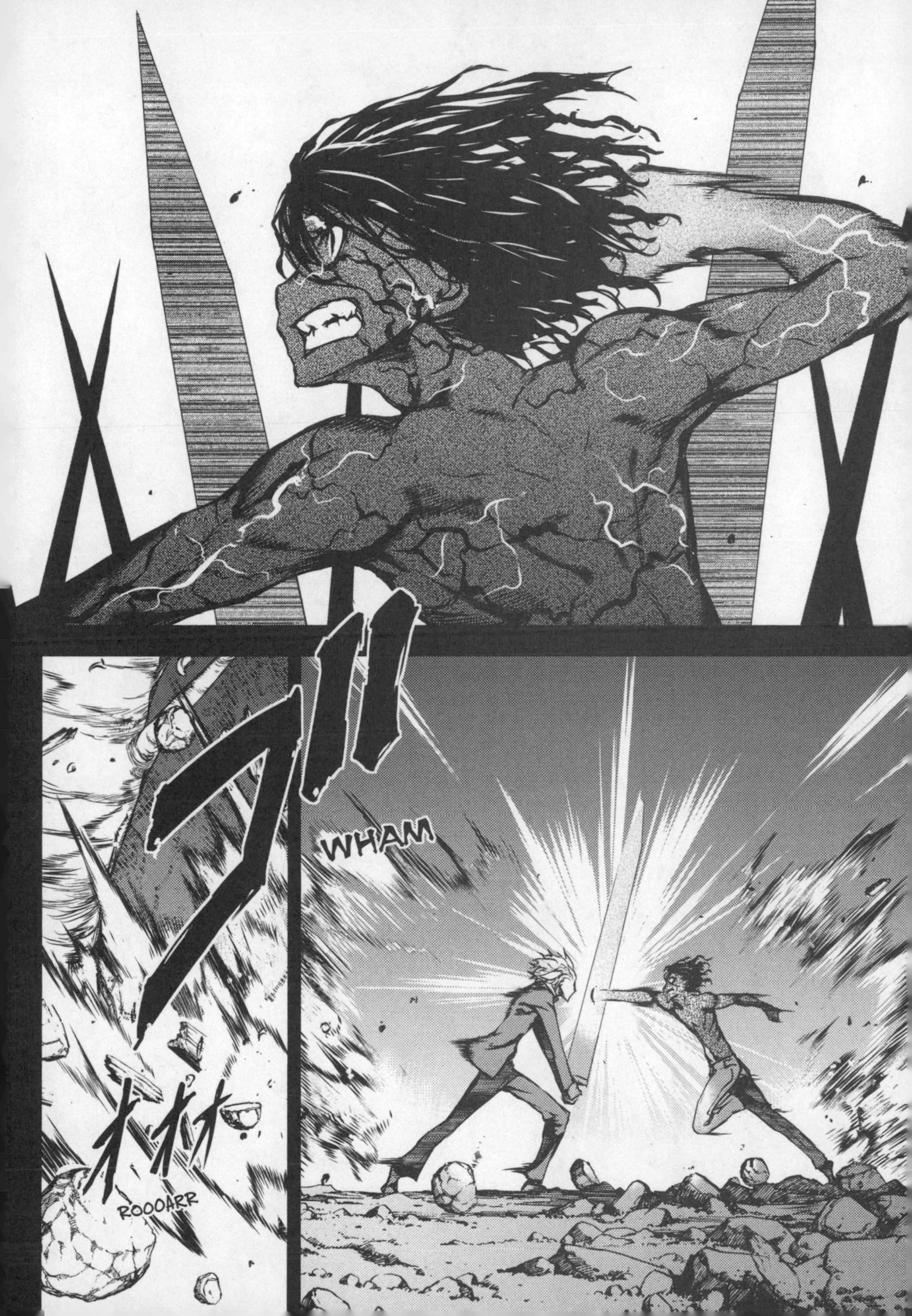
WHAM
ブ
オオオ
ROOOARR

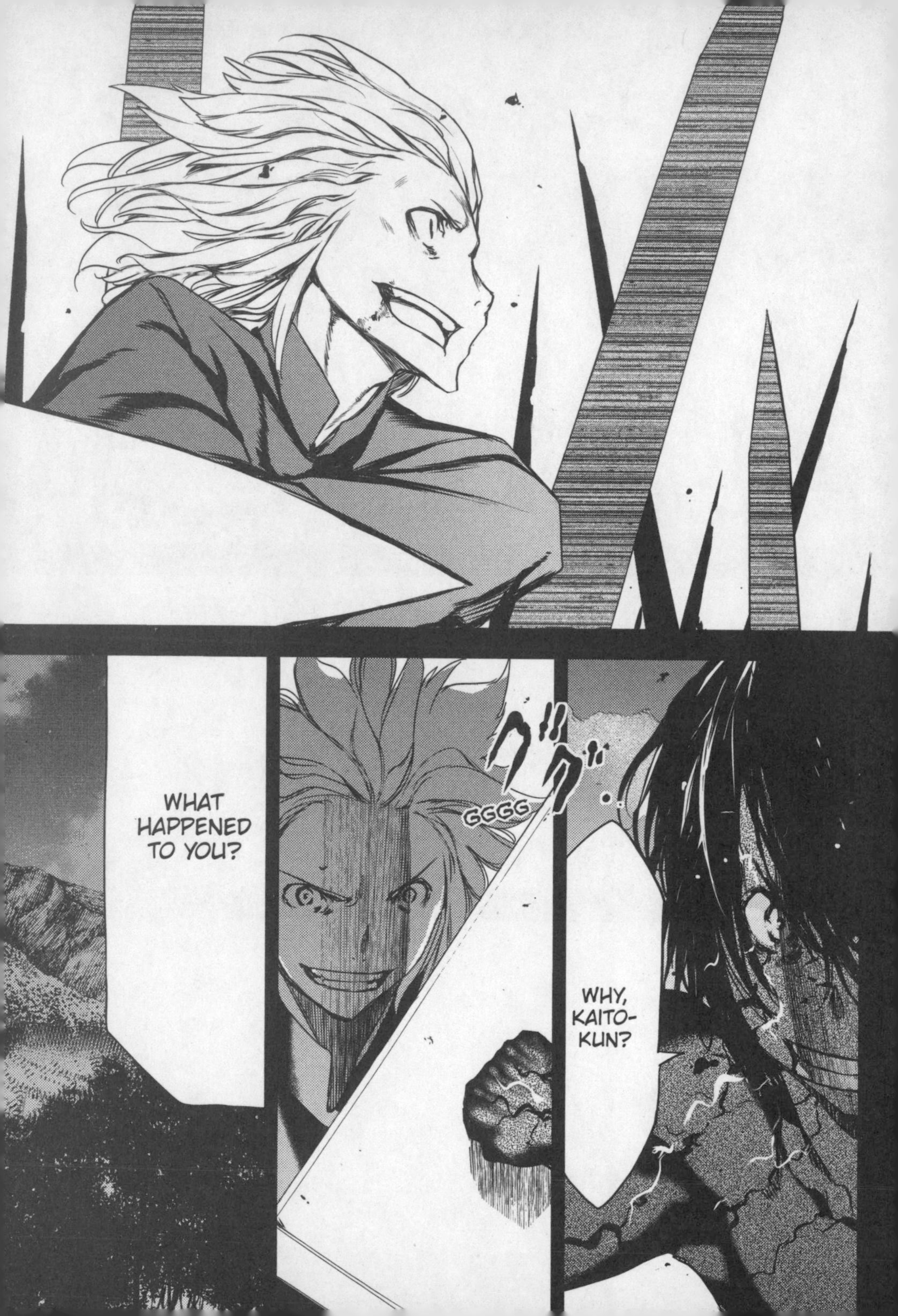
WHY, KAITO-KUN?
GGGG
WHAT HAPPENED TO YOU?

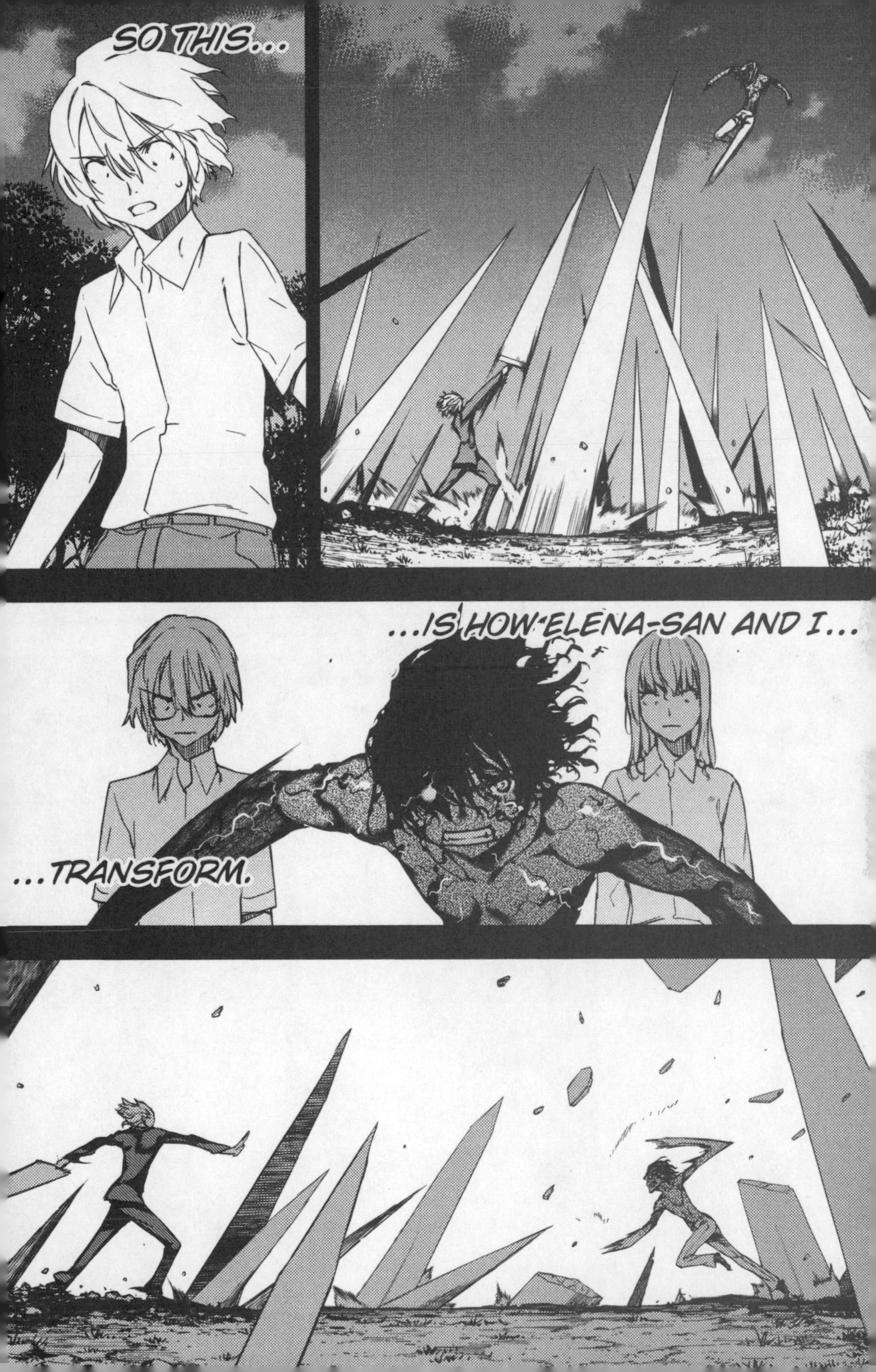
SO THIS...
...IS HOW ELENA-SAN AND I...
...TRANSFORM.

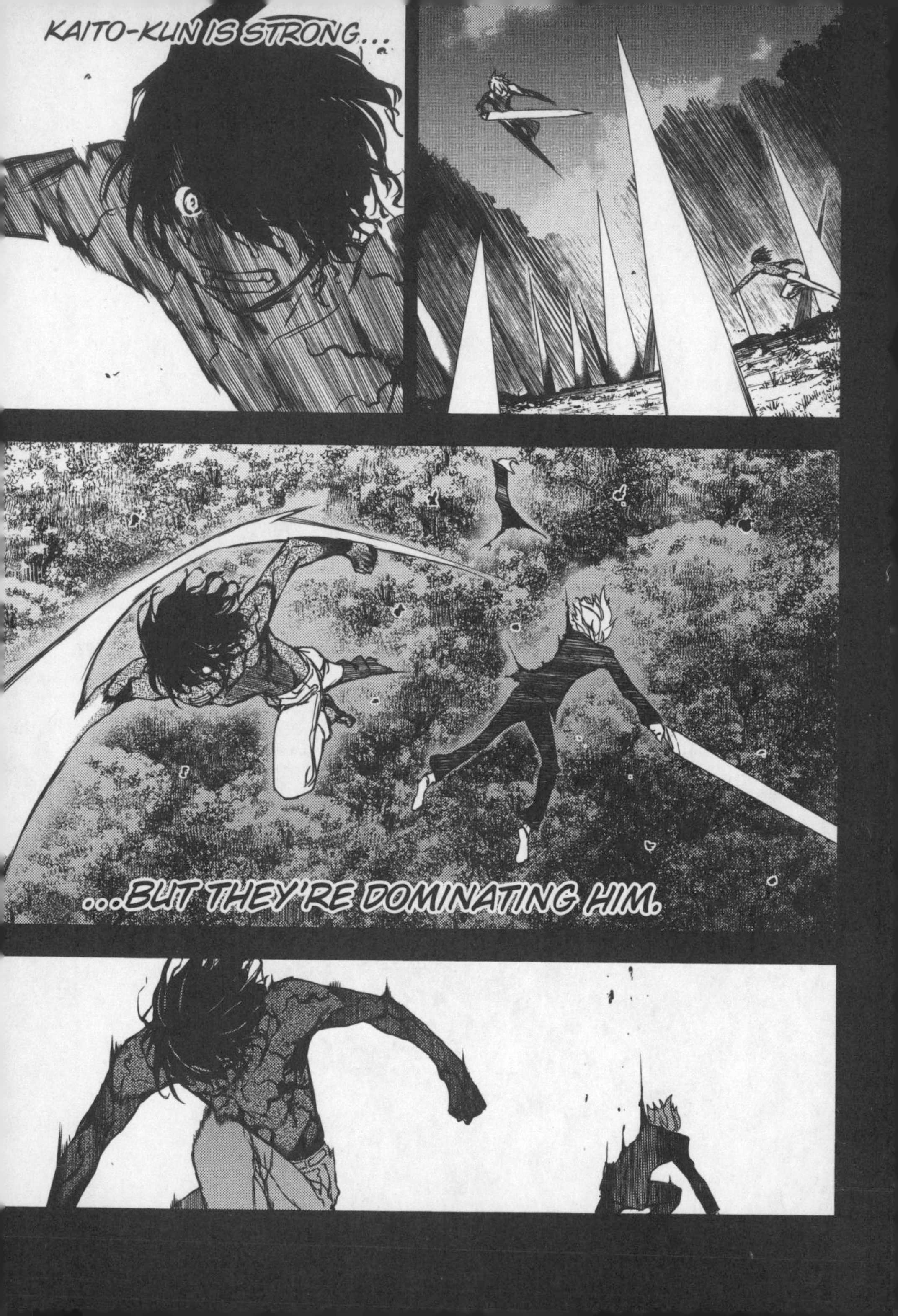
KAITO-KUN IS STRONG...
...BUT THEY'RE DOMINATING HIM.

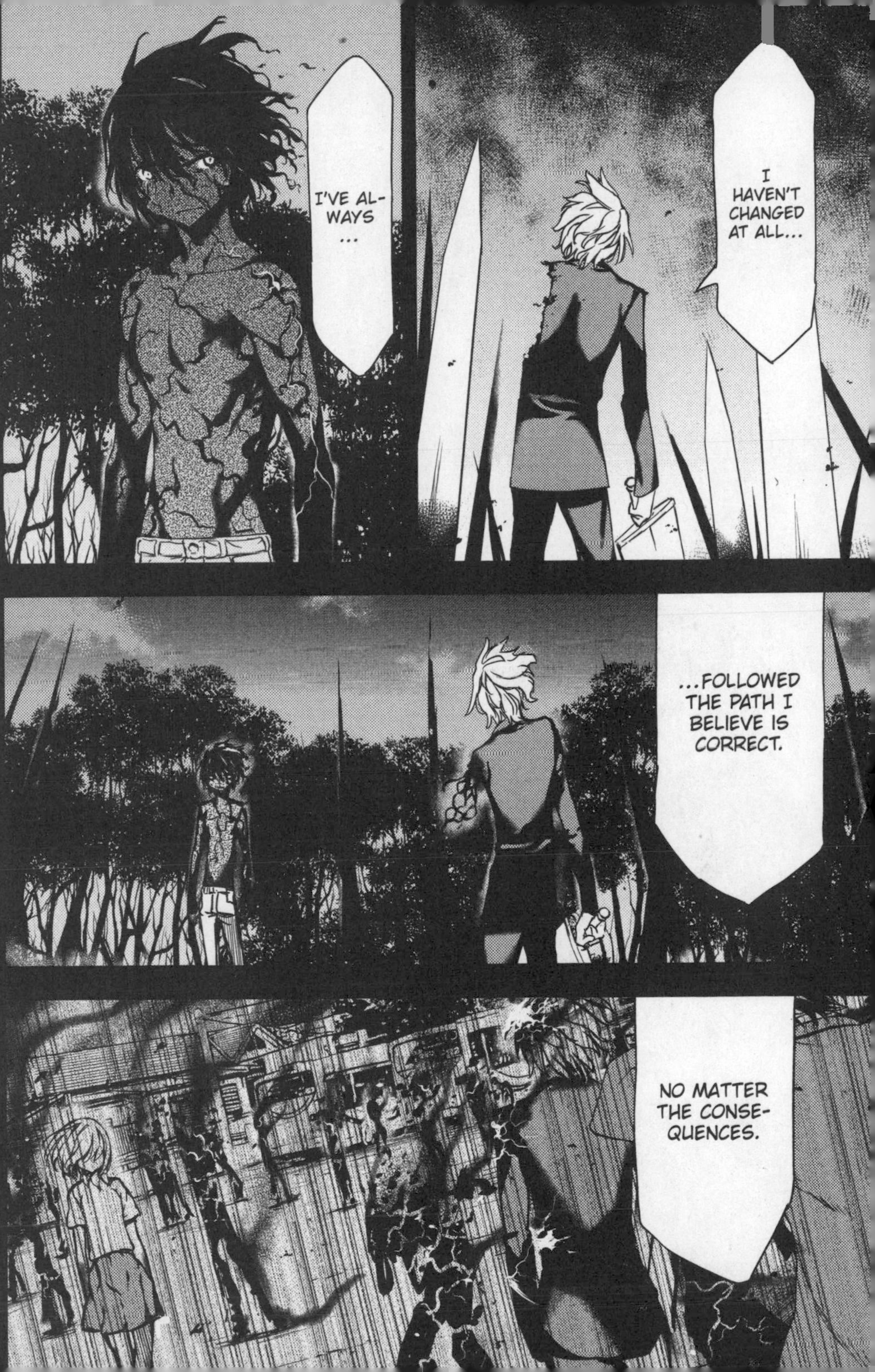
I HAVEN'T CHANGED AT ALL...
I'VE AL-WAYS ...
...FOLLOWED THE PATH I BELIEVE IS CORRECT.
NO MATTER THE CONSE-QUENCES.

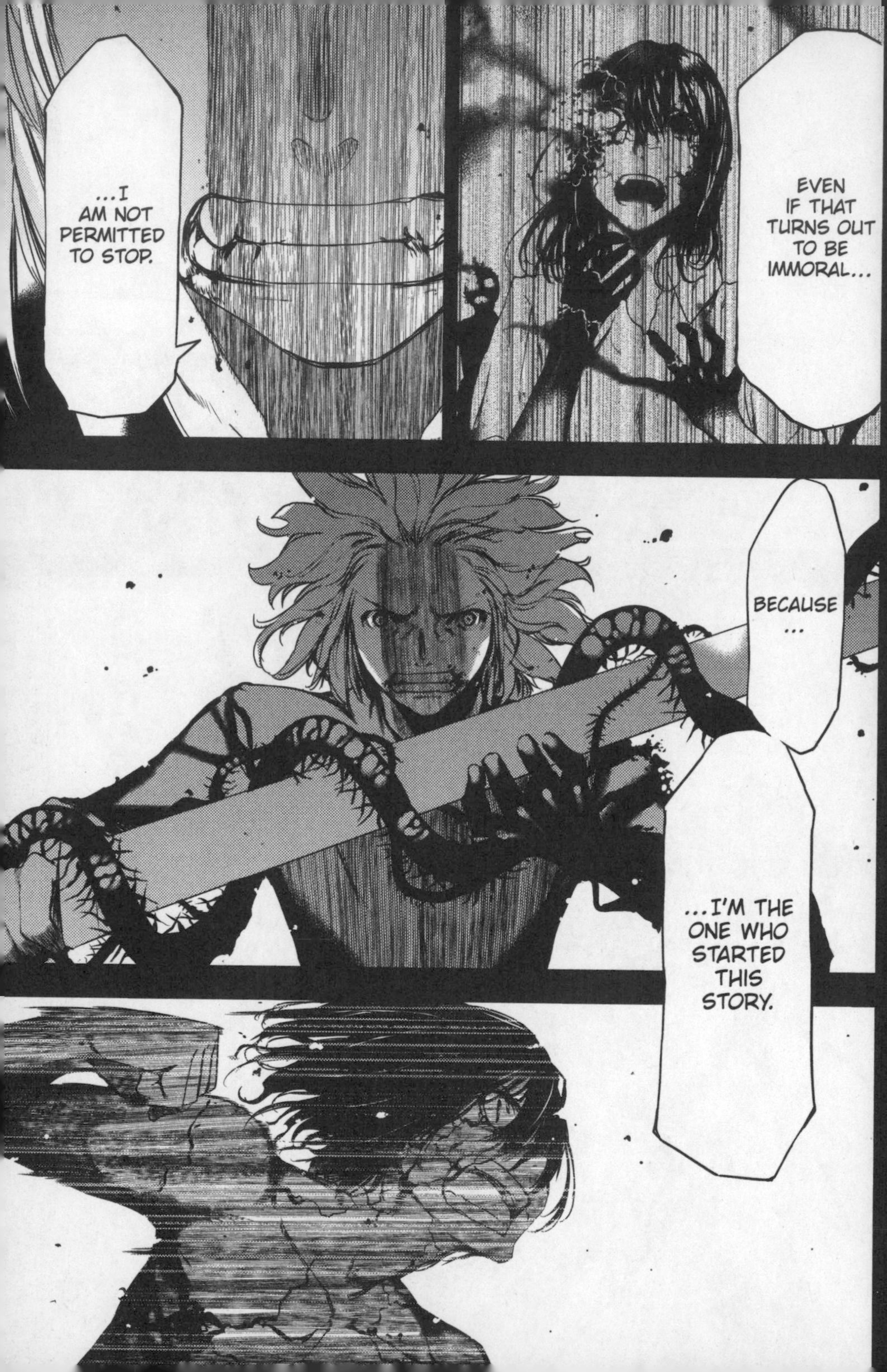
EVEN IF THAT TURNS OUT TO BE IMMORAL...
...I AM NOT PERMITTED TO STOP.
BECAUSE ...
...I'M THE ONE WHO STARTED THIS STORY.

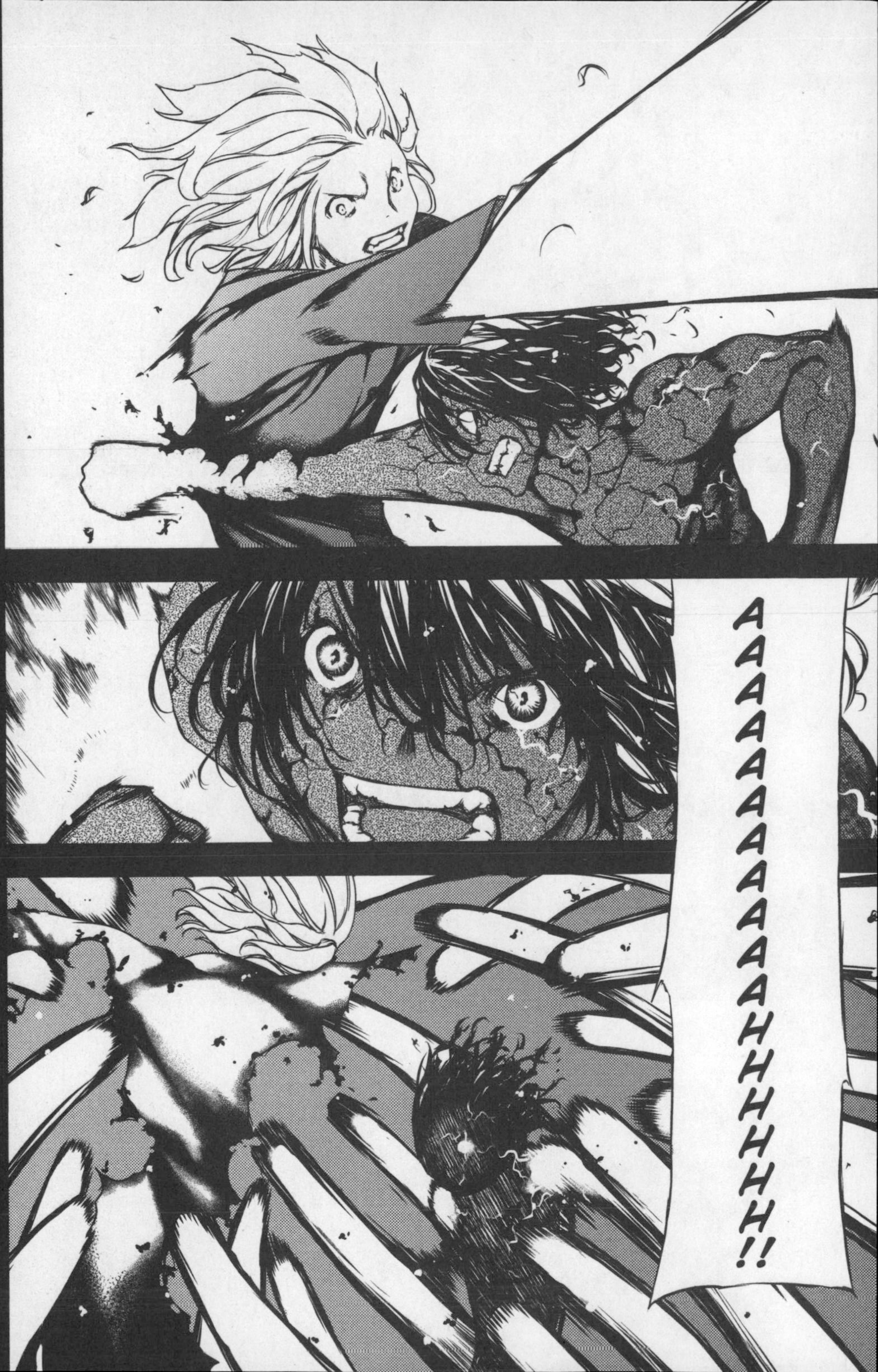
AAAAAAAAAAAAHHHHHH!!

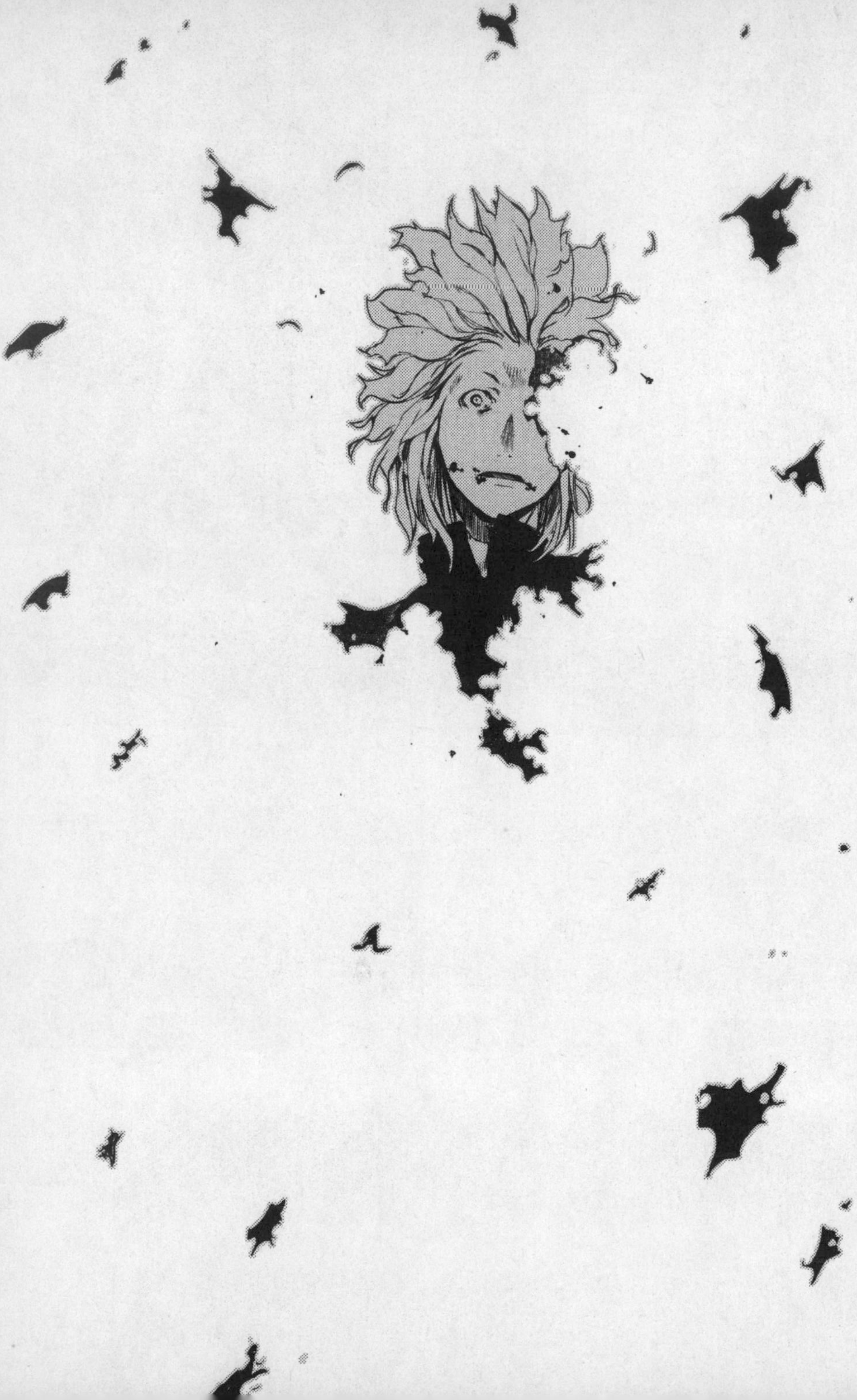

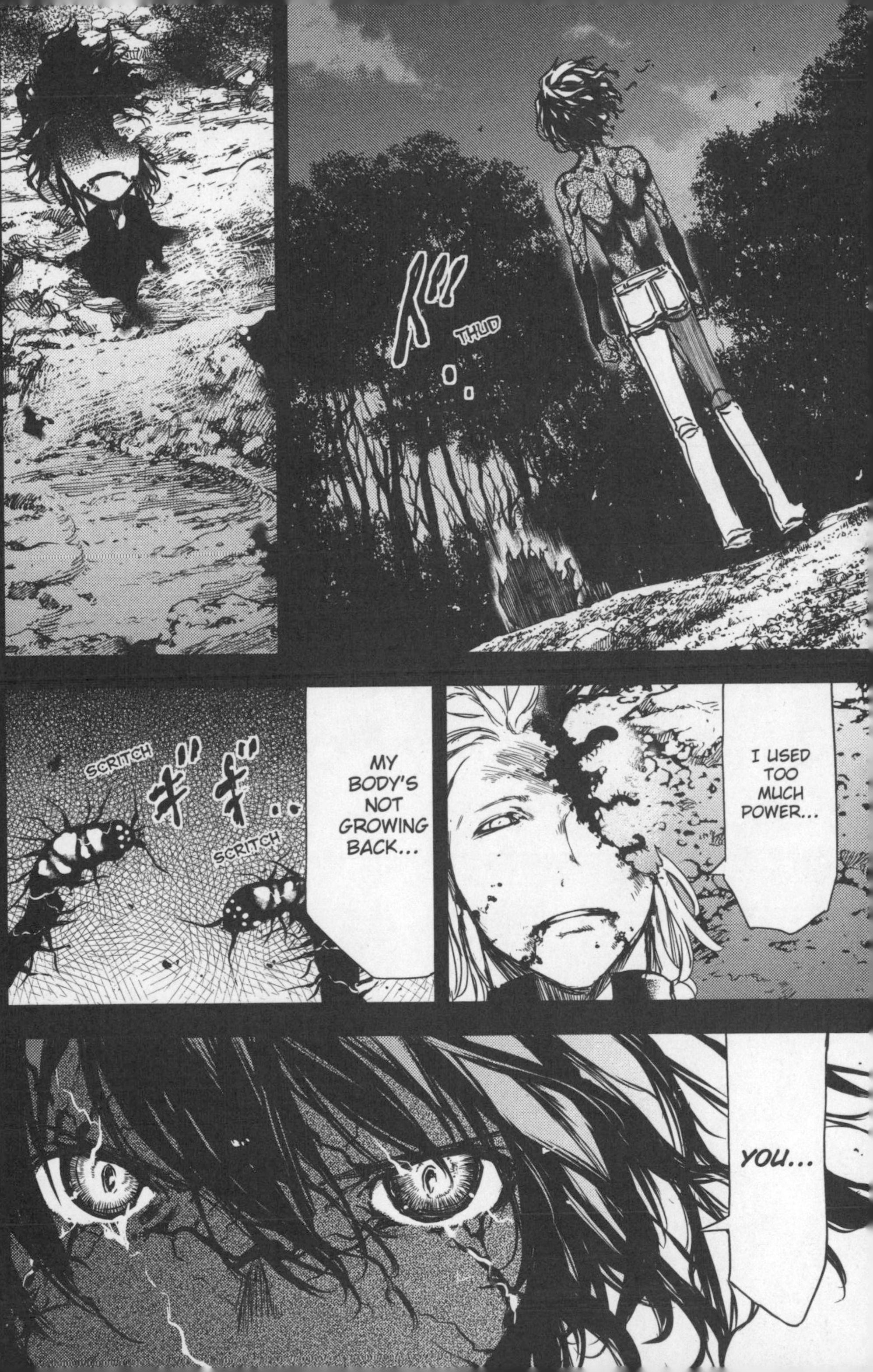
THUD
I USED TOO MUCH POWER...
MY BODY'S NOT GROWING BACK...
SCRITCH
ギギ..
SCRITCH
YOU...

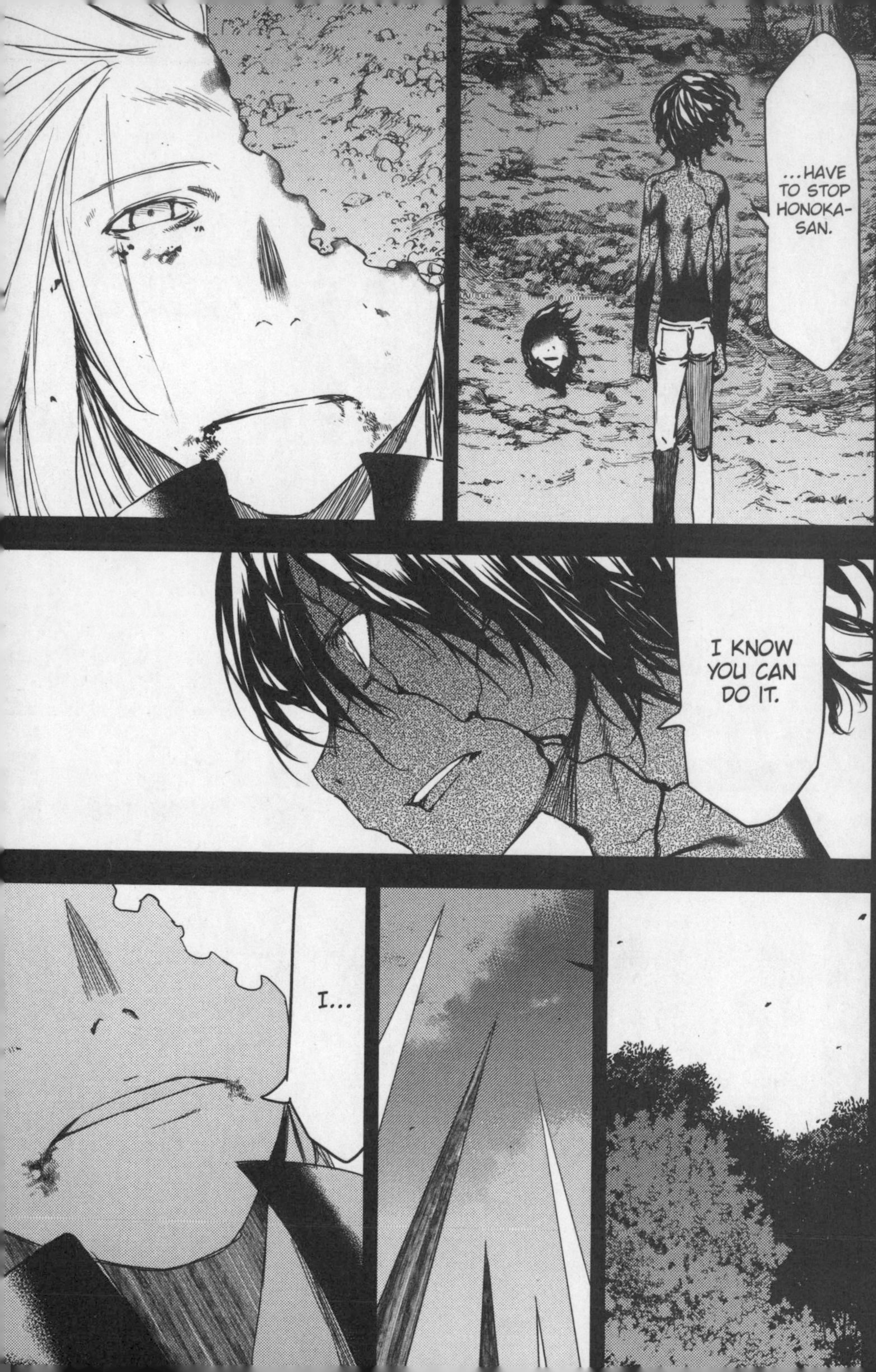
...HAVE TO STOP HONOKA-SAN.
I KNOW YOU CAN DO IT.
I...

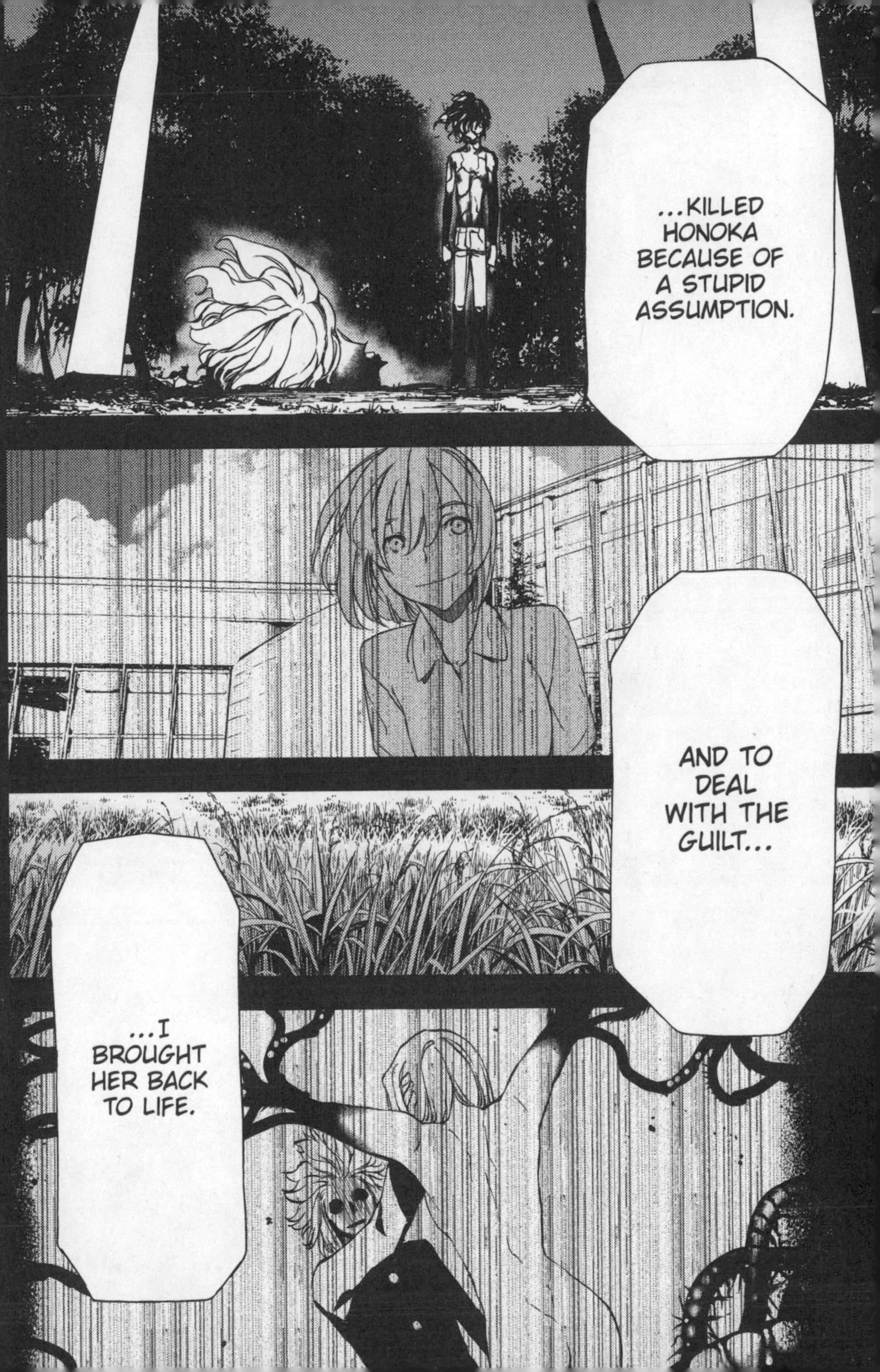
...KILLED HONOKA BECAUSE OF A STUPID ASSUMPTION.
AND TO DEAL WITH THE GUILT...
...I BROUGHT HER BACK TO LIFE.

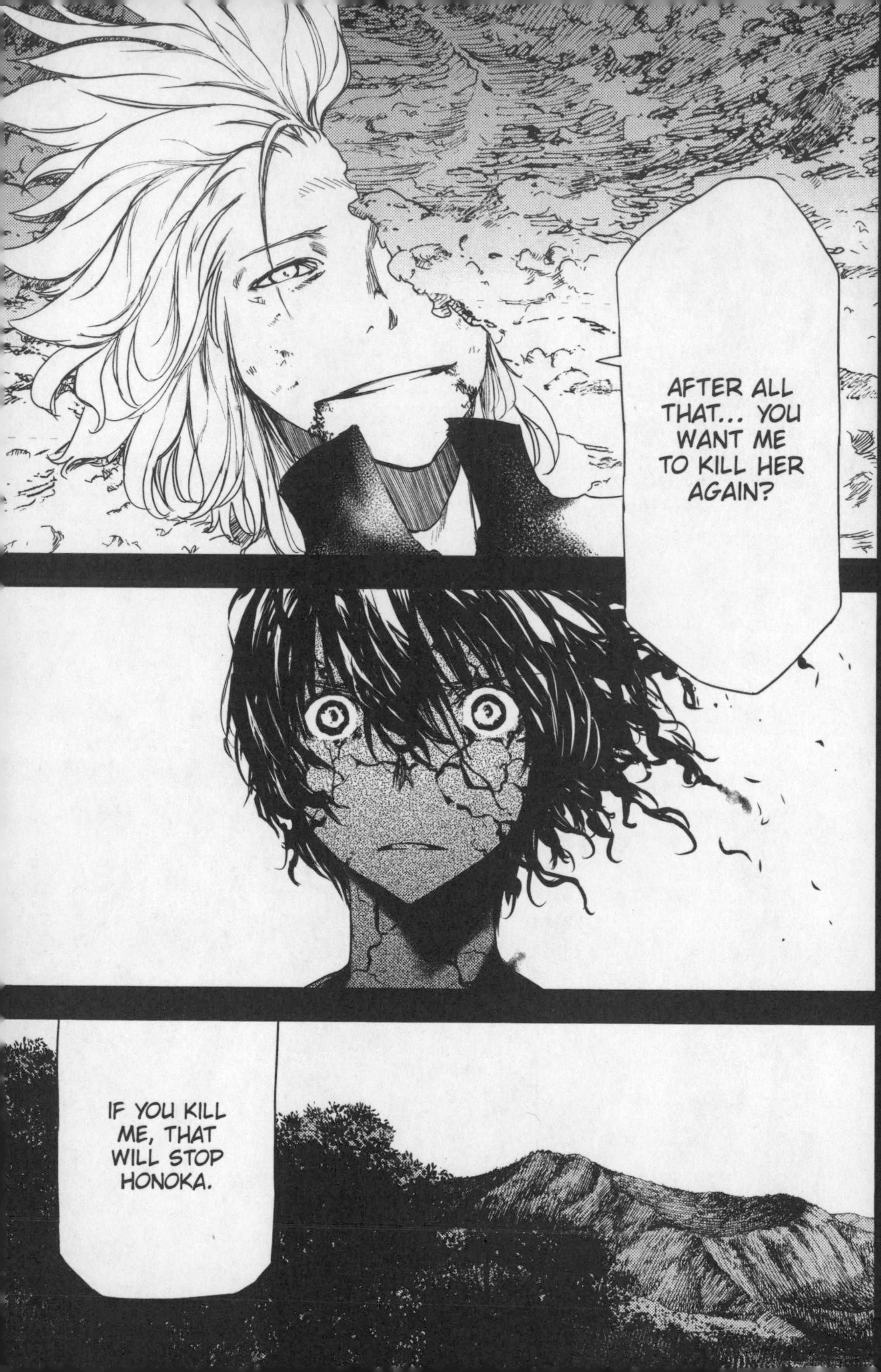
AFTER ALL THAT... YOU WANT ME TO KILL HER AGAIN?
IF YOU KILL ME, THAT WILL STOP HONOKA.

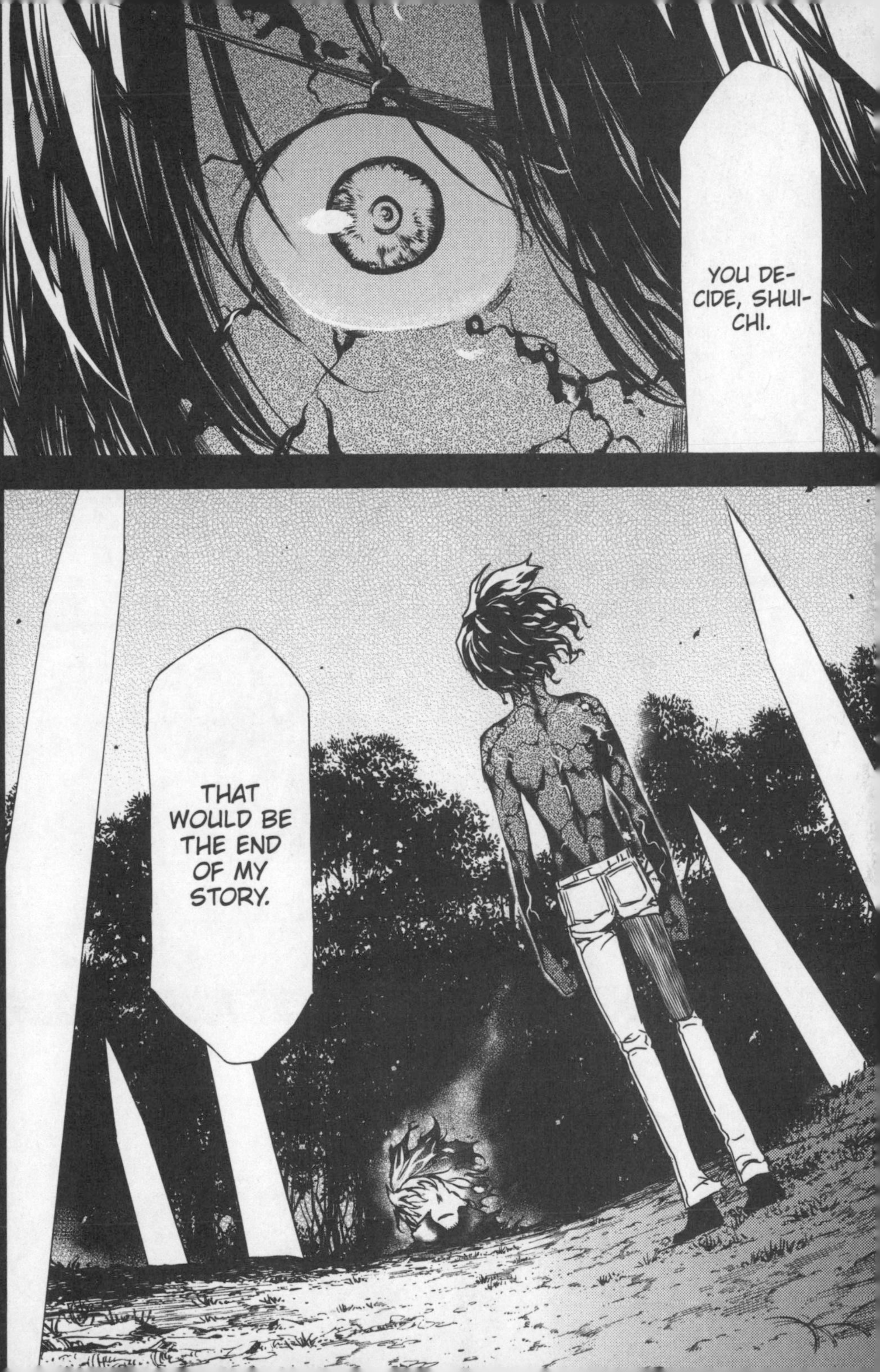
YOU DE-CIDE, SHUI-CHI.
THAT WOULD BE THE END OF MY STORY.

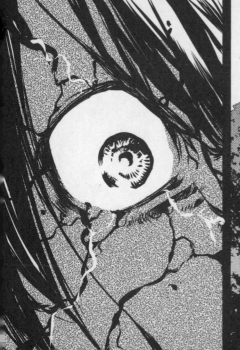

DO IT NOW, OR YOU'LL REGRET IT.

DO IT.

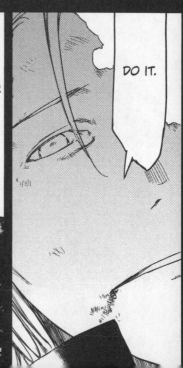

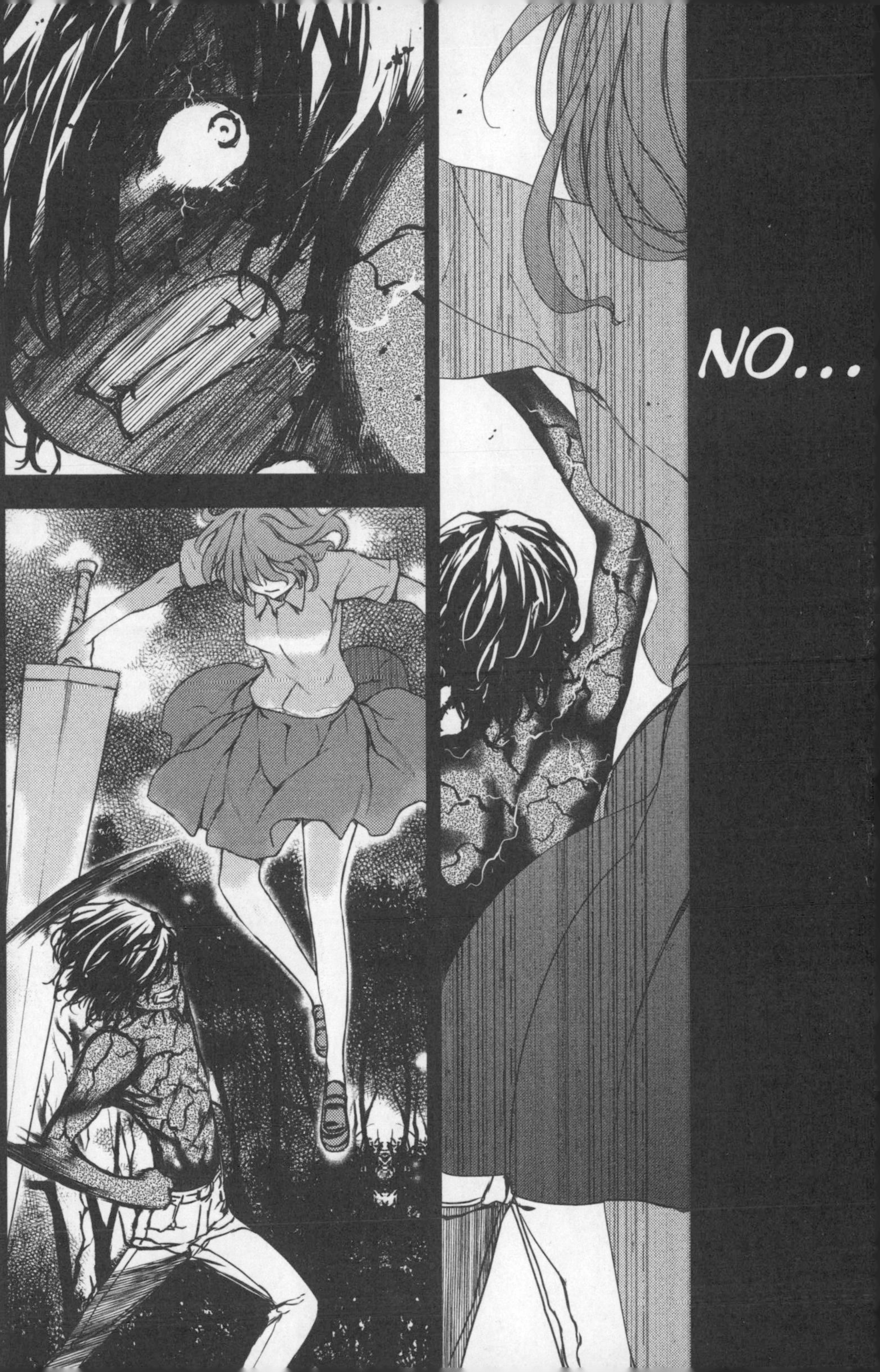
NO...

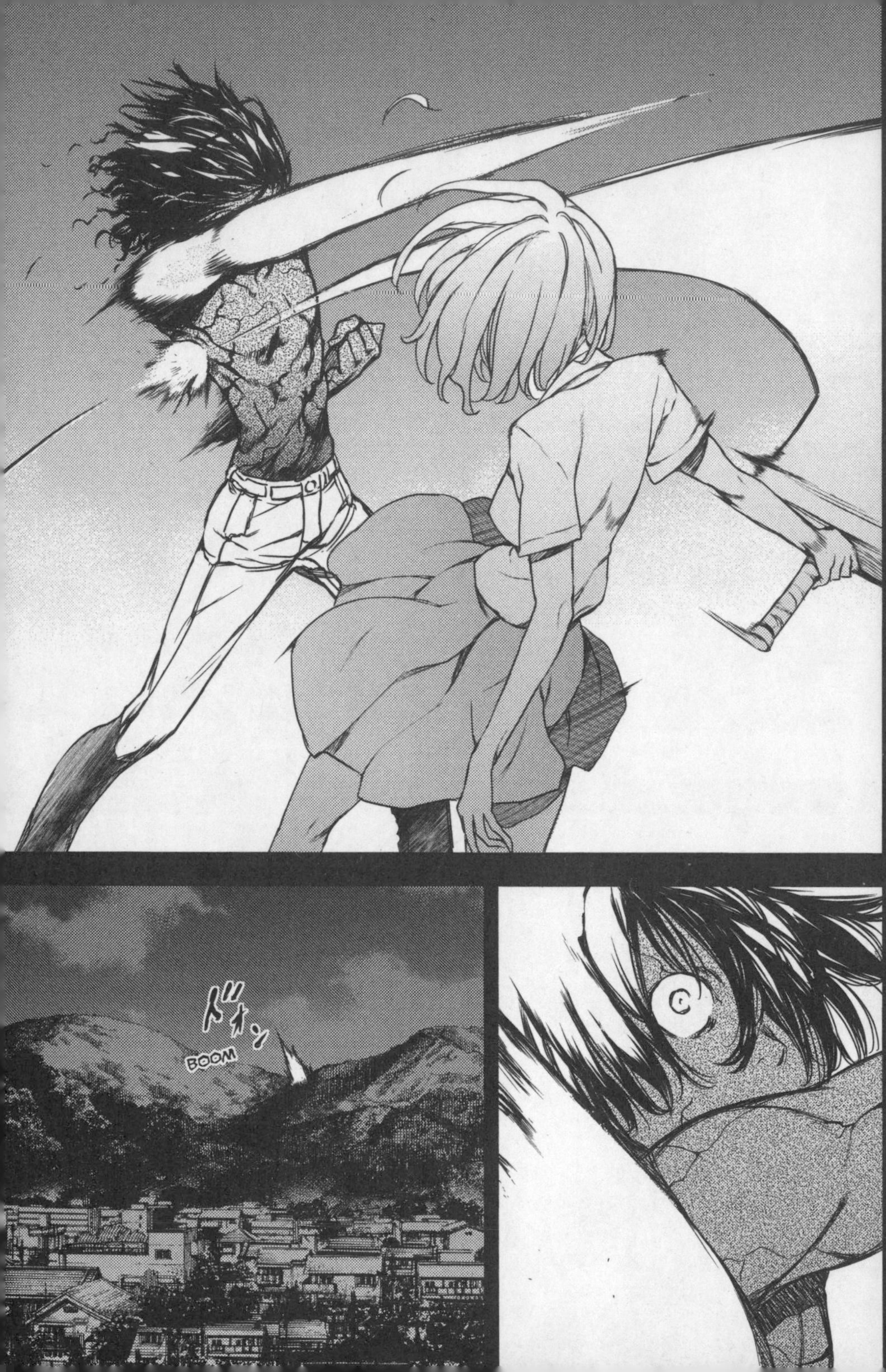
ドォン
BOOM

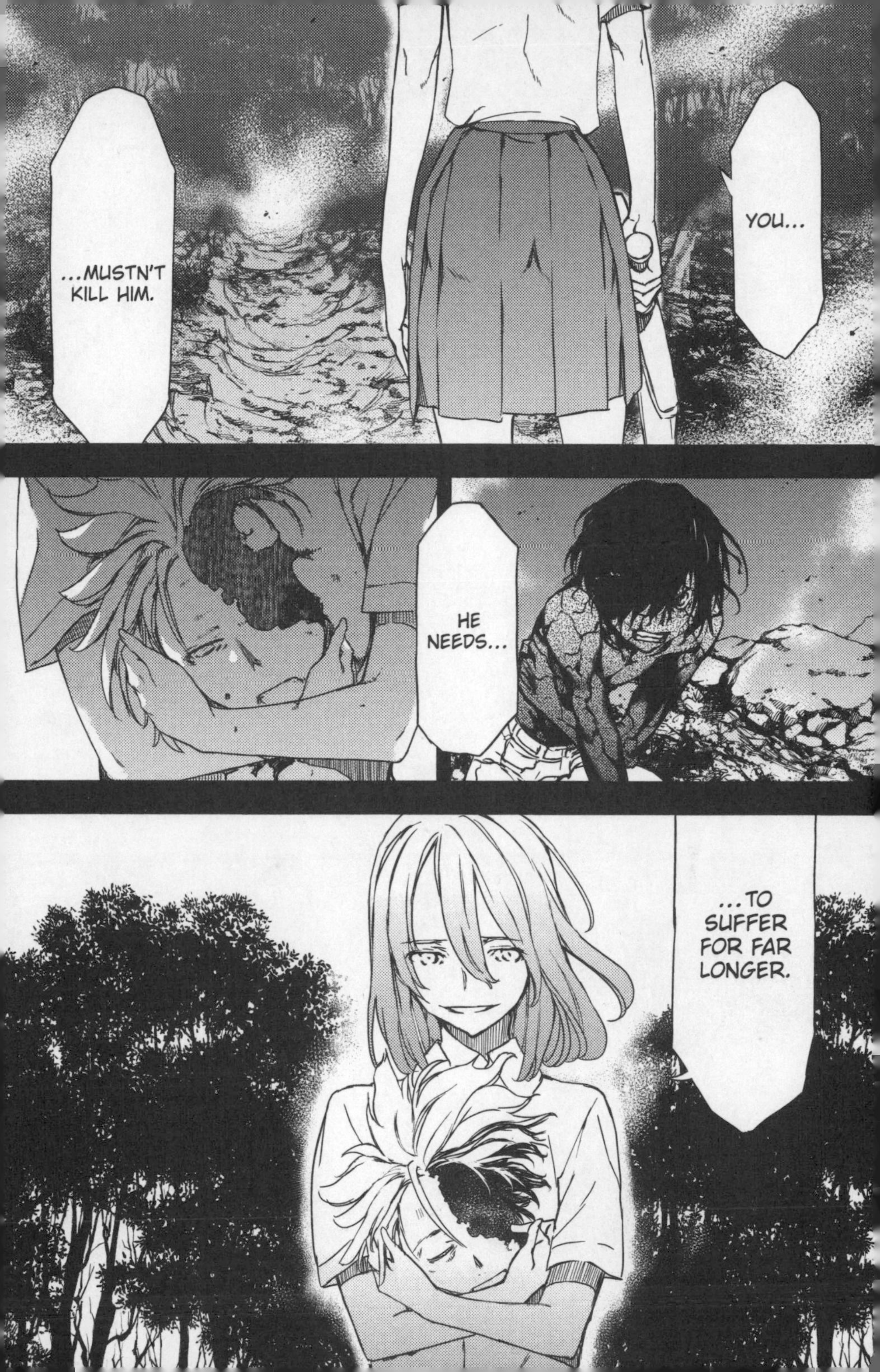
YOU...
...MUSTN'T KILL HIM.
HE NEEDS...
...TO SUFFER FOR FAR LONGER.

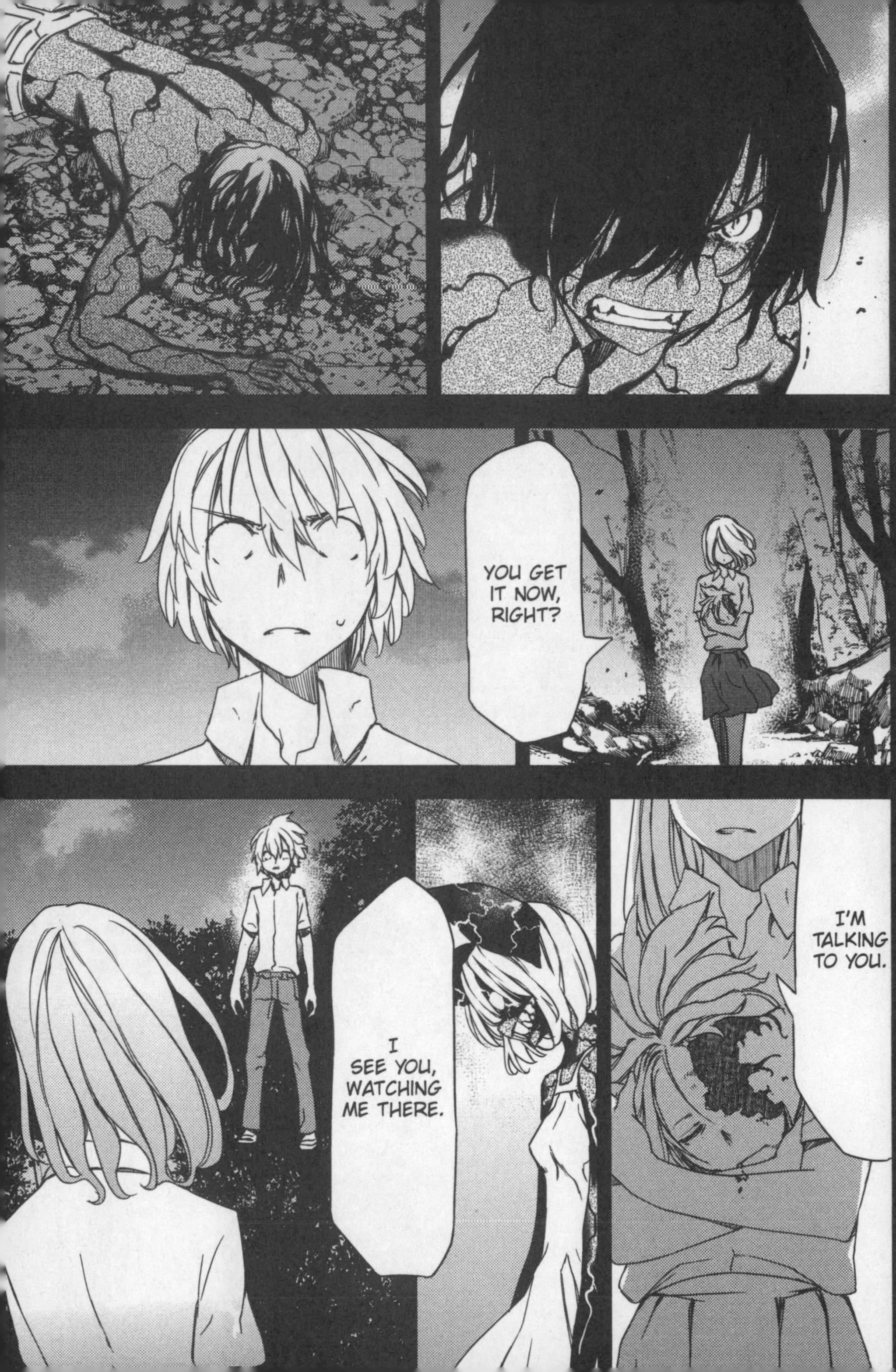
YOU GET IT NOW, RIGHT?
I'M TALKING TO YOU.
I SEE YOU, WATCHING ME THERE.

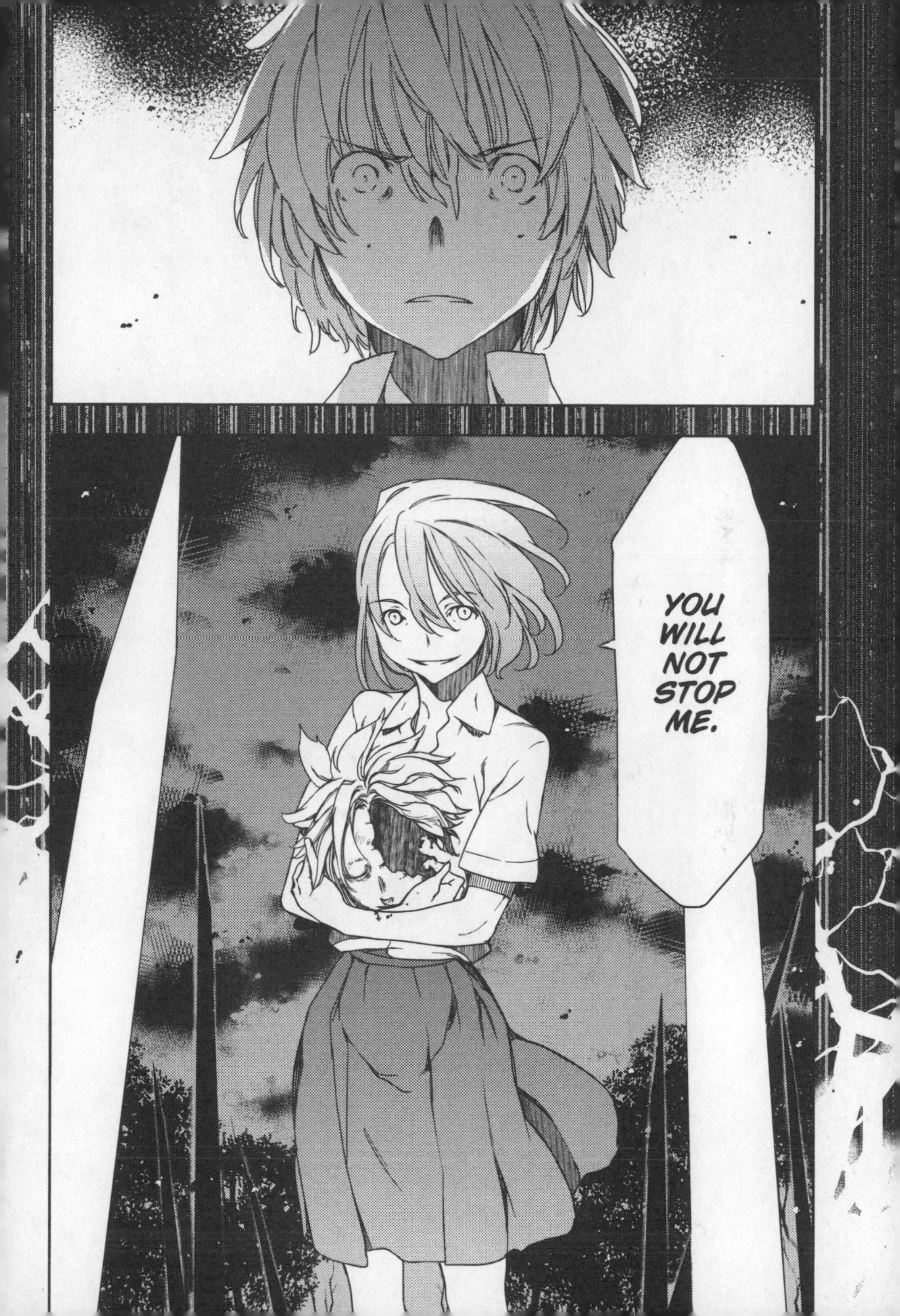
YOU WILL NOT STOP ME.

CONTINUED IN VOLUME 10

NEXT ISSUE

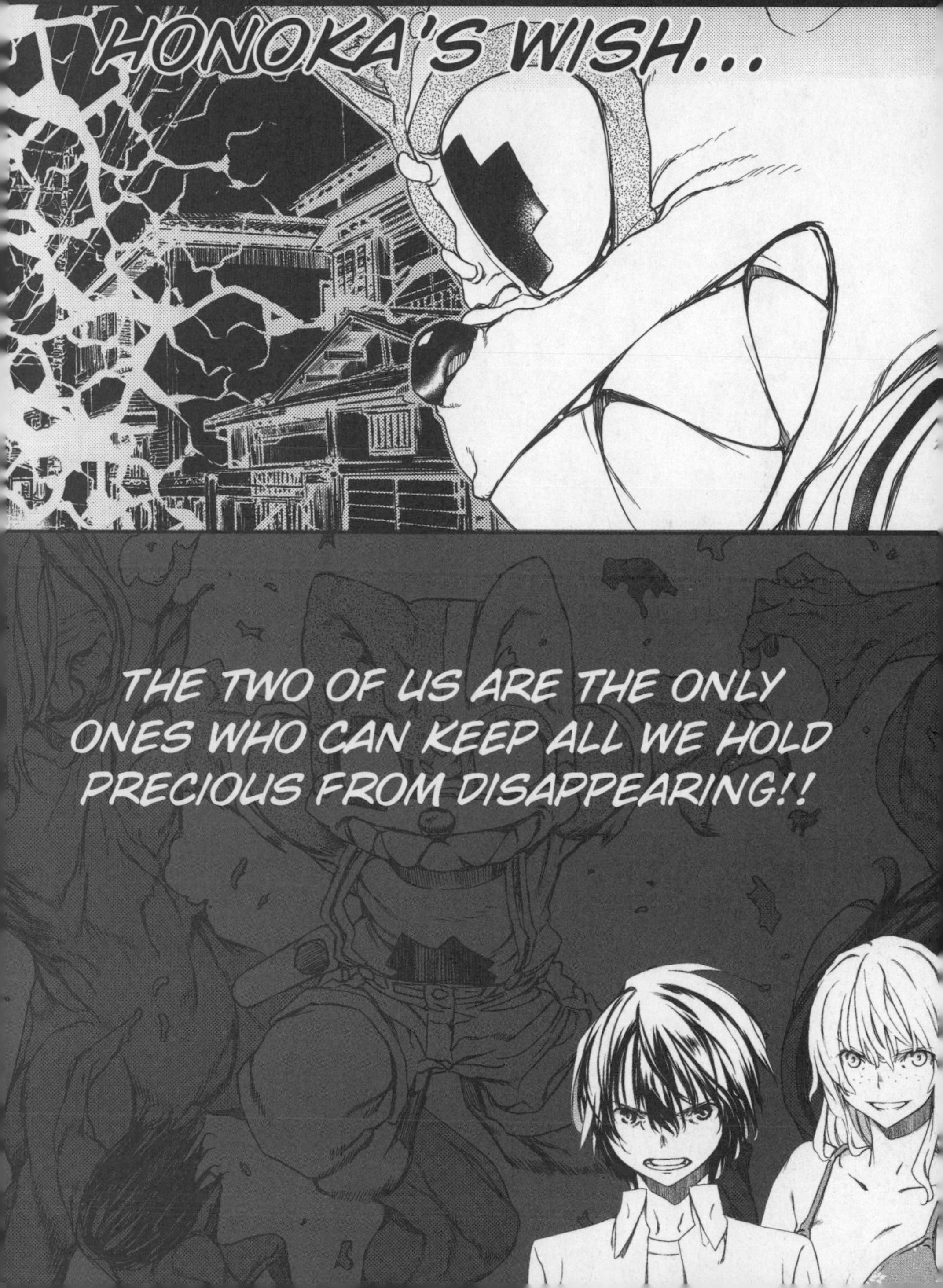
HONOKA'S WISH...
THE TWO OF US ARE THE ONLY ONES WHO CAN KEEP ALL WE HOLD PRECIOUS FROM DISAPPEARING!!